NOLO'S

everyday
LAW BOOK

answers to your most
frequently asked
legal questions

Edited by Attorney Shae Irving

NOLO PRESS · BERKELEY

Your Responsibility When Using a Self-Help Law Book

We've done our best to give you useful and accurate information in this book. But laws and procedures change frequently and are subject to differing interpretations. If you want legal advice backed by a guarantee, see a lawyer. If you use this book, it's your responsibility to make sure that the facts and general advice contained in it are applicable to your situation.

Nolo's everyday law book : answers to your most frequently asked legal questions / edited by Shae Irving.- -2nd ed.
    p.   cm.
    Includes index.
    ISBN 0-87337-426-6
    1. Law- -United States- -Popular works. 2. Law- -United States- -Miscellanea. I. Irving, Shae. II. Title: Everyday Law Book.
KF387.N65 1998
349.73- -DC21   98-10497
                             CIP

QUANTITY SALES: FOR INFORMATION ON BULK PURCHASES OR CORPORATE PREMIUM SALES, PLEASE CONTACT THE SPECIAL SALES DEPARTMENT. FOR ACADEMIC SALES OR TEXTBOOK ADOPTIONS, ASK FOR ACADEMIC SALES. 800-955-4775, NOLO PRESS, INC., 950 PARKER ST., BERKELEY, CA, 94710.

Keeping Up to Date

To keep its books up to date, Nolo Press issues new printings and new editions periodically. New printings reflect minor legal changes and technical corrections. New editions contain major legal changes, major text additions or major reorganizations. To find out if a later printing or edition of any Nolo book is available, call Nolo Press at 510-549-1976 or check our website at www.nolo.com.

To stay current, follow the "Update" service at our website: www.nolo.com. In another effort to help you use Nolo's latest materials, we offer a 25% discount off the purchase of the new edition of your Nolo book when you turn in the cover of an earlier edition. (See the "Special Upgrade Offer" in the back of the book.)

This book was last revised in: February 1999.

Second Edition .... *February 1999*
Editor .... *Shae Irving*
Cover & Book Design ..... *Linda Marie Wanczyk & Jackie Mancuso*
Index .... *Nancy Mulvany*
Proofreader .... *Joe Sadusky*
Printer .... *Bertelsmann Industry Services, Inc.*

Dedication

For Edward F. Dolan

Acknowledgments

First things first—thanks to Jake Warner for thinking this project up and dropping it in my lap; the work has been a privilege. And thanks to all the Nolo editors who kept me (and the book) on track, particularly Robin Leonard, my back-up editor, for rising above the call of duty, Mary Randolph for her eminent good judgment and Steve Elias for his relentless and contagious enthusiasm.

For diligent research help, I'd like to thank Naomi Starkman and Peri Pakroo. For helping me manage the changes through draft after draft, thanks go to Susan Cornell and Stephanie Harolde.

Jackie Mancuso made the book look great and was blessedly patient with someone who has very little color-confidence and doesn't know the difference between a border and a serif. Jaleh Doane, Susan Putney and Linda Marie Wanczyk brought their sharp minds and good humor to the design process, and made the whole thing even easier.

Finally, I'm grateful to every Nolo author and editor whose fine work has shaped these pages. You'll find many of these talented folks listed in the Contributors section on the following page. But I want to give special thanks to:

Paul Bergman and Sara Berman-Barrett, authors of *Represent Yourself in Court* and *The Criminal Law Handbook*

David W. Brown, author of *How to Change Your Name* and *Fight Your Ticket...and Win!*

Stephen Colwell and Ann Shulman, authors of *Trouble Free Travel...And What to Do When Things Go Wrong*

James Evans, author of *Law on the Net* and *Government on the Net*

Cora Jordan, author of *Neighbor Law: Fences, Trees, Boundaries and Noise* and co-author (with Denis Clifford) of *Plan Your Estate*

Mimi E. Lyster, author of *Child Custody: Building Agreements That Work*

Joseph Matthews, author of *How to Win Your Personal Injury Claim* and co-author (with Dorothy Matthews Berman) of *Social Security, Medicare and Pensions*

Tanya Starnes, author of *Mad at Your Lawyer*

Fred S. Steingold, author of *The Legal Guide for Starting and Running a Small Business* and *The Employer's Legal Handbook.*

Contributors

Denis Clifford (Estate and Gift Taxes). Denis is the author of several Nolo Press books, including *Nolo's Will Book, The Quick and Legal Will Book, Plan Your Estate* (with Cora Jordan) and *The Partnership Book* (with Ralph Warner). A graduate of Columbia Law School, where he was an editor of *The Columbia Law Review,* Denis has practiced law in various ways, and is convinced that people can do much of their own legal work.

Frederick W. Daily (Small Business Taxes, Dealing With the IRS). Fred graduated from the University of Florida College of Law in 1968. He later received a degree in tax law and is now a San Francisco tax attorney. He is the author of two Nolo Press books, *Stand Up to the IRS* and *Tax Savvy for Small Business.*

Stephen R. Elias (Patents, Copyrights, Trademarks, Criminal Law, Legal Research). Steve received a law degree from Hastings College of the Law in 1969. He has practiced law in California, Vermont and New York, working for a variety of programs delivering legal services to the poor. In 1980, he discovered Nolo Press and, referring to himself as a recovering lawyer, has never looked back. Steve has authored, co-authored or edited over 30 Nolo Press titles covering such topics as family law, patents, copyrights, trademarks and bankruptcy.

Patricia Gima (Child Custody and Visitation, Child Support, Guardian of Children, Conservatorships). Patricia received her law degree from Hastings College of the Law in 1992 and has been an editor and author at Nolo Press since 1993. Patricia has practiced law in the areas of copyright, trademark and software licensing. She now specializes in intellectual property and family law. She is currently the editor of several Nolo books, including *Trademark: Legal Care for Your Business and Product Name, Licensing Your Invention* and *The Guardianship Book.* She is co-author of *Nolo's Pocket Guide to California Law.*

Shae Irving (Wills, Durable Powers of Attorney for Finances, Spouses and Partners). Shae graduated from Boalt Hall School of Law at the University of California at Berkeley in 1993. She did a brief stint at a San Francisco law firm before she turned and ran screaming towards Nolo. She is the author (or co-author) of several Nolo books, including *The Financial Power of Attorney Workbook, Take Control of Your Student Loans* and the legal manual that accompanies Nolo's *Willmaker.* She edits many other Nolo titles, including this one.

Bethany K. Laurence (Workers' Compensation). Beth graduated from Hastings College of the Law at the University of California in 1993. She spent several years slaving for a corporate legal publisher before coming to Nolo Press. She joined Nolo's editorial staff in 1997 and has never been happier. Beth is the co-author of Nolo's *How to Create a Buy-Sell Agreement* and *Control the Destiny of Your Small Business* and the editor of several Nolo publications, including *Take Charge of Your Workers' Compensation Claim* and *Ten Tips to Avoiding Employee Lawsuits.*

Robin Leonard (Your Money, Cars and Driving, Traveling, Spouses and Partners, Dealing With Your Lawyer). Robin is an editor and author at Nolo Press who specializes in debt, credit, bankruptcy and family law. She earned her law degree from Cornell Law School in 1985 and practiced law in San Francisco before joining Nolo in 1987. Robin is the author (or co-author) of many Nolo books, including *Money Troubles: Legal Strategies to Cope With Your Debts, How to File for Bankruptcy, Nolo's Pocket Guide to Family Law, Take Control of Your Student Loans* and *Credit Repair*.

Peter Lovenheim (Mediation). A 1979 graduate of Cornell Law School, Peter has been an active mediator since 1986 and is founder and president of a private dispute resolution service. He is the author of *Mediate, Don't Litigate* (McGraw-Hill), *Reading Between the Lines: New Stories From the Bible*, with co-editor David Katz (Jason Aronson), and *Mediate Your Dispute* (Nolo Press). Peter lives in Rochester, New York, with his wife and three children.

Anthony Mancuso (Nonprofit Corporations). Tony is a California attorney and the author of Nolo's best-selling corporate law series, including *How to Form Your Own Corporation* (California, Florida, Texas, New York and computer editions). He is also the author of Nolo's *Taking Care of Your Corporation* series and the book *How to Form a Nonprofit Corporation*. Tony is a jazz guitarist and a licensed helicopter pilot.

Peri H. Pakroo (Adoption). Besides writing and editing Nolo's online news column, The Legal Word, Peri writes and edits small business titles for Nolo. She's the editor of *Starting and Running a Successful Magazine and Newsletter* and *Music Law: How to Run Your Band's Business*. She's also the author of *Open Your California Business in 24 Hours*. Peri received her law degree from the University of New Mexico in 1995.

Janet Portman (Tenants' Rights, Cars and Driving, Legal Research). Janet received undergraduate and graduate degrees from Stanford University and a law degree from the University of Santa Clara. She was a public defender before coming to Nolo and is the editor of several Nolo books, including *Legal Research: How to Find and Understand the Law* and *The Criminal Records Book*. She is the co-author of Nolo's *Every Landlord's Legal Guide*.

Mary Randolph (Deeds, Neighbors, Wills and Estate Planning). Mary has been editing and writing Nolo books and software for more than a decade. She earned her law degree from Boalt Hall School of Law at the University of California at Berkeley, and her undergraduate degree at the University of Illinois. She is the author of *Dog Law, The Deeds Book, 8 Ways to Avoid Probate* and the legal manual that accompanies Nolo's *Living Trust Maker* software.

Barbara Kate Repa (Workplace Rights, Final Arrangements, Body and Organ Donations, Healthcare Directives, Older Americans, Traffic Accidents). Barbara Kate, a lawyer, is an author and editor at Nolo Press, where her topics of concentration include aging, death, dying and, for some relief, workplace rights. She has written several books for Nolo, including *Your Rights in the Workplace, Sexual Harassment on the Job* and the legal manual that accompanies Nolo's *WillMaker*.

Marcia Stewart (Houses, Tenants' Rights). Marcia is an expert on landlord-tenant law, buying and selling houses and other issues of interest to consumers. She is the co-author of Nolo's *Every Landlord's Legal Guide, Every Tenant's Legal Guide, Leases & Rental Agreements* and *LeaseWriter* software as well as the editor of many other Nolo books. Marcia received a Master's degree in public policy from the University of California at Berkeley and has written and edited a wide variety of consumer publications for government agencies and private businesses.

Ralph Warner (Small Businesses, Courts and Mediation). Ralph is the co-founder and Publisher of Nolo Press. He is the author (or co-author) of a number of Nolo books, including *Every Landlord's Legal Guide, Everybody's Guide to Small Claims Court, The Partnership Book* and *Get a Life: You Don't Need a Million to Retire Well*. Ralph is a lawyer who became fed up with the legal system and as a result has dedicated his professional life to making law more accessible and affordable to all Americans.

Table of Contents

About This Book

Houses

Neighbors

Tenants' Rights

Workplace Rights

Small Businesses

Courts and Mediation

Criminal Law and Procedure

Legal Research

About this Book

Whether we like it or not, the law touches our personal lives in many ways each day. We may not think much about the laws that affect us as we carry out simple tasks such as driving a car, making a telephone call or buying milk at the corner grocery store. But every now and again, we're sure to need an answer to a common legal question that arises in the course of daily life:

What can I do about my noisy neighbor?

WHAT ARE MY RIGHTS IF I'M FIRED FROM MY JOB?

Do I really need to make a will?

What should I do if I can't pay the child support I owe?

And so on.

This book provides answers to frequently asked questions about more than 100 subjects you might encounter in your personal life—topics that range from buying a house to getting a divorce, from paying your debts to starting and running a small business. Obviously, we can't answer every question on a particular subject, but we've answered many common ones to get you started. Throughout each chapter, you'll find resource boxes listing sources for more information about a particular subject.

In addition, for those of you who are computer savvy, each chapter contains a list of online sites that will help you learn more about a particular area of the law. Look for the "Online Help" icon as you read. And if you need more information about finding the law, Chapter 19 contains a section that shows you how to do basic legal research—with a focus on searching the Internet.

Think of this book as a desk reference—a little encyclopedia that unpacks the law and puts it in your hands in a language you can understand. But remember that the law changes constantly as legislatures pass new laws and courts hand down their rulings. We will publish new, revised editions of this book periodically, but it will never be perfectly current. It's always your responsibility to be sure a law is up to date before you rely on it. Check the Legal Update Service on our wedsite at HTTP:// www.nolo.com/update.html for the most current legal information affecting Nolo books & Software.

Houses

Home is heaven for beginners.

—CHARLES H. PARKHURST

Buying or selling a house is a major undertaking. To do it right, you need to understand how houses are priced, financed and inspected; how to find and work with a real estate agent; how to protect your interests when negotiating a contract; and how legal transfer of ownership takes place. Once you own a home, you want to keep it safe and secure. This chapter covers many of the basic issues that buyers, sellers and owners need to know.

Buying a House

Before you look for a house, it's essential to determine how much you can afford to pay and what your financing options are. You'll also need to decide whether you want to work with a real estate agent or broker, and finally, even if you think you've found your dream home, you'll need to master the ins and outs of house inspections. This section gives you some answers that will help you find your way through the house-buying maze—and to your new front door.

I'm a first-time home buyer. Is there any easy way to determine how much house I can afford?

As a broad generalization, most people can afford to purchase a house worth about three times their total (gross) annual income, assuming a 20% down payment and a moderate amount of other long-term debts, such as car or student loan payments. With no other debts, you can probably afford a house worth up to four or even five times your annual income.

The most accurate way to determine whether you can afford a particular house is to total up the estimated monthly principal and interest payments plus one-twelfth of the yearly bill for property and homeowner's insurance. Now compare that to your gross monthly income.

Lenders normally want you to make all monthly housing payments with 28%-38% of your monthly income—the percentage depends on the amount of your down payment, the interest rate on the type of mortgage you want, your credit history, the level of your long-term debts and other factors. A bank or other lender can give you the paperwork you need to determine how much house you can afford.

Or you can run the numbers yourself, using an online mortgage calculator such as those on the Websites listed at the end of this chapter.

Once you've done the basic calculations, you can ask a lender or loan broker for a prequalification letter saying that loan approval for a specified amount is likely based on your income and credit history.

In competitive markets, you will want to do more than prequalify for a loan—you will want to be guaranteed for a specific loan amount. This means that the lender actually evaluates your financial situation, runs a credit check and preapproves you for a loan—rather than giving a general prequalification based on your own statement about your income and debts. Having lender preapproval for a loan makes you more attractive financially to sellers than simple loan prequalification.

How can I find the best home loan or mortgage?

Many entities, including banks, credit unions, savings and loans, insurance companies and mortgage bankers make home loans. Some lenders work statewide; others specialize in narrow geographical areas, types of housing or types of mortgages. Lenders and terms change frequently as new companies appear, old ones merge and market conditions fluctuate. To get the best deal, compare loans and fees with at least a half-dozen lenders. Fortunately, mortgage rates and fees are often published in the real estate sections of metropolitan newspapers, and are increasingly available online. (See the list of recommended Websites at the end of this chapter.)

Because many types of home loans are standardized to comply with rules established by the Federal National Mortgage Association (Fannie Mae), Federal Home Loan Mortgage Corporation (Freddie Mac) and other quasi-governmental corporations that purchase loans from lenders, comparison shopping is not difficult. You can also work with a loan broker, someone who specializes in matching a house buyer with an appropriate mortgage lender, normally collecting a fee from the lender.

You may also be eligible for a government-guaranteed loan, offered by the Federal Housing Administration or the U.S. Department of Veterans Affairs, or a loan from a state or local housing agency. These loans usually have low down payment requirements and sometimes offer better-than-market interest rates as well.

Finally, don't forget private sources of mortgage money—parents, other relatives, friends or even the seller of the house you want to buy. Borrowing money privately is usually the most cost-efficient mortgage of all.

What's the difference between a fixed and an adjustable rate mortgage?

With a fixed rate mortgage, the interest rate and the amount you pay each month remain the same over the entire mortgage term, traditionally 15, 20 or 30 years. With an adjustable rate mortgage (ARM), the interest rate fluctuates as the interest rates in the economy fluctuate. Initial interest rates of ARMs are usually discounted; the rates are lower than those for fixed rate mortgages. Over time, however, initial discounts are filtered out and ARM rates fluctuate as general interest rates go up or down. To avoid constant and drastic changes, ARMs typically regulate (cap) how much and how often the interest rate and/or payments can change in a year and over the life of the loan.

A number of variations are available for adjustable rate mortgages, including hybrids that change from a fixed to an adjustable rate after a period of years. A good loan officer or loan broker will walk you through all options and tradeoffs such as higher fees (or points) for a lower interest rate.

How do I decide whether to choose a fixed or an adjustable rate mortgage?

Because interest rates and mortgage options change often, your choice of a fixed or an adjustable rate mortgage should depend on the interest rates and mortgage options available when you're buying, your view of the future (generally, high inflation will mean that ARM rates will go up and lower inflation means that they will fall), and how willing you are to take a risk. Very risk-averse people usually prefer the certainty of a fixed rate mortgage, rather than take a chance that an ARM might be cheaper in the long run.

What's the best way to find and work with a real estate agent or broker?

Get recommendations from people who have purchased a house in the past few years and whose judgment you trust. Don't work with an agent you meet at an open house or find in the Yellow Pages or on the Internet unless and until you call references and thoroughly check the person out. The agent or broker you choose should be in the full-time business of selling real estate and should have the following five traits: integrity, business sophistication, experience with the type of services you need, knowledge of the area where you want to live and sensitivity to your tastes and needs.

All states regulate and license real estate agents and brokers. You may have different options as to the type of legal relationship you have with an agent or broker; typically, the seller pays the commission of the real estate salesperson who helps the buyer locate the seller's house. The commission is a percentage (usually 5% to 7%) of the sales price of the house. What this

means is that your agent or broker has a built-in conflict of interest: Unless you've agreed to pay her separately, she won't get paid until you buy a home, and the more you pay for a house, the bigger her cut.

In short, when you evaluate the suitability of a house, it's not wise to rely principally on the advice of a person with a significant financial stake in your buying it. You need to be knowledgeable about the house-buying process, your ideal affordable house and neighborhood, your financing needs and options, your legal rights and how to evaluate comparable prices.

My spouse and I want to buy a $300,000 house. We have good incomes and can make high monthly payments, but we don't have $60,000 to make a 20% down payment. Are there other options?

Assuming you can afford (and qualify for) high monthly mortgage payments and have an excellent credit history, you should be able to find a low (10% to 15%) down payment loan for a $300,000 house. However, you may have to pay a higher interest rate and loan fees than someone making a higher down payment. In addition, a buyer who puts less than 20% down should be prepared to purchase private mortgage insurance (PMI), which is designed to reimburse a mortgage lender if a buyer defaults and the foreclosure sale price is less than the amount owed the lender (the mortgage plus the costs of the sale).

I want to buy a newly built house. Is there anything special I need to know?

The most important factor in buying a newly built house is not what you buy (that is, the particular model), but rather from whom you buy. Shop for an excellent builder—someone who builds quality houses, delivers on time and stands behind his or her work. To check out a particular builder, talk to existing owners in the development you're considering, or ask an experienced contractor to look at other houses the developer is building.

Many developers of new housing will help you arrange financing; some will also pay a portion of your monthly mortgage or subsidize your interest payments for a short period of time (called a "buydown" of the mortgage). As with any loan, be sure you comparison shop before arranging financing through a builder.

Also, be sure to negotiate the prices of any add-ons and upgrades. These can add substantially to the cost of a new home. And finally, check out any restrictions on how you can use your property and the responsibilities of homeowners. These are called covenants, conditions and restrictions (CC&Rs). CC&Rs commonly limit the colors you can paint your house and even the type of front yard landscaping you can do. Some developments have so many restrictions that it's almost as if your house is part of a common park, over which you have little say.

How can I make sure that the house I'm buying is in good shape?

In some states, you may have the advantage of a law that requires sellers to disclose considerable information about the condition of the house. (See *Selling Your House*, below.) Regardless of whether the seller provides disclosures, however, you should have the property inspected for defects or malfunctions in the building's structure.

Start by conducting your own inspection. A good self-help book, such as *The Home Inspection Troubleshooter*, by Robert Irwin (Dearborn), can help you learn what to look for. Ideally, you should inspect a house before you make a formal written offer to buy it so that you can save yourself the trouble should you find serious problems.

If a house passes your inspection, hire a general contractor to check all major house systems from top to bottom, including the roof, plumbing, electrical and heating systems and drainage. This will take two or three hours and cost you anywhere from $200 to $500 depending on the location, size, age and type of home. You should accompany the inspector during the examination so that you can learn more about the maintenance and preservation of the house and get answers to any questions you may have, including which problems are important and which are relatively minor. Depending on the property, you may want to arrange specialized inspections for pest damage, hazards from floods, earthquakes and other natural disasters and environmental health hazards such as asbestos and lead.

Professional inspections should be done after your written purchase offer has been accepted by the seller. (Your offer should be contingent upon the house passing one or more inspections). To avoid confusion and disputes, be sure you get a written report of each inspection.

If the house is in good shape, you can proceed, knowing that you're getting what you paid for. If an inspector discovers problems—such as an antiquated plumbing system or a major termite infestation—you can negotiate with the seller to have him pay for necessary repairs, or you can back out of the deal, assuming your contract is properly written to allow you to do so.

I'm making an offer to buy a house, but I don't want to lock myself into a deal that might not work out. How can I protect myself?

Real estate offers almost always contain contingencies—events that must happen within a certain amount of time (such as 30 days) in order to finalize the deal. For example, you may want to make your offer contingent on your ability to qualify for financing, the house passing certain physical inspections or even your ability to sell your existing house first. Be aware, however, that the more contingencies you place in an offer, the less likely the seller is to accept it.

Strategies for Buying an Affordable House

To find a good house at a comparatively reasonable price, you must learn about the housing market and what you can afford, make some sensible compromises as to size and amenities and, above all, be patient. Here are some proven strategies to meet these goals:

Buy a cheap fixer-upper.

Buy a small house (with remodeling potential) and add on later.

Buy a house at an estate or probate sale.

Buy a house subject to foreclosure (when a homeowner defaults on his mortgage).

Buy a shared-equity house, pooling resources with someone other than a spouse or partner.

Rent out a room or two in the house.

Buy a duplex, triplex or house with an in-law unit.

Lease a house you can't afford now with an option to buy later.

Buy a limited-equity house built by a nonprofit organization.

Buy a house at an auction.

More Information About Buying a Home

100 Questions Every First-Time Home Buyer Should Ask, by Ilyce R. Glink (Times Books), is a substantial book designed to help first-time buyers through the maze of buying a house.

Buy Your First Home Now, by Peter G. Miller (Harper Collins), provides information to help you intelligently find and finance a home.

Your New House: The Alert Consumer's Guide to Buying and Building a Quality Home, by Alan & Denise Fields (Windsor Peak Press), offers advice for those who want to buy or build a new home.

The Home Inspection Troubleshooter, by Robert Irwin (Dearborn), shows how to inspect a house in order to discover major problems such as a bad foundation, leaky roof or malfunctioning fireplace.

How to Buy a House in California, by Ralph Warner, Ira Serkes and George Devine (Nolo Press), explains all the details of the California house-buying process and contains tear-out contracts and disclosure forms.

Selling Your House

If you're selling a home, you need to time the sale properly, price the home accurately and understand the laws, such as disclosure requirements, that cover house transactions. These questions and answers will get you started.

I'm trying to decide whether to put my house on the market or wait a while. What are the best and worst times to sell?

Too many people rush to sell their houses and lose money because of it. Ideally, you should put your house on the market when there's a large pool of buyers—causing prices to go up. This may occur in the following situations:

- your area is considered especially attractive—for example, because of the schools, low crime rate, weather or proximity to a major city
- mortgage interest rates are low
- the economic climate of your region is healthy and people feel confident about the future, or
- there's a jump in house buying activity, as often occurs in spring.

Of course, if you have to sell immediately—because of financial reasons, a divorce, a job move or an imperative health concern—and you don't have any of the advantages listed above, you may have to settle for a lower price, or help the buyer with financing, in order to make a quick sale.

I want to save on the real estate commission. Can I sell my house myself without a real estate broker or agent?

Usually, yes. This is called a FSBO (pronounced "fizzbo")—For Sale By Owner. You must be aware, however, of the legal rules that govern real estate transfers in your state, such as who must sign the papers, who can conduct the actual transaction and what to do if and when any problems arise that slow down the transfer of ownership. You also need to be aware of any state-mandated disclosures as to the physical condition of your house. (See the discussion below.)

If you want to go it alone, be sure you have the time, energy and ability to handle all the details—from setting a realistic price to negotiating offers and closing the deal. Also, be aware that FSBOs are usually more feasible in hot or sellers' markets where there's more competition for homes, or when you're not in a hurry to sell. For more advice on FSBOs, contact your state department of real estate. Also, check Abele Owners' Network, online at http://www.owners.com/.

Is there some middle ground where I can use a broker on a more limited (and less expensive) basis?

You might consider doing most of the work yourself—such as showing the house—and using a real estate broker's help with such crucial tasks as:

- setting the price of your house
- advertising your home in the local multiple listing service (MLS) of homes for sale in the area, published by local boards of realtors, and
- handling some of the more complicated paperwork when the sale closes.

If you work with a broker in a limited way, you may be able to negoti-ate a reduction of the typical 5%-7% broker's commission, or you may be able to find a real estate agent who charges by the hour for specified services such as reviewing the sales contract.

How much should I ask for my house?

The key is to determine how much your property is actually worth on the market—called "appraising" its value. The most important factors used to determine a house's value are recent sales prices of similar properties in the neighborhood (called "comps").

Real estate agents have access to sales data for the area ("comp books") and can give a good estimate of what your house should sell for. Many real estate agents will offer this service free, hoping that you will list your house with them. You can also hire a professional real estate appraiser to give you a documented opinion as to your house's value. Public record offices, such as the county clerk or recorder's office, may also have information on recent house sales. And *Consumer Reports* now offers this type of information by telephone: Call (800) 775-1212 for more information.

Finally, asking prices of houses still on the market can also provide guidance (adjusting for the fact that asking prices are typically 10% or more above the usual sales price). To find out asking prices, go to open houses and check newspaper real estate classified ads.

Preparing Your House for Sale

Making your house look as attractive as possible may put several thousand dollars in your pocket. Sweep the sidewalk; mow the lawn; clean the windows; fix chipped or flaking paint. Clean and tidy up all rooms; be sure the house smells good—hide the kitty litter box and bake some cookies. Check for loose steps, slick areas or unsafe fixtures, and deal with everything that might cause injury to a prospective buyer. Take care of real eyesores, such as a cracked window or overgrown front yard. Don't overlook small but obvious problems, such as a leaking faucet or loose doorknob. Find ways to improve the look of your house without spending much money—a new shower curtain and towels might really spruce up your bathroom.

Do I need to take the first offer that comes in?

Offers, even very attractive ones, are rarely accepted as written. More typically, you will respond with a written counteroffer accepting some, maybe even most, of the offer terms, but proposing certain changes. Most counteroffers correspond to these provisions of an offer:

- price—you want more money
- financing—you want a larger down payment
- occupancy—you need more time to move out
- buyer's sale of current house—you don't want to wait for this to occur
- inspections—you want the buyer to schedule them more quickly.

A contract is formed when either you or the buyer accept all of the terms of the other's offer or counteroffer in writing within the time allowed.

What are my obligations to disclose problems about my house, such as a basement that floods in heavy rains?

In most states, it is illegal to fraudulently conceal major physical defects in your property, such as your troublesome basement. And states are increasingly requiring sellers to take a pro-active role by making written disclosures on the condition of the property. California, for example, has stringent disclosure requirements. California sellers must give buyers a mandatory disclosure form listing such defects as a leaky roof, faulty plumbing, deaths that occurred within the last three years on the property, even the presence of neighborhood nuisances, such as a dog that barks every night. In addition, California sellers must disclose potential hazards from floods, earthquakes, fires, environmental hazards and other problems in a Natural Hazard Disclosure Statement.

Generally, you are responsible for disclosing only information within your personal knowledge. While it's not usually required, many sellers hire a general contractor to inspect the property. The information will help you determine which items need repair or replacement and will assist you in preparing any required disclosures. An inspection report is also useful in pricing your house and negotiating with prospective buyers.

Full disclosure of any property defects will also help protect you from legal problems from a buyer who seeks to rescind the sale or sues you for damages suffered because you carelessly or intentionally withheld important information about your property.

Check with your real estate broker or attorney, or your state department of real estate, for disclosures required in your state. Also, be aware that real estate brokers are increasingly requiring that sellers complete disclosure forms, regardless of whether it's legally required.

Sellers Must Disclose Lead-Based Paint and Hazards

If you are selling a house built before 1978, you must comply with the federal Residential Lead-Based Paint Hazard Reduction Act of 1992, also known as Title X (Ten). You must:

- disclose all known lead-based paint and hazards in the house
- give buyers a pamphlet prepared by the U.S. Environmental Protection Agency (EPA) called *Protect Your Family From Lead in Your Home*
- include certain warning language in the contract, as well as signed statements from all parties verifying that all disclosures (including giving the pamphlet) were made
- keep signed acknowledgments for three years as proof of compliance, and
- give buyers a ten-day opportunity to test the housing for lead.

If you fail to comply with the law, the buyer can sue you for triple the amount of damages suffered—for example, three times the cost of repainting a house previously painted with lead-based paint.

For more information, contact the National Lead Information Center, 800-424-LEAD (phone) or http://www.nsc.org/ehc/lead.htm (online).

What are home warranties, and should I buy one?

Home warranties are service contracts that cover major housing systems—electrical wiring, built-in appliances, heating, plumbing and the like—for one year from the date the house is sold. Most warranties cost $300-$500 and are renewable. If something goes wrong with any of the covered systems after escrow closes, the repairs are paid for (minus a modest service fee)—and the new buyer saves money. Many sellers find that home warranties make their house more attractive and easier to sell.

Before buying a home warranty, be sure you don't duplicate coverage. You don't need a warranty for the heating system, for example, if your furnace is just six months old and still covered by the manufacturer's three-year warranty.

Your real estate agent or broker can provide more information on home warranties.

What is the "house closing"?

The house closing is the final transfer of the ownership of the house from the seller to the buyer. It occurs after both you and the buyer have met all the terms of the contract and the deed is recorded. (See *Deeds*, below). Closing also refers to the time when the transfer will occur, such as "the closing on my house will happen on January 27 at 10:00 a.m."

Do I need an attorney for the house closing?

This varies depending on state law and local custom. In some states, attorneys are not typically involved in residential property sales, and an escrow or title company handles the entire closing process. In many other states, particularly in the eastern part of the country, attorneys (for both buyer and seller) have a more active role in all parts of the house transaction; they handle all the details of offer contracts and house closings. Check with your state department of real estate or your real estate broker for advice.

I'm selling my house and buying another. What are some of the most important tax considerations?

The 1997 Taxpayer Relief Act contained a big break for homeowners. If you sell your home, you may exclude up to $250,000 of your profit (capital gain) from tax. For married couples filing jointly, the exclusion is $500,000.

The law applies to sales after May 6, 1997. To claim the whole exclusion, you must have owned and lived in your residence an aggregate of at least two of five years before the sale. You can claim the exclusion once every two years.

Even if you haven't lived in your home a total of two years out of the last five, you are still eligible for a partial exclusion of capital gains if you sold because of a change in employment, health or unforeseen circumstances. You get a portion of the exclusion, based on the percentage of the two-year period you lived in the house. To calculate it, take the number of months you lived there before the sale and divide it by 24.

For example, if you're an unmarried taxpayer who's lived in your home for 12 months, and you sell it for a $100,000 profit, the entire amount would be excluded from capital gains. Because you lived in the house for half of the two-year period, you could claim half the exclusion, or $125,000. (12/24 x $250,000 = $125,000.) That's enough to exclude your entire $100,000 gain.

For more information on current tax laws involving real estate transactions, contact the IRS at 800-829-1040 or check their Website at www.irs.ustreas.gov. Ask for Form 2119, *Sale of Your Home*, and the general instructions for this form. If you're claiming the exclusion, you must file Form 2119 with your tax return.

More Information About Selling a Home

100 Questions Every Home Seller Should Ask, by Ilyce R. Glink (Times Books), is a complete guide to selling a house, from preparing for showing to signing the final contract to understanding the tax consequences of the sale.

Consumer Reports Home Price Service gives actual sales prices of houses and condos throughout the continental U.S.—by specific address, street or price range. For fee and order information, call 800-775-1212.

For Sale by Owner, by George Devine (Nolo Press), provides step-by-step advice on handling your own sale in California, from putting the house on the market to negotiating offers to transferring title.

Deeds

Castles in the air are the only property you can own without the intervention of lawyers. Unfortunately, there are no title deeds to them.

—J. FEIDOR REES

Remember playing Monopoly as a kid, where amassing deeds to property—those little color-coded cards—was all-important? Real-life deeds aren't nearly so colorful, but they're still very, very important. Here are some questions commonly asked about deeds.

What is a deed?

A deed is the document that transfers ownership of real estate. It contains the names of the old and new owners and a legal description of the property, and is signed by the person transferring the property.

Do I need a deed to transfer property?

Almost always. You can't transfer real estate without having something in writing. In some situations, a document other than a deed is used—for example, in a divorce, a court order may transfer real estate from the couple to just one of them.

I'm confused by all the different kinds of deeds—quitclaim deed, grant deed, warranty deed. Does it matter which kind of deed I use?

Probably not. Usually, what's most important is the substance of the deed: the description of the property being transferred and the names of the old and new owners. Here's a brief rundown of the most common types of deeds:

A *quitclaim* deed transfers whatever ownership interest you have in the property. It makes no guarantees about the extent of your interest. Quitclaim deeds are commonly used by divorcing couples; one spouse signs over all his rights in the couple's real estate to the other. This can be especially useful if it isn't clear how much of an interest, if any, one spouse has in property that's held in another spouse's name.

A *grant deed* transfers your ownership and implies certain promises— that the title hasn't already been transferred to someone else or been encumbered, except as set out in the deed. This is the most commonly used kind of deed, in most states.

A *warranty deed* transfers your ownership and explicitly promises the buyer that you have good title to the property. It may make other promises as well, to address particular problems with the transaction.

Does a deed have to be notarized?

Yes. The person who signs the deed (the person who is transferring the property) should take the deed to a notary public, who will sign and stamp it. The notarization means that a notary public has verified that the signature on the deed is genuine. The signature must be notarized before the deed will be accepted for recording (see the next question).

After a deed is signed and notarized, do I have to put it on file anywhere?

Yes. You should "record" (file) the deed in the land records office in the county where the property is located. This office goes by different names in different states; it's usually called the County Recorder's Office, Land Registry Office or Register of Deeds. In most counties, you'll find it in the courthouse.

Recording a deed is simple. Just take the signed, original deed to the land records office. The clerk will take the deed, stamp it with the date and some numbers, make a copy and give the original back to you. The numbers are usually book and page numbers, which show where the deed will be found in the county's filing system. There will be a small fee, probably about $5 a page, for recording.

What's a trust deed?

A trust deed (also called a deed of trust) isn't like the other types of deeds; it's not used to transfer property. It's really just a version of a mortgage, commonly used in some states.

A trust deed transfers title to land to a "trustee," usually a trust or title company, which holds the land as security for a loan. When the loan is paid off, title is transferred to the borrower. The trustee has no powers unless the borrower defaults on the loan; then the trustee can sell the property and pay the lender back from the proceeds, without first going to court.

More Information About Deeds

The Deeds Book, by Mary Randolph (Nolo Press), contains tear-out deed forms and instructions for transferring California real estate. For information about deeds in other states, check your local law library.

Home Safety

Most burglars prefer to enter an empty house and get in and out quickly. Here are ten ways to avoid making your house an easy target.

Burglar-proof your house.
If you've been meaning to get better locks, an alarm system, metal bars on windows or motion sensor lights, do it now. Cut down shrubbery that gives burglars a hiding place. Pay special attention to back doors and windows, where burglars often find the easiest entry. See if a police department representative will evaluate your home's security and recommend improvements.

Lock up.

Half of all burglaries occur through unlocked doors and windows. Don't hide keys in obvious places, such as under a doormat or flowerpot, on top of the door frame or under a plant. If you have to hide a key, put it in the spot where it is least likely to be discovered.

Have a trusted person house-sit.

Or ask a friend, relative or neighbor to keep an eye on things. Some police departments provide security checks for vacationers.

Give your house a lived-in look.

An overstuffed mailbox and yellowing newspapers signal that no one is home; have someone pick up your mail and newspapers, or have deliveries put on hold.

Arrange to have the lawn mowed, garden watered, leaves raked or snow shoveled. You may even want to have your neighbor put garbage in your garbage cans.

Fill up the driveway.

If you have two cars, leave one in the driveway, or ask a neighbor to park there.

Put lights on automatic timers.

Inexpensive timers turn lights and radios on and off at set times. For instance, a radio and lamp in the living room might be on in the early evening, and then a bedroom lamp could be on from 9:30 to midnight. You might also consider installing motion sensor lights for your back yard or back entrance, or other spots where someone might hide.

Leave drapes and shades the way you normally have them.

If you can, have someone open drapes during the day and shut them at night. A house that's shuttered up tight looks unoccupied.

Put valuables out of sight.

Don't leave valuables such as jewelry, art and electronic equipment in sight, close to windows. Even simple steps to hide your property may be effective if an intruder does manage to get in. A dusty hatbox in the top of a closet, empty food containers, a laundry hamper or a toy box are all places to stash valuables. As an extra precaution, consider leaving some valuables with a trusted neighbor, friend or relative—if that house is secure and someone will be home the entire time you're gone.

Consider a safe.

If you need to protect very expensive property, consider getting a safe deposit box or buying a good fireproof safe.

Make a home inventory.

If your home is burglarized, an up-to-date home inventory will make it easier to deal with police and your insurance company. Without one, you'll have to create a list of all your property from memory. (An inventory is also very useful if you lose property as a result of a fire, earthquake, flood or other natural disaster.)

Fortunately, making a home inventory isn't an onerous task. And doing so not only prepares you for possible losses—it can also help you prevent the loss itself. As you inventory your possessions, you'll become more aware of their vulnerability, and you can take steps to secure them.

Start by walking through your house with a pad of paper and a still or video camera. Take pictures and jot down a list of any items worth more than $25. Go room by room, and don't forget the garage, attic and basement. Be sure to include jewelry, clothing, stamp or coin collections, CD and record collections, silver, tools and electronic equipment. Then take a little time to formalize your inventory. Insurance companies often supply inventory forms. Making and updating an inventory can be even easier if you own a computer.

Keep your written and photographic inventory in a safe place, such as a fire-resistant file cabinet or safe, the freezer or a safe deposit box. Keep at least one copy away from home. If you take a long vacation, give a copy to a friend or neighbor; that way, if your house is broken into while you're gone, that person can determine what's missing and report it to the police.

What to Include in a Home Inventory

Your home inventory should include the following key information about each item:

- Complete description, including whether or not the item is marked with a serial number or an ID number such as your driver's license number. (You can buy an electric engraving pen for $20 or so at a hardware store.) ID and serial numbers will help police identify stolen goods. Also, remember to record the make and model of the item; this will help you justify its estimated value to your insurance company.
- Location. This will help you identify what you've lost if only one area, such as the garage, is hit.
- Location of ownership documents, receipts, owner's manuals and repair bills.
- Purchase price, current value and replacement cost. For most items, your best estimate will do. For antiques or other difficult-to-price items, such as a stamp collection, you may need a professional appraisal.

More Information About Home Security

Nolo's Personal RecordKeeper (Nolo Press) (software for Windows or Macintosh), allows you to create a complete home inventory on your computer.

http://www.nolo.com

Nolo Press offers self-help information on a wide variety of legal topics, including real estate matters.

http://www.homefair.com/home

The Homebuyer's Fair offers lots of information that will help you buy or sell a home or relocate to a new area. It's especially useful if you're deciding where to live based on home prices, schools, crime, salaries and other factors.

http://www.homescout.com

Home Scout will help you search over 800,000 real estate listings on hundreds of independent Websites.

http://www.ired.com

The Internet Real Estate Directory lists thousands of real estate Websites and ranks them based on the amount of traffic they receive.

http://www1.ashi.com

The American Society of Home Inspectors offers information on buying a home in good shape, including referrals to local home inspectors.

http://www.inman.com/

Real estate columnist Brad Inman provides the latest real estate news.

http://www.owners.com/

If you're selling your home without a broker, Abele Owners' Network allows you to list it for free. To post a photograph or detailed information, however, you must pay a fee.

http://www.realtylocator.com

Realty Locator provides over 100,000 real estate links nationwide, including property listings, agents, lenders and information resources on everything from home improvement to mortgage calculators.

http://www.homepath.com

Fannie Mae, the nation's largest source of home mortgage loans, offers several useful mortgage calculators to help you determine how much you can afford to spend on a house and what your monthly loan payments will be.

http://www.homeshark.com

HomeShark allows you to compare rates from various lenders, prequalify and apply for a home loan. It includes detailed advice on choosing the best type of mortgage, determining how much house you can afford, selecting a real estate broker and evaluating the value of a house. A similar online mortgage site is available from E-loan at www.eloan.com.

http://www.hsh.com

HSH Associates publishes detailed information on mortgage loans available from lenders across the U.S.

http://www.realtor.com

The official Website of the National Association of Realtors lists over one million homes for sale throughout the United States.

Neighbors

*People have discovered that they can fool
the devil, but they can't fool the neighbors*

—**EDGAR WATSON HOWE**

Years ago, problems between neighbors were resolved informally, perhaps with the help of a third person respected by both sides. These days, neighbors—who may not know each other well, if at all—are quicker to head for court. Usually, of course, lawsuits only exacerbate bad feelings and cost everyone money, and the courthouse should be the place of last, not first, resort. But knowing the legal ground rules is important; you may prevent small disputes from turning into big ones.

Boundaries

Most of us don't know, or care, exactly where our property boundaries are located. But if you or your neighbor wants to fence the property, build a structure or cut down a tree close to the line, you need to know where it actually runs.

How can I find the exact boundaries of my property?

You can hire a licensed land surveyor to survey the property and place official markers on the boundary lines. A simple survey usually costs about $500; if no survey has been done for a long time, or if the maps are unreliable and conflicting, be prepared to spend up to $1,000.

My neighbor and I don't want to pay a surveyor. Can't we just make an agreement about where we want the boundary to be?

You and the neighbor can decide where you want the line to be, and then make it so by signing deeds that describe the boundary. If you have a mortgage on the property, consult an attorney for help in drawing up the deeds. You may need to get the permission of the mortgage holder before you give your neighbor even a tiny piece of the land.

Once you have signed a deed, you should record (file) it at the county land records office, usually called the County Recorder's Office, Land Registry Office or something similar.

Deeds are discussed in more detail in Chapter 1.

What can I do if a neighbor starts using my property?

If a neighbor starts to build on what you think is your property, do something immediately. If the encroachment is minor—for instance, a small fence in the wrong place—you may think you shouldn't worry. But you're wrong. When you try to sell your house, a title company might refuse to issue insurance because the neighbor is on your land.

Also, if you don't act promptly, you could lose part of your property. When one person uses another's land for a long enough time, he can gain a legal right to continue to do so and, in some circumstances, gain ownership of the property.

Talk to your neighbor right away. Most likely, a mistake has been made because of a conflicting description in the neighbor's deed or just a mistaken assumption about the boundary line. If your neighbor is hostile and insists on proceeding, state that you will sue if necessary. Then send a firm letter—or have a lawyer send one on his or her letterhead. If the building doesn't stop, waste no time in having a lawyer get a judge's order to temporarily stop the neighbor until you can bring a civil lawsuit for trespass before the judge.

A Little Common Sense

If you are having no trouble with your property and your neighbors, yet you feel inclined to rush out to determine your exact boundaries just to know where they are, please ask yourself a question. Have you been satisfied with the amount of space that you occupy? If the answer is yes, then consider the time, money and hostility that might be involved if you pursue the subject.

If a problem exists on your border, keep the lines of communication open with the neighbor, if possible. Learn the law and try to work out an agreement. Boundary lines simply don't matter that much to us most of the time; relationships with our neighbors matter a great deal.

Fences

Local fence ordinances are usually strict and detailed. Most regulate height and location, and some control the material used and even appearance. Residents of planned unit developments and subdivisions are often subject to even pickier rules. On top of all this, many cities require you to obtain a building permit before you begin construction.

Fence regulations apply to any structure used as an enclosure or a partition. Usually, they include hedges and trees.

How high can I build a fence on my property?

In residential areas, local rules commonly restrict artificial (constructed) backyard fences to a height of six feet. In front yards, the limit is often four feet.

Height restrictions may also apply to natural fences—fences of bushes or trees—if they meet the ordinance's general definition of fences. Trees that are planted in a row and grow together to form a barrier are usually considered a fence. When natural fences are specifically mentioned in the laws, the height restrictions commonly range from five to eight feet.

If, however, you have a good reason (for example, you need to screen your house from a noisy or unsightly neighboring use, such as a gas station), you can ask the city for a one-time exception to the fence law, called a variance. Talk to the neighbors before you make your request, to explain your problem and get them on your side.

My neighbor is building a fence that violates the local fence law, but nothing's happening. How can I get the law enforced?

Cities are not in the business of sending around fence inspection teams, and as long as no one complains, a nonconforming fence may stand forever.

Tell the neighbor about the law as soon as possible. She probably doesn't know what the law is, and if the fence is still being built, may be able to modify it at a low cost. If she suggests that you mind your own business, alert the city. All it takes in most circumstances is a phone call to the planning or zoning department or the city attorney's office. The neighbor will be ordered to conform; if she doesn't, the city can fine her and even sue.

My neighbor's fence is hideous. Can I do anything about it?

As long as a fence doesn't pose a threat of harm to neighbors or those passing by, it probably doesn't violate any law just because it's ugly. Occasionally, however, a town or subdivision allows only certain types of new fences—such as board fences—in an attempt to create a harmonious architectural look. Some towns also prohibit certain materials—for example, electrically charged or barbed wire fences.

Even without such a specific law, if a fence is so poorly constructed that it is an eyesore or a danger, it may be prohibited by another law, such as a blighted property ordinance. And if the fence was erected just for meanness—it's high, ugly and has no reasonable use to the owner—it may be a "spite fence," and you can sue the neighbor to get it torn down.

The fence on the line between my land and my neighbor's is in bad shape. Can I fix it or tear it down?

Unless the property owners agree otherwise, fences on a boundary line belong to both owners when both are using the fence. Both owners are responsible for keeping the fence in good repair, and neither may remove it without the other's permission.

A few states have harsh penalties for refusing to chip in for maintenance after a reasonable request from the other owner. Connecticut, for example, allows one neighbor to go ahead and repair, and then sue the other owner for double the cost.

Of course, it's rare that a landowner needs to resort to a lawsuit. Your first step should be to talk to the neighbor about how to tackle the problem. Your neighbor will probably be delighted that you're taking the initiative to fix a fence that's already an eyesore and might deteriorate into a real danger.

Trees

WOODMAN, SPARE THAT TREE.

TOUCH NOT A SINGLE BOUGH:

IN YOUTH IT SHELTERED ME,

AND I'LL PROTECT IT NOW.

—GEORGE POPE MORRIS

We human beings exhibit some complicated, often conflicting, emotions over our trees. This is especially true when it comes to the trees in our own yards. We take ownership of our trees and their protection very seriously in this country, and this is reflected in the law.

Can I trim the branches of the neighbor's tree that hang over my yard?

You have the legal right to trim tree branches up to the property line. But you may not go onto the neighbor's property or destroy the tree itself.

Deliberately Harming a Tree

In almost every state, a person who intentionally injures someone else's tree is liable to the owner for two or three times the amount of actual monetary loss. These penalties protect tree owners by providing harsh deterrents to would-be loggers.

Most of a big oak tree hangs over my yard, but the trunk is on the neighbor's property. Who owns the tree?

Your neighbor. It is accepted law in all states that a tree whose trunk stands wholly on the land of one person belongs to that person.

If the trunk stands partly on the land of two or more people, it is called a boundary tree, and in most cases it belongs to all the property owners.

All the owners are responsible for caring for the tree, and one co-owner may not remove a healthy tree without the other owners' permission.

My neighbor dug up his yard, and in the process killed a tree that's just on my side of the property line. Am I entitled to compensation for the tree?

Yes. The basic rule is that someone who cuts down, removes or hurts a tree without permission owes the tree's owner money to compensate for the harm done. You can sue to enforce that right—but you probably won't have to, once you tell your neighbor what the law is.

My neighbor's tree looks like it's going to fall on my house any day now. What should I do?

You can trim back branches to your property line, but that may not solve the problem if you're worried about the whole tree coming down.

City governments often step in to take care of, or make the owner take care of, dangerous trees. Some cities have ordinances that prohibit maintaining any dangerous condition—including a hazardous tree—on private property. To enforce such an ordinance, the city can demand that the owner remove the tree or pay a fine. Some cities will even remove such a tree for the owner. To check on your city's laws and policies, call the city attorney's office.

You might also get help from a utility company, if the tree threatens its equipment. For example, a phone company will trim a tree that hangs menacingly over its lines.

If you don't get help from these sources, and the neighbor refuses to take action, you can sue. The legal theory is that the dangerous tree is a "nuisance" because it is unreasonable for the owner to keep it and it interferes with your use and enjoyment of your property. You can ask the court to order the owner to prune or remove the tree. You'll have to sue in regular court (not small claims court) and have proof that the tree really does pose a danger to you.

V i e w s

The privilege of sitting in one's home and gazing at the scenery is a highly prized commodity. And it can be a very expensive one. Potential buyers, sometimes overwhelmed by a stunning landscape, commit their life savings to properties, assuming that the view is permanent. Sometimes it is not.

If a neighbor's addition or growing tree blocks my view, what rights do I have?

Unfortunately, you have no right to light, air or view, unless it has been granted in writing by a law or subdivision rule. The exception to this general rule is that someone may not deliberately and maliciously block another's view with a structure that has no reasonable use to the owner.

This rule encourages building and expansion, but the consequences can be harsh. If a view becomes blocked, the law will help only if:

- a local law protects views
- the obstruction violates private subdivision rules, or
- the obstruction violates some other specific law.

How can a view ordinance help?

A few cities that overlook the ocean or other desirable vistas have adopted view ordinances. These laws protect a property owner from having his view (usually, the view that he had when he bought the property) obstructed by growing trees. They don't cover buildings or other structures that block views.

The ordinances allow someone who has lost a view to sue the tree owner for a court order requiring him to restore the view. A neighbor who wants to sue must first approach the tree owner and request that the tree be cut back. The complaining person usually bears the cost of trimming or topping, unless the tree was planted after the law became effective, or the owner refuses to cooperate.

Some view ordinances contain extensive limitations that take most of the teeth out of them. Some examples:

- Certain species of trees may be exempt, especially if they grew naturally.
- A neighbor may be allowed to complain only if the tree is within a certain distance from his or her property.
- Trees on city property may be exempt.

Cities Without View Ordinances

If, like most cities, your city doesn't have a view ordinance, you might find help from other local laws. Here are some laws that may help restore your view:

Fence Height Limits. If a fence is blocking your view, it may be in violation of a local law. Commonly, local laws limit artificial (constructed) fences in back yards to six feet high and in front yards to three or four feet. Height restrictions may also apply to natural fences, such as hedges.

Tree Laws. Certain species of trees may be prohibited—for example, trees that cause allergies or tend to harm other plants. Laws may also forbid trees that are too close to a street (especially an intersection), to power lines or even to an airport.

Zoning Laws. Local zoning regulations control the size, location and uses of buildings. In a single-family area, buildings are usually limited to 30 or 35 feet. Zoning laws also usually require a certain setback, or distance between a structure and the boundary lines. They also limit how much of a lot can be occupied by a structure. For instance, many suburban cities limit a dwelling to 40% to 60% of the property.

I live in a subdivision with a homeowners' association. Will that help me in a view dispute?

Often, residents of subdivisions and planned unit developments are subject to a detailed set of rules called Covenants, Conditions and Restrictions (CC&Rs). They regulate most matters that could concern a neighbor, including views. For example, a rule may state that trees can't obstruct the view from another lot, or simply limit tree height to 15 feet.

If someone violates the restrictions, the homeowners' association may apply pressure (for example, removing the privilege of using a swimming pool) or even sue. A lawsuit is costly and time-consuming, however, and the association may not want to sue except for serious violations of the rules.

If the association won't help, you can take the neighbor to court yourself, but be prepared for a lengthy and expensive experience.

I want to buy a house with a great view. Is there anything I can do to make sure I won't ever lose the view—and much of my investment?

First, ask the property owner or the city planning and zoning office if the property is protected by a view ordinance. Then check with the real estate agent to see if neighbors are subject to restrictions that would protect your view. Also, if the property is in a planned unit development, find out whether a homeowners' association actively enforces the restrictions.

Check local zoning laws for any property that might affect you. Could the neighbor down the hill add a second-story addition?

Finally, look very closely from the property to see which trees might later obstruct your view. Then go introduce yourself to their owners and explain your concerns. A neighbor who also has a view will probably understand your concern. If someone is unfriendly and uncooperative, you stand warned.

How to Approach a View Problem

Before you approach the owner of a tree that has grown to block your view, answer these questions:

- Does the tree affect the view of other neighbors? If it does, get them to approach the tree owner with you. Trimming costs may be divided among you.
- Which part of the tree is causing view problems for you—one limb, the top, one side of it?
- What is the least destructive action that could be taken to restore your view? Maybe the owner will agree to a limited and careful pruning.
- How much will the trimming cost? Be ready to pay for it. Remember that every day you wait and grumble is a day for the trees to grow and for the job to become more expensive. The loss of your personal enjoyment is probably worth more than the trimming cost, not to mention the devaluation of your property (which can be thousands of dollars).

N o i s e

Nothing so needs reforming as other people's habits.

—MARK TWAIN

If you are a reasonable person and your neighbor is driving you wiggy with noise, the neighbor is probably violating a noise law.

Do I have any legal recourse against a noisy neighbor?

You bet. The most effective weapon you have to maintain your peace and quiet is your local noise ordinance. Almost every community prohibits excessive, unnecessary and unreasonable noise, and police enforce these laws.

Most laws designate certain "quiet hours"—for example, from 10 p.m. to 7 a.m. on weekdays, and until 8 or 9 a.m. on weekends. So running a power mower may be perfectly acceptable at 10 a.m. on Saturday, but not at 7 a.m. Many towns also have decibel level noise limits. When a neighbor complains, they measure the noise with electronic equipment. To find out what your town's noise ordinance says, ask at the public library or the city attorney's office.

If your neighbor keeps disturbing you, you can also sue, and ask the court for money damages or to order the neighbor to stop the noise ("abate the nuisance," in legal terms). For money damages alone, you can use small claims court. For a court order telling somebody to stop doing something, you'll have to sue in regular court.

Of course, what you really want is for the nuisance to stop. But getting a small claims court to order your neighbor to pay you money can be amazingly effective. And suing in small claims court is easy and inex-

pensive, and it doesn't require a lawyer.

Noise that is excessive and deliberate may also be in violation of state criminal laws against disturbing the peace or disorderly conduct. This means that, in very extreme circumstances, the police can arrest your neighbor. Usually, these offenses are punishable by fines or short jail sentences.

The neighbor in the apartment next to mine is very noisy. Isn't the landlord supposed to keep tenants quiet?

In addition to the other remedies all neighbors have, you have another arrow in your quiver: You can lean on the landlord to quiet the neighbor. Standard rental and lease agreements contain a clause entitled "Quiet Enjoyment." This clause gives tenants the right to occupy their apartments in peace, and also imposes upon them the responsibility not to disturb their neighbors. It's the landlord's job to enforce both sides of this bargain.

If the neighbor's stereo is keeping you up every night, the tenants are probably violating the rental agreement, and could be evicted. Especially if several neighbors complain, the landlord will probably order the tenant to comply with the lease or face eviction. For more information about your rights as a tenant, see Chapter 3.

*Tips for Handling
a Noise Problem*

- Know the law and stay within it.
- Be reasonably tolerant of your neighbors.
- Assert your rights.
- Communicate with your neighbors—both the one causing the problem and others affected by it.
- Ask the police for help when it is appropriate.
- Use the courts when necessary.

My neighbor's dog barks all the time, and it's driving me crazy. What can I do?

Usually, problems with barking dogs can be resolved without resorting to police or courts. If you do eventually wind up in court, however, a judge will be more sympathetic if you made at least some effort to work things out first. Here are the steps to take when you're losing patience (or sleep) over a neighbor's noisy dog:

1. Ask your neighbor to keep the dog quiet. Sometimes owners are blissfully unaware that there's a problem. If the dog barks for hours every day—but only when it's left alone—the owner may not know that you're being driven crazy.

If you can establish some rapport with the neighbor, try to agree on specific actions to alleviate the problem: for example, that your neighbor will take the dog to obedience school or consult with an animal behavior

specialist, or that the dog will be kept inside after 10 p.m. After you agree on a plan, set a date to talk again in a couple of weeks.

2. Try mediation. Mediators, both professional and volunteers, are trained to listen to both sides, identify problems, keep everyone focused on the real issues and suggest compromises. A mediator won't make a decision for you, but will help you and your neighbor agree on a resolution.

Many cities have community mediation groups which train volunteers to mediate disputes in their own neighborhoods. Or ask for a referral from:

- the small claims court clerk's office
- the local district attorney's office—the consumer complaint division, if there is one
- radio or television stations that offer help with consumer problems, or
- a state or local bar association.

3. Look up the law. In some places, barking dogs are covered by a specific state or local ordinance. If there's no law aimed specifically at dogs, a general nuisance or noise ordinance makes the owner responsible. Local law may forbid loud noise after 10 p.m., for example, or prohibit any "unreasonable" noise. And someone who allows a dog to bark after numerous warnings from police may be arrested for disturbing the peace.

To find out what the law is where you live, go to a law library and check the state statutes and city or county ordinances yourself. Look in the index under "noise," "dogs," "animals" or "nuisance." Or call the local animal control agency or city attorney.

4. Ask animal control authorities to enforce local noise laws. **Be** persistent. Some cities have special programs to handle dog complaints.

5. Call the police, if you think a criminal law is being violated. Generally, police aren't too interested in barking dog problems. And summoning a police cruiser to a neighbor's house obviously will not improve your already-strained relations. But if nothing else works, and the relationship with your neighbor is shot anyway, give the police a try.

http://www.nolo.com
Nolo Press offers self-help information about a wide variety of legal topics, including neighbor law.

More Information About Neighbor Law

Neighbor Law: Fences, Trees, Boundaries and Noise, by Cora Jordan (Nolo Press), explains laws that affect neighbors and shows how to resolve common disputes without lawsuits.

Dog Law, by Mary Randolph (Nolo Press), is a guide to the laws that affect dog owners and their neighbors.

Landlords and Tenants

Property has its duties as well as its rights.

–THOMAS DRUMMOND

Thirty years ago, custom, not law, controlled how most landlords and tenants interacted with each other. This is no longer true. Today, whether you focus on leases and rental agreements; habitability; discrimination; the amount, use and return of security deposits; how and when a landlord may enter a rental unit; or a dozen other issues, both landlord and tenant must understand their legal rights and responsibilities.

Because landlord-tenant laws vary significantly depending on where you live, remember to check your state and local laws for specifics. A list of state statutes, including URLs for those that are online, is included at the end of this chapter.

Leases and Rental Agreements

It's important to carefully read—and fully understand—the terms of your lease or rental agreement. This piece of paper is the contract that forms the legal basis for the landlord-tenant relationship.

Why is it important to sign a lease or rental agreement?

The lease or rental agreement is the key document of the tenancy, setting out important issues such as:

- the length of the tenancy
- the amount of rent and deposits the tenant must pay
- the number of people who can live on the rental property
- who pays for utilities
- whether the tenant may have pets
- whether the tenant may sublet the property
- the landlord's access to the rental property, and
- who pays attorney fees if there is a lawsuit.

Leases and rental agreements should always be in writing, even though most states allow them to be oral (spoken). While oral agreements may seem easy and informal, they often lead to disputes. If a tenant and landlord later disagree about key agreements, such as whether or not the tenant can sublet, the end result is all too likely to be a court argument over who said what to whom, when and in what context. This is particularly a problem with long-term leases, so most states prohibit oral agreements that last for one year or more.

What's the difference between a rental agreement and a lease?

The biggest difference is the period of occupancy. A written rental agreement provides for a tenancy of a short period (often 30 days). The tenancy is automatically renewed at the end of this period unless the tenant or landlord ends it by giving written notice, typically 30 days. For these month-to-month rentals (meaning the rent is paid monthly), the landlord can change the terms of the agreement with proper written notice, subject to any rent control laws. This notice is usually 30 days, but can be shorter in some states if the rent is paid weekly or bi-weekly.

A written lease, on the other hand, gives a tenant the right to occupy a rental unit for a set term—most often for six months or a year, but sometimes longer—if the tenant pays the rent and complies with other lease provisions. Unlike a rental agreement, when a lease expires it does not usually automatically renew itself. A tenant who stays on with the landlord's consent will generally be considered a month-to-month tenant.

In addition, with a fixed-term lease, the landlord cannot raise the rent or change other terms of the tenancy during the lease, unless the changes are specifically discussed in the lease or the tenant agrees.

What happens if a tenant breaks a long-term lease?

As a general rule, a tenant may not legally break a lease unless the landlord significantly violates its terms—for example, by failing to make necessary repairs. A few states have laws that allow tenants to break a lease because health problems or a job relocation require a permanent move. A tenant who breaks a lease without good cause will be responsible for the remainder of the rent due under the lease term. In most states, however, a landlord has a legal duty to try to find a new tenant as soon as possible—no

matter what the tenant's reason for leaving—rather than charge the tenant for the total remaining rent due under the lease.

When can a landlord legally break a lease and end a tenancy?

A landlord may legally break a lease if a tenant significantly violates its terms or the law—for example, by paying the rent late, keeping a dog in violation of a no-pets clause in the lease, substantially damaging the property or participating in illegal activities on or near the premises, such as selling drugs.

A landlord must first send the tenant a notice stating that the tenancy has been terminated. State laws set out very detailed requirements as to how a landlord must write and deliver (serve) a termination notice. Depending on what the tenant has done wrong, the termination notice may state that the tenancy is over and warn the tenant that he or she must vacate the premises or face an eviction lawsuit. Or, the notice may give the tenant a few days to clean up his or her act—for example, pay the rent or find a new home for the dog. If the tenant fixes the problem or leaves as directed, no one goes to court. If a tenant doesn't comply with the termination notice, the landlord can file a lawsuit to evict the tenant.

Tenant Selection

Choosing tenants is the most important decision any landlord makes. To do it well, landlords need a reliable system that helps weed out tenants who will pay their rent late, damage the rental unit or cause legal or practical problems later.

What's the best way for landlords to screen tenants?

Savvy landlords should ask all prospective tenants to fill out a written rental application that includes the following information:
- employment, income and credit history
- Social Security and driver's license numbers
- past evictions or bankruptcies, and
- references.

Before choosing tenants, landlords should check with previous landlords and other references; verify income, employment and bank account information; and obtain a credit report. The credit report is especially important because it will indicate whether a particular person has a history of paying rent or bills late, has gone through bankruptcy, has been convicted of a crime or has ever been evicted.

How can a landlord avoid discrimination lawsuits when choosing a tenant?

Fair housing laws specify clearly illegal reasons to refuse to rent to a tenant. (For details, see *Housing Discrimination*, below.) Landlords are legally free to choose among prospective tenants as long as their decisions comply with these laws and are based on legitimate business criteria. For example, a landlord is entitled to reject someone with a poor credit history, insufficient income to pay the rent or past behavior—such as damaging property—that makes the person a bad risk. A valid occupancy policy limiting the number of people per rental unit—one that is clearly tied to health and safety—can also be a legal basis for refusing tenants.

Housing Discrimination

Not so long ago, a landlord could refuse to rent to an applicant, or could evict a tenant, for almost any reason. If a landlord didn't like your race or religion, or the fact that you had children, you might find yourself out on the street. But times have changed. To protect every American's right to be treated fairly and to help people find adequate housing, Congress and state legislatures passed laws prohibiting discrimination, most notably the federal Fair Housing Acts.

What types of housing discrimination are illegal?

The federal Fair Housing Act and Fair Housing Amendments Act prohibit landlords from choosing tenants on the basis of a group characteristic such as:

- race
- religion
- ethnic background or national origin
- sex
- age
- the fact that the prospective tenant has children (except in certain designated senior housing), or
- a mental or physical disability.

In addition, some state and local laws prohibit discrimination based on a person's marital status or sexual orientation.

On the other hand, landlords are allowed to select tenants using criteria that are based on valid business reasons, such as requiring a minimum income or positive references from previous landlords, as long as these standards are applied equally to all tenants.

Examples of Housing Discrimination

The Fair Housing Act and Amendments prohibit landlords from taking any of the following actions based on race, religion or any other protected category:

- advertising or making any statement that indicates a preference based on group characteristic, such as skin color
- falsely denying that a rental unit is available
- setting more restrictive standards, such as higher income, for certain tenants
- refusing to rent to members of certain groups
- refusing to accommodate the needs of disabled tenants, such as allowing a guide dog, hearing dog or service dog
- setting different terms for some tenants, such as adopting an inconsistent policy of responding to late rent payments, or
- terminating a tenancy for a discriminatory reason.

How does a tenant file a discrimination complaint?

A tenant who thinks that a landlord has broken a federal fair housing law should contact the U.S. Department of Housing and Urban Development (HUD), the agency which enforces the Fair Housing Act. To find the nearest office, call HUD's Fair Housing Information Clearinghouse at (800) 343-3442, or check the HUD Website at www.hud.gov. HUD will provide a complaint form and will investigate and decide the merits of the claim. A tenant must file his or her complaint within one year of the alleged discriminatory act. HUD will typically appoint a mediator to negotiate with the landlord and reach a settlement (called a "conciliation"). If a settlement can't be reached, the fair housing agency will hold an administrative hearing to determine whether discrimination has occurred.

If the discrimination is a violation of a state fair housing law, the tenant may file a complaint with the state agency in charge of enforcing the law. In California, for example, the Department of Fair Employment and Housing enforces the state's two fair housing laws.

Also, instead of filing a complaint with HUD or a state agency, tenants may file lawsuits directly in federal or state court. If a state or federal court or housing agency finds that discrimination has taken place, a tenant may be awarded damages, including any higher rent he or she had to pay as a result of being turned down, and damages for humiliation or emotional distress.

Rent and Security Deposits

Landlords may charge any dollar amount for rent, except in certain areas covered by rent control. Many states do, however, have rules as to

when and how rent must be paid and how it may be increased.

Security deposits are more strictly regulated by state law. Most states dictate how much money a landlord can require, how the funds can be used—for example, to cover unpaid rent—and when and how the deposit must be returned.

What laws cover rent due dates, late rent and rent increases?

By custom, leases and rental agreements usually require rent to be paid monthly, in advance. Often rent is due on the first day of the month. However, it is usually legal for a landlord to require rent to be paid at different intervals or on a different day of the month. Unless the lease or rental agreement specifies otherwise, there is no legally-recognized grace period—in other words, if a tenant hasn't paid the rent on time, the landlord can usually start eviction proceedings the day after it is due. Some landlords charge fees for late payment of rent or for bounced checks; these fees are usually legal if they are reasonable. The laws on late fees can be found in your state's landlord-tenant statutes, listed at the end of this chapter.

For month-to-month rentals, the landlord can raise the rent (subject to any rent control laws) with proper written notice, typically 30 days. With a fixed-term lease, the landlord may not raise the rent during the lease, unless the increase is specifically called for in the lease or the tenant agrees.

How Rent Control Works

Communities in only five states—
California, the District of Columbia,
Maryland, New Jersey and New York—
have laws that limit the amount of rent
landlords may charge. Rent control
ordinances (also called rent stabilization,
maximum rent regulation or a similar
term) typically set a base rent for each
rental unit, and limit the circumstances
and times rent may be increased. Many
rent control laws require landlords to
have a legal or just cause (that is, a
good reason) to evict a tenant—for
example, if the tenant doesn't pay rent or
if the landlord wants to move a family
member into the rental unit. Landlords
and tenants in New York City, Newark,
San Francisco and other cities with rent
control should be sure to get a current
copy of the ordinance and any
regulations interpreting it. Check the
phone book for the address and phone
number of the local rent control board, or
contact the mayor or city manager's
office.

How much security deposit can a landlord charge?

All states allow landlords to collect a
security deposit when the tenant
moves in; the general purpose is to
assure that the tenant pays rent when
due and keeps the rental unit in good
condition. Half the states limit the
amount landlords can charge, usually
not more than a month or two worth
of rent—the exact amount depends on
the state.

Many states require landlords to
put deposits in a separate account, and
some require landlords to pay tenants
the interest on deposits.

What are the rules for returning security deposits?

The rules vary from state to state, but
landlords usually have a set amount of
time in which to return deposits, usually 14 to 30 days after the tenant
moves out—either voluntarily or by
eviction.

Landlords may normally make certain deductions from a tenant's security deposit, provided they do it correctly and for an allowable reason.
Many states require landlords to provide a written itemized accounting of
deductions for unpaid rent and for
repairs for damages that go beyond
normal wear and tear, together with
payment for any deposit balance.

A tenant may sue a landlord who
fails to return his or her deposit when
and how required, or who violates
other provisions of security deposit
laws such as interest requirements;
often these lawsuits may be brought
in small claims court. In some states,
a tenant may recover the entire deposit—sometimes even two or three
times this amount—plus attorney fees
and other damages.

The rules for the keeping and return of security deposits can be found
in state landlord-tenant statutes,
listed at the end of this chapter.

Tenants' Privacy Rights

In most states, the tenant's duty to pay rent is conditioned on the landlord's proper repair and mainte-nance of the premises. This means that landlords have a legal responsi-bility to keep fairly close tabs on the condition of the property. To balance landlords' responsibilities with ten-ants' rights to privacy in their homes, laws in many states set rules about when and how landlords may legally enter rented premises.

Under what circumstances may a landlord enter rental property?

Typically, a landlord has the right to legally enter rented premises in cases of emergency, in order to make needed repairs (in some states, just to determine whether repairs are neces-sary) or to show the property to pro-spective new tenants or purchasers.

Several states allow landlords the right of entry during a tenant's ex-tended absence (often defined as seven days or more) to maintain the prop-erty as necessary and to inspect for damage and needed repairs. In most cases, a landlord may not enter just to check up on the tenant and the rental property.

Must landlords provide notice of entry?

States typically require landlords to provide advance notice (usually 24 hours) before entering a rental unit. Without advance notice, a landlord or manager may enter rented premises while a tenant is living there only in an emergency, such as a fire or serious water leak, or when the tenant gives permission.

To find out how much notice a landlord must give a tenant before entering, check your state's landlord-tenant statutes, listed at the end of this chapter.

Is it legal for a landlord to answer questions about a tenant's credit?

Creditors, banks and prospective land-lords may ask a landlord to provide credit or other information about a current or former tenant. A landlord who sticks to the facts that are rel-evant to the tenant's creditworthiness (such as whether the tenant paid rent on time) is allowed to respond to these inquiries. To be extra careful, some landlords insist that tenants sign a release giving the landlord permis-sion to respond to such requests.

Repairs and Maintenance

In 1863, an English judge wrote that "Fraud apart, there is no law against letting [leasing] a tumble-down house." But in 20th century America, it's no longer legal to be a slumlord. Landlords must repair and maintain their rental property or face financial losses and legal problems from tenants—who may withhold rent and pursue other legal remedies—and from government agencies that enforce housing codes.

What are the landlord's repair and maintenance responsibilities?

Under most state and local laws, rental property owners must offer and maintain housing that satisfies basic habitability requirements, such as adequate weatherproofing; available heat, water and electricity; and clean, sanitary and structurally safe premises. Local building or housing codes typically set specific standards, such as the minimum requirements for light, ventilation and electrical wiring. Many cities require the installation of smoke detectors in residential units and specify security measures involving locks and keys.

To find out more about state laws on repair and maintenance responsibilities, check your state's landlord-tenant statutes listed at the end of this chapter. Your local building or housing authority, and health or fire department, can provide information on local housing codes and penalties for violations.

What are a tenant's rights if the landlord refuses to maintain the property?

If a landlord doesn't meet his or her legal responsibilities, a tenant usually has several options, depending on the state. These options include:
- paying less rent
- withholding the entire rent until the problem is fixed
- making necessary repairs
- hiring someone to make necessary repairs and deducting the cost from the next month's rent
- calling the local building inspector, who can usually order the landlord to make repairs, or
- moving out, even in the middle of a lease.

A tenant can also sue the landlord for a partial refund of past rent, and in some circumstances can sue for the discomfort, annoyance and emotional distress caused by the substandard conditions.

Tenants should check state and local laws and understand remedies available before taking any action such as withholding rent.

What must tenants do to keep the rental property in good shape?

All tenants have the responsibility to keep their own living quarters clean and sanitary. And a landlord can usually delegate his repair and maintenance tasks to the tenant in exchange for a reduction in rent. If the tenant fails to do the job well, however, the landlord is not excused from his responsibility to maintain habitability. In addition, tenants must carefully use common areas and facilities, such as lobbies, garages and pools.

Is a landlord liable if a tenant or visitor is injured on the rental property?

A landlord may be liable to the tenant—or others—for injuries caused by dangerous or defective conditions on the rental property. In order to hold the landlord responsible, the tenant must prove that the landlord was negligent, and that the landlord's negligence caused an injury. To do this, the tenant must show that:

- the landlord had control over the problem that caused the injury
- the accident was foreseeable
- fixing the problem (or at least giving adequate warnings) would not have been unreasonably expensive or difficult
- a serious injury was the probable consequence of not fixing the problem

- the landlord failed to take reasonable steps to avert the accident
- the landlord's failure—his negligence—caused the tenant's accident, and
- the tenant was genuinely hurt.

For example, if a tenant falls and breaks his ankle on a broken front door step, the landlord will be liable if the tenant can show that:

- It was the landlord's responsibility to maintain the steps (this would usually be the case, because the steps are part of the common area, which is the landlord's responsibility).
- An accident of this type was foreseeable (falling on a broken step is highly likely).
- A repair would have been easy or inexpensive (fixing a broken step is a minor job).
- The probable result of a broken step is a serious injury (a fall certainly qualifies).
- The landlord failed to take reasonable measures to maintain the steps (this will be easy to prove if the step was broken for weeks, or even days, but less so if the step broke five minutes earlier and showed no previous signs of weakening).
- The broken step caused the injury (this is easy to prove if the tenant has a witness to the fall, but might be hard if there are no witnesses and the landlord claims that the tenant really injured himself somewhere else and is attempting to pin the blame on the landlord), and

- He is really hurt (in the case of a broken bone, this is easy to establish).

A tenant can file a personal injury lawsuit for medical bills, lost earnings, pain and other physical suffering, permanent physical disability and disfigurement and emotional distress. A tenant can also sue for property damage that results from faulty maintenance or unsafe conditions.

More Information on Personal Injury Lawsuits

How to Win Your Personal Injury Claim, by Joseph L. Matthews (Nolo Press), provides step-by-step details on how to understand what a claim is worth, prepare a claim for compensation, negotiate a fair settlement and manage a case even if a lawyer is not involved.

How can property owners minimize financial losses and legal problems related to repairs and maintenance?

Landlords who offer and maintain housing in excellent condition can avoid many problems. Here's how:

- Clearly set out responsibilities for repair and maintenance in the lease or rental agreement.

- Use a written checklist to inspect the premises and fix any problems before new tenants move in.
- Encourage tenants to immediately report plumbing, heating, weatherproofing or other defects or safety or security problems—whether in the tenant's unit or in common areas such as hallways and parking garages.
- Keep a written log of all tenant complaints and repair requests with details as to how and when problems were fixed.
- Handle urgent repairs as soon as possible. Take care of major inconveniences, such as a plumbing or heating problem, within 24 hours. For minor problems, respond in 48 hours. Always keep tenants informed as to when and how the repairs will be made, and the reasons for any delays.

- Twice a year, give tenants a checklist on which to report potential safety hazards or maintenance problems that might have been overlooked. Use the same checklist to inspect all rental units once a year.

Landlord Liability for Criminal Acts and Activities

Can a law-abiding citizen end up financially responsible for the criminal acts of a total stranger? Yes—if it's a landlord who owns rental property where an assault or other crime occurred. Rental property owners are being sued with increasing frequency by tenants injured by criminals, with settlements and jury awards typically ranging from $100,000 to $1 million. What are the landlord's responsibilities for tenant safety and security?

Property owners are responsible for keeping their premises safe for tenants and guests. Landlords in most states now have at least some degree of legal responsibility to protect their tenants from would-be assailants and thieves and from the criminal acts of fellow tenants. Landlords must also protect the neighborhood from their tenants' illegal activities, such as drug dealing. These legal duties stem from building codes, ordinances, statutes and, most frequently, court decisions.

How can a landlord limit responsibility for crime committed by strangers on the rental property?

Effective preventive measures are the best response to possible liabilities from criminal acts and activities. The following steps will not only limit the likelihood of crime, but also reduce the risk that the property owner will be found responsible if a criminal assault or robbery does occur. A landlord should:

- Meet or exceed all state and local security laws that apply to the rental property, such as requirements for deadbolt locks on doors, good lighting and window locks.
- Realistically assess the crime situation in and around the rental property and neighborhood and design a security system that provides reasonable protection for the tenants—both in individual rental units and common areas such as parking garages and elevators. Local police departments, the landlord's insurance company and private security professionals can all provide useful advice on security measures. If additional security requires a rent hike, the landlord should discuss the situation with his or her tenants. Many tenants will pay more for a safer place to live.
- Educate tenants about crime problems in the neighborhood, and describe the security measures provided and their limitations.
- Maintain the rental property and conduct regular inspections to spot and fix any security problems, such as broken locks or burned out exterior flood lights. Asking tenants for their suggestions as part of an ongoing repair and maintenance system is also a good idea.
- Handle tenant complaints about dangerous situations, suspicious

activities or broken security items immediately. Failing to do this may saddle a landlord with a higher level of legal liability should a tenant be injured by a criminal act after a relevant complaint is made.

The Costs of Crime

The money a landlord spends today on effective crime-prevention measures will pale in comparison to the costs that may result from crime on the premises. The average settlement paid by landlords' insurance companies for horrific crimes such as rape and assault is $600,000, and the average jury award (when cases go to trial) is $1.2 million.

What kind of legal trouble do landlords face from tenants who deal drugs on the property?

Drug-dealing tenants can cause landlords all kinds of practical and legal problems:

- It will be difficult to find and keep good tenants and the value of the rental property will plummet.
- Anyone who is injured or annoyed by drug dealers—be it other tenants or people in the neighborhood— may sue the landlord on the grounds that the property is a public nuisance that seriously threatens public safety or morals.
- Local, state or federal authorities may levy stiff fines against the landlord for allowing the illegal activity to continue.

- Law enforcement authorities may seek criminal penalties against the landlord for knowingly allowing drug dealing on the rental property.
- In extreme cases, the presence of drug dealers may result in the government confiscating the rental property.

How can a property owner avoid legal problems from tenants who deal drugs or otherwise break the law?

There are several practical steps landlords can take to avoid trouble from tenants and limit their exposure to any lawsuits that are filed:

- Screen tenants carefully and choose tenants who are likely to be law-abiding and peaceful citizens. Weed out violent or dangerous individuals to the extent allowable under privacy and anti-discrimination laws that may limit questions about a tenant's past criminal activity, drug use or mental illness.
- Keep the results of background checks that show that the tenants' rent appeared to come from legitimate sources (jobs and bank accounts).
- Don't accept cash rental payments.
- Do not tolerate tenants' disruptive behavior. Include an explicit provision in the lease or rental agreement prohibiting drug dealing and other illegal activity and promptly evict tenants who violate the clause.
- Be aware of suspicious activity, such as heavy traffic in and out of the rental premises.

- Respond to tenant and neighbor complaints about drug dealing on the rental property. Get advice from police immediately upon learning of a problem.
- Consult with security experts to do everything reasonable to discover and prevent illegal activity on the rental property.

Protecting Tenant From the Manager

Rental property owners should be particularly careful hiring a property manager—the person who interacts with all tenants and has access to master keys. Landlords should scrupulously check a manager's background to the fullest extent allowed by law, and closely supervise his or her job performance. A tenant who gets hurt or has property stolen or damaged by a manager could sue the property owner for failing to screen the manager properly. If tenants complain about illegal acts by a manager, landlords should pay attention. Finally, property owners should make sure their insurance covers illegal acts of their employees.

Landlord Liability for Lead Poisoning

Landlords are increasingly likely to be held liable for tenant health problems resulting from exposure to lead and other environmental toxins, even if the landlord didn't cause—or even know about—the danger.

What are a landlord's legal responsibilities regarding lead in rental property?

Because of the health problems caused by lead poisoning, the Residential Lead-Based Paint Hazard Reduction Act was enacted in 1992. This law is commonly known as Title X (ten). Environmental Protection Agency (EPA) regulations implementing Title X apply to rental property built before 1978.

Under Title X, before signing or renewing a lease or rental agreement, a landlord must give every tenant the EPA pamphlet, *Protect Your Family From Lead in Your Home,* or a state-approved version of this pamphlet. Both the landlord and tenant must sign an EPA-approved disclosure form to prove that the landlord told the tenants about any known lead-based paint or hazards on the premises. Property owners must keep this disclosure form as part of their records for three years from the date that the tenancy begins.

A landlord who fails to comply with EPA regulations faces penalties of up to $10,000 for each violation. And a landlord who is found liable for tenant injuries from lead may have to pay three times what the tenant suffered in damages.

More Information on Lead Hazard Resources

Information on the evaluation and control of lead dust, and copies of *Protect Your Family From Lead in Your Home* may be obtained by calling the National Lead Information Center at 800-424-LEAD, or checking its Website at www.nsc.org/ehc/lead.htm. In addition, state housing departments have information on state laws and regulations governing the evaluation and control of lead hazards.

Are there any rental properties exempt from Title X regulations?

These properties are not covered by Title X:
- housing for which a construction permit was obtained, or on which construction was started, after January 1, 1978
- housing certified as lead-free by a state-accredited lead inspector
- lofts, efficiencies and studio apartments
- short-term vacation rentals of 100 days or less

- a single room rented in a residential dwelling
- housing designed for persons with disabilities, unless any child less than six years old lives there or is expected to live there
- retirement communities (housing designed for seniors, where one or more tenants is at least 62 years old), unless children under the age of six are present or expected to live there.

Landlord's Liability for Exposure to Asbestos

In addition to lead, property owners may be liable for tenant health problems caused by exposure to other environmental hazards, such as asbestos. Regulations issued by the Occupational Safety and Health Administration (OSHA) set strict standards for the testing, maintenance and disclosure of asbestos in buildings constructed before 1981. For information call OSHA at (202) 219-8148 or check OSHA's Website at www.osha.gov.

Insurance

Both tenants and landlords need insurance to protect their property and bank accounts. Without adequate insurance, landlords risk losing hundreds of thousands of dollars of property from fire or other hazards. While tenants may not have as much at stake financially, they also need insurance—especially tenants with expensive personal belongings. Tenant losses from fire or theft are not covered by the landlord's insurance.

How can insurance help protect a rental property business?

A well-designed insurance policy can protect rental property from losses caused by many perils, including fire, storms, burglary and vandalism. (Earthquake and flood insurance are typically separate.) A comprehensive policy will also include liability insurance, covering injuries or losses suffered by others as the result of defective conditions on the property.

Equally important, liability insurance covers the cost (mostly lawyer's bills) of defending personal injury lawsuits.

Here are some tips on choosing insurance:

- Purchase enough coverage to protect the value of the property and assets.
- Be sure the policy covers not only physical injury but also libel, slander, discrimination, unlawful and retaliatory eviction and invasion of privacy suffered by tenants and guests.
- Carry liability insurance on all vehicles used for business purposes, including the manager's car or truck if he or she will use it on the job.

If you need more information, *The Legal Guide for Starting and Running a Small Business*, by Fred S. Steingold

(Nolo Press), contains a detailed discussion of small business law, including how to insure your rental property.

What does renter's insurance cover?

The average renter's policy covers tenants against losses to their belongings occurring as a result of fire and theft, up to the amount stated on the face of the policy, such as $25,000 or $50,000.

Most renter policies include deductible amounts of $250 or $500. This means that if a tenant's apartment is burglarized, the insurance company will pay only for the amount of the loss over and above the deductible amount.

In addition to fire and theft, most renter's policies include personal liability coverage ($100,000 is a typical amount) for injuries or damage caused by the tenant—for example, if a tenant's garden hose floods the neighbor's cactus garden, or a tenant's guest is injured on the rental property due to the tenant's negligence.

Renter's insurance is a package of several types of insurance designed to cover tenants for more than one risk. Each insurance company's package will be slightly different—types of coverage offered, exclusions, the dollar amounts specified and the deductible will vary. Tenants who live in a flood or earthquake-prone area will need to pay extra for coverage. Policies covering flood and earthquake damage can be hard to find; tenants should shop around until they find the type of coverage that they need.

Resolving Disputes

Legal disputes—actual and potential—come in all shapes and sizes for landlords and tenants. Whether it's a disagreement over a rent increase, responsibility for repairs or return of a security deposit, rarely should lawyers and litigation be the first choice for resolving a landlord-tenant dispute.

How can landlords and tenants avoid disputes?

Both landlords and tenants should follow these tips to avoid legal problems:

- Know your rights and responsibilities under federal, state and local law.
- Make sure the terms of your lease or rental agreement are clear and unambiguous.
- Keep communication open. If there's a problem—for example, a disagreement about the landlord's right to enter a tenant's apartment—see if you can resolve the issue by talking it over, without running to a lawyer.
- Keep copies of any correspondence and make notes of conversations about any problems. For example, a tenant should ask for repairs in writing and keep a copy of the letter. The landlord should keep a copy of the repair request and note when and how the problem was repaired.

We've talked about the problem and still don't agree. What should we do next?

If you can't work out an agreement on your own, but want to continue the rental relationship, consider mediation by a neutral, third party. Unlike a judge, the mediator has no power to impose a decision but will simply work to help find a mutually acceptable solution to the dispute. Mediation is often available at little or no cost from a publicly-funded program.

More Information About Mediation

For information on local mediation programs, call your mayor's or city manager's office, and ask for the staff member who handles "landlord-tenant mediation matters" or "housing disputes." That person should refer you to the public office, business or community group that handles landlord-tenant mediations.

You can learn more about mediation by reading Chapter 17 of this book, *Courts and Mediation*.

If mediation doesn't work, is there a last step before going to a lawyer?

If you decide not to mediate your dispute, or mediation fails, it's time to pursue other legal remedies. If the disagreement involves money, such as return of the security deposit, you can take the case to small claims court. A few states use different names for this type of court (such as "Landlord-Tenant Court"), but traditionally the purpose has been the same: to provide a speedy, inexpensive resolution of disputes that involve relatively small amounts of money.

Keep in mind that your remedy in small claims court may be limited to an award of money damages. The maximum amount you can sue for varies from $3,000 to $7,500, depending on your state.

You can find more information about small claims court in Chapter 17, *Courts and Mediation*.

Landlord-Tenant Statutory Codes

Here are some of the key statutes pertaining to landlord-tenant law in each state.

ALABAMA
Ala. Code §§ 35-9-1 to -100

ALASKA
Alaska Stat. §§ 34.03.010 to .380

ARIZONA
Ariz. Rev. Stat. Ann. §§ 12-1171 to -1183; §§ 33-1301 to -1381

ARKANSAS
Ark. Code Ann. §§ 18-16-101 to -306

CALIFORNIA
Cal. [Civ.] Code §§ 1925-1954, 1961-1962.7, 1995.010-1997.270

COLORADO
Colo. Rev. Stat. §§ 38-12-101 to -104, -301 to -302

CONNECTICUT
Conn. Gen. Stat. Ann. §§ 47a-1 to -50a

DELAWARE
Del. Code. Ann. tit. 25, §§ 5101-7013

DISTRICT OF COLUMBIA
D.C. Code Ann. §§ 45-1401 to -1597, -2501 to -2593

FLORIDA
Fla. Stat. Ann. §§ 83.40-.66

GEORGIA
Ga. Code Ann. §§ 44-7-1 to -81

HAWAII
Haw. Rev. Stat. §§ 521-1 to -78

IDAHO
Idaho Code §§ 6-301 to -324 and §§ 55-201 to -313

ILLINOIS
Ill. Rev. Stat. ch. 765 para. 705/0.01-740/5

INDIANA
Ind. Code Ann. §§ 32-7-1-1 to 37-7-19

IOWA
Iowa Code Ann. §§ 562A.1-.36

KANSAS
Kan. Stat. Ann. §§ 58-2501 to -2573

KENTUCKY
Ky. Rev. Stat. Ann. §§ 383.010-.715

LOUISIANA
La. Rev. Stat. Ann. §§ 9:3201-:3259; La. Civ. Code Ann. art. 2669-2742

MAINE
Me. Rev. Stat. Ann. tit. 14, §§ 6001-6045

MARYLAND
Md. Code Ann., [Real Prop.] §§ 8-101 to -501

MASSACHUSETTS
Mass. Gen. Laws Ann. ch. 186 §§ 1-21

MICHIGAN
Mich. Comp. Laws Ann. § 554.601-.640

MINNESOTA
Minn. Stat. Ann. §§ 504.01-.35

MISSISSIPPI
Miss. Code Ann. §§ 89-8-1 to -27

MISSOURI
Mo. Ann. Stat. §§ 441.010-.650; and §§ 535.150-.300

MONTANA
Mont. Code Ann. §§ 70-24-101 to -25-206

NEBRASKA
Neb. Rev. Stat. §§ 76-1401 to -1449

NEVADA
Nev. Rev. Stat. Ann. §§ 118A.010-.520

NEW HAMPSHIRE
N.H. Rev. Stat. Ann. §§ 540:1-540-A:8

NEW JERSEY
N.J. Stat. Ann. §§ 46:8-1 to -49

NEW MEXICO
N.M. Stat. Ann. §§ 47-8-1 to -51

NEW YORK
N.Y. [Gen. Oblig.] Law §§ 7-101 to -109; N.Y. [Real Prop.] Law §§ 220-238; N.Y. [Mult. Dwell.] Law §§ 1-11; N.Y. [Mult. Resid.] Law §§ 305

NORTH CAROLINA
N.C. Gen. Stat. §§ 42-1 to -56

NORTH DAKOTA
N.D. Cent. Code §§ 47-16-01 to -41

OHIO
Ohio Rev. Code Ann. §§ 5321.01-.19

OKLAHOMA
Okla. Stat. tit. 41, §§ 1-136

OREGON
Or. Rev. Stat. §§ 90.100-.435

PENNSYLVANIA
Pa. Stat. Ann. tit. 68, §§ 250.101-.342

RHODE ISLAND
R.I. Gen. Laws §§ 34-18-1 to -19

SOUTH CAROLINA
S.C. Code Ann. §§ 27-40-10 to -910

SOUTH DAKOTA
S.D. Codified Laws Ann. §§ 43-32-1 to -26

TENNESSEE
Tenn. Code Ann. §§ 66-28-101 to -517

TEXAS
Tex. [Prop.] Code Ann. §§ 91.001-92.301

UTAH
Utah Code Ann. §§ 57-17-1 to -5, -22-1 to -6

VERMONT
Vt. Stat Ann. tit. 9, §§ 4451-4468

VIRGINIA
Va. Code Ann. §§ 55-218.1 to -248.40

WASHINGTON
Wash. Rev. Code Ann. §§ 59.04.010-.900, .18.010-.910

WEST VIRGINIA
W. Va. Code §§ 37-6-1 to -30

WISCONSIN
Wis. Stat. Ann. §§ 704.01-.40

WYOMING
Wyo. Stat. §§ 34-2-125 to -130

More Information About Landlord-Tenant Law

From the landlord's point of view:

Every Landlord's Legal Guide, by Marcia Stewart, Ralph Warner and Janet Portman (Nolo Press). This 50-state book provides extensive legal and practical information on leases, tenant screening, rent, security deposits, privacy, repairs, property managers, discrimination, roommates, liability, tenancy termination and much more. It includes more than 25 legal forms and agreements as tear-outs and on disk.

Lease Writer (Nolo Press)(CD-ROM for Windows/Macintosh). This software program generates a customized legal residential lease or rental agreement, plus more than a dozen key documents and forms every landlord and property manager needs. It includes a database to track tenants and rental properties, and a log for rental payments, repairs and problems. The program gives you instant access to state-specific landlord-tenant information, and extensive online legal help.

From the tenant's point of view:

Every Tenant's Legal Guide, by Janet Portman and Marcia Stewart (Nolo Press). This book gives tenants in all 50 states the legal and practical information they need to deal with their landlords and protect their rights when things go wrong. It covers all important issues of renting, including signing a lease, getting a landlord to make needed repairs, fighting illegal discrimination, protecting privacy rights, dealing with roommates, getting the security deposit returned fairly, moving out and much more.

For both landlords and tenants:

Everybody's Guide to Small Claims Court, by Attorney Ralph Warner (National and California Editions)(Nolo Press). The book explains how to evaluate your case, prepare for court and convince a judge you're right. It also tells you what remedies (money only, or enforcement of the lease) are available in your state.

How to Mediate Your Dispute, by Peter Lovenheim (Nolo Press), explains how to choose a mediator, prepare a case and navigate the mediation process.

Additionally, tenants' unions and rental property owners' associations are good sources of advice. Look in your telephone book's white pages for names of these organizations.

http://www.nolo.com
Nolo Press offers self-help information about a wide variety of legal topics, including landlord-tenant law.

http://tenant.net/main.html
TenantNet provides information about landlord-tenant law, with a focus on tenants' rights. TenantNet is designed primarily for tenants in New York City, but the site offers information about the law in many other states. The site also provides the text of the federal fair housing law.

State Landlord-Tenant Statutes Online

The following states have made their statutes available online. By the time you read this, there will undoubtedly be more.

ALASKA
http://www.touchngo.com/lglcntr/akstats/statutes.htm

ARIZONA
http://www.azleg.state.az.us/ars/ars.htm

CALIFORNIA
http://www.leginfo.ca.gov/calaw.html

COLORADO
http://crs.aescon.com (Note: subscription fee)

CONNECTICUT
http://www.cslnet.ctstateu.edu/statutes/index.htm

FLORIDA
http://www.scri.fsu.edu/fla-leg/statutes/

IDAHO
http://www.idwr.state.id.us/idstat/TOC/idstTOC.html

INDIANA
http://www.law.indiana.edu/codes/in/incode.html

IOWA
http://www2.legis.state.ia.us/Code.html

KENTUCKY
http://www.lrc.state.ky.us/KRS/383-00/CHAPTER.HTM

LOUISIANA
http://www.state.la.us/osr/lac/lac.htm

MICHIGAN
http://www.icle.org/leg-sums/leglist.htm

MINNESOTA
http://www.leg.state.mn.us/leg/statutes.htm

MISSISSIPPI
http://www.mscode.com/

MISSOURI
http://www.house.state.mo.us/homestat.htm

MONTANA
http://www.nfoweb.com/folio.pgi/MTCODE/doc/

NEBRASKA
http://unicam1.lcs.state.ne.us/folio.pgi/statutes.nfo/

NEVADA
http://www.leg.state.nv.us/law1.htm

NEW JERSEY
http://www.njleg.state.nj.us/

NEW YORK
http://assembly.state.ny.us/ALIS/laws.html

OKLAHOMA
http://www.onenet.net/oklegal/statutes.basic.html

OREGON
http://www.efn.org/%7Ebobl/index4.html

SOUTH CAROLINA
http://www.lpitr.state.sc.us/newlaws.htm

UTAH
http://www.le.state.ut.us/~code/code.htm

VERMONT
http://www.leg.state.vt.us/statutes/statutes.htm

VIRGINIA
http://leg1.state.va.us/000/src.htm

WASHINGTON
http://leginfo.leg.wa.gov/www/rcw.htm

WISCONSIN
http://www.legis.state.wi.us/rsb/weblinks.html

WYOMING
http://legisweb.state.wy.us/titles/statutes.htm

Workplace Rights

I LIKE WORK; IT FASCINATES ME.

I CAN SIT AND LOOK AT IT FOR HOURS.

—JEROME K. JEROME

If you're like most workers, you have experienced occasional job-related problems or have questions about whether you are being fairly and legally treated on the job. Here are several common problems:

- You were not hired for a job and you have good reason to suspect it was because of your race, age or sex, or because you are disabled.
- Your employer promoted a less-qualified person—perhaps someone who is younger than you are—to fill a position you were promised.
- You are regularly asked to work overtime but are not offered extra pay. Or, you are paid for working extra hours, but you do not receive a premium rate, such as time-and-a-half.
- You need to take a leave of absence from your job to care for a sick parent, but you are concerned that this will jeopardize your job or your eligibility for a promotion.
- You have been called to serve on a jury and wonder if your employer must pay you for this time.
- You have just been laid off and you want to know whether, if business at your company picks up in the future, you have any right to get your job back. You also want to know whether you're entitled to unemployment payments, or whether your employer owes you severance pay.

It is reassuring for many workers to learn that they do not face these issues alone. In recent years, a number of laws have been passed to protect your rights in the workplace. Federal laws now establish some basic guarantees for most workers—such as the right to be paid fairly and on time and to work free from discrimination. And state laws may place their own twists on your workplace rights—regulat-

ing, for example, both your right to smoke and to work in a smoke-free place, or whether or not you are entitled to time off work to vote or to care for a sick child.

Fair Pay and Time Off

I do not like work even when someone else does it.

—MARK TWAIN

These days, most of us spend at least half of our waking hours working. Ideally, this time will be spent on jobs that are fulfilling. But whether or not we enjoy our work, the bottom line for almost all of us is to be paid fairly and on time. Fortunately, both state and federal laws protect this right.

I suspect my employer is bending some of the rules on paying employees. What are the legal controls on pay for work?

The most important and far-reaching law guaranteeing a worker's right to be paid fairly is the federal Fair Labor Standards Act or FLSA. The FLSA:
- defines the 40-hour workweek
- covers the federal minimum wage (currently $5.15 per hour)
- sets requirements for overtime, and
- places restrictions on child labor.

The FLSA is the single law most often violated by employers. But employers must also comply with other local, state or federal workplace laws that sometimes set higher standards. So in addition to determining whether you are being paid properly for overtime under the FLSA, you may need to check other laws that apply to your situation. Begin by contacting the local office of your state department of labor, which should be able to supply you with written materials setting forth your legal rights to be paid for your work.

Check Your Paystubs

Many employers either become confused by the nuances and exceptions in the wage and hour law (FLSA)—or they bend the rules to suit their own pocketbooks. Whatever the cause, you would do well to doublecheck your employer's math. A few simple rules distilled from the law may help.

Hourly. Hourly employees must be paid at least the minimum wage for all hours worked. Your employer cannot take an average—or pay you less than minimum wage for some hours worked and more for others.

Fixed rate or salary. Employees paid at a fixed rate can check their wages by dividing the amount they are paid in a pay period by the number of hours worked. The resulting average must be at least the minimum wage.

Commissions and piece rates. Your total pay divided by the number of hours you worked must average at least the minimum hourly wage rate.

My boss says that because I'm a supervisor, I am not legally entitled to overtime pay. Is this true?

It may be. Some employees are exempt from the FLSA—and the biggest and most abused exemption is for executive, administrative and professional workers. To qualify as an exempt executive, the employee must, among other things, spend at least 80% of worktime managing other workers. The definitions of administrative and professional employees are similar, but contain minor differences. For example, employees categorized as professionals must perform work that is primarily intellectual. The definitions also change with the employee's salary level. For example, if the weekly salary of the executive, administrative or professional employee exceeds a certain minimum, fewer factors are required to qualify for the exemption.

The portion of the law setting out restrictions on overtime pay is particularly complex and convoluted. If you have a question about whether your particular job is exempt, it may be worth your while to go to the nearest law library and carefully read the Fair Labor Standards Act, 29 U.S.C. §§ 201 and following. You can also read this law online by visiting the U.S. Department of Labor site at http://www.dol.gov. If questions remain, workers at your state department of labor may be able to help.

I put in more than forty hours on the job each week, without overtime pay. Am I entitled to time off to compensate for this?

Most workers are familiar with compensatory or comp time—the practice of offering employees time off from work in place of cash payments for overtime. What comes as a shock to many is that the practice is illegal in most situations. Under the FLSA, only state or government agencies may legally allow their employees time off in place of wages (29 U.S.C. § 207(o)). Even then, comp time may be awarded only:

- according to the terms of an agreement arranged by union representatives, or
- if the employer and employee agree to the arrangement before work begins.

When compensatory time is allowed, it must be awarded at the rate of one and one-half times the overtime hours worked—and comp time must be taken during the same pay period that the overtime hours were worked.

Some states do allow private employers to give employees comp time instead of cash. But there are complex, often conflicting laws controlling how and when it may be given. A common control, for example, is that employees must voluntarily request in writing that comp time be given instead of overtime pay—before the extra hours are worked. Check with your state's labor department for special laws on comp time in your area.

Many employers and employees routinely violate the rules governing the use of compensatory time in place of cash overtime wages. However, such violations are risky. Employees can find themselves unable to collect money due them if a company goes out of business or they are fired. And employers can end up owing large amounts of overtime pay to employees as the result of a labor department prosecution of compensatory time violations.

I work as a waitress and make good tips. But my boss says that because I get this extra money at work, I can be paid lower than the hourly minimum wage. Is this true?

It depends on how much money you make in tips. Employers must pay all employees covered by the federal wage law (FLSA) not less than the minimum wage—currently $5.15 per hour. And some states, including Alaska, Connecticut, the District of Columbia, Hawaii and Massachusetts have established a minimum wage that is higher than the federal one; if you live in one of these states, you are entitled to the higher rate.

But the matter of minimum wage becomes trickier when an employee routinely receives at least $30 per month in tips. Employers are allowed to credit half of those tips against the minimum wage requirement—that is, they can credit up to $2.12 an hour of the tips received toward their wage obligation and actually pay you only $2.13 an hour. However, the employer's offset must not exceed the tips the employee actually receives.

EXAMPLE

Alphonse is employed as a waiter and earns more than $10 per hour in tips. Denis, the restaurant's owner, is required to pay Alphonse at least $2.13 per hour on top of his tips for the first 40 hours worked in each week.

If business slows and Alphonse's tips dip to, say, $1 an hour, Denis may credit the tip amount toward Alphonse's hourly minimum wage. Denis must pay the additional salary required to make up the full amount of minimum wage Alphonse is owed: $5.15 an hour.

I am required to carry a beeper 24 hours a day, every day of the week for my job. I am occasionally called on my vacation, holidays and other days off. Am I entitled to be paid anything for on-call time?

Vacation days, holidays and other paid days off work should be just that—days off work—and you are entitled to enjoy them free from the reins of your beeper. When your employer requires you to be on-call but does not require you to stay on the company's premises, the following two rules generally apply:

- On-call time that you control and use for your own enjoyment or benefit is not counted as payable time.
- On-call time over which you have little or no control and which you cannot use for your own enjoyment or benefit is payable time.

Disputes usually boil down to the slipperiness in the definition of control and use of time. If the occasional beep beckons you only to call in to give advice, but you are otherwise free to spend your time any way you want, your employer need only pay for the time you spend answering the beeper. However, if your employer insists that you be available to return to work on demand and puts constraints on your behavior between beeper calls—you cannot consume alcohol, or you must stay within a certain radius of work, for example—you may be entitled to compensation for your on-call time.

Independent Contractors Are Exempt

The Fair Labor Standards Act covers only employees, not independent contractors, who are considered independent business people. Whether a person is an employee for purposes of the FLSA, however, generally turns on whether that worker is employed by a single employer, and not on the sometimes more lax Internal Revenue Service definition of an independent contractor.

If nearly all of your income comes from one company, a court would probably rule that you are an employee of that company for purposes of the FLSA, regardless of whether other details of your worklife would appear to make you an independent contractor.

The FLSA was passed to clamp down on employers who cheated workers of their fair wages. As a result, employee status is broadly interpreted so that as many workers as possible come within the protections of the law. In recent cases determining close questions of employment status, growing numbers of courts have found workers to be employees rather than independent contractors.

Courts are more likely to find that workers are employees when:
- the relationship appears to be permanent
- the worker lacks bargaining power with regard to the terms of his or her employment, and
- the individual worker is economically dependent upon the business to which he or she gives service.

What laws ensure my right to take vacations?

Here's a surprising legal truth that most workers would rather not learn: no law requires employers to pay you for time off, such as vacation or holidays. This means that if you receive a paid vacation, it's because of custom, not law.

And just as vacation benefits are discretionary with each employer, so is the policy of how and when they accrue. For example, it is perfectly legal for an employer to require a certain length of employment—six months or a year are common—before an employee is entitled to any vacation time. It is also legal for employers to prorate vacations for part-time employees, or to deny them the benefit completely. Employers are also free to set limits on how much paid time off employees may store up before it must be taken or is lost.

If your employer does have a policy of offering employees paid time off, however, it cannot discriminate in offering it—all employees must be subject to the same rules.

If I lose or leave my job, when will I receive my final paycheck?

Unfortunately, there is no easy answer to this question. Many state laws, but not all, mandate that a worker who is fired must be paid all accrued wages and promised vacation pay immediately. Furthermore, state laws often set short limits—generally 72 hours—as the time in which this payment must be made if an employee quits. But you'll need to check with your state's deparment of labor to learn the details of the law that applies to you.

Am I entitled to take time off from work if I get sick?

No law requires an employer to offer paid time off for illness. As with paid vacation time, however, an employer who offers paid sick time to some workers cannot discriminate by denying it to others.

Though you may not be entitled to paid time off, the Family and Medical Leave Act (FMLA), a federal law passed in 1993, gives workers some rights to unpaid leave for medical reasons. Under the FMLA, you may be eligible for up to 12 weeks of unpaid sick leave during any 12-month period. Your employer can count your accrued paid benefits—vacation, sick leave and personal leave days—toward the 12 weeks of leave allowed under the law. But many employers give employees the option of deciding whether or not to include paid leave time as part of their 12 weeks of sick leave.

The FMLA applies to all private and public employers with 50 or more employees—an estimated one-half of the workforce. To be covered under the law, you must have:
• been employed at the same workplace for a year or more, and
• worked at least 1,250 hours (about 24 hours a week) during the year preceding the leave.

There are a number of loopholes in the FMLA. Companies with fewer than 50 employees working at offices within a 75-mile radius are exempt from the FMLA—this means that small regional companies of even the largest corporations may not need to comply with the Act. The law also allows companies to exempt the highest paid 10% of employees. And finally, schoolteachers and instructors who work for educational agencies and private elementary or secondary schools may have restrictions on their FMLA leave.

Note, however, that a number of states have passed their own versions of family leave laws—and most of them give workers more liberal leave rights. A number of laws apply, for example, to smaller workplaces and extend to workers who have been on the job only a short time. Check with your state's department of labor for more information.

What if a member of my family gets sick—can I take time off to care for him or her?

Possibly. Workers' rights under the Family and Medical Leave Act

(FMLA)—or under your state's version of it—also apply if a member of your close family gets sick, or if you give birth to or adopt a child. The rights for new parents apply to both mothers and fathers in all situations—birth or adoption.

My employer refused to grant me the time off for sick leave guaranteed by the FMLA. What can I do?

The FMLA is enforced by the U.S. Department of Labor. If you have specific questions about this emerging law, including how to file a claim against your employer for failing to comply, contact your local Department of Labor office. You should be able to find a listing under U.S. Government, Department of Labor, in the phone book.

You generally must file a claim under the FMLA within two years of an employer's violation. If the violation was willful (intentional), you'll have up to three years to file. Because this law is relatively new, many interpretations of its language—including what constitutes a willful violation by an employer—will be decided by courts in years to come.

More Information About Wages, Hours and Time Off

You can check into your employer's wage and payment policies by calling the local U.S. Labor Department, Wage and Hour Division office, listed in the federal government section of your telephone directory.

Most of the exemptions to FLSA coverage are listed in federal statute, 29 U.S.C. §213. The most direct way to become familiar with these exemptions is to read about them in an annotated edition of the U.S. Code, which is what your local law library (or even a large public library) is most likely to have.

Also, the United States Department of Labor, 200 Constitution Avenue, NW, Washington, DC 20210, 202-219-7316, offers pamphlets describing federal wage and hours laws and the Family Medical Leave Act. Or, visit their Website at http://www.dol.gov.

Workplace Health and Safety

Over the past 20 years, workers have pushed strongly for laws to protect their health and safety on the job. And they have been somewhat successful. Several laws now establish basic safety standards aimed at reducing the number of illnesses, injuries and deaths in workplaces. Because most workplace safety laws rely for their effectiveness on employees who are willing to report job hazards, most laws also prevent employers from firing or discriminating against employees who report unsafe conditions to proper authorities.

Do I have any legal rights if I feel that my workplace is unsafe or unhealthy?

The main federal law covering threats to workplace safety is the Occupational Safety and Health Act of 1970 (OSHA). OSHA requires employers to provide a workplace that is free of dangers that could physically harm employees.

The law quite simply requires that your employer protect you from "recognized hazards" in the workplace. It does not specify or limit the types of dangers covered. Instead, it includes everything from equipment that might cause a serious cut or bruise to the unhealthy effects of long-term exposure to radiation, chemicals or airborne pollutants.

Basically, to prove an OSHA violation, you must produce evidence that:
- your employer failed to keep the workplace free of a hazard, and
- the particular hazard was recognized as being likely to cause death or serious physical injury.

Most states now have their own OSHA laws, most of which offer protections similar to the federal law. State laws typically concentrate on protecting workers who complain

about safety violations from being demoted or fired. A few states, including California, require all employers to fashion workplace safety plans. And Texas, big in its approach to most everything, has instituted a 24-hour hotline to receive complaints; the state prohibits employers from discriminating against those who call in.

How do I assert my rights to a safe workplace?

If you feel that your workplace is unsafe, your first action should be to make your supervisor aware of the danger. If your employer doesn't take prompt action, follow up in writing. Then, if you are still unsuccessful in getting your company to correct the safety hazard, you can file a complaint at the nearest OSHA office. Look under the U.S. Labor Department in the federal government section of your local telephone directory.

Preventing Additional Injuries

Workplace hazards often become obvious only after they cause an injury. For example, an unguarded machine part that spins at high speed may not seem dangerous until someone's clothing or hair becomes caught in it. But even after a worker has been injured, employers sometimes fail—or even refuse—to recognize that something that hurt one person is likely to hurt another.

If you have been injured at work by a hazard that should be eliminated before it injures someone else, take the following steps as quickly as possible after obtaining the proper medical treatment:

- Immediately file a claim for workers' compensation benefits so that your medical bills will be paid and you will be compensated for your lost wages and injury. In some states, the amount you receive from a workers' comp claim will be larger if a violation of a state workplace safety law contributed to your injury. (For more information about workers' compensation, see the next series of questions in this chapter.)

- Point out to your employer that a continuing hazard or dangerous condition exists. As with most workplace safety complaints, the odds of getting action will be greater if other employees join in your complaint.

- If your employer does not eliminate the hazard promptly, file a complaint with OSHA and any state or local agency that you think may be able to help. For example, if your complaint is about hazardous waste disposal, you may be able to track down a specific local group that has been successful in investigating similar complaints in the past.

Does OSHA protect against the harmful effects of tobacco smoke in the workplace?

OSHA rules apply to tobacco smoke only in rare and extreme circumstances, such as when contaminants created by a manufacturing process combine with tobacco smoke to create a dangerous workplace air supply that fails OSHA standards.

Workplace air quality standards and measurement techniques are so technical that typically only OSHA agents or consultants who specialize in environmental testing are able to determine when the air quality falls below allowable limits.

If OSHA won't protect me from secondhand tobacco smoke at work, is there anything I can do to limit or avoid exposure?

If your health problems are severely aggravated by co-workers' smoking, there are a number of steps you can take.

Check local and state laws. A growing number of local and state laws prohibit smoking in the workplace. Most of them also set out specific procedures for pursuing complaints. Your state's labor department should have up-to-date information about these. If you can't find local laws that prohibit smoking in workplaces, check with a national nonsmokers' rights group, such as Americans for Nonsmokers Rights, 2530 San Pablo Avenue, Suite J, Berkeley, CA 94702, 510-841-3032.

Ask your employer for an accommodation. Successful accommodations to smoke-sensitive workers have included installing additional ventilation systems, restricting smoking areas to outside or special rooms and segregating smokers and nonsmokers.

Consider filing a federal complaint. Most claims for injuries caused by secondhand smoke in the workplace are pressed and processed under the

Americans with Disabilities Act. In the strongest complaints, workers proved that smoke sensitivity rendered them disabled in that they were unable to perform a major life activity: breathing freely.

Consider income replacement programs. If you are unable to work out a plan to resolve a serious problem with workplace smoke, you may be forced to leave the workplace. But you may qualify for workers' compensation or unemployment insurance benefits. See *Losing or Leaving Your Job*, below.

More Information About Workerplace Health and Safety

OSHA in the Real World, by John Hartnett (Merritt Publishing), is written for employers, but provides a detailed overview of federal workplace safety rules and regulations for anyone who wants to know more about them.

The Occupational Safety and Health Administration, 200 Constitution Avenue, NW, Washington, DC 20210, 202-219-7162, publishes pamphlets about workplace safety laws. You can also visit OSHA online at http://www.osha.gov.

Workers' Compensation

If you are injured on the job—or suffer a work-related illness or disease that prevents you from working—you are eligible to receive benefits from your state workers' compensation program. You are also entitled to free medical care. If your disability is classified as permanent or results in death, additional benefits are available to you and your family.

Who pays workers' compensation benefits?

In most states, employers are required to purchase insurance for their employees from a workers' compensation insurance company—also called an insurance carrier. In some states, larger employers who are clearly solvent are allowed to self-insure or act as their own insurance companies, while smaller companies (with fewer than three or four employees) are not required to carry workers' compenstation insurance at all. When a worker is injured, her claim is filed with the insurance company—or self-insuring employer—who pays medical and disability benefits according to a state-approved formula.

Are all on-the-job injuries covered by workers' compensation?

Most are. The workers' compensation system is designed to provide benefits to injured workers no matter whether an injury is caused by the employer's or employee's negligence. But there are some limits. Generally, injuries caused because an employee is intoxicated or using illegal drugs are not covered by workers' compensation. Coverage may also be denied in situations involving:

- self-inflicted injuries (including those caused by a person who starts a fight)
- injuries suffered while a worker was committing a serious crime
- injuries suffered while an employee was not on the job, and
- injuries suffered when an employee's conduct violated company policy.

Does an injury have to have a definite date of onset in order to be covered?

Not necessarily. Your injury does not need to be caused by an accident—such as a fall from a ladder. Many workers, for example, receive compensation for repetitive stress injuries, including carpal tunnel syndrome and back problems, that are caused by overuse or misuse over a long period of time. You may also be compensated for some illnesses and diseases that are the gradual result of work conditions—for example, heart conditions, lung disease and stress-related digestive problems.

Are You Covered by Workers' Compensation?

Most workers are eligible for workers' compensation coverage, but every state excludes some workers. Exclusions often include:

- business owners
- independent contractors
- casual workers
- domestic employees in private homes
- farm workers
- maritime workers
- railroad employees, and
- unpaid volunteers.

Check the workers' compensation law of your state to see whether these exclusions affect you.

Federal government employees are also excluded from state workers' compensation coverage, but they receive workers' compensation benefits under a separate federal law.

Employees who aren't covered by workers' compensation usually must sue the employer for damages or, in some cases, they can sue the maker of a faulty piece of equipment.

Do I have to be injured at my workplace to be covered by workers' compensation?

No. As long as your injury is job-related, it's covered. For example, you'll be covered if you are injured while traveling on business, doing a work-related errand or even attending a required, business-related social function.

How do I claim workers' compensation benefits?

First, promptly report the work-related injury or sickness to your employer. Most states require that this be done within two to 30 days following an injury. If an injury occurs over time (for example, a breathing problem or carpal tunnel syndrome), you must report your condition soon after you discover it and realize that it is caused by your work.

Next, get the medical treatment you need and follow the doctor's instructions exactly. (This may include an "off-work order" or a "limited-duties work order.") Finally, file a claim with your workers' compensation carrier. Necessary forms must be provided by your employer. Ask someone in the personnel or benefits department.

Finally, make sure you save copies of all correspondence with your employer, its insurance carrier and your doctor concerning your workers' comp claim.

What kind of benefits will I receive?

The workers' compensation system provides replacement income, medical expenses and sometimes vocational rehabilitation benefits—that is, on the job training, schooling or job placement assistance. The benefits paid through workers' compensation, however, are almost always limited to relatively modest amounts.

If you become temporarily unable to work, you'll usually receive two-thirds of your average wage up to a fixed ceiling. But because these payments are tax-free, if you received decent wages prior to your injury, you'll fare reasonably well in most states. You will be eligible for these wage-loss replacement benefits as soon as you've lost a few days of work because of an injury or illness that is covered by workers' compensation.

If you become permanently unable to do the work you were doing prior to the injury, or unable to do any work at all, you may be eligible to receive long-term or lump-sum benefits. The amount of the payment you may be entitled to receive varies greatly with the nature and extent of your injuries. If you anticipate a permanent work disability, contact your local workers' compensation office as soon as possible; these benefits are rather complex and may take a while to process.

Social Security Benefits for the Permanently Disabled

If you're permanently unable to return to work, you may qualify for Social Security Disability benefits. Social Security will, over the long run, provide more benefits than workers' compensation—but be forewarned that these benefits are hard to get. They are reserved for seriously injured workers. To qualify, your injury or illness:

- must prevent you from doing any "substantial gainful work," and
- must be expected to last at least twelve months, or to result in death.

If you think you may meet the above requirements, contact your local Social Security office. For more information about Social Security benefits, see Chapter 14.

Can I be treated by my own doctor and, if not, can I trust a doctor provided by my employer?

In some states, you have a right to see your own doctor if you make this request in writing before the injury occurs. More typically, however, injured workers are referred to a doctor or health plan recruited and paid for by their employer.

Your doctor's report will have a big impact upon the benefits you receive. While it's crucial that you tell the doctor the truth about both your injury and your medical history (your benefits may be denied based on fraud if you don't), be sure to clearly identify all possible job-related medical problems and sources of pain. In short, this is no time to downplay or gloss over the presence of a pain.

Keep in mind that a doctor paid for by your employer's insurance company is not your friend. The desire to get future business may motivate a doctor to minimize the seriousness of your injury or to identify it as a pre-existing condition. For example, if you injure your back and the doctor asks you if you have ever had back problems before, it would be unwise to treat the doctor to a 20-year history of every time you suffered a minor pain or ache. Just say "no" unless you really have suffered a significant previous injury or chronic condition.

If I am initially treated by an insurance company doctor, do I have a right to see my own doctor at some point?

State workers' compensation systems establish technical and often tricky rules in this area. Often, you have the right to ask for another doctor at the insurance company's expense if you clearly state you don't like the one the insurance company provides, although there is sometimes a waiting period before you can get a second doctor. Also, if your injury is serious, you usually have the right to a second opinion. And in some states, after you are treated by an insurance company's doctor for a certain period (90 days is typical), you may have the automatic right to transfer your treatment to your own doctor or health plan—with the cost being paid for by the workers' comp insurance company.

To understand your rights, get a copy of your state's rules—or, if necessary, research your state workers' compensation laws and regulations in the law library. Chapter 19 contains information about how to do your own legal research.

Suppose I suffer an injury to a part of my body that had been injured previously—will I still be covered?

If the previous injury was also work-related, workers' compensation should provide full coverage. If it wasn't, you may receive lower-level benefits.

If your earlier injury occurred at a former job, it's generally up to your current employer's insurance company and your former employer to sort out who's responsible for paying your benefits—sometimes they will split the costs between them.

How do I find a good workers' compensation lawyer —and how much will it cost?

You usually don't need a lawyer unless you suffer a permanent disability, or all or part of your workers' compensation claim is denied. If one of these situations occurs, you'll probably want to do some research to familiarize yourself with your rights and duties. For example, many claims are denied based on a doctor's report claiming that you are not injured. If you dispute this, you may have a right to obtain a second doctor's opinion paid for by the workers' comp insurer.

If your claim is denied, consider hiring an experienced workers' compensation lawyer to help you navigate the appeals process. The best way to find a good lawyer is often through word of mouth—talk to other injured workers or check with a local union or other workers' organization.

In most states, fees for legal representation in workers' compensation cases are limited to between 10% and 15% of any eventual award. Because these fees are relatively modest, workers' compensation lawyers customarily take on many clients and, as a result, do not have time to provide much individual attention. Most of your contacts with your attorney's office

will be with paralegals and other support personnel. This is not a bad thing in itself, if the office is well run by support staff. Be sure the office is able to stay on top of paperwork and filing deadlines, and that a knowledgeable person is available to answer your questions clearly and promptly.

What to Do When the Insurance Company Won't Pay

Some workers' compensation carriers take an aggressive stance and deny legitimate claims for workers' compensation. When this happens, it's often because the insurer claims you haven't been injured or, if you have, that it's not serious enough to qualify you for temporary or total disability. Commonly, this is done after a private investigator hired by the insurance company follows you and obtains photographs showing you engaging in fairly strenuous physical activity, such as lifting a box or mowing the lawn, despite claiming a back injury.

If your legitimate benefits are denied, you should immediately file an appeal with your state appeals agency—called the Industrial Accidents Board, the Workers' Compensation Appeals Board or something similar. You may also want to hire an attorney to help you press your claim.

If I receive workers' compensation, can I also sue my employer in court?

Generally, no. The workers' compensation system was established as part of a legal trade-off. In exchange for giving up the right to sue an employer in court, you get workers' compensation benefits no matter who was at fault. Before the workers' comp system was passed, if you went to court, you stood to recover a large amount of money, but only if you could prove the injury was caused by your employer.

Today, you may be able to sue in court if your injury was caused by someone other than your employer (a visitor or outside contractor, for example) or if it was caused by a defective product (such as a flaw in the construction of the equipment you were working with).

What if my employer tells me not to file a workers' compensation claim or threatens to fire me if I do?

In most states, it is a violation of the workers' compensation laws to discriminate against an employee for filing a workers' compensation claim. If this happens, immediately report it to your local workers' compensation office.

More Information About Workers' Compensation

How to Handle Your Workers' Compensation Claim, by Christopher Ball (Nolo Press), includes all forms and instructions for filing a workers' compensation claim in California. The book is also useful for people who live elsewhere, given the absence of self-help resources for other states; it provides a good overview of how the system works.

Age Discrimination

By working faithfully eight hours a day, you may eventually get to be a boss and work twelve hours a day.

—ROBERT FROST

America's workforce is aging. And as workers stay on the job longer, they generally move up the compensation ladder, acquiring more benefits and higher salaries. They also become more expensive for employers to keep around. This has led to a problem for many older workers, who increasingly face lay-offs (quaintly known as company downsizing or "right" sizing) and difficulties finding new jobs. New laws afford some protection to older workers who face discrimination in the workplace—and also help protect their pension rights when they leave.

My employer has just cut the workforce in half, singling out older workers who have higher salaries. Is there any legal protection for us?

Possibly. The federal Age Discrimination in Employment Act (ADEA) provides that workers over the age of 40 cannot be arbitrarily discriminated against because of age in any employment decision. Perhaps the single most important rule under the ADEA is that no worker can be forced to retire.

Under the ADEA, there has to be a valid reason—not related to age—for all employment decisions, especially lay-offs. Examples of valid reasons would be poor job performance by the employee or an employer's economic trouble. If lay-offs have been announced or are in the wind, talk with other affected workers. If most people who are laid off are 40 or older, and the majority of workers kept on are younger, you may have the basis for an ADEA complaint or lawsuit. This is especially likely if the employer has hired younger workers to take the places of workers over 40.

Does the ADEA protect all workers from age discrimination?

Unfortunately not; there are limits on both the employees and the employers who are covered. The ADEA only applies to employees age 40 and older—and to workplaces with 20 or more employees. But unlike several other federal workplace laws, the ADEA covers employees of labor organizations and local, state and federal governments as well as those who work in the private sector.

In addition to workers employed by companies which have fewer than 20 employees, there are several other exceptions to the broad protection of the ADEA:

- Executives or people "in high policy-making positions" can be forced to retire at age 65 if they would receive annual retirement pension benefits worth $44,000 or more.
- There are special exceptions for police and fire personnel, tenured university faculty and certain federal employees having to do with law enforcement and air traffic control. If you are in one of these categories, check with your personnel office or benefits plan office for details.
- An additional exception to the federal age discrimination law is made when age is an essential part of a particular job—referred to by the legal jargon of a "bona fide occupational qualification" (BFOQ). For example, if an employer who sets age limits on a particular job can prove that the limit is necessary

because a worker's ability to adequately perform the particular job does, in fact, diminish after the age limit is reached, it's okay to discriminate. However, it has become more difficult for employers to prove a BFOQ because the law protects workers as young as age 40.

If I'm not protected by the ADEA, is an employer free to discriminate against me because of my age?

That depends on where you live. Most states have laws against age discrimination in employment, and those laws often provide greater protection than the federal law. For example, several states provide age discrimination protection to workers before they reach age 40, and other states protect against the actions of employers with fewer than 20 employees.

If you work in a state with such a law, you can choose to file a complaint under either state law or the federal law (ADEA), or both.

I've noticed a pattern where I work: Older workers tend to be laid off just before their pension rights lock in or vest. Is that legal?

Using various ploys like this one to cheat workers out of their promised pensions is a technique some employers use to save money. But it's not legal. When the federal Older Workers Benefit Protection Act was passed in 1990, it became clearly illegal for employers:

- to use an employee's age as the basis for discrimination in benefits, and
- to target older workers for their staff cutting programs.

Does the law restrict my employer from offering a Golden Parachute—a benefits package that seems contrived to get me into early retirement?

Maybe. One provision of the Older Workers Benefit Protection Act regulates the legal waivers that employers are increasingly asking employees to sign in connection with so-called early retirement programs. For more information, see *Out From Under the Golden Parachute*, below.

If your employer offers you the opportunity to participate in a staff reduction program, the Act indirectly puts you in a position to negotiate the terms of your departure. The fact that your employer has offered an incentive suggests that the company wants you gone and is worried that you might file a lawsuit for wrongful discharge. So, although the company may say that you have only two choices—accept or reject the offer—there is nothing preventing you from making a counteroffer.

How can I enforce my rights under the laws that protect against age discrimination?

If you believe that an employer has discriminated against you because of your age, you can file a complaint with the federal Equal Employment Opportunity Commission (EEOC) just as you would against any other workplace discrimination. Call 800-669-3362 to find the EEOC office nearest you. If the EEOC does not resolve your complaint to your satisfaction, you may decide to pursue your complaint through a lawsuit.

Out From Under the Golden Parachute

A growing number of employers ask older workers to sign waivers—also called releases or agreements not to sue. In return for signing the waivers, the employer offers the employee an incentive to leave the job voluntarily, such as a significant amount of severance pay. The Older Workers Benefit Protection Act places a number of restrictions on such waivers:

- Your employer must make the waiver understandable to the people who are likely to use it.

- The waiver may not cover any rights or claims that you discover are available after you sign it, and it must specify that it covers your rights under the ADEA.
- Your employer must offer you something of value (such as severance pay)—over and above what is already owed to you—in exchange for your signature on the waiver.
- Your employer must advise you, in writing, that you have the right to consult an attorney before you sign the waiver.
- If the offer is being made to a group or class of employees, your employer must inform you in writing how the class of employees is defined; the job titles and ages of all the individuals to whom the offer is being made; and the ages of all the employees in the same job classification or unit of the company to whom the offer is not being made.
- You must be given a fixed time in which to make a decision on whether or not to sign the waiver.

More Information About Age Discrimination

Several organizations offer help and information on age discrimination in employment. Among the most helpful are:

American Association of Retired Persons
601 E Street, NW
Washington, DC 20049
800-424-3410
http://www.aarp.org (online)

AARP is a nonprofit membership organization of older Americans open to anyone age 50 or older. It offers a wide range of publications on retirement planning, age discrimination and employment-related topics. Networking and direct services are available through local chapters.

Older Women's League
666 Eleventh Street, NW, Suite 700
Washington, DC 20001
202-783-6686

The Older Women's League provides advice on discrimination and other issues facing elderly men and women.

Sexual Harassment

Sexual harassment on the job took a dramatic leap into public awareness in October 1991, when Professor Anita Hill made known her charges against Judge Clarence Thomas after his nomination to the U.S. Supreme Court. Many other incidents have erupted since then, including investigations into the Navy after the Tailhook incident and into government officials after Senator Bob Packwood was accused of harassing several female staffers. Paula Jones dominated headlines for months with her claim that President Clinton harassed her while a conventioneering governor. And more recently, Mitsubishi Motors agreed to pay a record $34 million settlement to hundreds of women harassed at its auto assembly plant.

Enforcement of the laws prohibiting sexual harassment has been stepped up in the last few years. But in workplaces across America, the issue is far from settled. Sexual harassment is still a daily problem for many workers, especially women.

What is sexual harassment?

In legal terms, sexual harassment is any unwelcome sexual advance or conduct on the job that creates an intimidating, hostile or offensive working environment. In real life, sexually harassing behavior ranges from repeated offensive or belittling jokes to a workplace full of offensive pornography to an outright sexual assault.

Are there laws that protect against sexual harassment on the job?

Yes. But surprisingly, those laws are fairly new. In 1980, the Equal Employment Opportunity Commission (EEOC) issued regulations defining sexual harassment and stating it was a form of sex discrimination prohibited by the Civil Rights Act, which had been originally passed in 1964. In 1986, the U.S. Supreme Court first ruled that sexual harassment was a form of job discrimination—and held it to be illegal.

Today, there is greater understanding that the Civil Rights Act prohibits sexual harassment at work. In addition, most states have their own fair employment practices laws that prohibit sexual harassment—many of them more strict than the federal law.

To find out the law in your state, call 800-669-3362 and ask for the federal EEOC office nearest you.

Are men ever sexually harassed? Can workers harass co-workers of the same gender?

The laws prohibiting sexual harassment on the job protect all workers. Men can—and do—sexually harass other men, and the U.S. Supreme Court recently sanctioned a harassed male worker's right to sue his same-sex harassers. Women can—and do—sexually harass men and sometimes other women.

But in the overwhelming majority of cases of sexual harassment, it's a male co-worker or supervisor who is harassing a female worker. No one is sure why this is so. Socialization probably plays a part: Men are more likely than women to find sexual advances flattering, women more likely to be perceived as the gatekeepers of sexual conduct. Economics probably enter, too. There are simply more women in the workforce than ever before—and at least some male workers feel the influx as a threat to their own livelihoods. Finally, sexual harassment is usually a power ploy, a way to keep some workers in lower-paid, less respected positions—or force them out of the workplace altogether.

I'm being sexually harassed at work. What should I do?

Tell the harasser to stop. Surprisingly often—some experts say up to 90% of the time—this works.

When confronted directly, harassment is especially likely to end if it is at a fairly low level: off-color jokes, inappropriate comments about your appearance, tacky cartoons tacked onto the office refrigerator or repeated requests for dates after you have said no.

But clearly saying you want the offensive behavior to stop does more than let the harasser know that the behavior is unwelcome. It is also a crucial first step if you later decide to take more formal action against the harasser, whether through your company's complaint procedure or through the legal system. And give serious thought to documenting what's going on by keeping a diary or journal; your case will be stronger if you can later prove that the harassment continued after you confronted the harasser.

What if the harassment doesn't stop even after I've confronted the harasser?

It may be time to get help from either your employer or a state or federal agency. Prepare to do this by collecting as much detailed evidence as possible about the specifics of your harassment.

Be sure to save any offensive letters, photographs, cards or notes you receive. And if you were made to feel uncomfortable because of jokes, pin-ups or cartoons posted at work, confiscate them—or at least make copies. An anonymous, obnoxious photo or joke posted on a bulletin board is not anyone else's personal property, so you are free to take it down and keep it as evidence. If that's not possible, photograph the workplace walls. Note the dates the offensive material was posted—and whether there were hostile reactions when you took it down or asked another person to do so.

Also, keep a detailed journal. Write down the specifics of everything that feels like harassment. Include the names of everyone involved, what happened, and where and when it took place. If anyone else saw or heard the harassment, note that as well. Be as specific as possible about what was said and done—and how it affected you, your health or your job performance.

If your employer has conducted periodic evaluations of your work, make sure you have copies. In fact, you may want to ask for a copy of your entire personnel file—before you tip your hand that you are considering taking action against a harassing co-worker. Your records will be particularly persuasive evidence if your evaluations have been good but after you complain, your employer retaliates by trying to transfer or fire you, claiming poor job performance.

If You're Afraid of Offending

The super-cautious advice—don't talk with co-workers about anything but business—is surely overkill. The better approach is to use common sense. There is plenty of room to be friendly and personable without behaving in a way that is likely to offend workers of either gender.

Some rough guides for evaluating your own workplace behavior:

- If you wouldn't say or do something in front of your spouse or parents, it's probably a poor idea to say or do it at work.
- Would you say or do it in front of a colleague of the same gender?
- How would you feel if your mother, wife, sister or daughter were subjected to the same words or behavior?
- How would you feel if another man said or did the same things to you?
- Does it need to be said or done at all?

If you are truly concerned that your words or conduct may be offensive to a co-worker, there is one surefire way to find out: ask.

If the harassment still doesn't stop, what are my options short of filing a lawsuit or a complaint with a government agency?

If the harasser has ignored your oral requests to stop, or you are uncomfortable making the request, write a succint letter demanding an end to the behavior. If that doesn't end the harassment, you may want to take more forceful action. Consider giving a copy of your letter to the harasser's supervisor—along with a memo explaining that the behavior has become more outrageous.

If the harassment still does not abate—or if you believe the supervisor is sympathetic to the harassment or the harasser—send the letter to the next-ranked worker or official at your workplace. Include a cover letter in which you offer your own remedy for the situation—something realistic that might help end the discomfort, such as transferring the harasser to a more distant worksite. If it's your own supervisor who has been harassing you, consider asking to be assigned a different supervisor.

These days, most workplaces have specific written policies prohibiting sexual harassment. If you have followed the steps that seem reasonable to you but the harassment continues, your next option is to pursue any procedure your company has established for handling harassment.

What legal steps can I take to end the harassment?

If all investigation and settlement attempts fail to produce satisfactory results, one option is to file a civil lawsuit for damages either under the federal Civil Rights Act or under a state fair employment practices statute.

Even if you intend right from the beginning to file such a lawsuit, you sometimes must first file a claim with a government agency. For example, an employee pursuing a claim under the Civil Rights Act must first file a claim with the federal EEOC, and a similar complaint procedure is required under some state laws. The EEOC or state agency may decide to prosecute your case on its own, but that happens only occasionally.

More commonly, at some point, the agency will issue you a document referred to as a "right-to-sue" letter that allows you to take your case to court. When filing an action for sexual harassment, you will almost always need to hire a lawyer for help.

More Information About Sexual Harassment

Sexual Harassment on the Job, by William Petrocelli and Barbara Kate Repa (Nolo Press), explains what sexual harassment is and how to stop it.

9to5, National Association of Working Women
614 Superior Avenue, NW
Cleveland, OH 44113
216-566-9308 (general information)
800-522-0925 (hotline)

9to5 is a national nonprofit membership organization for working women. It provides counseling, information and referrals for problems on the job, including family leave, pregnancy disability, termination, compensation and sexual harassment. 9to5 also offers a newsletter and publications. There are local chapters throughout the country.

Disability Discrimination

Many individuals fortunate enough to be healthy in mind and body—and to be employed—lament the difficulties a workplace can impose. But for those with physical or mental disabilities, many workplaces can be truly daunting. Fortunately, the Americans with

Disabilities Act (ADA), a fairly new federal law whose kinks are still being tested and interpreted by the courts, has helped to level the playing field.

What laws protect disabled workers from workplace discrimination?

The Americans with Disabilities Act (ADA) prohibits employment discrimination on the basis of workers' disabilities. Generally, the ADA prohibits employers from:

- discriminating on the basis of virtually any physical or mental disability
- asking job applicants questions about their past or current medical conditions
- requiring job applicants to take medical exams, and
- creating or maintaining worksites that include substantial physical barriers to the movement of people with physical disabilities.

The ADA covers companies with 15 or more employees. Its coverage broadly extends to private employers, employment agencies and labor organizations. A precursor of the ADA, the Vocational Rehabilitation Act, prohibits discrimination against disabled workers in state and federal government.

In addition, many state laws protect against discrimination based on physical or mental disability.

Exactly whom does the ADA protect?

The ADA's protections extend to disabled workers—defined as people who:

- have a physical or mental impairment that substantially limits a major life activity
- have a record of impairment, or
- are regarded as having an impairment.

An impairment includes physical disorders, such as cosmetic disfigurement or loss of a limb, as well as mental and psychological disorders.

The ADA protects job applicants and employees who, although disabled as defined above, are still qualified for a particular job. In other words, they would be able to perform the essential functions of a job with some form of accommodation, such as wheelchair access, a voice-activated computer or a customized workspace. As with other workers, whether a disabled worker is deemed qualified for a given job depends on whether he or she has appropriate skill, experience, training or education for the position.

How can I tell if a particular accommodation offered by my employer is reasonable?

The ADA points to several specific accommodations that are likely to be deemed reasonable—some of them changes to the physical set-up of the workplace, some of them changes to how or when work is done. They include:

- making existing facilities usable by disabled employees—for example, by modifying the height of desks and equipment, installing computer screen magnifiers or installing telecommunications devices for the deaf

- restructuring jobs—for example, allowing a ten-hour/four-day workweek so that a worker can receive weekly medical treatments
- modifying exams and training materials—for example, allowing more time for taking an exam, or allowing it to be taken orally instead of in writing
- providing a reasonable amount of additional unpaid leave for medical treatment
- hiring readers or interpreters to assist an employee, and
- providing temporary workplace specialists to assist in training.

These are just a few possible accommodations. The possibilities are limited only by an employee's and employer's imaginations—and the reality that might make one or more of these accommodations financially impossible in a particular workplace.

When can an employer legally claim that a particular accommodation is simply not feasible?

The ADA does not require employers to make accommodations that would cause them an undue hardship—a weighty concept defined in the ADA only as "an action requiring significant difficulty or expense."

The Equal Employment Opportunity Commission (EEOC), the federal agency responsible for enforcing the ADA, has set out some of the factors that will determine whether a particu-

lar accommodation presents an undue hardship on a particular employer:

- the nature and cost of the accommodation
- the financial resources of the employer (a large employer may be expected to foot a larger bill than a mom and pop business)
- the nature of the business (including size, composition and structure of the workforce), and
- accommodation costs already incurred in the workplace.

It is not easy for employers to prove that an accommodation is an undue hardship, as financial difficulty alone is not usually sufficient. Courts will look at other sources of money, including tax credits and deductions available for making some accommodations, as well as the disabled employee's willingness to pay for all or part of the costs.

Taking Action Under the ADA

The ADA is enforced by the Equal Employment Opportunity Commission (EEOC). To start an investigation of your claim, file a complaint at the local EEOC office. Call 800-669-3362 to find the office nearest you.

If you live in a state with laws that protect workers against discrimination based on physical or mental disability, you can choose to file a complaint under your state's law, the ADA or both.

For additional information on the ADA, contact:

Office of the Americans
with Disabilities Act
Civil Rights Division
U.S. Department of Justice
P.O. Box 66118
Washington, DC 20035-6118
202-514-0301 (voice)
202-514-0383 (TDD)
http://www.usdoj.gov/
crt/ada/adahom1.htm (online).

Losing or Leaving Your Job

Nothing is really work unless you would rather be doing something else.

—SIR JAMES A. BARRIE

The possibility of being laid off or fired looms large in the list of fears of most workers. Employers have traditionally had a free hand to hire and fire, but a number of recent laws and legal rulings restrict these rights. As a result, many soon-to-be-former employees are pleased to find out that they have the power to negotiate severance pay and other benefits on the way out the door in exchange for giving up claims of discrimination.

For what reasons can I be fired?

Unless you have a written contract with your employer establishing a set number of years for your employment (for example, you are a football coach with a five-year employment contract), you can be fired for a host of traditional and obvious reasons: incompetence, excessive absences, violating certain laws or company rules or sleeping or taking drugs on the job. And you can also be fired or laid off because of company downsizing due to a downturn in revenue, reexamination of the company's mission, a merger with another company or transferring work to a factory in a lower-wage area. In most cases, an employer does not need to provide any notice before giving an employee walking papers.

Still, there are limits. Employers do not have the right to discriminate against you illegally or to violate state or federal laws, such as those controlling wages and hours. Most state discrimination laws are quite broad. In addition to protecting against the traditional forms of discrimination based on race, color, religion, national origin and age, many also protect against discrimination based on sexual orientation, physical and mental disability, marital status and receiving public funds.

Separate state laws protect workers from being fired or demoted for taking advantage of laws protecting them from discrimination and unsafe workplace practices. And there are a number of other more complex reasons that may make it illegal for an employer to fire you—all boiling down to the fact that an employer must deal with you fairly and honestly.

I've just received a warning from my employer, and I suspect I will be fired soon. What should I do?

If you find yourself on the receiving end of a disciplinary notice you consider to be unfair, there are several steps you should take to avoid losing your job.

First, be sure you understand exactly what work behavior is being challenged. Check your company handbook to see if there is a clear policy against what you've done. If you are unclear, ask for a meeting with your supervisor or human resources staff to discuss the issue more thoroughly.

If you disagree with allegations that your work performance or behavior is poor, you may want to ask for the assessment in writing. You can then write a clarification and ask that it be inserted in your personnel file. But do this only if you feel your employer's assessment is clearly inaccurate; otherwise you may risk escalating a minor verbal reprimand into a more major incident that will be permanently recorded in your file. Before you sit down to write, take some time to reflect and perhaps discuss your situation with friends.

If you think you are likely to be fired, see if any policy in the employee handbook will buy you time—for example, the right to file an appeal—so the controversy can die down and, if necessary, you can change your work habits.

Finally, read between the lines to see whether your employer's action may be discriminatory or in other ways unfair. Look particularly at the timing. For example, if you were let go shortly before your rights in the company pension plan were permanently locked in or vested, the company may be guilty of age discrimination. Look also at uneven applications of discipline: Are women more often given substandard performance reviews or fired before they could be elevated to supervisor?

What can I do to protect any legal rights I might have before leaving my job?

Even if you decide not to challenge the legality of your firing, you will be in a much better position to enforce all of your workplace rights if you keep careful written records of everything that happens. For example, if you apply for unemployment insurance benefits and your former employer challenges that application, you will probably need to prove that you were dismissed for reasons that were not related to your misconduct.

There are a number of ways to document events. The easiest is to keep an employment diary where you record and date each significant work-related event such as performance reviews, commendations or reprimands, salary increases or decreases and even informal comments your supervisor makes to you about your work. Note the date, time and location for each event, which members of management were involved and whether or not witnesses were present. Whenever possible, back up your log with materials issued by your employer, such as copies of the employee handbook, memos, brochures, employee orientation videos and any written evaluations, commendations or criticisms of your work. In addition, if a problem develops, ask to see your personnel file and make a copy of all reports and reviews in it.

Am I entitled to severance pay if I'm fired?

No law requires an employer to provide severance pay. Nevertheless, many employers voluntarily offer one or two months' salary to employees who are laid off. A few are more generous to long-term employees, basing severance pay on a formula such as one month's pay for every year an employee worked for the company.

An employer may be legally obligated to give you some severance pay if you were promised it, as evidenced by:

- a written contract stating that severance will be paid
- a promise in an employee handbook of severance pay
- a long history of the company paying severance to other employees in your position, or
- an oral promise to pay you severance—although you may run into difficulties proving the promise existed.

My biggest concern about losing my job is losing health insurance coverage. Do I have any rights?

Ironically, workers have more rights to health insurance coverage after they lose their jobs than while employed.

This is because of a 1986 law, the Consolidated Omnibus Budget Reconciliation Act (COBRA). Under COBRA, employers with 20 or more employees must offer them the option of continuing to be covered by the company's group health insurance plan at the workers' own expense for a specific period—often 18 months—after employment ends. Family coverage is also included. In some other circumstances, such as the death of the employee, that employee's dependents can continue coverage for up to 36 months.

A relatively new federal law, the Health Insurance Act, should make it easier for employees to change jobs without the fear of losing insurance coverage—and should make it easier for many employees to get coverage in the first place. The law imposes some restrictions on group health plans, including HMOs: under this law:

- Employees with preexisting conditions may not be denied coverage under a new health insurance plan if they have been continuously covered for 12 months under another plan. Employees who do not have this prior coverage may be denied coverage based on a preexisting condition for only one year.
- No group health plan may discriminate in eligibility for coverage or premiums based on health status, physical or mental condition, claims experience, receipt of healthcare, medical history, genetic information, evidence of insurability or disability of the individual or dependents seeking coverage.

Getting Money When You're Out of Work

If you've lost your job, you may be desperately seeking income. It's best to act quickly to apply for unemployment and other possible benefits, as there is often a delay—in a few states, as long as six weeks—between the time you apply and the date on which you actually receive a check.

Here is a brief breakdown of what is covered by each of the three major income replacement programs.

Unemployment insurance . This program may provide some financial help if you lose your job, temporarily or permanently, through no fault of your own. Benefits will be less than your former pay and temporary—often lasting for about 26 weeks.

Workers' compensation . When you cannot work because of a work-related injury or illness, this program is designed to provide you with prompt replacement income. It may also pay the medical bills resulting from a workplace injury or illness; compensate you for a permanent injury, such as the loss of a limb; and provide death benefits to the survivors of workers who die from a workplace injury or illness. For more information, see the questions and answers on workers' compensation that appear earlier in this chapter.

Social Security disability insurance . This is intended to provide income to adults who, because of injury or illness, cannot work for at least 12 months. Unlike the workers' compensation program, it does not require that your disability be caused by a workplace injury or illness.

Also consider possible income from a private disability insurance program if you were paying for it through payroll withholdings, or if your employer paid for such premiums.

In addition, a few states—including California, Hawaii, New Jersey, New York and Rhode Island—offer disability benefits as part of their unemployment insurance programs. Typical program requirements mandate that you submit your medical records and show that you requested a leave of absence from your employer. Some may also require proof that you intend to return to your job when you recover. Call the local unemployment insurance and workers' compensation insurance offices to determine whether your state is one that maintains this kind of coverage.

http://www.nolo.com

Nolo Press offers self-help information about a wide variety of legal topics, including workplace rights.

http://www.workdoctor.com

Work Doctor—Employee Advocates offers candid advice for dealing with bothersome workplace behavior that doesn't quite rise to the level of a legal infraction: bullying, power plays, other displays of insecurity. Includes an e-mail advice column and timely tips for bullybusting.

http://fatty.law.cornell.edu/topics/ employment_discrimination.html

The Legal Information Institute at Cornell Law School provides information about discrimination in the workplace, including relevant codes and regulations.

http://www.vix.com/pub/men/ harass/harass.html

The Sexual Harassment Site offers articles and other materials on sexual harassment, including relevant laws and perspectives on court opinions.

http://www.anipubs.com/FAQ/ index.html

The Alexander Hamilton Institute serves up common sense packaged as FAQs about many aspects of employment, from benefits to safety and health concerns. The information is aimed at managers, but it's helpful for employees, too.

Small Businesses

Business is never so healthy as when,
like a chicken, it must do a certain
amount of scratching for what it gets.

—HENRY FORD

For all sorts of personal and economic reasons, more Americans are starting and running their own businesses today than ever before. This trend has been helped by the increasing availability of powerful and affordable data storage and communications equipment, most notably the personal computer. Because of this accessible technology, today's savvy small-time operator can often accomplish tasks that just a few decades ago could be tackled only by large corporations.

But not all change has been positive. When it comes to the law, the relatively informal world of just 40 years ago—where deals were often sealed with a handshake—has given way to a world where legal rules affect almost every small business relationship, including organizing the business, dealing with co-owners, hiring and supervising employees and relating to customers and suppliers. Staying on top of all these rules is as necessary as it is challenging. Fortunately, by using affordable, good quality self-help legal resources and getting additional help from a knowledgeable small business lawyer, you can master the laws you need to know to keep your business healthy.

Before You Start

Your imagination is your preview of life's coming attractions.

—ALBERT EINSTEIN

No matter what type of business you're thinking of starting, there are some practical and legal issues you'll face right away, including choosing a name and location for your business, deciding whether or not to hire employees, writing a business plan, choosing a legal structure (sole proprietorship, partnership, corporation or limited liability company), establishing a system for reporting and paying taxes and adopting policies to deal with your customers. This section addresses many of these concerns. As you read, don't be discouraged by the details. If you have chosen a business that you will truly enjoy and, after creating a tight business plan, are confident you'll make a decent profit, your big jobs are done. Furthermore, many people and affordable sources of information are available to help you cope with the practical details we discuss here.

I'm thinking of starting my own business. What should I do first?

Be sure you are genuinely interested in what the business does. If you aren't, you are unlikely to succeed in the long run—no matter how lucrative your work turns out to be. Yes, going into business with a firm plan to make a good living is important, but so, too, is choosing a business that fits your life goals in an authentic way. Here are a few things you might want to consider before you take the leap:

- Do you know how to accomplish the principal tasks of the business? (Don't open a transmission repair shop if you hate cars, or a restaurant if you can't cook.)

- If the business involves working with others, do you do this well? If not, look into the many opportunities to begin a one-person business.
- Do you understand basic business tasks, such as bookkeeping and how to prepare a profit-and-loss forecast and cash-flow analysis? If not, learn before, not after, you begin.
- Does the business fit your personality? If you are a shy introvert, stay away from businesses that require lots of personal selling. If you are easily bored, find a business which will allow you to deal with new material on a regular basis (publishing a newsletter, for example).

What should I keep in mind when choosing a name for my business?

First, assume that you will have competitors and that you will want to market your products or services under the name you choose. (This will make your name a trademark.) For marketing purposes, the best names are those that customers will easily remember and associate with your business. Also, if the name is memorable, it will be easier to stop others from using it in the future.

Most memorable business names are made-up words, or are somehow fanciful or surprising, such as Exxon and Kodak (made-up words), Double Rainbow ice cream and Penguin Books. And some notable names are cleverly suggestive, such as The Body Shop (a store that sells personal hygiene products) and Accuride tires.

Names that tend to be forgotten by consumers are common names (names of people), geographic terms and names that literally describe some aspect of a product or service. For instance, Steve's Web Designs may be very pleasing to Steve as a name, but it's not likely to help Steve's customers remember his company when faced with competitors such as Sam's Web Designs and Sheri's Web Designs. Similarly, names like Central Word Processing Services or Robust Health Foods are not particularly memorable.

Of course, over time even a common name can become memorable through widespread use and advertising, as with Ben and Jerry's Ice Cream. And unusual names of people can sometimes be very memorable indeed, as with Fuddrucker's (restaurants and family entertainment centers).

How do I find out whether I'm legally permitted to use the business name I've chosen?

Your first step depends on whether you plan to incorporate your business. If you do, you should check with the Secretary of State's office in your state capital to see whether your proposed name is the same or confusingly similar to an existing corporate name in your state. If it is, you'll have to choose a different name. If you don't plan to incorporate, check with your county clerk to see whether your proposed name is already on the list maintained for fictitious or assumed business names in your county. In the few states where assumed business name registrations are statewide, check with your Secretary of State's office. (The county clerk should be able to tell you whether you'll need to check the name at the state level.) If you find that your chosen name (or a very similar name) is listed on a fictitious or assumed name register, you shouldn't use it.

If my proposed business name isn't listed on a county or state register, am I free to use it however I like?

Not necessarily. Even if you are permitted to use your chosen name as a corporate or assumed business name in your state or county, you might not be able to use the name as a trademark or service mark in either area. To understand what all this is about, consider the potential functions of a business name:

- A business name may be a tradename that describes the business for purposes of bank accounts, invoices and taxes.

- A business name may be a trademark or servicemark used to identify and distinguish products or services sold by the business (for example, Ford Motor Co. sells Ford automobiles, and McDonald's Corporation offers McDonald's fast food services).

While your corporate or assumed business name registration may legally clear the name for the first purpose, it doesn't speak to the second. For example, if your business is organized as a limited liability company (LLC) or corporation, you may get the green light from your Secretary of State to use IBM Toxics as your business name (if no other corporation of LLC in your state is using it or something confusingly similar), but if you try to use that name out in the mar-

ketplace, you're asking for a claim of trademark violation from the IBM general counsel's office.

To find out whether you can use your proposed name as a trademark or servicemark, you will need to do what's known as a trademark search. See Chapter 8, *Trademarks*.

I've found out that the name I want to use is available. What do I need to do to reserve it for my business?

If you are incorporating or forming an LLC, every state has a procedure—operated by the Secretary of State's office—under which a proposed name can be reserved for a certain period of time, usually for a fee. Additional reservation periods can usually be purchased for additional fees. (For more information about corporations, see *Legal Structures for Small Businesses*, below.) If you are not incorporating or forming an LLC, then you need to file a fictitious or assumed business name statement with the agency who handles these registrations in your state (usually the county clerk, but sometimes the Secretary of State).

If you plan to use your business name as a trademark or servicemark, and your service or product will be marketed in more than one state (or across territorial or international borders), you can file an application with the U.S. Patent and Trademark Office to reserve the name for your use. See Chapter 8, *Trademarks*.

What should I keep in mind when choosing a location for my business?

Commercial real estate brokers are fond of saying the three most important factors in establishing a business are location, location and location. While true for a few types of businesses—such as a retail sandwich shop that depends on lunchtime walk-in trade—for most, locating in a popular, high-cost area is a mistake. For example, if you design computer software, repair tile, import jewelry from Indonesia or do any one of ten thousand other things that don't rely on foot traffic, your best bet is to search out convenient, low-cost, utilitarian surroundings. And even if yours is a business that many people will visit, consider the possibility that a low-cost, offbeat location may make more sense than a high-cost, trendy one.

What about zoning and other rules which restrict where a business may locate?

Never sign a lease without being absolutely sure you will be permitted to operate your business at that location. If the rental space is in a shopping center or other retail complex, this involves first checking carefully with management, because many have contractual restrictions (for example, no more than two pizza restaurants in the Mayfair Mall). If your business will be located in a non-shopping center area, you'll need to be sure that you meet applicable zoning rules, which typically divide a municipality into residential, commercial, industrial and mixed-use areas. You'll also need to find out whether any other legal restrictions will affect your operations. For example,

some cities limit the number of certain types of business—such as fast food restaurants or coffee bars—in certain areas, and others require that a business provide off-street parking, close early on weeknights, limit advertising signs or meet other rules as a condition of getting a permit. Fortunately, many cities have business development offices which help small business owners understand and cope with restrictions.

What is a business plan, and do I need to write one?

A business plan is a written document that describes the business you want to start and how it will become profitable. The document usually starts with a statement outlining the purpose and goals of your business and how you plan to realize them, including a detailed marketing plan. It should also contain a formal profit-and-loss projection and cash-flow analysis designed to show that if the business develops as expected, it will be profitable. Your business plan enables you to explain your business prospects to potential lenders and investors in a language they can understand. Even more important, the intellectual rigor of creating a tight business plan will help you see whether the business you hope to start is likely to meet your personal and financial goals. Many times when budding entrepreneurs take an honest look at their financial numbers, they see that hoped-for profits are unlikely to materialize. Or, put another way, one of the most important purposes of writing a good business plan is to talk you out of starting a bad business.

I plan to sell products and services directly to the public. What do I need to know to comply with consumer protection laws?

Many federal and state laws regulate the relationship between a business and its customers. These laws cover such things as advertising, pricing, door-to-door sales, written and implied warranties and, in a few states, layaway plans and refund policies. You can find out more about consumer protection laws by contacting the Federal Trade Commission, 6th and Pennsylvania Avenue, NW, Washington DC 20850, 202-326-2222, http:// ftc.gov/, and by contacting your state's consumer protection agency.

Although it's essential to understand and follow the rules that protect consumers, most successful businesses regard them as only a foundation for building friendly customer service policies designed to produce a high level of customer satisfaction. For example, many enlightened businesses tell their customers they can return any purchase for a full cash refund at any time for any reason. Not only does this encourage existing customers to continue to patronize the business, but it can be a highly effective way to get them to brag about it to their friends.

Selling Goods and Services on Consignment

Many small business people, especially those who produce art, crafts and specialty clothing items, sell on consignment.

In a consignment agreement, the owner of goods (in legal jargon, the consignor) puts the goods in the hands of another person or business—usually a retailer (the consignee)—who then attempts to sell them. If the goods are sold, the consignee receives a fee, which is usually a percentage of the purchase price, and the rest of the money is sent to the consignor. For example, a sculptor (the consignor) might place his or her work for sale at an art gallery (the consignee) with the understanding that if the artwork sells, the gallery keeps 50% of the sale price. Or a homeowner might leave old furniture with a resale shop that will keep one-third of the proceeds if the item sells. Typically, the consignor remains the owner of the goods until the consignee sells them.

As part of any consignment of valuable items, the consignor (owner) wants to be protected if the goods are lost or stolen while in the consignee's possession. The key here is to establish that the consignee has an insurance policy which will cover any loss. When extremely valuable items are being consigned, it's often appropriate to ask to be named as a co-insured so that you can receive a share of the insurance proceeds if a loss occurs.

If you're a consignee, check your insurance coverage. Before you accept the risk of loss or theft, make sure your business insurance policy covers you for loss of "personal property of others" left in your possession—and that the amount of coverage is adequate. Getting full reimbursement for the selling price of consigned goods may require an added supplement (called an endorsement) to your insurance policy. Check with your insurance agent or broker.

More Information About Starting Your Small Business

The Legal Guide for Starting and Running a Small Business, Volume 1, by Fred S. Steingold (Nolo Press), provides clear, plain-English explanations of the laws that affect business owners every day. It covers partnerships, corporations, limited liability companies, leases, trademarks, contracts, franchises, insurance, hiring and firing and much more.

The Legal Guide for Starting and Running a Small Business, Volume 2: Legal Forms, by Fred S. Steingold (Nolo Press), contains the forms and instructions you need to accomplish many routine legal tasks, such as borrowing money, leasing property and contracting for goods and services.

Small Time Operator, by Bernard Kamoroff, C.P.A. (Bell Springs Publishing), is the best single source of practical information on getting a small business off the ground—from business licenses, to taxes, to basic accounting. It includes ledgers and worksheets to get you started.

Running a One-Person Business, by Claude Whitmyer and Salli Rasberry (Ten Speed Press), covers the nuts and bolts of doing business on your own: finances, time management, marketing and more.

How to Write a Business Plan, by Mike McKeever (Nolo Press), shows you how to write the business plan and loan package necessary to finance your business and make it work. It includes up-to-date sources of financing.

Guerrilla Marketing, by Jay Conrad Levinson (Houghton Mifflin), contains hundreds of ideas and strategies to help you market your business.

Marketing Without Advertising, by Michael Phillips and Salli Rasberry (Nolo Press), shows you how to generate sales and encourage customer relations without spending a lot of money on advertising.

Legal Structures for Small Businesses

There is no one legal structure that's best for all small businesses. Whether you're better off starting as a sole proprietor or choosing one of the more complicated organizational structures, such as a partnership, corporation or limited liability company (LLC), usually depends on several factors, including the size and profitability of your business, how many people will own it and whether it will entail liability risks not covered by insurance.

What's the easiest way to structure my business?

The vast majority of small business people begin as sole proprietors, because it's cheap, easy and fast. With a sole proprietorship, there's no need to draft a partnership agreement or go to the trouble and expense of registering a corporation or limited liability company (LLC) with your state regulatory agency. All it usually entails is getting a local business license, and unless you are doing business under your own name, filing and possibly publishing a fictitious name statement.

If it's so simple, why aren't all businesses sole proprietorships?

There are several reasons why doing business as a sole proprietor is not appropriate for everyone. First, the owner of a sole proprietorship is personally responsible for all business debts, whereas limited liability companies and corporations normally shield their owners' assets from such debts. Second, a sole proprietorship is possible only when a business is owned by one person or a husband and wife. And finally, unlike a corporation (or a partnership or LLC that elects to be taxed as a corporation), which is normally taxed separately from its owners (something that can result in lower taxes for many small businesses—see below), a sole proprietor and her business are considered to be the same legal entity for tax purposes.

I'm starting my business with several other people. What are the advantages and disadvantages of forming a partnership?

One big advantage of a partnership is that you don't have to register with your state and pay an often-hefty fee, as you do to establish a corporation or limited liability company. And because a partnership is normally a "pass through" tax entity (the partners, not the partnership, are taxed), filing income tax returns is easier than it is for a regular corporation, where separate tax returns must be filed for the corporate entity and its owners. But it is essential that you go into business with a partner or partners you completely trust, given that the business-related acts of one partner legally bind all others. It is also essential that you prepare a written partnership agreement establishing, among other things, each partner's share of profits or losses, day-to-day duties and what happens if one partner dies or retires.

Finally, a major disadvantage of doing business as a partnership is that all partners are personally liable for business debts and liabilities (for example, a judgment in a lawsuit). While it's true that a good insurance policy can do much to reduce lawsuit worries and that many small, savvy businesses do not face debt problems, it's also true that businesses which face significant risks in either of these areas should probably organize themselves as a corporation or LLC.

What exactly is "limited liability"— and why is it so important?

Some types of businesses—corporations and limited liability companies are the most common—shield their owners from personal responsibility for business debts. That is, if the business goes bankrupt, its owners are not usually required to use their personal assets to make good on business losses— unless they voluntarily assume responsibility. Other types of business—sole proprietorships and partnerships—do not provide this shield, which means their owners are personally responsible for business liabilities. To see how this works, assume a large court judgment is obtained against an incorporated business. Because corporate stockholders are not personally liable for business debts, their houses and other assets can't be grabbed even if the corporation files for bankruptcy. By comparison, if a sole proprietorship or partnership gets into the same kind of trouble, the houses, bank accounts and other valuable personal assets of the business's owners can be attached to satisfy the debt.

Why do so many small business owners choose not to take advantage of limited liability protection?

Many small businesses simply don't have major debt or lawsuit worries, so they don't need limited liability protection. For example, if you run a small service business (perhaps you are a graphic artist, management consultant or music teacher), your chances of being sued or running up big debts are low. And when it comes to liability for many types of debts, achieving limited liability status makes little practical difference for newly created businesses: If you want to borrow money from a commercial lender or establish credit with a vendor, you will probably be required to pledge your personal assets (waive limited liability status) should your business be unable to pay.

Finally, even if your business faces serious and predictable risks (say, the risk that a customer may trip and fall on your premises or that your products may malfunction), organizing your business to achieve limited liability status is no substitute for purchasing a good insurance policy. After all, without a decent insurance policy, if a serious injury occurs, all the assets of your business—which will probably amount to a large portion of your net worth—can be grabbed to satisfy any resulting court judgment. It follows that if you purchase comprehensive business insurance, your personal assets are not at significant risk and you may therefore sensibly conclude you don't need limited liability status.

Given all its limitations, when is it wise for a small business person to seek limited liability status?

You should consider limited liability status if:

- your business subjects you to a risk of lawsuits in an area where insurance coverage is unaffordable or incomplete, or
- your business is well established and has a good credit rating so that you no longer need to personally guarantee every loan or credit application.

The easiest and most popular way to gain limited liability status is to form a corporation or a limited liability company (LLC).

SMALL BUSINESS STRUCTURES: AN OVERVIEW

Type of Entity	Main Advantages	Main Drawbacks
Sole Proprietorship	Simple and inexpensive to create and operate Owner reports profit or loss on his or her personal tax return	Owner personally liable for business debts
General Partnership	Simple and inexpensive to create and operate Owners (partners) report their share of profit or loss on their personal tax returns	Owners (partners) personally liable for business debts
Limited Partnership	Limited partners have limited personal liability for business debts as long as they don't participate in management General partners can raise cash without involving outside investors in management of business	General partners personally liable for business debts More expensive to create than general partnership Suitable mainly for companies that invest in real estate
Regular Corporation	Owners have limited personal liability for business debts Fringe benefits can be deducted as business expense Owners can split corporate profit among owners and corporation, paying lower overall tax rate	More expensive to create than partnership or sole proprietorship Paperwork can seem burdensome to some owners Separate taxable entity
S Corporation	Owners have limited personal liability for business debts Owners report their share of corporate profit or loss on their personal tax returns Owners can use corporate loss to offset income from other sources	More expensive to create than partnership or sole proprietorship More paperwork than for a limited liability company, which offers similar advantages Income must be allocated to owners according to their ownership interests Fringe benefits limited for owners who own more than 2% of shares
Professional Corporation	Owners have no personal liability for malpractice of other owners	More expensive to create than partnership or sole proprietorship Paperwork can seem burdensome to some owners All owners must belong to the same profession
Nonprofit Corporation	Corporation doesn't pay income taxes Contributions to charitable corporation are tax-deductible Fringe benefits can be deducted as business expense	Full tax advantages available only to groups organized for charitable, scientific, educational, literary or religious purposes Property transferred to corporation stays there; if corporation ends, property must go to another nonprofit

Type of Entity	Main Advantages	Main Drawbacks
Limited Liability Company	Owners have limited personal liability for business debts even if they participate in management	More expensive to create than partnership or sole proprietorship
	Profit and loss can be allocated differently than ownership interests	State laws for creating LLCs may not reflect latest federal tax changes
	IRS rules now allow LLCs to choose between being taxed as partnership or corporation	
Professional Limited Liability Company	Same advantages as a regular limited liability company	Same as for a regular limited liability company
	Gives state-licensed professionals a way to enjoy those advantages	Members must all belong to the same profession
Limited Liability Partnership	Mostly of interest to partners in old line professions such as, law, medicine and accounting	Unlike a limited liability company or a professional limited liability company, owners (partners) remain personally liable for many types of obligations owed to business creditors, lenders and landlords
	Owners (partners) aren't personally liable for the malpractice of other partners	
	Owners report their share of profit or loss on their personal tax returns	Not available in all states
		Often limited to a short list of professions

Is forming a corporation difficult?

No, as long as you and close associates and family members will own all stock and none will be sold to the public, the necessary documents—principally your Articles of Incorporation and Corporate Bylaws—can usually be prepared in a few hours. The first step is to check with your state's corporate filing office (usually either the Secretary of State or Corporations Commissioner) and conduct a trade-mark search to be sure the name you want to use is legally available. You then fill in blanks in a preprinted form (available from commercial publishers or your state's corporate filing office) listing the purpose of your corporation, its principal place of business and the number and type of shares of stock. You'll file these documents with the appropriate office, along with a registration fee which will usually be between $200 and $1,000, depending on the state.

You'll also need to complete, but not file, Corporate Bylaws. These will outline a number of important corporate housekeeping details, such as when annual shareholder meetings will be held, who can vote and the manner in which shareholders will be notified if there is need for an additional "special" meeting.

Fortunately, good self-help books exist in many states which make it easy and safe to incorporate your business without a lawyer.

What about operating my corporation? Aren't ongoing legal formalities involved?

Assuming your corporation has not sold stock to the public, conducting corporate business is remarkably straightforward and uncomplicated. Often it amounts to little more than recording key corporate decisions (for example, borrowing money or buying real estate) and holding an annual meeting. Even these formalities can often be done by written agreement and don't usually necessitate a face-to-face meeting.

Doesn't forming a corporation mean income will be taxed twice—once at the corporate level and then again when dividends are paid to the corporation's owners (shareholders)?

Taxation of business is complicated; we'll be able to cover only the high spots here. First, understand that most types of businesses—sole proprietorships and corporations that have qualified for Subchapter S Status, as well as partnerships and limited liability companies that have not elected to be taxed as regular, or C Corporations—are known as pass-through tax entities, meaning that all business profits are reflected on the individual tax returns of the owners.

For example, if a sole proprietor's convenience store turns a yearly profit of $85,000, this amount goes right on his personal tax return. By contrast, a regular profit corporation (and any partnership or LLC that elects to be taxed like a corporation) is a separate tax entity—meaning that the business files a tax return and pays its own tax.

But the fact that a corporation is taxed separately from its owners doesn't mean that profits will be taxed twice. That's because owners of most incorporated small businesses are also employees of those businesses; the money they receive in the form of salaries and bonuses is tax-deductible to the corporation as an ordinary and necessary business expense. After surplus money is paid to owners in the form of salaries and bonuses, a corporation often shows no profit and therefore pays no corporate income tax.

Are there tax advantages to forming a corporation?

Frequently, yes. Corporations pay federal income tax at a far lower rate than do most individuals for the first $75,000 of their profits—15% of the first $50,000 of profit, and 25% of the next $25,000. By contrast, in a sole proprietorship or partnership, where all profits are taxed to the business owner(s), up to 39.6% could be subject to federal income tax.

A corporation can often reduce taxes by paying its owner-employees a decent salary (which, of course, is tax-deductible to the corporation but taxable to the employee), and then retaining additional profits in the business (say, for future expansion).

Recently I've heard a lot about limited liability companies. How do they work?

For many years, small business people have been torn between operating as a sole proprietor (if several people are involved, as a partnership) or incorporating. On the one hand, many owners are attracted to the tax reporting simplicity of being a sole proprietor or partner. On the other, they desire the personal liability protection offered by incorporation. Until the mid 1990s it was possible to safely achieve these dual goals only by forming a corporation at the state level and then complying with a number of technical rules to gain S-corp status from the IRS. Then the limited liability company (LLC) was introduced and slowly gained full IRS acceptance. LLCs can have many of the most popular attributes of both partnerships (pass-through tax status) and corporations (limited personal liability for the owners). You can establish an LLC by filing a document called Articles or Certificate of Organization with your state's corporate filing office (often the Secretary or Department of State).

Can any small business register as a limited liability company?

Most can, because limited liability companies are recognized by all states. In California, the District of Columbia, Florida, Massachusetts, New Jersey, South Dakota and Tennessee, however, an LLC requires at least two owners, meaning they are not suitable for sole proprietors except where a spouse is included as a co-owner.

Are there any drawbacks to forming a limited liability company?

Very few, beyond the fact that LLCs require a moderate amount of paperwork at the outset. These papers include the Articles of Organization and an Operating Agreement. You must file the Articles with your state's Secretary of State, along with a filing fee that will range from a few hundred dollars in some states to almost $1,000 in others.

More Information About Choosing a Structure for Your Small Business

The Legal Guide to Starting and Running a Small Business, by Fred Steingold (Nolo Press), explains what you need to know to choose the right form for your business and shows you what to do to get started.

Nonprofit Corporations

In the long run you hit only what you aim at. Therefore, though you should fail immediately, you had better aim at something high.

—HENRY DAVID THOREAU

A nonprofit corporation is a group of people who join together to do some activity that benefits the public, such as running a homeless shelter, an artists' performance group or a low-cost medical clinic. Making a profit from these activities is allowed under legal and tax rules, but the primary purpose of the organization should be to do good work, not make money. Nonprofit goals are typically educational, charitable or religious.

How are nonprofit organizations structured?

Most nonprofits start out as small, loosely-structured organizations. Volunteers perform the work, and the group spends what little money it earns to keep the organization afloat. Because there is no profit, the group does not file tax returns. Formal legal papers (such as a nonprofit charter or bylaws) are rarely prepared in the beginning. Legally, groups of this sort are considered nonprofit associations, and each member can be held personally liable for organizational debts and liabilities.

Once a nonprofit association gets going and starts to make money, or wishes to obtain a tax exemption to attract public support and qualify for grant funds, it formalizes its structure. Usually a decision is made to incorporate, but forming a nonprofit association by adopting a formal association charter and operating bylaws is an alternative. Most groups form a nonprofit corporation because it is the traditional form—the IRS and grant agencies are very familiar with it. Also, once incorporated, the individual members of the nonprofit are not personally liable for debts of the organization—a big legal advantage of the corporate form over the unincorporated association.

Is forming a nonprofit corporation difficult?

Legally, no. To form a nonprofit corporation, one of the organization's founders prepares and files standard Articles of Incorporation—a short legal document that lists the name and directors of the nonprofit plus other basic information. The Articles are filed with the Secretary of State's office for a modest filing fee. After the Articles are filed, the group is a legally recognized nonprofit corporation.

Is there more to forming a nonprofit than this simple legal task?

Taxwise, there is more. You will want to apply for and obtain a federal and state nonprofit tax exemption. In fact, it's often best to obtain your state tax exemption before filing Articles with the Secretary of State—by doing this, you get to file your Articles without making the tax payments that your state requires of nonexempt corporations. For example, in California, if you file nonprofit Articles after getting your state tax exemption, you pay just $30; if you file before you get the exemption, the fee is $830 (you pay the extra $800 required to form a nonexempt corporation).

The Benefits of a Nonprofit Tax Exemption

In addition to qualifying for lower filing fees, your nonprofit tax exemption offers many benefits, including:

- an exemption from payment of annual income taxes on profits made from engaging in your nonprofit activities
- eligibility for charitable tax-deductible contributions from donors
- eligibility for grant funds from private and public sources
- nonprofit mailing rates, and
- local real and personal property tax exemptions.

What type of tax exemption do most nonprofits get?

Most organizations obtain a federal tax exemption under Section 501(c)(3) of the Internal Revenue Code for charitable, education, religious, scientific or literary purposes. States typically follow the federal lead and grant state tax-exempt status to nonprofits recognized by the IRS as 501(c)(3)s.

How do I get a 501(c)(3) tax exemption?

You'll need to get the IRS Package 1023 exemption application. This is a lengthy and technical application with many references to the federal tax code. Most nonprofit organizers need help in addition to the IRS instructions that accompany the form. But you can do it on your own if you have a good self-help resource by your side such as Nolo's *How to Form Your Own Nonprofit Corporation*, by Anthony Mancuso, which shows you, line-by-line, how to complete your application.

Are there any restrictions imposed on 501(c)(3) nonprofits?

You must meet the following conditions to qualify for a 501(c)(3) IRS tax exemption:

- The assets of your nonprofit must be irrevocably dedicated to charitable, educational, religious or similar purposes. If your 501(c)(3) nonprofit dissolves, any assets it owns must be transferred to another 501(c)(3) organization. (You don't have to name the specific organization that will receive your assets—a broad dedication clause will do.)
- Your organization cannot campaign for or against candidates for public office, and political lobbying activity is restricted.
- If your nonprofit makes a profit from activities unrelated to its exempt-purposes activities, it must pay taxes on the profit (but up to $1,000 of unrelated income can be earned tax-free).

More Information About Nonprofit Corporations

How to Form a Nonprofit Corporation, by Anthony Mancuso (Nolo Press), shows you how to form a tax-exempt corporation in all 50 states. In California, look for *The California Nonprofit Corporation Handbook*, also by Anthony Mancuso (Nolo Press).

The Law of Tax Exempt Organizations, by Bruce Hopkins (Wiley), is an in-depth guide to the legal and tax requirements for obtaining and maintaining a 501(c)(3) tax exemption and public charity status with the IRS.

Small Business Taxes

THE MAN WHO IS

ABOVE HIS BUSINESS

MAY ONE DAY FIND HIS

BUSINESS ABOVE HIM.

—SAMUEL DREW

Taxes are a fact of life for every small business. Those that take the time to understand and follow the rules will have little trouble with tax authorities. By contrast, those who are sloppy or dishonest are likely to be dogged by tax bills, audits and penalties. The moral is simple: Meeting your obligations to report business information and pay taxes is the cornerstone of operating a successful business.

I want to start my own small business. What do I have to do to keep out of trouble with the IRS?

Start by learning a new set of "3 Rs"—recordkeeping, recordkeeping and (you guessed it) recordkeeping. IRS studies show that poor records, not dishonesty, cause most small business people to lose at audits or fail to comply with their tax reporting obligations, with resulting fines and penalties. Even if you hire someone to keep your records, you need to know how to supervise him—because if he goofs up, you'll be held responsible.

I don't have enough money in my budget to hire a business accountant or tax preparer. Is it safe and sensible for me to keep my own books?

Yes, if you remember to keep thorough, current records. Consider using a check register-type computer program such as *Quicken* (Intuit) to track your expenses, and if you are doing your own tax return, use Intuit's companion program, *Turbotax* (or *MacIntax*) for Business. To ensure that you're on the right track, it's a good idea to run your bookkeeping system by a savvy small business tax pro. With just a few hours of work, she should help you avoid most common mistakes and show you how to dovetail your bookkeeping system with tax filing requirements.

When your business is firmly in the black and your budget allows for it, consider hiring a bookkeeper. He can do your day-to-day payables and receivables. And hire an outside tax pro to handle your heavy duty tax work—not only are his fees a tax-deductible business expense, but chances are your business will benefit if you put more of your time into running it and less into completing routine paperwork.

Recordkeeping Basics

Keep all receipts and canceled checks for business expenses. It will help if you separate your documents by category, such as:

- auto expenses
- rent
- utilities
- advertising
- travel
- entertainment, and
- professional fees.

Organize your documents by putting them into individual folders or envelopes, and keep them in a safe place. If you are ever audited, the IRS is most likely to zero in on business deductions for travel and entertainment, and car expenses.

Remember that the burden will be on you—not the IRS—to explain your deductions. If you're feeling unsure about how to get started or what documents you need to keep, consult a tax professional familiar with recordkeeping for small businesses.

I've been operating my own business for several years, but I'm still often confused as to what is—and isn't—a tax-deductible business expense. Can you help me?

Just about any "ordinary, necessary and reasonable" expense that helps you earn business income is deductible. This term reflects the purpose for which the expense is made. For example, buying a computer, or even a sound system, for your office or store is an "ordinary and necessary" business expense, but buying the same items for your family room obviously isn't. In the latter case, the computer and stereo would be nondeductible personal expenses. The property must be used in a "trade or business," which means it is used with the expectation of generating income.

In addition to the "ordinary and necessary" rule, a few things are specifically prohibited by law from being tax deductable—for instance, you can't deduct a bribe paid to a public official. Other deduction no-nos are traffic tickets, your home telephone line and clothing you wear on the job, unless it is a required uniform. As a rule, if you think it is necessary for your business, it is probably deductible. Just be ready to explain it to an auditor.

Business Costs That Are Never Deductible

A few expenses are not deductible even if they are business related, because they violate "public policy." (IRC 162.) These expenses include:

- any type of government fine, such as a tax penalty paid to the IRS, or even a parking ticket
- bribes and kickbacks
- any kind of payment made for referring a client, patient or customer, if it is contrary to a state or federal law
- expenses for lobbying and social club dues.

Thankfully, very few other business expenses are affected by these rules.

If I use my car for business, how much of that expense can I write off?

You must keep track of how much you use your car for business in order to figure out your deduction. (You'll also need to produce these records if you're ever audited.) Start by keeping a log showing the miles for each business use, always noting the purpose of the trip. Then, at the end of the year, you will usually be able to figure your deduction by using either the "mileage method" (as of 1998 you can take 31.5¢ per mile deduction for business usage) or the "actual expense" method (you can take the total you pay for gas and repairs plus depreciation according to a tax code schedule, multiplied by the percentage of business use).

Figure it both ways and take the method that benefits you most.

Can I claim a deduction for business-related entertainment?

You may deduct only 50% of expenses for entertaining clients, customers or employees, no matter how many martinis or Perriers you swigged. (Yes, this is a change. In the old days you could write off 100% of every entertainment expense, and until a few years ago, 80%.) Qualified business entertainment includes taking a client to a ball game, a concert or dinner at a fancy restaurant, or just inviting a few of your customers over for a Sunday barbecue at your home.

Parties, picnics and other social events you put on for your employees and their families are an exception to the 50% rule—such events are 100% deductible. Keep in mind that if you are audited, you must be able to show some proof that the expense was either directly related to, or associated with, business. So, keep a guest list and note the business (or potential) relationship of each person entertained.

Commonly Overlooked Business Expenses

Despite the fact that most people keep a sharp eye out for deductible expenses, it's not uncommon to miss a few. Some overlooked routine deductions include:

advertising giveaways and promotion
audio and video tapes
related to business skills
bank service charges
business association dues
business gifts
business-related magazines and books
(like the one in your hand)
casual labor and tips
casualty and theft losses
charitable contributions
coffee service
commissions
consultant fees
credit bureau fees
education to improve business skills
interest on credit cards for
business expenses
interest on personal loans used for
business purposes
office supplies
online computer services related to
business
parking and meters
petty cash funds
postage
promotion and publicity
seminars and trade shows
taxi and bus fare
telephone calls away from the business

I've heard that some types of business supplies and equipment can be fully deducted in the year they are purchased but the purchase price of others must be deducted over several years. Is this true?

Current expenses, which include the everyday costs of keeping your business going, such as office supplies, rent and electricity, can be deducted from your business's total income in the year you incurred them. But expenditures for things that will generate revenue in future years—for example, a desk, copier or car—must be "capitalized," that is, written off or "amortized" over their useful life—usually three, five or seven years—according to IRS rules. There is one important exception to this rule, discussed next.

I want to purchase a new computer system for my business. Does this mean that, even if I buy the entire system this year, I must spread the deduction over a period of five years?

Not necessarily. Normally the cost of "capital equipment"—usually equipment that has a useful life of more than one year—must be deducted over a number of years, but there is one major exception. Internal Revenue Code § 179 allows you to deduct up to $18,500 worth of capital assets in any one year against your business income. Even if you buy the computer on credit, with no money down, you can still qualify for this deduction.

New Law: Increasing § 179 Deductions to $25,000

Beginning in 1998, the annual limit on expensing of business assets under IRC § 179 increases as follows: 1998: $18,500; 1999: $19,000; 2000: $20,000; 2001: $24,000; 2002: $25,000.

Business Assets That Must Be Capitalized

Buildings

Cellular phones and beepers

Computer components and software

Copyrights and patents

Equipment

Improvements to business property

Inventory

Office furnishings and decorations

Small tools and equipment

Vehicles

Window coverings

A friend told me that corporations get the best tax breaks of any type of business, so I am thinking of incorporating my startup. What do you recommend?

There's a seed of truth in what your friend told you, but keep in mind that most tax benefits flow to profitable, established businesses, not to startups in their first few years. For example, corporations, and LLCs which elect to be taxed like corporations, can offer more tax-flexible pension plans and greater medical deductions than sole proprietors or partnerships; few startups have the cash flow needed to take advantage of this tax break. Similarly, the ability to split income between a corporation and its owners—thereby keeping income in lower tax brackets—is only effective if the business is solidly profitable. And incorporating adds a lot of state fees, as well as legal and accounting charges, to your expense load. So unless you are sure that substantial profits will begin to roll in immediately, hold off.

For more information about choosing the right structure for your business, see *Legal Structures for Small Businesses*, above.

I am thinking about setting up a consulting business with two of my business associates. Do we need to have partnership papers drawn up? Does it make any difference tax-wise?

If you go into business with other people and split the expenses and profits, under the tax code you are in partnership whether you have signed a written agreement or not. (The only exception to this rule is for a husband and wife, who have a choice: They can be a sole proprietorship or a partnership.) This means that you will have to file a partnership tax return every year, in addition to your individual tax return.

Even though a formal partnership agreement doesn't affect your tax status, it's essential to prepare one to establish

all partners' rights and responsibilities vis-à-vis each other. For more information about partnerships, see *Legal Structures for Small Businesses*, above.

I am a building contractor with a chance to land a big job. If I get it, I'll need to hire people quickly. Should I hire independent contractors or employees?

If you will be telling your workers where, when and how to do their jobs, you should treat them as employees, because that's how the IRS will classify them. Generally, you can treat workers as independent contractors only if they have their own businesses and offer their services to several contractors—for example, a specialty sign painter with his own shop who you hire to do a particular job. If in doubt, err on the side of treating workers as employees.

While misclassifying your workers would save you money in the short run (you wouldn't have to pay the employer's share of payroll taxes or have an accountant keep records and file payroll tax forms), it may get you into big trouble if the IRS later audits you. The IRS will reclassify your "independent contractors" as employees—with the result that you are assessed hefty back taxes, penalties and interest.

I've heard that I can no longer claim a deduction for an office in my home. But I also see that the IRS has a form for claiming home office expenses. What's the story?

It's not as confusing as it sounds. A while back, the Supreme Court told a doctor who was taking work home from the hospital that he couldn't take a depreciation deduction for the space used at his condo. But this is quite different from maintaining a home-based business. If you run a business out of your home, and you devote most of the time you dedicate to that business working in your home office, you can claim a deduction for the portion of the home used for business. Also, you can deduct related costs—utilities, insurance, remodeling—whether you own or rent.

For more information about running a home-based business, see the next set of questions.

I am planning a trip to Los Angeles to attend a trade show. Can I take my family along for a vacation and still be able to deduct the expenses?

If you take others with you on a business trip, you can deduct business expenses for the trip no greater than if you were traveling alone. If on the trip your family rides in the back seat of the car and stays in one standard motel room, then you can fully deduct your automobile and hotel expenses. You can also fully deduct the cost of air tickets even if they feature a two-for-one or "bring along the family" discount. You can't

claim a deduction for your family's meals or jaunts to Disneyland or Universal Studios, however. And if you extend your stay and partake in some of the fun after the business is over, the expenses attributed to the nonbusiness days aren't deductible, unless you extended your stay to get discounted airfare (the "Saturday overnight" requirement). In this case, your hotel room and your own meals would be deductible.

More Information About Small Business Taxes

Tax Savvy for Small Business, by Frederick W. Daily (Nolo Press), tells small business owners what they need to know about federal taxes and shows them how to make the right tax decisions.

Hiring Independent Contractors: A Legal Guide for Employers, by Stephen Fishman (Nolo Press), explains who qualifies as an independent contractor, describes applicable tax rules and shows employers how to set up effective working agreements with independent contractors.

Wage Slave No More: Law and Taxes for the Self-Employed, by Stephen Fishman (Nolo Press), is designed for the estimated 20 million Americans who are self-employed and offer their services on a contract basis.

Home-Based Businesses

As technology advances, it becomes more and more convenient and economical to operate a business from home. Depending on local zoning rules, as long as the business is small, quiet and doesn't create traffic or parking problems, it's usually legal to do so. But as with any other business endeavor, it pays to know the rules before you begin.

Is a home-based business legally different from other businesses?

No. The basic legal issues, such as picking a name for your business and deciding whether to operate as a sole proprietorship, partnership, limited liability company or corporation, are the same. Similarly, when it comes to signing contracts, hiring employees and collecting from your customers, the laws are identical whether you run your business from home or the top floor of a high-rise.

Are there laws that restrict a person's right to operate a business from home?

Municipalities have the legal right to establish rules about what types of activities can be carried out in different geographical areas. For example, they often establish zones for stores and offices (commercial zones), factories (industrial zones) and houses (residential zones). In some residential areas—especially in affluent communities—local zoning ordinances absolutely prohibit all types of business. In the great majority of municipalities, however, residential zoning rules allow small nonpolluting home businesses, as long as any home containing a business is used primarily as a residence and the business activities don't negatively affect neighbors.

How can I find out whether residential zoning rules allow the home-based business I have in mind?

Get a copy of your local ordinance from your city or county clerk's office, the city attorney's office or your public library, and read it carefully. Zoning ordinances are worded in many different ways to limit business activities in residential areas. Some are extremely vague, allowing "customary home-based occupations." Others allow homeowners to use their houses for a broad—but, unfortunately, not very specific—list of business purposes (for example, "professions and domestic occupations, crafts or services"). Still others contain a detailed list of approved occupations, such as "law, dentistry, medicine, music lessons, photography, cabinet making." If you read your ordinance and still aren't sure whether your business is okay, you may be tempted to talk to zoning or planning officials. But until you figure out what the rules and politics of your locality are, it may be best to do this without identifying and calling attention to yourself. (For example, have a friend who lives nearby make inquiries.)

The business I want to run from home is not specifically allowed or prohibited by my local ordinance. What should I do to avoid trouble?

Start by understanding that in most areas zoning and building officials don't actively search for violations. The great majority of home-based businesses that run into trouble do so when a neighbor complains—often because of noise or parking problems, or even because of the unfounded fear that your business is doing something illegal such as selling drugs. It follows that your best approach is often to explain your business activities to your neighbors and make sure that your activities are not worrying or inconveniencing them. For example, if you teach piano lessons or do physical therapy from your home and your students or clients will often come and go, make sure your neighbors are not bothered by noise or losing customary on-street parking spaces.

Will the local ordinance regulating home-based businesses include rules about specific activities, such as making noise, putting up signs or having employees?

Quite possibly. Many ordinances—especially those which are fairly vague as to the type of business you can run from your home—restrict how you can carry out your business. The most frequent rules limit your use of on-street parking, prohibit outside signs, limit car and truck traffic and restrict the number of employees who can work at your house on a regular basis (some prohibit employees altogether). In addition, some zoning ordinances limit the percentage of your home's floor space that can be devoted to the business. Again, you'll need to study your local ordinance carefully to see how these rules will affect you.

If Municipal Officials Say No to Your Home-Based Business

In many cities and counties, if a planning or zoning board rejects your business, you can appeal—often to the city council or county board of supervisors. While this can be an uphill battle, it is likely to be less so if you have the support of all affected neighbors. You may also be able to get an overly-restrictive zoning ordinance amended by your municipality's governing body. For example, in some communities, people are working to amend ordinances that prohibit home-based businesses entirely or only allow "traditional home-based businesses" to permit those that rely on the use of computers and other high tech equipment—businesses that are usually unobtrusive, but far from traditional.

I live in a planned development which has its own rules for home-based businesses. Do these control my business activities or can I rely on my city's home-based business ordinance, which is less restrictive?

In an effort to protect residential property values, most subdivisions, condos and planned unit developments create special rules—typically called Covenants, Conditions and Restrictions (CC&Rs)—that govern many aspects of property use. Rules pertaining to home-based businesses are often significantly stricter than those found in city ordinances. But so long as the rules of your planned development are reasonably clear and consistently enforced, you must follow them.

I sell my consulting services to a number of businesses. Does maintaining a home office help me establish independent contractor status with the IRS?

No. An independent contractor is a person who controls both the outcome of a project and the means of accomplishing it, and who offers services to a number of businesses or individual purchasers. Although having an office or place of business is one factor the IRS looks at in determining whether an individual qualifies as an independent contractor, it makes no difference whether your office is located at home or in a traditional business setting.

Are there tax advantages to working from home?

Almost all ordinary and necessary business expenses (everything from wages to computers to paper clips) are tax-deductible, no matter where they are incurred—in a factory or office, while traveling or at home. In addition, if you operate your business from home and qualify under IRS rules, you may be able to deduct part of your rent from your income taxes—or if you own your home, take a depreciation deduction.

Finally, you may also be eligible to deduct a portion of your total utility, home repair and maintenance, property tax and house insurance costs, based on the percentage of your residence you use for business purposes. To qualify to take this deduction, the IRS requires that three legal tests be met:

- your home must be the principal place where you conduct your business
- the business must occupy a separate and identifiable space (for example, a den or garage), and
- you must use your business space regularly and exclusively for business purposes.

In addition, the amount of your deduction can't exceed your home-based business's total profit.

Insuring Your Home-Based Business

It's a mistake to rely on a homeowner's or renter's insurance policy to cover your home-based business. These policies often exclude or strictly limit coverage for business equipment and liability for injuries to business visitors. For example, if your computer is stolen or a client or business associate trips and falls on your steps, you may not be covered. Fortunately, it's easy to avoid these nasty surprises. Sit down with your insurance agent and fully disclose your planned business operation. You'll find that it's relatively inexpensive to add business coverage to your homeowner's policy—and it's a tax-deductible expense. But be sure to check prices—some insurance companies provide special cost-effective policies designed to protect both homes and home-based businesses.

I have a full-time job, but I also operate a separate part-time business from home. Can I claim a tax deduction?

Yes, as long as you meet the IRS rules mentioned in the previous answer. It makes no difference that you work only part-time at your home-based business or that you have another occupation. But your business must be more than a disguised hobby—it has to pass muster with the IRS as a real business. The IRS defines a business as "any activity engaged in to make a profit." If a venture makes money—even a small amount—in three of five consecutive years, it is presumed to possess a profit motive. (IRC §183(d).) However, courts have held that some activities that failed to meet this three-profitable-years-out-of-five test still qualify as a business if they are run in a businesslike manner. When determining whether a nonprofitable venture qualifies for a deduction, courts may look at whether you kept thorough business records, had a separate business bank account, prepared advertising or other marketing materials and obtained any necessary licenses and permits (a business license from your city, for example).

How big will my home office tax deduction be if my business qualifies under IRS rules?

To determine your deduction, you first need to figure out how much of your home you use for business as compared to other purposes. Do this by dividing the number of square feet used for your home business by the total square footage of your home. The resulting percentage of business usage determines how much of your rent (or, if you are a homeowner, depreciation), insurance, utilities and other expenses are deductible. But remember, the amount of the deduction can't be larger than the profit your home-based business generates. (Additional technical rules apply to calculating depreciation on houses you own to allow for the fact that the structure, but not the land, depreciates.) For more information, contact the IRS to order Publication 587, *Business Use of Your Home*.

Do I need to watch out for any tax traps when claiming deductions for my home office?

Claiming a home office deduction increases your audit risk slightly, but this needn't be a big fear if you carefully follow the rules.

Keep in mind that if you sell your house, all the home-based office deductions you have previously taken will be subject to income tax in that year, whether you made a profit or not. And you can't use the $250,000 per person "exclusion of profits" on the sale of a home to offset this tax. For example, if your home office deductions total $15,000 for the last seven years, you will be taxed on this amount in the year you sell your house. Despite this tax, it's generally wise to continue to take your home office deductions each year. Especially for people who don't plan to sell their houses anytime soon, it's usually beneficial to receive a tax break today that you won't have to repay for many years. You can use your tax savings to help your business grow.

More Information About Home-Based Business

Working From Home, Everything You Need to Know About Living and Working Under the Same Roof, by Paul & Sarah Edwards (Tarcher-Putnam), covers all aspects of doing business at home, from zoning, credit and insurance prob-

lems to personal concerns (juggling family, friends, children and work).

The Best Home Businesses for the 90s, by Paul & Sarah Edwards (Tarcher-Putnam), profiles 95 workable home-based businesses, including information about how each business works and what sets of skills and opportunities are necessary to succeed.

Wage Slave No More: Law and Taxes for the Self-Employed, by Stephen Fishman (Nolo Press), shows independent contractors how to meet business start-up requirements, comply with strict IRS rules and make sure they get paid in full and on time.

Employers' Rights & Responsibilities

At some point during your business venture, you may need to hire people to help you manage your workload. When you do, you'll be held accountable to a host of state and federal laws that regulate your relationship with your employees. Among the things you'll be expected to know and understand:

- proper hiring practices, including how to write appropriate job descriptions, conduct interviews and respect privacy rights
- wage and hour laws, as well as the laws that govern retirement plans, healthcare benefits and life insurance benefits

- workplace safety rules and regulations
- how to write an employee handbook and conduct performance reviews, including what you should and shouldn't put in an employee's personnel file
- how to avoid sexual harassment as well as discrimination based on gender, age, race, pregnancy, sexual orientation and national origin, and
- how to avoid trouble if you need to fire an employee.

This section provides you with an overview of your role as an employer. And you can find more guidance elsewhere in this book. Employee's rights—including questions and answers about wages, hours and workplace safety—are discussed in Chapter 4; pension plans are covered in Chapter 14.

First things first. How can I write advertisements that will attract the best pool of potential employees—without getting in legal hot water?

Many small employers get tripped up when summarizing a job in an advertisement. This can easily happen if you're not familiar with the legal guidelines. Nuances in an ad can be used as evidence of discrimination against applicants of a particular gender, age or marital status.

There are a number of pitfalls to avoid in job ads:

DON'T USE	USE
Salesman	Salesperson
College Student	Part-time Worker
Handyman	General Repair Person
Gal Friday	Office Manager
Married Couple	Two-Person Job
Counter Girl	Retail Clerk
Waiter	Wait Staff
Young	Energetic

Also, requiring a high school or college degree may be discriminatory in some job categories. You can avoid problems by stating that an applicant must have a "degree or equivalent experience."

Probably the best way to write an ad that meets legal requirements is to stick to the job skills needed and the basic responsibilities. Some examples:

"Fifty-unit apartment complex seeks experienced manager with general maintenance skills."

"Mid-sized manufacturing company has opening for accountant with tax experience to oversee interstate accounts."

"Cook trainee position available in new vegetarian restaurant. Flexible hours."

Help Wanted ads placed by federal contractors must state that all qualified applicants will receive consideration for employment without regard to race, color, religion, sex or national origin. Ads often express this with the phrase, "An Equal Opportunity Employer." To show your intent to be fair, you may want to include this phrase in your ad even if you're not a federal contractor.

Any tips on how to conduct a good, forthright interview—and again, avoid legal trouble?

Good preparation is your best ally. Before you begin to interview applicants for a job opening, write down a set of questions focusing on the job duties and the applicant's skills and experience. For example:

"Tell me about your experience in running a mailroom."

"How much experience did you have in making cold calls on your last job?"

"Explain how you typically go about organizing your workday."

"Have any of your jobs required strong leadership skills?"

By writing down the questions and sticking to the same format at all interviews for the position, you reduce the risk that a rejected applicant will later complain about unequal treatment. It's also smart to summarize the applicant's answers for your files—but don't get so involved in documenting the interview that you forget to listen closely to the applicant. And don't be so locked in to your list of questions that you don't follow up on something significant that an applicant has said, or try to pin down an ambiguous or evasive response.

To break the ice, you might give the applicant some information about the job—the duties, hours, pay range, benefits and career opportunities. Questions about the applicant's work history and experience that may be relevant to the job opening are always appropriate. But don't encourage the applicant to divulge the trade secrets of a present or former employer—especially a competitor. That can lead to a lawsuit. And be cautious about an applicant who volunteers such information or promises to bring secrets to the new position; such an applicant will probably play fast and loose with your own company's secrets, given the chance.

I've heard horror stories about employers who get sued for discriminating—both by employees and even by people they've interviewed but decided not to hire. What's the bottom line?

Federal and state laws prohibit you from discriminating against an employee or applicant because of race, color, gender, religious beliefs, national origin, physical disability—or age if the person is at least 40 years old. Also, many states and cities have laws prohibiting employment discrimination based on marital status or sexual orientation.

A particular form of discrimination becomes illegal when Congress, a state legislature or a city council decides that a characteristic—race, for example—bears no legitimate relationship to employment decisions. As an employer, you must be prepared to show that your hiring and promotion decisions have been based on objective criteria and that the more qualified applicant has always succeeded.

Still, when hiring, you can exercise a wide range of discretion based on business considerations. You remain free to hire, promote, discipline and fire employees and to set their duties and salaries based on their skills, experience, performance and reliability—factors that are logically tied to valid business purposes.

The law also prohibits employer practices that seem neutral, but may have a disproportionate impact on a particular group of people. Again, a policy is legal only if there's a valid business reason for its existence. For example, refusing to hire people who don't meet a minimum height and weight is permissible if it's clearly related to the physical demands of the particular job—felling and hauling huge trees, for instance. But applying such a requirement to exclude applicants for a job as a cook or receptionist wouldn't pass legal muster.

How can I check out a prospective employee without violating his or her right to privacy?

As an employer, you likely believe that the more information you have about job applicants, the better your hiring decisions will be. But make sure any information you seek will actually be helpful to you. It's often a waste of time and effort to acquire and review transcripts and credit reports—although occasionally they're useful. If you're hiring a bookkeeper, for example, previous job experience is much more important than the grades the applicant received in a community college bookkeeping program 10 years ago. On the other hand, if the applicant is fresh out of school and has never held a bookkeeping job, a transcript may yield some insights. Similarly, if you're hiring a switchboard operator, information on a credit report would be irrelevant. But if you're filling a job for a bar manager who will be handling large cash receipts, you might want to see a credit report to learn if the applicant is in financial trouble.

To avoid claims that you've invaded a prospective employee's privacy, always obtain the applicant's written consent before you contact a former employer, request a credit report or send for high school or college transcripts.

Finally, it's usually not wise to resort to screening applicants through personality tests; laws and court rulings restrict your right to use them in most states.

Protection for Recovering Addicts

With drug and alcohol use on the rise—along with increased pressure to make solid hiring decisions—many employers are resorting to drug and blood tests in an attempt to weed out problem employees before they're hired.

The legal rules on whether this testing is permissible are a bit complicated. What may be most mystifying is what you can do with information you discover. For example, after you've made a conditional offer of employment and as part of a pre-employment medical screening, you may discover that a job applicant had a drug problem in the past. The Americans with Disabilities Act (ADA) prohibits you from discriminating against people because of past drug problems. This includes people who no longer use drugs illegally and are receiving treatment for drug addiction or who have successfully recovered from an addiction.

To make sure that drug use isn't recurring, however, you may request evidence that a person is participating in a drug rehab program. You may also ask for the results of a drug test.

You can refuse to hire someone with a history of alcoholism or illegal drug use if you can show that the person poses a direct threat to health or safety. You must show that there's a high probability that the person will return to the illegal drug use or alcohol abuse, and a high probability of substantial harm to the person or others—harm that you can't reduce or eliminate through what the ADA deems a reasonable accommodation, such as changing the employee's job duties to eliminate working with toxic chemicals or heavy machinery.

How do I avoid legal problems when giving employee evaluations?

Be honest and consistent with your employees. If a fired employee initiates a legal action against you, a judge or jury will analyze not only your evaluations, but other actions regarding that employee as well. For example, a jury will sense that something is wrong if you consistently rate a worker's performance as poor or mediocre—but continue to hand out generous raises or perhaps even promote the person. The logical conclusion: You didn't take seriously the criticisms in your evaluation report, so you shouldn't expect the employee to take them seriously, either.

It's just as damaging to give an employee glowing praise in report after report—perhaps to make the employee feel good—and then to fire him or her for a single infraction. That strikes most people as unfair. And unfair employers often lose court fights, especially in situations where a sympathetic employee appears to have been treated harshly.

If your system is working, employees with excellent evaluations should not need to be fired for poor performance. And employees with poor performance shouldn't be getting big raises.

As a small employer, what should I keep in personnel files—and what right do employees have to see what's inside?

Create a file for each employee in which you keep all job-related information, including:
- job description
- job application
- offer of employment
- INS form I-9, the Employment Eligibility Verification, and supporting documents
- IRS form W-4, the Employee's Withholding Allowance Certificate

- receipt for employee handbook
- periodic performance evaluations
- sign-up forms for employee benefits
- complaints from customers and co-workers
- awards or citations for excellent performance
- warnings and disciplinary actions, and
- notes on an employee's attendance or tardiness.

Medical Records: A Serious Case

The Americans with Disabilities Act (ADA) imposes very strict limitations on how you must handle information obtained from post-offer medical examinations and inquiries. You must keep the information in medical files that are separate from nonmedical records, and you must store the medical files in a separate locked cabinet. To further guarantee the confidentiality of medical files, designate a specific person to have access to those files.

The ADA allows very limited disclosure of medical information. Under the ADA, you may:

- inform supervisors about necessary restrictions on an employee's duties and about necessary accommodations
- inform first aid and safety workers about a disability that may require emergency treatment and about specific procedures that are needed if the workplace must be evacuated, and
- provide medical information required by government officials and by

insurance companies that require a medical exam for health or life insurance.

Otherwise, don't disclose medical information about employees. Although the confidentiality provisions of the ADA protect only some disabled workers, the best policy is to treat all medical information about all employees as confidential.

Many states have laws giving employees—and former employees—access to their own personnel files. How much access varies from state to state. Typically, if your state allows employees to see their files, you can insist that you or another supervisor be present to make sure nothing is taken, added or changed. Some state laws allow employees to obtain copies of items in their files, but not necessarily all items. For example, a law may limit the employee to copies of documents that he or she has signed, such as a job application. If an employee is entitled to a copy of an item in the file or if you're inclined to let the employee have a copy of any document in the file, you—rather than the employee—should make the copy.

Usually, you won't have to let the employee see sensitive items such as information assembled for a criminal investigation, reference letters and information that might violate the privacy of other people. In a few states, employees may insert rebuttals to information in their personnel files with which they disagree.

I hear a lot about disabled workers being protected by the Americans with Disabilities Act (ADA), but the law is long and hard to understand. How can I make sure I comply?

The ADA states that when making hiring and employment decisions, it's illegal to discriminate against anyone because of a disability. If a person is qualified to do the work, or to do it once a reasonable accommodation is made, you must treat that person the same as all other applicants and employees. Although the concept is simple, the ADA requirements are immensely complicated—primarily because the statute is poorly drafted.

Many of the legal battles involving the ADA are waged over this imprecise language—particularly the meaning of "reasonable accommodation." The idea is quite simple: You may have to make some changes to help a disabled person do a job. This can take a number of forms, such as changing the job, an employment practice or the work environment. And you need not be psychic. Generally, the person with the disability needs to ask an employer to make the change.

The added twist is that the ADA doesn't require you to accommodate a disabled applicant or employee if it would place an undue hardship on the business—that is, if it would require significant difficulty or expense.

For employers, the ADA has its heaviest impact on the hiring process. For example, you must:

- write job descriptions that focus on essential tasks so that a person with a disability isn't eliminated because he or she can't perform a marginal job duty
- avoid questions in job applications and interviews that focus on possible disabilities, and
- defer pre-employment medical exams and inquiries until after you've made a conditional offer of employment.

See *Disability Discrimination*, in Chapter 4, for more information about the ADA.

ADA Coverage Is Broad

Under the ADA, you can't discriminate against a person with a disability in any aspect of employment, including:

- applications
- interviews
- testing
- hiring
- job assignments
- evaluations
- disciplinary actions
- training
- promotion
- medical exams
- layoffs
- firing
- compensation
- leave, and
- benefits.

In addition, you can't deny a job to someone or discriminate against an employee because that person is related to or associates with a person who has a disability. For example, you can't:

- refuse to hire someone because that person's spouse, child or other dependent has a disability
- refuse to hire someone because that person's spouse, child or other dependent has a disability that's not covered by your current health insurance plan or that may cause increased healthcare costs, or
- fire an employee because that the employee has a roommate or close friend who has AIDS, or because the employee does volunteer work for people who have AIDS.

My employees' religious differences are causing strife in the workplace. What am I required to do?

This is a tricky area. An increasing number of employees are claiming religious discrimination. And unfortunately, the law in this delicate area is unclear.

First, make sure your own plate is clean. You have the legal right to discuss your own religious beliefs with an employee, if you're so inclined, but you can't persist to the point that the employee feels you're being hostile, intimidating or offensive. So if an employee objects to your discussion of religious subjects or you get even an inkling that your religious advances are unwelcome, back off. Otherwise, you may find yourself embroiled in a lawsuit or administrative proceeding.

If employees complain to you that a co-worker is badgering them with

religious views, you have a right—if not a duty—to intervene, although you must, of course, use the utmost tact and sensitivity.

While you may feel that the best way to resolve these knotty problems is to simply banish religion from the workplace, that's generally not a viable alternative. You're legally required to accommodate the religious needs of employees—for example, allowing employees to pick and choose the paid holidays they would like to take during the year. You don't, however, need to do anything that would cost more than a minimum amount or that would cause more than minimal inconvenience.

Some of my employees insist they have a right to smoke during breaks and at lunch, and another group claims they'll quit if I allow smoking on the premises. I'm caught in the middle. What should I do?

It's well established that second hand tobacco smoke can harm the health of nonsmokers. Consequently, in many states and municipalities, employers are legally required to limit smoking in the workplace. And a number of locales have specific laws that ban or limit smoking in public places; if your workplace falls within the legal definition of a public place—a bar, restaurant or hotel, for example—your legal rights and responsibilities will be clearly spelled out in the law.

A rule proposed recently by the Occupational Health and Safety Administration (OSHA) would allow only two choices: you'd have to either prohibit smoking in the workplace, or limit it to areas that are enclosed and ventilated directly to the outdoors. Under the rule, you couldn't require employees to enter the smoking areas when performing their normal job duties.

Given the scientific facts and the general direction in which the law is moving, your safest legal course is to restrict smoking in the workplace—and a total ban may be the only practical solution. That's because in many modern buildings, it's too expensive—maybe even impossible—to provide a separate ventilation system for a smokers' room.

In addition to meeting the specific requirements of laws and regulations that limit or prohibit smoking in the workplace, be aware that you may be legally liable to nonsmoking employees if you don't take appropriate actions on their complaints.

It's been a bad year for my business—and it looks as though I may have to lay off some workers. Are there legal problems to avoid?

Generally, you're free to lay off or terminate employees because business conditions require it. But if you do cut back, don't leave your business open to claims that the layoffs were really a pretext for getting rid of employees for illegal reasons.

Be sensitive to how your actions may be perceived. If the layoff primarily affects workers of a particular race, or women or older employees, someone may well question your motives. It's better to spread the pain around; don't let the burden fall on just one group of employees.

I have to give a reference for a former employee I had to fire. I don't want to be too positive about him, but I am also afraid he might sue me for unflattering remarks. Advice?

The key to protecting yourself is to stick to the facts and act in good faith. You'll get in trouble only if you exaggerate or cover up the truth—or are motivated by a desire to harm your former employee.

Former employees who feel maligned can sue for defamation—called slander if the statements were spoken or libel if they were written. To win a defamation case, a former employee must prove that you gave out false information and that the information harmed his or her reputation. If you can show that the information you provided was true, the lawsuit will be dismissed.

And even if it turns out that the information provided is untrue, employers in most states are entitled to some protection in defamation cases. This protection is based on a legal doctrine called "qualified privilege." To receive the benefits, you must show that:

• you made the statement in good faith

• you and the person to whom you disclosed the information shared a common interest, and

• you limited your statement to this common interest.

The law recognizes that a former employer and a prospective employer share a common interest in the attributes of an employee. To get the protection of the qualified privilege, your main task is to stick to facts that you've reasonably investigated and to lay aside your personal feelings about the former employee.

A practical policy—and one that gives you a high degree of legal protection—is simply not to discuss an employee with prospective employers if you can't say something positive. Just tell the person inquiring that it's not your policy to comment on former workers.

Where an employee's record is truly mixed, it's usually possible to accent the positive while you try to put negative information into a more favorable perspective.

More Information About Employers' Rights and Responsibilities

The Employer's Legal Handbook, by Fred Steingold (Nolo Press), explains employers' legal rights and responsibilities in detail.

Reference Checking Handbook, published by the Society for Human Resource Management, provides helpful information about the Ps and Qs of checking references. Call 612-885-5588 for price and ordering information.

In a concise publication called *Credit Reports: What Employers Should Know About Using Them,* the Federal Trade Commission offers examples to illustrate situations where it is and is not a good idea to check job applicants' credit records. To order, call the FTC's Office of Consumer and Business Education at 202-326-3650.

Many state trade associations publish newsletters or magazines to help keep their members informed of changes in employment law. Your state chamber of commerce may also have helpful publications on this subject.

General Sites for Small Businesses

http://www.nolo.com
Nolo Press offers self-help information on a wide variety of subjects, including starting and running your small business.

http://www.americanexpress.com/smallbusiness
The American Express Small Business Exchange helps you find information, resources and customers for your small business.

http://www.claris.com/smallbiz/experts/
Claris's Small Business Expert Advice offers dozens of FAQs written by experts on various small business matters. Topics include start-up issues, staying competitive, tax strategies and using the Internet for small business.

http://www.nfibonline.com/
The National Federation of Independent Business provides news, workshops and action alerts for small business owners. The NFIB is the nation's largest advocacy organization for small and independent businesses.

http://www.smalloffice.com
Smalloffice.com offers useful tips on marketing, sales and financing, as well as advice on how to use software, computers and other technology to help your business.

http://www.sbaonline.sba.gov/
The Small Business Administration provides information about starting, financing and expanding your small business.

http://www.yahoo.com/Business/Small_Business_Information
Yahoo offers an abundance of links to resources for small business people.

Sites for Nonprofit Corporations

http://www.igc.org/igc/issues/activis/index.html
The Institute for Global Communication offers an extensive list of links to resources for activism and nonprofit development.

http://www.ncnb.org/home.html
The National Center for Nonprofit Boards provides information and publications to help you run a successful nonprofit organization.

Sites for Independent Contractors and Home-Based Businesses

http://www.hoaa.com/
The Home Office Association of America is a national association for home-based business people. It offers resources, ideas and benefits to help you run a more profitable business from home. The site also contains an extensive list of links to other sites of interest to the self-employed.

http://www.ssa.gov/
The Social Security Administration provides lots of information on regulations and benefits for self-employed people.

Patents

To invent, you need a good imagination and a pile of junk.

—THOMAS EDISON

Many of us muse about the million-dollar idea: the invention that will make life easier for others and more lucrative for us. Most of these ideas never get off the ground, however; we decide it's not really worth the time and effort to create the perfect dog toothbrush, clothes hanger or juice squeezer. But every now and then we may hit on a winner—an idea worth developing, marketing and protecting. In these cases, we must turn to the patent laws for help.

This chapter addresses the basic legal issues that arise in the patent area, answering questions such as:

- What is a patent?
- When does a particular invention qualify for a patent?
- How do you get a patent in the U.S. or abroad?
- How are patent rights enforced?
- How can you profit from your patent?

Qualifying for a Patent

THERE IS NOTHING WHICH

PERSEVERING EFFORT AND UNCEASING

AND DILIGENT CARE CANNOT

ACCOMPLISH.

—SENECA

A patent is a document issued by the U.S. Patent and Trademark Office (PTO) that grants a monopoly for a limited period of time on the manufacture, use and sale of an invention. These exclusive rights last between 14 and 20 years, depending on the type of invention.

What types of inventions can be patented?

The PTO issues three different kinds of patents: utility patents, design patents and plant patents.

To qualify for a utility patent—by far the most common type of patent—an invention must be:

- a process or method for producing a useful, concrete and tangible result (such as a genetic engineering procedure, an investment strategy or computer software)
- a machine (usually something with moving parts or circuitry, such as a cigarette lighter, sewage treatment system, laser or photocopier)
- an article of manufacture (such as an eraser, tire, transistor or hand tool)
- a composition of matter (such as a chemical composition, drug, soap or genetically altered life form), or
- an improvement of an invention that fits within one of the first four categories.

Often, an invention will fall into more than one category. For instance, a laser can usually be described both as a process (the steps necessary to produce the laser beam) and a machine (a device that implements the steps to produce the laser beam). Regardless of the number of categories into which a particular invention fits, it can receive only one utility patent.

If an invention fits into one of the categories described above, it is known as "statutory subject matter" and has passed the first test in qualifying for a patent. But an inventor's creation must overcome several additional hurdles before the PTO will issue a patent. The invention must also:

- have some utility, no matter how trivial

- be novel (that is, it must be different from all previous inventions in some important way), and
- be nonobvious (a surprising and significant development) to somebody who understands the technical field of the invention.

For design patents, the law requires that the design be novel, nonobvious and nonfunctional. For example, a new shape for a car fender, bottle or flashlight that doesn't improve its functionality would qualify.

Finally, plants may qualify for a patent if they are both novel and nonobvious. Plant patents are issued less frequently than any other type of patent.

More Examples of Patentable Subject Matter

The following items are just some of the things that might qualify for patent protection: biological inventions; carpet designs; new chemical formulas, processes or procedures; clothing accessories and designs; computer hardware and peripherals; computer software; containers; cosmetics; decorative hardware; electrical inventions; electronic circuits; fabrics and fabric designs; food inventions; furniture design; games (board, box and instructions); housewares; jewelry; laser light shows; machines; magic tricks or techniques; mechanical inventions; medical accessories and devices; medicines; musical instruments; odors; plants; recreational gear; and sporting goods (designs and equipment).

What types of inventions are not eligible for patent protection?

Some types of inventions will not qualify for a patent, no matter how interesting or important they are. For example, mathematical formulas, laws of nature, newly discovered substances that occur naturally in the world, and purely theoretical phenomena—for instance, a scientific principle like superconductivity without regard to its use in the real world—have long been considered unpatentable. This means, for example, that you can't patent a general mathematical approach to problem solving or a newly discovered pain killer in its natural state.

In addition, the following categories of inventions don't qualify for patents:

- processes done entirely by human motor coordination, such as choreographed dance routines or a method for meditation
- most protocols and methods used to perform surgery on humans
- printed matter that has no unique physical shape or structure associated with it
- unsafe new drugs
- inventions useful only for illegal purposes, and
- nonoperable inventions, including "perpetual motion" machines (which are presumed to be nonoperable because to operate they would have to violate certain bedrock scientific principles).

Can computer software qualify for patent protection?

Yes. Even though you can't get a patent on a mathematical formula per se, you may be able to get protection for a specific application of a formula. Thus, software may qualify for a patent if it produces a useful, concrete and tangible result. For example, the PTO will not issue a patent on the complex mathematical formulae that are used in space navigation, but will grant a patent for the software and machines that translate those equations and make the space shuttle go where it's supposed to go.

Is it possible to obtain a patent on forms of life?

Forms of life, from bacteria to cows, that are genetically altered to have new and useful characteristics or behaviors may qualify for utility patents. Also patentable are sequences of DNA that have been created to test genetic behaviors and the methods used to accomplish this sequencing. With the advent of cloning techniques and the ability to mix genes across species—for example, the human immune system genetic code transplanted into a mouse for testing purposes—the question of what life forms can and cannot be patented promises to be a subject of fierce debate for years to come.

What makes an invention novel?

In the context of a patent application, an invention is considered novel when it is different from all previous inventions (called "prior art") in one or more of its constituent elements. When deciding whether an invention is novel, the PTO will consider all prior art that existed as of the date the inventor files a patent application on the invention, or if necessary, as of the date the inventor can prove he or she first built and tested the invention. If prior art is uncovered, the invention may still qualify for a Patent if the inventor can show that he or she conceived of the invention before the prior art existed and was diligent in building and testing the invention or filing a patent application on it.

An invention will flunk the novelty test if it was described in a published document or put to public use more than one year prior to the date the patent application was filed. This is known as the one-year rule.

When is an invention considered nonobvious?

To qualify for a patent, an invention must be nonobvious as well as novel. An invention is considered nonobvious if someone who is skilled in the particular field of the invention would view it as an unexpected or surprising development.

For example, in August of 1998, Future Enterprises invents a portable high quality virtual reality system. A virtual reality engineer would most likely find this invention to be truly surprising and unexpected. Even though increased portability of a computer-based technology is always expected in the broad sense, the specific way in which the portability is accomplished by this invention would be a breakthrough in the field and thus unobvious. Contrast this with a bicycle developer who uses a new, light but strong metal alloy to build his bicycles. Most people skilled in the art of bicycle manufacturing would consider the use of the new alloy in the bicycle to be obvious, given that lightness of weight is a desirable aspect of high-quality bicycles.

Knowing whether an invention will be considered nonobvious by the PTO is difficult because it is such a subjective exercise—what one patent examiner considers surprising, another may not. In addition, the examiner will usually be asked to make the nonobviousness determination well after the date of the invention, because of delays inherent in the patent process. The danger of this type of retroactive assessment is that the examiner may unconsciously be affected by the intervening technical improvements. To avoid this, the examiner generally relies only on the prior-art references (documents describing previous inventions) that existed as of the date of invention.

As an example, assume that in 2001, Future Enterprises' application for a patent on the 1998 invention is being examined in the Patent and Trademark Office. Assume further that by 2001, you can find a portable virtual reality unit in any consumer electronics store for under $200. The patent examiner will have to go back to the time of the invention to fully appreciate how surprising and unexpected it was when it was first conceived, and ignore the fact that in 2001 the technology of the invention is very common.

What makes an invention useful?

Patents may be granted for inventions that have some type of usefulness (utility), even if the use is humorous, such as a musical condom or a motorized spaghetti fork. However, the invention must work—at least in theory. Thus, a new approach to manufacturing superconducting materials may qualify for a patent if it has a sound theoretical basis—even if it hasn't yet been shown to work in practice. But a new drug that has no theoretical basis and which hasn't been tested will not qualify for a patent.

Remember that to qualify for a design or plant patent, the other two types of patents obtained in the U.S., the inventor need not show utility

Are You the First?

As discussed previously, patents are awarded only on new and nonobvious inventions. How can an inventor find out whether his or her invention is really new? The place to start is to see whether it has ever been patented. Although a number of great inventions have never received a patent, most have. A quick spin through the patent database can provide a good headstart on finding out just how innovative an invention really is.

The World Wide Web can be used for free access to patents issued since 1971. Both the U.S. Patent and Trademark Office and the IBM Corporation provide free online databases where you simply type in words which describe your invention—called keywords. Only words that appear on the front page of the patent can be searched in this manner. However, the front page includes the title of the invention and the invention abstract (a one-paragraph description of the invention). So if the invention involves technology that has arisen since 1971, a relatively thorough search over the Internet is possible. The USPTO database is located at http://www.uspto.gov, and the IBM Corporation Patent Search Site is located at http://patent.womplex.ibm.com.

Sometimes an inventor needs to search for patents issued before 1971. All patents since the founding of the United States count when deciding whether an invention is sufficiently new to deserve a patent. And if the invention involves time-less technology (another way to core an apple), these pre-1971 patents are as important as those that were issued later.

A great resource for complete patent searching—from the first patent ever issued to the latest—is a network of special libraries called Patent and Trademark Depository Libraries (PTDLs). Every state but Connecticut has at least one. While a complete patent search can be done for free in these libraries, many of them also offer computer searches for a reasonable fee. To find a PTDL, see the list in Chapter 8.

Obtaining a Patent

Many times a day I realize how much my own outer and inner life is built upon the labors of my fellow men, both living and dead, and how earnestly I must exert myself in order to give in return as much as I have received.

—ALBERT EINSTEIN

Because a patent grants the inventor a monopoly on his or her invention for a relatively long period of time (between 14 and 20 years depending upon the invention), patent applications are rigorously examined by the Patent and Trademark Office (PTO). Typically, a patent application travels back and forth between the applicant and the patent examiner until both sides agree on which aspects of an invention the patent will cover, if any. This process typically takes between one and two years.

If an agreement is reached, the PTO "allows" the application and publishes a brief description of the patent in a weekly publication called the *Official Gazette*. If no one objects to the patent as published, and the applicant pays the required issuance fee, the PTO provides the applicant with a document called a patent deed, which we colloquially refer to as a patent. The patent deed consists primarily of the information submitted in the patent application, as modified during the patent examination process.

What information is typically included in a patent application?

There is no such thing as an automatic patent through creation or usage of an invention. To receive patent protection, an inventor must file an application, pay the appropriate fees and obtain a patent. To apply for a U.S. patent, the inventor must file the application with a branch of the U.S. Department of Commerce known as the U.S. Patent and Trademark Office, or PTO. A U.S. patent application typically consists of:

- an Information Disclosure Statement—that is, an explanation of why the invention is different from all previous and similar developments (the "prior art")

- a detailed description of the structure and operation of the invention (called a patent specification) that teaches how to build and use the invention
- a precise description of the aspects of the invention to be covered by the patent (called the patent claims)
- all drawings that are necessary to fully explain the specification and claims
- a Patent Application Declaration—a statement under oath that the information in the application is true, and
- the filing fee.

In addition, small inventors often include a declaration asking for a reduction in the filing fee.

Understanding the Provisional Patent Application

Often inventors want to have a patent application on file when they go out to show their invention to prospective manufacturers because it will discourage ripoffs. Also, inventors like to get their invention on record as early as possible in case someone else comes up with the same invention. To accomplish both these goals, an inventor may file what is known as a Provisional Patent Application (PPA). The PPA need only contain a complete description of the structure and operation of an invention and any drawings that are necessary to understand it—it need not contain claims, formal drawings, a Patent Application Declaration or an Information Disclosure Statement. The PPA isn't examined when submitted. Instead, it sits in a PTO file and is examined only if the inventor files a regular patent application on the same invention within a one-year period and the applicant wishes to claim the earlier filing date. (An inventor would need to claim the earlier date only if prior art surfaced after the PPA's filing date but before the filing date of the regular application, or if a patent application for the same invention was filed by another inventor and the PTO has to decide which applicant should get the patent.)

What happens if there are multiple applications for the same invention?

If a patent examiner discovers that another pending application involves the same invention and that both in-ventions appear to qualify for a patent, the patent examiner will declare that a conflict (called an interference) exists between the two applications. In that event, a hearing is held to determine who is entitled to the patent.

Who gets the patent depends on such variables as who first conceived the invention and worked on it dili-gently, who first built and tested the invention and who filed the first pro-visional or regular patent application. Because of the possibility of a patent interference, it is wise to document all invention-related activities in a signed and witnessed inventor's notebook so that you can later prove the date the invention was conceived and the steps you took to build and test the inven-tion or quickly file a patent applica-tion.

How are U.S. patents protected abroad?

Patent rights originate in the U.S. Constitution and are implemented exclusively by federal laws passed by Congress. These laws define the kinds of inventions that are patentable and the procedures that must be followed to apply for, receive and maintain patent rights for the duration of the patent.

All other industrialized countries offer patent protection as well. While patent requirements and rules differ from country to country, several inter-national treaties (including the Patent Cooperation Treaty and the Paris Con-vention) allow U.S. inventors to obtain patent protection in other countries that have adopted the treaties if the inventors take certain required steps, such as filing a patent application in the countries on a timely basis and paying required patent fees.

Enforcing a Patent

Once a patent is issued, it is up to the owner to enforce it. If friendly negotiations fail, enforcement involves two basic steps:

• making a determination that the patent is being illegally violated (infringed), and

• filing a federal court action to enforce the patent.

Because enforcing a patent can be a long and expensive process, many patent infringment suits that could have been filed, aren't. Instead, the patent owner often settles with the infringer. Frequently, an infringer will pay a reasonable license fee that allows the infringer to continue using the invention.

What constitutes infringement of a patent?

To decide whether an inventor is violating a patent, it is necessary to carefully examine the patent's claims (most patents contain more than one of these terse statements of the scope of the invention) and compare the elements of each claim with the elements of the accused infringer's device or process. If the elements of a patent claim match the elements of the de-

vice or process (called "reading on" or "teaching" the device or process), an infringement has occurred. Even if the claims don't literally match the infringing device, it is possible that a court would find an infringement by applying what's known as the "doctrine of equivalents," that is, the invention in the patent and the allegedly infringing device or process are sufficiently equivalent in what they do and how they do it to warrant a finding of infringement.

For example, Steve invents a tennis racket with a score keeper embedded in the racket handle's end. The invention is claimed as a tennis racket handle that combines grasping and score keeping functions. Steve receives a patent on this invention. Later, Megan invents and sells a tennis racket with a transparent handle that provides a more sophisticated score keeping device than Steve's racket. Even though Megan's invention improves on Steve's invention in certain respects, it will most likely be held to be an infringement of Steve's invention, for one of two reasons:

• Megan's invention teaches the same elements as those claimed in Steve's patent (a tennis racket handle with two functions), or

• when considering what it is and how it works, Megan's invention is the substantial equivalent of Steve's invention (the doctrine of equivalents).

What remedies are available for patent infringement?

A patent owner may enforce his patent by bringing a patent infringement action (lawsuit) in federal court against anyone who uses his invention without permission. If the lawsuit is successful, the court will take one of two approaches. It may issue a court order (called an injunction) preventing the infringer from any further use or sale of the infringing device, and award damages to the patent owner. Or, the court may work with the parties to hammer out an agreement under which the infringing party will pay the patent owner royalties in exchange for permission to use the infringing device.

Bringing a patent infringement action can be tricky, because it is possible for the alleged infringer to defend by proving to the court that the patent is really invalid (most often by showing that the PTO made a mistake in issuing the patent in the first place). In a substantial number of patent infringement cases, the patent is found invalid and the lawsuit dismissed, leaving the patent owner in a worse position than before the lawsuit.

When does patent protection end?

Patent protection usually ends when the patent expires. For all utility patents filed before June 8, 1995, the patent term is 20 years from date of filing, or 17 years from date of issuance, whichever period is longer. For utility patents filed on or after June 8, 1995, the patent term is 20 years from the date of filing. For design patents, the period is 14 years from date of issuance. For plant patents, the period is 17 years from date of issuance.

A patent may expire if its owner fails to pay required maintenance fees. Usually this occurs because attempts to commercially exploit the underlying invention have failed and the patent owner chooses to not throw good money after bad.

Patent protection ends if a patent is found to be invalid. This may happen if someone shows that the patent application was insufficient or that the applicant committed fraud on the PTO, usually by lying or failing to disclose the applicant's knowledge about prior art that would legally prevent issuance of the patent. A patent may also be invalidated if someone shows that the inventor engaged in illegal conduct when using the patent—such as conspiring with a patent licensee to exclude other companies from competing with them.

Once a patent has expired, the invention described by the patent falls into the public domain: It can be used by anyone without permission from the owner of the expired patent. The basic technologies underlying television and personal computers are good examples of valuable inventions that are no longer covered by in-force patents.

The fact that an invention is in the public domain does not mean that subsequent developments based on the original invention are also in the public domain. Rather, new inventions that improve public domain technology are constantly being conceived and patented. For example, televisions and personal computers that roll off today's assembly lines employ many recent inventions that are covered by in-force patents.

The Life of an Invention

Although most inventors are concerned with the rights a patent grants during its monopoly or in-force period (from the date the patent issues until it expires), the law actually recognizes five "rights" periods in the life of an invention. These five periods are as follows:

1. Invention conceived but not yet documented. When an inventor conceives an invention but hasn't yet made any written, signed, dated and witnessed record of it, the inventor has no rights whatsoever.

2. Invention documented but patent application not yet filed. After making a proper signed, dated and witnessed documentation of an invention, the inventor has valuable rights against any inventor who later conceives the same invention and applies for a patent. The invention may also be treated as a "trade secret"—that is, kept confidential. This gives the inventor the legal right to sue and recover damages against anyone who immorally learns of the invention—for example, through industrial spying.

3. Patent pending (patent application filed but not yet issued). During the patent pending period, including the one-year period after a provisional patent application is filed, the inventor's rights are the same as in Period 2 above. A patent application gives an inventor no rights whatsoever—only the hope of a future monopoly that doesn't begin until a patent issues. However, most companies that manufacture a product that is the subject of a pending patent application will mark the product "patent pending" in order to warn potential copiers that if they copy the product, they may have to stop later (and thus scrap all their molds and tooling) if and when a patent issues. The PTO must keep all patent applications preserved in secrecy. The patent pending period usually lasts from one to three years.

4. In-force patent (patent issued but hasn't yet expired). After the patent issues, the patent owner can bring and maintain a lawsuit for patent infringement against anyone who makes, uses or sells the invention without permission. The patent's in-force period lasts from the date it issues until it expires. Also, after the patent issues, it becomes a public record or publication that prevents others from getting patents on the same or similar inventions—that is, it becomes "prior art" to anyone who files a subsequent patent application.

5. Patent expired. After the patent expires, the patent owner has no further rights, although infringement suits can still be brought for any infringement that occurred during the patent's in-force period as long as the suit is filed within the time required by law. An expired patent remains a valid "prior-art reference" forever.

Putting a Patent to Work

OUR ASPIRATIONS ARE OUR

POSSIBILITIES.

—ROBERT BROWNING

On its own, a patent has no value. Value arises only when a patent owner takes action to realize commercial gain from his or her monopoly position. There are several basic approaches to making money from a patent.

How can an inventor make money with a patent?

Some inventors start new companies to develop and market their patented inventions. This is not typical, however, because the majority of inventors would rather invent than run a business. More often, an inventor makes arrangements with an existing company to develop and market the invention. This arrangement usually takes the form of a license (contract) under which the developer is authorized to commercially exploit the invention in exchange for paying the patent owner royalties for each invention sold. Or, in a common variation of this arrangement, the inventor may sell all the rights to the invention for a lump sum.

What does it mean to license an invention?

A license is written permission to use an invention. A license may be exclusive (if only one manufacturer is licensed to develop the invention) or nonexclusive (if a number of manufacturers are licensed to develop it). The license may be for the duration of the patent or for a shorter period of time.

The developer itself may license other companies to market or distribute the invention. The extent to which the inventor will benefit from these sub-licenses depends on the terms of the agreement between the inventor and the developer. Especially when inventions result from work done in the course of employment, the employer-business usually ends up owning the patent rights, and receives all or most of the royalties based on subsequent licensing activity. (See the next question.)

In many cases, a developer will trade licenses with other companies—called cross-licensing—so that companies involved in the trade will benefit from each other's technology. For example, assume that two computer companies each own several patents on newly-developed remote-controlled techniques. Because each company would be strengthened by being able to use the other company's inventions as well as its own, the companies will most likely agree to swap permissions to use their respective inventions.

MECHANICAL CLOTHESPIN
No. 732,072

Can inventors who are employed by a company benefit from their inventions?

Typically, inventor-employees who invent in the course of their employment are bound by employment agreements that automatically assign all rights in the invention to the employer. While smart research and development companies give their inventors bonuses for valuable inventions, this is a matter of contract rather than law.

If there is no employment agreement, the inventor may retain the right to exploit the invention, but the employer is given a nonexclusive right to use the invention for its internal purposes (called shop rights). For example, Robert is a machinist in a machine shop and invents a new process for handling a particular type of metal. If Robert hasn't signed an employment agreement giving the shop all rights to the invention, Robert can patent and exploit the invention for himself. The shop, however, would retain the right to use the new process without having to pay Robert.

How Patents Differ From Copyrights and Trademarks

While it is possible to invent definitions that draw clear lines between the areas of patent, copyright and trademark (the three major types of intellectual property protection), there are complications when it comes to certain innovative designs. In some cases, a design may be subject to patent, trademark and copyright protection all at the same time.

How do patents differ from copyrights?

With the exception of innovative designs, patents are closely associated with things and processes which are useful in the real world. Almost at the opposite end of the spectrum, copyright applies to expressive arts such as novels, fine and graphic arts, music, phonorecords, photography, software, video, cinema and choreography. While it is possible to get a patent on technologies used in the arts, it is copyright that keeps one artist from stealing another artist's creative work.

An exception to the general rule that patents and copyright don't overlap can be found in product designs. It is theoretically possible to get a design patent on the purely ornamental (nonfunctional) aspects of the product design and also claim a copyright in this same design. For example, the stylistic fins of a car's rear fenders may qualify for both a design patent (because they are strictly ornamental) and copyright (as to their expressive elements). In practice, however, a product is usually granted one type of protection or the other—not both.

For more information about copyright law, see Chapter 7.

What's the difference between patent and trademark?

Generally speaking, patents allow the creator of certain kinds of inventions that contain new ideas to keep others from making commercial use of those ideas without the creator's permission. Trademark, on the other hand, is not concerned with how a new technology is used. Rather, it applies to the names, logos and other devices—such as color, sound and smell—that are used to identify the source of goods or services and distinguish them from their competition.

Generally, patent and trademark laws do not overlap. When it comes to a product design, however—say, jewelry or a distinctively shaped musical instrument—it may be possible to obtain a patent on a design aspect of the device while invoking trademark law to protect the design as a product identifier. For example, a surfboard manufacturer might receive a patent for a surfboard design that mimics the design used in a popular surfing film.

Then, if the design is intended to be—and actually is—used to distinguish the particular type of surfboard in the marketplace, trademark law may kick in to protect the appearance of the board.

For more information about trademarks, see Chapter 8.

More Information About Patents

Patent It Yourself, by David Pressman (Nolo Press), takes you step by step through the process of getting a patent without hiring a patent lawyer. *Patent It Yourself* software (for Windows) is also available. *The Patent Drawing Handbook* by Jack Lo and David Pressman (Nolo Press), takes you step by step through the process of making your own patent drawing, and *License Your Invention* by Richard Stim (Nolo Press), walks you through the process of realizing your invention's commercial potential.

Patent, Copyright and Trademark, by Stephen Elias (Nolo Press), provides concise definitions and examples of the important words and phrases commonly used in patent law.

http://www.nolo.com
Nolo Press offers self-help information about a wide variety of legal topics, including patent law.

http://www.uspto.gov
The U.S. Patent and Trademark Office is the place to go for recent policy and statutory changes and transcripts of hearings on various patent law issues. The U.S. Patent and Trademark Office maintains a seachable electronic database of the front page of all patents issued since 1971. This site is an excellent way to initiate a search for relevant patents. Also, the USPTO has announced that it is putting the full U.S. patent database online for free searching near the end of 1998.

http://patent.womplex.ibm.com
This IBM site maintains a searchable electronic database of the first page and claims of all patents issued since 1973. In addition, the database contains pictures of the entire patent, including drawings, which makes this site a good place to follow up a search on the USPTO site.

http://www.detroit.lib.mi.us/glptc
The Great Lakes Patent and Trademark Center (GLPTC) offers quality patent and trademark searches for a reasonable fee. This site is maintained by one of the two former Patent and Trademark Depository Libraries that has entered into a partnership with the U.S. Patent and Trademark Office. The other partner is the Sunnyvale Center for Invention, Innovation and Ideas at http://www.sci3.com.

http://www.findlaw.com
This general purpose online legal catalog is a good place to start for researching patent law. Click on intellectual property in the legal subjects section of the home page and then click on the Patent WWW Sites and Resources link.

http://www.spi.org
The Software Patent Institute lets you search for previous software developments that may affect whether your software qualifies for a patent.

Copyrights

People seldom improve when they have no other model but themselves to copy after.

—OLIVER GOLDSMITH

It has long been recognized that everyone benefits when creative people are encouraged to develop new intellectual and artistic works. When the United States Constitution was written in 1787, the framers took care to include a copyright clause (Article I, Section 8) giving Congress the power to "promote the Progress of Science and useful Arts" by passing laws that give creative people exclusive rights in their own artistic works for a limited period of time.

Copyright laws are not designed to enrich creative artists, but to promote human knowledge and development. These laws encourage artists in their creative efforts by giving them a mini-monopoly over their works—called a copyright. But this monopoly is limited when it conflicts with the overriding purpose of encouraging people to create new works of scholarship or art.

This chapter introduces you to copyright law and guides you through the first steps of creating, owning and protecting a copyright. To learn about how copyrights differ from—and work with—patents and trademarks, see Chapters 6 and 8.

Copyright Basics

IT IS NECESSARY TO ANY ORIGINALITY

TO HAVE THE COURAGE TO BE AN

AMATEUR.

—WALLACE STEVENS

Copyright is a legal device that gives the creator of a work of art or literature, or a work that conveys information or ideas, the right to control how that work is used. The Copyright Act of 1976—the federal law providing for copyright protection—grants authors a bundle of exclusive rights over their works, including the right to reproduce, distribute, adapt or perform them.

An author's copyright rights may be exercised only by the author—or by a person or entity to whom the author has transferred all or part of her rights. If someone wrongfully uses the material covered by a copyright, the copyright owner can sue and obtain compensation for any losses suffered.

What types of creative work does copyright protect?

Copyright protects works such as poetry, movies, CD-ROMs, video games, videos, plays, paintings, sheet music, recorded music performances, novels, software code, sculptures, photographs, choreography and architectural designs.

To qualify for copyright protection, a work must be "fixed in a tangible medium of expression." This means that the work must exist in some physical form for at least some period of time, no matter how brief. Virtually any form of expression will qualify as a tangible medium, including a computer's random access memory (RAM), the recording media that capture all radio and television broadcasts and the scribbled notes on the back of an envelope that contain the basis for an impromptu speech.

In addition, the work must be original—that is, independently created by the author. It doesn't matter if an author's creation is similar to existing works, or even if it is arguably lacking in quality, ingenuity or aesthetic merit. So long as the author toils without copying from someone else, the results are protected by copyright.

Finally, to receive copyright protection, a work must be the result of at least some creative effort on the part of its author. There is no hard and fast rule as to how much creativity is enough. As one example, a work must be more creative than a telephone book's white pages, which involve a straightforward alphabetical listing of telephone numbers rather than a creative selection of listings.

Does copyright protect an author's creative ideas?

No. Copyright shelters only fixed, original and creative expression, not the ideas or facts upon which the expression is based. For example, copyright may protect a particular song, novel or computer game about a romance in space, but it cannot protect the underlying idea of having a love affair among the stars. Allowing authors to monopolize their ideas would thwart the underlying purpose of copyright law, which is to encourage people to create new work.

For similar reasons, copyright does not protect facts—whether scientific, historical, biographical or news of the day. Any facts that an author discovers in the course of research are in the public domain, free to all. For instance, anyone is free to use information included in a book about how the brain works, an article about the life and times of Neanderthals or a TV documentary about the childhood of President Clinton—provided that they express the information in their own words.

Facts are not protected even if the author spends considerable time and effort discovering things that were previously unknown. For example, the author of the book on Neanderthals takes ten years to gather all the necessary materials and information for her work. At great expense, she travels to hundreds of museums and excavations around the world. But after the book is published, any reader is free to use the results of this ten-year research project to write his or her own book on Neanderthals—without paying the original author.

How long does a copyright last?

For works published after 1977, the copyright lasts for the life of the author plus 70 years. However, if the work is a work for hire (that is, the work is done in the course of employment or has been specifically commissioned) or is published anonymously or under a pseudonym, the copyright lasts between 95 and 120 years, depending on the date the work is published.

All works published in the United States before 1923 are in the public domain. Works published after 1922, but before 1978, are protected for 95 years from the date of publication. If the work was created, but not published, before 1978, the copyright lasts for the life of the author plus 70 years. However, even if the author died over 70 years ago, the copyright in an unpublished work lasts until December 31, 2002. And if such a work is published before December 31, 2002, the copyright lasts until December 31, 2047.

Is the Work Published?

In the complicated scheme of copyright laws, which law applies to a particular work depends on when that work is published. A work is considered published when the author makes it available to the public on an unrestricted basis. This means that it is possible to distribute or display a work without publishing it if there are significant restrictions placed on what can be done with the work and when it can be shown to others. For example, Andres Miczslova writes an essay called "Blood Bath" about the war in Bosnia, and distributes it to five human rights organizations under a non exclusive license that places restrictions on their right to disclose the essay's contents. "Blood Bath" has not been "published" in the copyright sense. If Miczslova authorizes posting of the essay on the Internet, however, it would likely be considered published.

Copyright Ownership

HE WHO CAN COPY, CAN DO.

—LEONARDO DA VINCI

A copyright is initially owned by a creative work's author or authors. But under the law, a person need not actually create the work to be its "author" for copyright purposes. A protectible work created by an employee as part of his or her job is initially owned by the employer—that is, the employer is considered to be the work's author. Such works are called "works made for hire." Works created by nonemployees (independent contractors) may also be works made for hire if they sign written agreements to that effect.

Like any other property, a copyright can be bought and sold. Transfers of copyright ownership are unique in one respect, however: Authors or their heirs have the right to terminate any transfer of copyright ownership 35 to 40 years after it is made.

What are the exceptions to the rule that the creator of a work owns the copyright?

Copyrights are generally owned by the people who create the works of expression, with some important exceptions:

- If a work is created by an employee in the course of his or her employment, the employer owns the copyright.
- If the work is created by an independent contractor and the independent contractor signs a written agreement stating that the work shall be "made for hire," the commissioning person or organization owns the copyright only if the work is (1) a part of a larger literary work, such as an article in a magazine or a poem or story in an anthology; (2) part of a motion picture or other audiovisual work, such as a screenplay; (3) a translation; (4) a supplementary work such as an afterword,

introduction, chart, editorial note, bibliography, appendix or index; (6) an instructional text; (7) a test; (8) answer material for a test; or (9) an atlas. Works that don't fall within one of these nine categories constitute works made for hire only if created by an employee within the scope of his or her employment.

- If the creator has sold the entire copyright, the purchasing business or person becomes the copyright owner.

Who owns the copyright in a joint work?

When two or more authors prepare a work with the intent to combine their contributions into inseparable or interdependent parts, the work is considered joint work and the authors are considered joint copyright owners. The most common example of a joint work is when a book or article has two or more authors. However, if a book is written primarily by one author, but another author contributes a specific chapter to the book and is given credit for that chapter, then this probably wouldn't be a joint work because the contributions aren't inseparable or interdependent.

The U.S. Copyright Office considers joint copyright owners to have an equal right to register and enforce the copyright. Unless the joint owners make a written agreement to the contrary, each copyright owner has the right to commercially exploit the copyright, provided that the other copyright owners get an equal share of the proceeds.

Can two or more authors provide contributions to a single work without being considered a joint authors?

Yes. If at the time of creation, the authors did not intend their works to be part of an inseparable whole, the fact that their works are later put together does not create a joint work. Rather, the result is considered a collective work. In this case, each author owns a copyright in only the material he or she added to the finished product. For example, in the 1950s, Vladimir writes a famous novel full of complex literary allusions. In the 1980s, his publisher issues a student edition of the work with detailed annotations written by an English professor. The student edition is a collective work. Vladimir owns the copyright in the novel, but the professor owns the annotations.

What rights do copyright owners have under the Copyright Act?

The Copyright Act of 1976 grants a number of exclusive rights to copyright owners, including:

- reproduction right—the right to make copies of a protected work
- distribution right—the right to sell or otherwise distribute copies to the public
- right to create adaptations (called derivative works)—the right to prepare new works based on the protected work, and

- performance and display rights—the rights to perform a protected work (such as a stageplay) or to display a work in public.

This bundle of rights allows a copyright owner to be flexible when deciding how to realize commercial gain from the underlying work; the owner may sell or license any of the rights.

Can a copyright owner transfer some or all of his specific rights?

Yes. When a copyright owner wishes to commercially exploit the work covered by the copyright, the owner typically transfers one or more of these rights to the person or entity who will be responsible for getting the work to market, such as a book or software publisher. It is also common for the copyright owner to place some limitations on the exclusive rights being transferred. For example, the owner may limit the transfer to a specific period of time, allow the right to be exercised only in a specific part of the country or world or require that the right be exercised only through certain media, such as hardcover books, audiotapes, magazines or computers.

If a copyright owner transfers all of his rights unconditionally, it is generally termed an "assignment." When only some of the rights associated with the copyright are transferred, it is known as a "license." An exclusive license exists when the transferred rights can be exercised only by the owner of the license (the licensee), and no one else—including the person

who granted the license (the licensor). If the license allows others (including the licensor) to exercise the same rights being transferred in the license, the license is said to be nonexclusive.

The U.S. Copyright Office allows buyers of exclusive and non-exclusive copyright rights to record the transfers in the U.S. Copyright Office. This helps to protect the buyers in case the original copyright owner later tries to transfer the same rights to another party.

Copyright Protection

Probably the most important fact to grasp about copyright protection is that it automatically comes into existence when the protected work is created. However, the degree of protection that copyright laws extend to a protected work can be influenced by later events.

What role does a copyright notice play?

Until 1989, a published work had to contain a valid copyright notice to receive protection under the copyright laws. But this requirement is no longer in force—works first published after March 1, 1989 need not include a copyright notice to gain protection under the law.

But even though a copyright notice is not required, it's still important to include one. When a work contains a valid notice, an infringer cannot claim in court that he or she didn't know it was copyrighted. This makes it much easier to win a copyright infringement case and perhaps collect enough damages to make the cost of the case worthwhile. And the very existence of a notice might discourage infringement.

Finally, including a copyright notice may make it easier for a potential infringer to track down a copyright owner and legitimately obtain permission to use the work.

What is a valid copyright notice?

A copyright notice should contain:
- the word "copyright"
- a "c" in a circle (©)
- the date of publication, and
- the name of either the author or the owner of all the copyright rights in the published work.

For example, the correct copyright for the fourth edition of *The Copyright Handbook*, by Stephen Fishman (Nolo Press), is *Copyright © 1998 by Stephen Fishman.*

International Copyright Protection

Copyright protection rules are fairly similar worldwide, due to several international copyright treaties, the most important of which is the Berne Convention. Under this treaty, all member countries— and there are more than 100, including virtually all industrialized nations—must afford copyright protection to authors who are nationals of any member country. This protection must last for at least the life of the author plus 50 years, and must be automatic, without the need for the author to take any legal steps to preserve the copyright.

In addition to the Berne Convention, the GATT (General Agreement on Tariffs and Trade) treaty contains a number of provisions that affect copyright protection in signatory countries. Together, the Berne Copyright Convention and the GATT treaty allow U.S. authors to enforce their copyrights in most industrialized nations, and allow the nationals of those nations to enforce their copyrights in the U.S.

When can I use a work without the author's permission?

When a work becomes available for use without permission from a copyright owner, it is said to be "in the public domain." Most works enter the public domain because their copyrights have expired.

To determine whether a work is in the public domain and available for use without the author's permission, you first have to find out when it was published. Then you can apply the periods of time set out earlier in this chapter. (See *How long does a copyright last?*, above.) If the work was published between 1923 and 1963, however, you must check with the U.S. Copyright Office to see whether the copyright was properly renewed. If the author failed to renew the copyright, the work has fallen into the public domain and you may use it.

The Copyright Office will check renewal information for you, at a charge of $20 per hour. (Call the Reference & Bibliography Section at 202-707-6850.) You can also hire a private copyright search firm to see if a renewal was filed. Finally, you may be able to conduct a renewal search yourself. The renewal records for works published from 1950 to the present are available online at http://lcweb.loc.gov/copyright. Renewal searches for earlier works can be conducted at the Copyright Office in Washington DC or by visiting one of the many government depository libraries throughout the country. Call the Copyright Office for more information.

With one important exception, you should assume that every work is protected by copyright unless you can establish that it is not. As mentioned above, you can't rely on the presence or absence of a copyright notice (©) to make this determination, because a notice is not required for works published after March 1, 1989. And even for works published before 1989, the absence of a copyright notice may not affect the validity of the copyright—

for example, if the author made diligent attempts to correct the situation.

The exception is for materials put to work under the "fair use rule." This rule recognizes that society can often benefit from the unauthorized use of copyrighted materials when the purpose of the use serves the ends of scholarship, education or an informed public. For example, scholars must be free to quote from their research resources in order to comment on the material. To strike a balance between the needs of a public to be well informed and the rights of copyright owners to profit from their creativity, Congress passed a law authorizing the use of copyrighted materials in certain circumstances deemed to be "fair"— even if the copyright owner doesn't give permission.

Often, it's difficult to know whether a court will consider a proposed use to be fair. The fair use statute requires the courts to consider the following questions in deciding this issue:

- Is it a competitive use? (In other words, if the use potentially affects the sales of the copied material, it's probably not fair.)
- How much material was taken compared to the entire work of which the material was a part? (The more someone takes, the less likely it is that the use is fair.)
- How was the material used? (Criticism, comment, news reporting, research, scholarship and nonprofit educational uses are most likely to be judged fair uses. Uses motivated primarily by a desire for a commercial gain are less likely to be fair use.)

As a general rule, if you are using a small portion of somebody else's work in a noncompetitive way and the purpose for your use is to benefit the public, you're on pretty safe ground. On the other hand, if you take large portions of someone else's expression for your own purely commercial reasons, the rule usually won't apply.

If You Want to Use Material on the Internet

Each day, people post vast quantities of creative material on the Internet—material that is available for downloading by anyone who has the right computer equipment. Because the information is stored somewhere on an Internet server, it is fixed in a tangible medium and potentially qualifies for copyright protection. Whether it does, in fact, qualify depends on other factors that you would have no way of knowing about, such as when the work was first published (which affects the need for a copyright notice), whether the copyright in the work has been renewed (for works published before 1978), whether the work is a work made for hire (which affects the length of the copyright) and whether the copyright owner intends to dedicate the work to the public domain. If you want to download the material for use in your own work, you should be cautious. It's best to track down the author of the material and ask for permission. The only exception to this advice is for situations where you want to use only a very small portion of text for educational or nonprofit purposes. (See

the previous question for a discussion of the "fair use rule.")

Copyright Registration and Enforcement

Although every work published after 1989 is automatically protected by copyright, you can strengthen your rights by registering your work with the U.S. Copyright Office. This registration makes it possible to bring a lawsuit to protect your copyright if someone violates (infringes) it. The registration process is straightforward and inexpensive, and can be done without a lawyer.

Why register your work with the U.S. Copyright Office?

You must register your copyright with the U.S. Copyright Office before you are legally permitted to bring a lawsuit to enforce it.

You can register a copyright at any time, but filing promptly may pay off in the long run. "Timely registration"—that is, registration within three months of the work's publication date or before any copyright infringement actually begins—makes it much easier to sue and recover money from an infringer. Specifically, timely registration creates a legal presumption that your copyright is valid, and allows you to recover up to $100,000 (and possibly lawyer's fees) without having to prove any actual monetary harm.

How do you register a copyright?

You can register your copyright by filing a simple form and depositing one or two samples of the work (depending on what it is) with the U.S. Copyright Office. There are different forms for different types of works—for example, form TX is for literary works while form VA is for a visual art work. Forms and instructions may be obtained from the U.S. Copyright Office by telephone, (202) 707-9100, or online at http://www.loc.gov/copyright. Registration currently costs $20 per work. If you're registering several works that are part of one series, you may be able to save money by registering the works together (called "group registration").

How are copyrights enforced? Is going to court necessary?

If someone violates the rights of a copyright owner, the owner is entitled to file a lawsuit in federal court asking the court to:

- issue orders (restraining orders and injunctions) to prevent further violations

- award money damages if appropriate, and
- in some circumstances, award attorney fees.

Whether the lawsuit will be effective and whether damages will be awarded depends on whether the alleged infringer can raise one or more legal defenses to the charge. Common legal defenses to copyright infringement are:

- too much time has elapsed between the infringing act and the lawsuit (the statute of limitations defense)
- the infringement is allowed under the fair use doctrine (discussed above)
- the infringement was innocent (the infringer had no reason to know the work was protected by copyright)
- the infringing work was independently created (that is, it wasn't copied from the original), or
- the copyright owner authorized the use in a license.

If someone has good reason to believe that a use is fair—but later finds herself on the wrong end of a court order—she is likely to be considered an innocent infringer at worst. Innocent infringers usually don't have to pay any damages to the copyright owner, but do have to cease the infringing activity or pay the owner for the reasonable commercial value of that use.

More Information About Copyrights

The Copyright Handbook: How to Protect and Use Written Works, by Stephen Fishman (Nolo Press), is a complete guide to the law of copyright. The book includes forms for registering a copyright.

Copyright Your Software, by Stephen Fishman (Nolo Press), explains copyright protection for computer software and include all the forms and instructions necessary for registering a software copyright.

Patent, Copyright and Trademark, by Stephen Elias (Nolo Press), provides concise definitions and examples of the important words and phrases commonly used in copyright law.

If you wish to visit a law library, you will be able to answer just about any copyright question by studying *Nimmer on Copyright*, a five-volume legal treatise, published by Matthew Bender.

http://www.nolo.com
Nolo Press offers self-help information about a wide variety of legal topics, including copyright law.

http://lcweb.loc.gov/copyright
The U.S. Copyright office offers regulations, guidelines, forms and links to other helpful copyright sites.

http://www.findlaw.com
This online catalog has an excellent collection of links to copyright resources of all types. Click the intellectual property link on the homepage (under the legal subject index link) and then click the WWW copyright sites and resources link.

http://www.kuesterlaw.com
The Jeffrey R. Kuester law firm provides an online reference service that will lead you to other copyright resources on the World Wide Web.

Trademarks

A good name lost is seldom regained
—JOEL HAWES

Most of us encounter many trademarks each day; we might eat Kellogg's cornflakes for breakfast, drive our Ford car to work and sit down at an IBM computer. But as we go about our daily tasks, we rarely think about the laws behind the familiar words and images that identify the products and services we use.

Trademark law consists of the legal rules that govern how businesses may:

- distinguish their products or services in the marketplace to prevent consumer confusion, and
- protect the means they've chosen to identify their products or services against use by competitors.

This chapter will introduce you to trademark law and answer common questions about choosing, using and protecting a trademark.

Types of Trademarks

The term trademark is commonly used to describe many different types of devices that label, identify and distinguish products or services in the marketplace. The basic purpose of all these devices is to inform potential customers of the origin and quality of the underlying products or services.

What is a trademark?

A trademark is a distinctive word, phrase, logo, graphic symbol, slogan or other device that is used to identify the source of a product and to distinguish a manufacturer's or merchant's products from others. Some examples are Nike sports apparel, Gatorade beverages and Microsoft software. In the trademark context, "distinctive" means unique enough to help customers recognize a particular product in the marketplace. A mark may either

be inherently distinctive (the mark is unusual in and of itself, such as Double Rainbow ice cream) or may become distinctive over time because customers come to associate the mark with the product or service (for example, Safeway markets).

Consumers often make their purchasing choices on the basis of recognizable trademarks. For this reason, the main thrust of trademark law is to make sure that trademarks don't overlap in a manner that causes customers to become confused about the source of a product. However, in the case of trademarks that have become famous—for example, McDonald's—the courts are willing to prohibit all use of the trademark (or anything close to it) by anyone other than the famous mark's owner. For instance, McDonald's was able to prevent the use of the mark McSleep by a motel chain because McSleep traded on the McDonald's mark reputation for a particular type of service (quick, inexpensive, standardized). This type of sweeping protection is authorized by federal and state statutes (referred to as anti-dilution laws) designed to prevent the weakening of a famous mark's reputation for quality.

What is a servicemark?

For practical purposes, a servicemark is the same as a trademark—but while trademarks promote products, servicemarks promote services and events. As a general rule, when a business uses its name to market its goods or services in the yellow pages, on signs or in advertising copy, the name qualifies as a servicemark. Some familiar servicemarks: Jack in the Box (fast food service), Kinko's (photocopying service), ACLU (legal service), Blockbuster (video rental service), CBS's stylized eye in a circle (television network service) and the Olympic Games' multicolored interlocking circles (international sporting event).

What is a certification mark?

A certification mark is a symbol, name or device used by an organization to vouch for products and services provided by others—for example, the "Good Housekeeping Seal of Approval." This type of mark may cover characteristics such as regional origin, method of manufacture, product quality and service accuracy. Some other examples of certification marks: Stilton cheese (a product from the Stilton locale in England), Carneros wines (from grapes grown in the Carneros region of Sonoma/Napa counties) and Harris Tweeds (a special weave from a specific area in Scotland).

What is a collective mark?

A collective mark is a symbol, label, word, phrase or other mark used by members of a group or organization to identify goods, members, products or

services they render. Collective marks are often used to show membership in a union, association or other organization.

The use of a collective mark is restricted to members of the group or organization that owns the mark. Even the group itself—as opposed to its members—cannot use the collective mark on any goods it produces. If the group wants to identify its product or service, it must use its own trademark or servicemark.

EXAMPLE

The letters "ILGWU" on a shirt label is the collective mark that identifies the shirt as a product of a member of the International Ladies Garment Workers Union. If, however, the ILGWU wanted to start marketing its own products, it could not use the ILGWU collective mark to identify them; the union would have to get a trademark of its own.

What is trade dress?

In addition to a label, logo or other identifying symbol, a product may come to be known by its distinctive packaging—for example, Kodak film or the Galliano liquor bottle—and a service by its distinctive decor or shape, such as the decor of Banana Republic clothing stores. Collectively, these types of identifying features are commonly termed "trade dress." Because trade dress often serves the same function as a trademark or servicemark—the identification of goods and services in the marketplace—trade dress can be protected under the federal trademark laws and in some cases registered as a trademark or servicemark with the Patent and Trademark Office.

What kinds of things can be considered trademarks or service marks?

Most often, trademarks are words or phrases that are clever or unique enough to stick in a consumer's mind. Logos and graphics that become strongly associated with a product line or service are also typical. But a trademark or servicemark can also consist of letters, numbers, a sound, a smell, a color, a product shape or any other nonfunctional but distinctive aspect of a product or service that tends to promote and distinguish it in the marketplace. Titles, character names or other distinctive features of movies, television and radio programs can also serve as trademarks or servicemarks when used to promote a service or product. Some examples of unusual trademarks are the sound of a Harley Davidson motorcycle, the pink color of housing insulation manufactured by Owens-Corning and the shape of the Galliano liquor container.

What's the difference between a business name and a trademark or servicemark?

The name that a business uses to identify itself is called a "trade name." This is the name the business uses on its stock certificates, bank accounts, invoices and letterhead. When used to identify a business in this way—as an entity for nonmarketing purposes— the business name is given some protection under state and local corporate and fictitious business name registration laws, but it is not considered a trademark or entitled to protection under trademark laws.

If, however, a business uses its name to identify a product or service produced by the business, the name will then be considered a trademark or servicemark and will be entitled to protection if it is distinctive enough. For instance, Apple Computer Corporation uses the trade name Apple as a trademark on its line of computer products.

Although trade names by themselves are not considered trademarks for purposes of legal protection, they may still be protected under federal and state unfair competition laws against a confusing use by a competing business.

If my trade name is registered with the Secretary of State as a corporate name, or placed on a fictitious business name list, can I use it as a trademark?

Not necessarily. When you register a corporate name with a state agency or place your name on a local fictitious business name register, there is no guarantee that the name has not already been taken by another business as a trademark. It is only the trade name aspect of the name that is affected by your registration. This means that before you start using your business name as a trademark, you will need to make sure it isn't already being used as a trademark by another company in a context that precludes your using it. For more information about trademark searches, see *Conducting a Trademark Search,* below.

Trademark Protection

If a trademark or servicemark is protected, the owner of the mark can:
- prevent others from using it in a context where it might confuse consumers, and
- recover money damages from someone who used the mark knowing that it was already owned by someone else.

Trademark law also protects famous marks by allowing owners to sue to prevent others from using the same or similar mark, even if customer confusion is unlikely.

Not all marks are entitled to an equal amount of protection, however—and some aren't entitled to any protection at all.

What laws offer protection to trademark owners?

The basic rules for resolving disputes over who is entitled to use a trademark come from decisions by federal and state courts (the common law). These rules usually favor the business that first used the mark where the second use would be likely to cause customer confusion. A number of additional legal principles used to protect owners against improper use of their marks derive from federal statutes known collectively as the Lanham Act (Title 15 U.S.C. §§ 1051 to 1127). And all states have statutes that govern the use and protection of marks within the state's boundaries.

In addition to laws that specifically protect trademark owners, all states have laws that protect one business against unfair competition by another business, including the use by one business of a name already used by another business in a context that's likely to confuse customers.

What types of marks are entitled to the most legal protection?

As a general rule, trademark law grants the most legal protection to the owners of names, logos and other marketing devices that are distinctive—that is, memorable because they are creative or out of the ordinary, or because they have become well known to the public through their use over time or because of a marketing blitz.

Inherently Distinctive Marks

Trademarks that are unusually creative are known as inherently distinctive marks. Typically, these marks consist of:
- unique logos or symbols (such as the McDonald's Golden Arch and the IBM symbol)
- made-up words, such as Exxon or Kodak (called "coined marks")
- words that invoke imaginative images in the context of their usage, such as Double Rainbow ice cream (called "fanciful marks")
- words that are surprising or unexpected in the context of their usage, such as Time Magazine or Diesel for a bookstore (called "arbitrary marks"), and

• words that cleverly connote qualities about the product or service, such as Slenderella diet food products (called "suggestive or evocative marks").

Which marks receive the least protection?

Trademarks and servicemarks consisting of common or ordinary words are not considered inherently distinctive and receive less protection under federal and state laws. Typical examples of trademarks using common or ordinary words are:

• people's names, such as Pete's Muffins or Smith Graphics
• geographic terms, such as Northern Dairy or Central Insect Control, and
• descriptive terms—that is, words that attempt to literally describe the product or some characteristic of the product, such as Rapid Computers, Clarity Video Monitors or Ice Cold Ice Cream.

However, nondistinctive marks may be come distinctive through use over time or through intensive marketing efforts. And marks consisting of common terms or names may be distinctive because the words are combined into a clever phrase or slogan, such as "Taco John's" or "Don't Leave Home Without It," or because the name itself is highly unusual, as with Orville Redenbacher's popcorn products. See the next question.

What about Ben and Jerry's Ice Cream? Even though Ben and Jerry are common names, isn't the Ben and Jerry's trademark entitled to maximum protection?

Absolutely. Even if a mark is not inherently distinctive, it may become distinctive if it develops great public recognition through long use and exposure in the marketplace. A mark that becomes protected in this way is said to have acquired a "secondary meaning." In addition to Ben and Jerry's, examples of otherwise common marks that have acquired a secondary meaning and are now considered to be distinctive include Sears (department stores) and Park 'n Fly (airport parking services.)

Are there marks that can't be protected under the trademark laws?

Yes. When a trademark is used to describe a type of product rather than a brand of product, the mark is said to be generic and won't be given any protection. Sometimes an inherently distinctive mark is so successful that people start to consider the mark to be synonymous with the product itself, and the mark becomes generic. For example, aspirin was originally a highly distinctive brand name for a type of analgesic (salicylic acid). After a while, aspirin became synonymous with salicylic acid itself and was no longer considered distinctive. Escalator and cellophane were once distinctive marks, as well. And not too long ago, the Xerox mark for photocopiers was in grave danger of losing protection because of the common use of the term as a noun (a xerox) and a verb (to xerox something). To prevent this from happening, Xerox launched an expensive campaign urging the public to use "Xerox" as a proper noun (Xerox brand photocopiers).

Sometimes the name originally chosen for a mark is simply too descriptive of the underlying product to qualify for trademark status. For instance, assume that a new cellular telephone manufacturer calls its product "The Cellular." Because the term "cellular" is the descriptive name for the product itself, it cannot legally be considered a trademark or servicemark. If the term "cellular" were used on a facial creme, however, it would be considered suggestive, and therefore distinctive, in that context.

Are Internet domain names— names for sites on the World Wide Web—covered by trademark law?

The short answer is yes. Most people are familiar with Website names like http://www.times.com or http://

www.uspto.gov. The words between "www" and the extension following the period—for example, com, org, gov or edu—are typically used to identify the business that owns the Website or a well-known product or service that is featured on the site. Frequently, this identifier is an abbreviation of the company or product name. The U.S. Patent and Trademark Office allows these identifiers to be registered as trademarks as long as they are being used in connection with a site that is, in fact, providing goods or services. And the courts offer them the same protection as other types of trademarks.

Using and Enforcing a Trademark

Generally, a trademark is owned by the business that first uses it in a commercial context—that is, attaches the mark to a product or uses the mark when marketing a product or service. A business may also obtain trademark protection if it files for trademark registration before anyone else uses the mark. (Trademark registration is discussed in more detail in the series of questions, *Registering a Trademark,* below.)

Once a business owns a trademark, it may be able to prevent others from using that mark, or a similar one, on their goods and services.

More specifically, what does it mean to "use" a trademark?

In trademark law, "use" means that the mark is at work in the market-place, identifying the underlying goods or services. This doesn't mean that the product or service actually has to be sold, as long as it is legitimately offered to the public under the mark in question. For example, Robert creates a Website where he offers his new invention—a humane mouse-trap—for sale under the trademark "MiceFree." Even if Robert doesn't sell any traps, he is still "using" the trademark as long as "MiceFree" appears on the traps or on tags attached to them and the traps are ready to be shipped when a sale is made. Similarly, if Kristin, a trademark attorney, puts up a Website to offer her services under the servicemark Trademark Queen, her servicemark will be in use as long as she is ready to respond to customer requests for her advice.

How can a business reserve a trademark for future use?

It is possible to acquire ownership of a mark by filing an "intent-to-use" (ITU) trademark registration application with the U.S. Patent and Trademark Office before someone else has actually started using the mark. The filing date of this application will be considered the date of first use of the mark if the applicant actually uses the mark within the required time limits—six months to three years after the PTO approves the mark, depending on whether the applicant seeks and pays for extensions of time.

For more information about trademark registration, see *Registering a Trademark*, below.

When can the owner of a trademark stop others from using it?

Whether the owner of a trademark can stop others from using it depends on such factors as:
- whether the trademark is being used on competing goods or services (goods or services compete if the sale of one is likely to affect the sale of the other)
- whether consumers would likely be confused by the dual use of the trademark, and
- whether the trademark is being used in the same part of the country or is being used on related goods (goods that will probably be noticed by the same customers, even if they don't compete with each other).

In addition, under federal and state laws known as "anti-dilution statutes," a trademark owner may go to court to prevent its mark from being used by someone else if the mark is famous and the later use would dilute the mark's strength—that is, weaken its reputation for quality (called tarnishment) or render it common through overuse in different contexts.

Anti-dilution statutes can apply even if there is no way customers would be likely to confuse the source of the goods or services designated by the later mark with the famous mark's owner. For instance, consumers would not think that Microsoft Bakery is associated with Microsoft, the software company, but Microsoft Bakery could still be forced to choose another name under federal and state anti-dilution laws.

How does a trademark owner prevent others from using the mark?

Typically, the owner will begin by sending a letter, called a "cease and desist letter," to the wrongful user, demanding that it stop using the mark. If the wrongful user continues to infringe the mark, the owner can file a lawsuit to stop the improper use. The lawsuit is usually filed in federal court if the mark is used in more than one state or country, and in state court if the dispute is between purely local marks. In addition to preventing further use of the mark, a trademark owner can sometimes obtain money damages from the wrongful user.

When can a trademark owner get money from someone who has infringed the owner's mark?

If a trademark owner proves in federal court that the infringing use is likely to confuse consumers and that it suffered economically as a result of the infringement, the competitor may have to pay the owner damages based on the loss. And if the court finds that the competitor intentionally copied the owner's trademark, or at least should have known about the mark, the competitor may have to give up the profits it made by using the mark as well as pay other damages, such as punitive

damages, fines or attorney fees. On the other hand, if the trademark's owner has not been damaged, a court has discretion to allow the competitor to continue to use the trademark under limited circumstances designed to avoid consumer confusion.

Do people have the right to use their last names as marks even if someone else is already using them for a similar business?

It depends on the name. A mark that is primarily a surname (last name) does not qualify for protection under federal trademark law unless the name becomes well known as a mark through advertising or long use. If this happens, the mark is said to have acquired a "secondary meaning."

If a surname acquires a secondary meaning, it is off limits for all uses that might cause customer confusion, whether or not the name is registered. Sears, McDonald's, Hyatt, Champion, Howard Johnson's and Calvin Klein are just a few of the hundreds of surnames that have become effective and protected marks over time.

Also, a business that tries to capitalize on the name of its owner to take advantage of an identical famous name being used as a trademark may be forced, under the state or federal anti-dilution laws, to stop using the name. This may happen if the trademark owner files a lawsuit.

"TM" and ®: What do they mean?

Many people like to put a "TM" (or "SM" for servicemark) next to their mark to let the world know that they are claiming ownership of it. However, it is not legally necessary to provide this type of notice; the use of the mark itself is the act that confers ownership.

The "R" in a circle (®) is a different matter entirely. This notice may not be put on a mark unless it has been registered with the U.S. Patent and Trademark Office—and it should accompany a mark after registration is complete. Failure to put the notice on a registered trademark can greatly reduce the possibility of recovering significant damages if it later becomes necessary to file a lawsuit against an infringer.

Conducting a Trademark Search

If you want to find out whether the trademark you've chosen for your products or services is available, you'll need to conduct a trademark search—an investigation to discover potential conflicts between your desired mark and any existing marks. Ideally, the search should be done before you begin to use a mark; this will help you avoid the expensive mistake of infringing a mark belonging to someone else.

Why do I need to conduct a trademark search?

The consequences of failing to conduct a reasonably thorough trademark search may be severe, depending on how widely you intend to use your mark and how much it would cost you to change it if a conflict later develops. If the mark you want to use has been federally registered by someone else, a court will presume that you knew about the registration—even if you did not. You will be precluded from using the mark in any context where customers might become confused. And if you do use the mark improperly, you will be cast in the role of a "willful infringer." Willful infringers can be held liable for large damages and payment of the registered owner's attorney fees; they can also be forced to stop using the mark altogether.

My business is local. Why should I care what name or mark someone else in another part of the country is using?

Most small retail or service-oriented business owners well know the mantra for success: location, location, location. But as the Internet takes firm hold in the late 1990s, the concept of location, while still central to business success, takes on a whole new meaning. Instead of being rooted in physical space, businesses are now required to jockey for locations in the virtual or electronic space known as the Internet. In particular, the World Wide Web, because of its ability to handle graphics and mouse clicks, has become a powerful new type of "Yellow Pages" extending to all parts of the country and many parts of the world.

Vast numbers of businesses—even local enterprises—are putting up their own Websites, creating a new potential for competition (and confusion) in the marketplace. Because of this, every business owner must pay attention to whether a proposed name or mark has already been taken by another business, regardless of the location or scope of that business.

Can I do my own trademark search?

Yes. You can do your own search for free on the Internet by visiting the U.S. Patent and Trademark Office's Website, http://www.uspto.gov. Or, you can visit one of the Patent and Trademark Depository Libraries available in every state. These libraries offer a combination of hardcover directories of federally registered marks and an online database of both registered marks and marks for which a registration application is pending. Most of these libraries also have step-by-step instructions for searching registered and pending marks.

In addition to searching for registered or pending marks, you may also use product guides and other materials available in these libraries to search for possibly conflicting marks that haven't been registered. This can be important because an existing mark, even if it's unregistered, would preclude you from:

- registering the same or a confusingly similar mark in your own name, and
- using the mark in any part of the country or commercial transaction where customers might be confused.

To find the Patent and Trademark Depository Library nearest you, see the list below.

PATENT AND TRADEMARK DEPOSITORY LIBRARIES

State	Library	Phone
Alabama	Auburn University Libraries	334-844-1747
	Birmingham Public Library	205-226-3620
Alaska	Anchorage: Z.J. Loussac Public Library	907-562-7323
Arizona	Tempe: Noble Library, Arizona State University	602-965-7010
Arkansas	Little Rock: Arkansas State Library	501-682-2053
California	Los Angeles Public Library	213-228-7220
	Sacramento: California State Library	916-654-0069
	San Diego Public Library	619-236-5813
	San Francisco Public Library	415-557-4500
	Santa Rosa: Bruce Sawyer Center (not a PTDL, but useful)	707-524-1773
	Sunnyvale Center for Innovation	408-730-7290
Colorado	Denver Public Library	303-640-6220
Connecticut	Hartford: Hartford Public Library	(not yet operational)
	New Haven: New Haven Free Public Library	(not yet operational)
Delaware	Newark: University of Delaware Library	302-831-2965
District of Columbia	Washington: Howard University Libraries	202-806-7252
Florida	Fort Lauderdale: Broward County Main Library	954-357-7444
	Miami: Dade Public Library	305-375-2665
	Orlando: University of Central Florida Libraries	407-823-2562
	Tampa: Tampa Campus Library, University of South Florida	813-974-2726
Georgia	Atlanta: Price Gilbert Memorial Library, Georgia Institute of Technology	404-894-4508
Hawaii	Honolulu: Hawaii State Public Library System	808-586-3477
Idaho	Moscow: University of Idaho Library	208-885-6235
Illinois	Chicago Public Library	312-747-4450
	Springfield: Illinois State Library	217-782-5659
Indiana	Indianapolis: Marion County Public Library	317-269-1741
	West Lafayette: Purdue University Libraries	317-494-2872
Iowa	Des Moines: State Library of Iowa	515-281-4118
Kansas	Wichita: Ablah Library, Wichita State University	316-978-3155

State	Library	Phone
Kentucky	Louisville Free Public Library	502-574-1611
Louisiana	Baton Rouge: Troy H. Middleton Library, Louisiana State University	504-388-8875
Maine	Orono: Raymond H. Fogler Library, University of Maine	207-581-1678
Maryland	College Park: Engineering and Physical Sciences Library, University of Maryland	301-405-9157
Massachusetts	Amherst: Physical Sciences Library, University of Massachusetts	413-545-1370
	Boston Public Library	617-536-5400, Ext. 265
Michigan	Ann Arbor: Media Union Library, University of Michigan	313-647-5735
	Big Rapids: Abigail S. Timme Library, Ferris State University	616-592-3602
	Detroit Public Library	313-833-3379
Minnesota	Minneapolis Public Library and Information Center	612-630-6120
Mississippi	Jackson: Mississippi Library Commission	601-359-1036
Missouri	Kansas City: Linda Hall Library	816-363-4600
	St. Louis Public Library	314-241-2288, Ext. 390
Montana	Butte: Montana College of Mineral Science & Technology Library	406-496-4281
Nebraska	Lincoln: Engineering Library, University of Nebraska	402-472-3411
Nevada	Reno: University of Nevada-Reno Library	702-784-6500, Ext. 257
New Hampshire	Concord: New Hampshire State Library	603-271-2239
New Jersey	Newark Public Library	973-733-7779
	Piscataway: Library of Science & Medicine, Rutgers University	732-445-2895
New Mexico	Albuquerque: University of New Mexico General Library	505-277-4412
New York	Albany: New York State Library	518-474-5355
	Buffalo and Erie County Public Library	716-858-7101
	New York Science, Industry & Business Library	212-592-7000
	Stony Brook: Engineering Library, SUNY	516-632-7148
North Carolina	Raleigh: D.H. Hill Library, North Carolina State University	919-515-2935
North Dakota	Grand Forks: Chester Fritz Library, University of North Dakota	701-777-4888
Ohio	Akron: Summit County Public Library	330-643-9075
	Cincinnati and Hamilton County, Public Library of	513-369-6971

State	Library	Phone
	Cleveland Public Library	216-623-2870
	Columbus: Ohio State University Libraries	614-292-6175
	Toledo/Lucas County Public Library	419-259-5212
Oklahoma	Stillwater: Oklahoma State University Library	405-744-7086
Oregon	Portland: Paul L. Boley Law Library, Lewis & Clark College	503-768-6786
Pennsylvania	Philadelphia, The Free Library of	215-686-5331
	Pittsburgh, Carnegie Library of	412-622-3138
	University Park: Pattee Library, Pennsylvania State University	814-865 4861
Puerto Rico	Mayaguez General Library, University of Puerto Rico	787-832-4040, Ext. 3459
Rhode Island	Providence Public Library	401-455-8027
South Carolina	R.M. Cooper Library, Clemson University	864-656-3024
South Dakota	Rapid City: Devereaux Library, South Dakota School of Mines and Technology	605-394-1275
Tennessee	Memphis & Shelby County Public Library and Information Center	901-725-8877
	Nashville: Stevenson Science Library, Vanderbilt University	615-322-2717
Texas	Austin: McKinney Engineering Library, University of Texas at Austin	512-495-4500
	College Station: Sterling C. Evans Library, Texas A & M University	409-845-3826
	Dallas Public Library	214-670-1468
	Houston: The Fondren Library, Rice University	713-527-8101, Ext. 2587
	South Central Intellectual Property Partnership at Rice University (SCIPPR)	713-285-5196
	Lubbock: Texas Tech University	806-742-2282
Utah	Salt Lake City: Marriott Library, University of Utah	801-581-8394
Vermont	Burlington: Bailey/Howe Library, University of Vermont	802-656-2542
Virginia	Richmond: James Branch Cabell Library, Virginia Commonwealth University	804-828-1104
Washington	Seattle: Engineering Library, University of Washington	206-543-0740
West Virginia	Morgantown: Evansdale Library, West Virginia University	304-293-2510 Ext. 5113
Wisconsin	Madison: Kurt F. Wendt Library, University of Wisconsin	608-262-6845
	Milwaukee Public Library	414-286-3051
Wyoming	Casper: Natrona County Public Library	307-237-4935

Reprinted with permission from *Patent It Yourself*, by David Pressman (Nolo Press).

Can the World Wide Web help me with my trademark search?

Yes. In addition to searching for registered and pending marks in the PTO's database at http://www.uspto.gov, you can now conduct a very thorough search for unregistered marks by using one or more of the powerful Internet search engines to find out if and where your proposed mark is being used on the World Wide Web. For instance, by entering your proposed name in the search field on the Alta Vista home page (http://www.altavista.digital.com), you will get a report of every instance where the name appears on Web pages that the Alta Vista search engine has indexed. Because no search engine is 100% complete, an especially thorough search will include several additional search engines, such as Infoseek (http://www.infoseek.com) and Excite (http://www.excite.com).

In addition, a number of product guides are being put up on the World Wide Web that may be individually searched for possible matches. For example, if you are selecting a mark for a new toy you invented, you can visit "eToys"—an online toy store at http://www3.etoys.com/shopping/etoys/html/home.shtml. Once there, you can browse 250 brands of toys and do a keyword search for any toy mark that is similar to yours. This same approach can be used for any type of product by clicking the shopping category link on one of the popular search engines, such as Infoseek.

How can I find out whether a mark I want to use is already being used as a domain name (the name of a site on the World Wide Web)?

Every Website is identified by a unique phrase known as a "domain name." For example, the domain name for Nolo Press is Nolo.com. Because so much business is now being done online, most people will want to be able to use their proposed mark as a domain name so that their customers can easily locate them on the Web.

There are two ways to find out via the World Wide Web whether you will be able to use your proposed mark as a domain name. One is to buy a domain name search from Thompson and Thompson: http://ttdomino.thomson-thomson.com. The other is to do your own search using Tabnet: http://www.tabnet.com. While it is possible to simply enter your proposed name in the WWW address (URL) box and see what comes up, this approach will not produce domain names that are slightly different from yours but similar enough to be confusing.

Would it be better to have a professional firm conduct my trademark search?

Many people do prefer to pay a professional search firm to handle a trademark search. This can make sense if your financial plans justify an initial outlay of several hundred dollars, the minimum cost for a thorough professional search for both registered and unregistered marks. Depending on the search firm, you may also get a legal opinion as to whether your proposed mark is legally safe to use in light of existing registered and unregistered marks. Obtaining a legal opinion may provide important protection down the road if someone later sues you for using the mark.

How do I find a professional search firm?

The best place to start is the Sunnyvale Center for Invention, Innovation and Ideas, on the Web at http://www.sci3.com. This Patent and Trademark Depository Library conducts full bore trademark searches at very competitive prices.

Professional search firms can also be found in the Yellow Pages of the nearest good-sized city under Trademark Consultants or Information Brokers. Or, you can consult a legal journal or magazine for your area. In these journals, you'll find the ads of a number of trademark search firms—the ads are aimed at lawyers, but many will also do searches for individuals and businesses.

For direct hit searches—finding out whether your proposed mark is already registered or pending in the Patent and Trademark Office—expect to pay between $25 and $50 per mark searched. For more complete searches of registered and pending marks—finding out whether there are any similar marks that consumers might confuse with yours—expect to pay between $75 and $200 per mark

searched. For a complete search of registered and unregistered marks, expect to pay between $250 and $500.

Registering a Trademark

It is possible to register certain types of trademarks and servicemarks with the U.S. Patent and Trademark Office (PTO). Federal registration puts the rest of the country on notice that the trademark is already taken, and makes it easier to protect a mark against would-be copiers.

How does a mark qualify for federal registration?

To register a trademark with the PTO, the mark's owner first must put it into use "in commerce that Congress may regulate." This means the mark must be used on a product or service that crosses state, national or territorial lines or that affects commerce crossing such lines—for example, a catalog business or a restaurant or motel that caters to interstate or international customers. Even if the owner files an intent-to-use (ITU) trademark application (ITU applications are discussed in the previous set of questions), the mark will not actually be registered until it is used in commerce.

Once the PTO receives a trademark registration application, the office must answer the following questions:

- Is the trademark the same as or similar to an existing mark used on similar or related goods or services?
- Is the trademark on the list of prohibited or reserved names?
- Is the trademark generic—that is, does the mark describe the product itself rather than its source?
- Is the trademark too descriptive (not distinctive enough) to qualify for protection?

If the answer to each question is "no," the trademark is eligible for registration and the PTO will continue to process the application.

I know the PTO won't register a mark if it's not distinctive or already in use. But are there other types of marks that are ineligible for federal registration?

Yes. The PTO won't register any marks that contain:

- names of living persons without their consent
- the U.S. flag
- other federal and local governmental insignias
- the name or likeness of a deceased U.S. President without his widow's consent
- words or symbols that disparage living or deceased persons, institutions, beliefs or national symbols, or
- marks that are judged immoral, deceptive or scandalous.

As a general rule the PTO takes a liberal view of the terms immoral and scandalous and will rarely refuse to register a mark on those grounds.

If the PTO decides that a mark is eligible for federal registration, what happens next?

Next, the PTO publishes the trademark in the *Official Gazette* (a publication of the U.S. Patent and Trademark Office). The *Gazette* states that the mark is a candidate for registration; this provides existing trademark owners with an opportunity to object to the registration. If someone objects, the PTO will schedule a hearing to resolve the dispute.

Is it possible to federally register a mark made up of common or ordinary words?

Yes, if the combination of the words is distinctive. But even if the entire mark is judged to lack sufficient distinctiveness, it can be placed on a list called the supplemental register. (Marks that are considered distinctive—either inherently or because they have become well known—are placed on a list called the principal register.) Marks on the supplemental register receive far less protection than do those on the principal register. The benefits granted by each type of registration are discussed in more detail in the next question.

What are the benefits of federal trademark registration?

It depends on which register carries the mark. Probably the most important benefit of placing a mark on the principal register is that anybody who later initiates use of the same or a confusingly similar trademark may be presumed by the courts to be a "willful infringer" and therefore liable for large money damages.

Placing a trademark on the supplemental register produces significantly fewer benefits, but still provides notice of ownership. This notice makes it far less likely that someone will use that identical mark; the fear of being sued for damages should keep potential infringers away. Also, if the trademark remains on the supplemental register for five years—meaning that the registration isn't canceled for some reason—and the mark remains in use during that time, it may be moved to the principal register under the secondary meaning rule (secondary meaning will be presumed).

Even if a mark is not registered, it is still possible for the owner to sue the infringer under a federal statute which forbids use of a "false designation of origin" (Title 15 U.S.C. § 1125). It is usually much easier to prove the case and collect large damages, however, if the mark has been registered.

How long does federal registration last?

Once a trademark or servicemark is placed on the principal register, the owner receives a certificate of registration good for an initial term of ten years. The registration may lapse before the ten-year period expires, however, unless the owner files a form within six years of the registration date (called the Sections 8 and 15 Affidavit) stating that the mark is either still in use in commerce or that

the mark is not in use for legitimate reasons.

The original registration may be renewed indefinitely for additional ten-year periods if the owner files the required renewal applications (called a Section 9 Affidavit) with the U.S. Patent and Trademark Office. Failure to renew a registration does not void all rights to the mark, but if the owner fails to re-register, the special benefits of federal registration will be lost.

What happens if there is a conflict between an Internet domain name and an existing trademark?

To establish a Website, the owner must first register the site name with a nonprofit organization called InterNic. As a general rule, InterNic will register any name that it hasn't already registered, without regard to whether the name is in fact a trademark owned by a different company. This has led to a number of instances where companies with famous marks have initially not been able to use these marks when establishing Websites because someone already used the name to identify another site.

Courts have generally sided with the trademark owners in these disputes and ordered the domain name user to stop using the offending name, even when no goods or services were being offered on the Website.

Also, to respond to the legitimate interests of trademark owners—and to keep from getting sued as an enabling (contributory) infringer—InterNic lets an established trademark owner contest the use of a domain name that infringes the owner's mark, and in some cases requires the domain name owner to either stop using the name or post a bond to cover any damages suffered by the trademark owner while the dispute is settled in court.

Can a business register its mark at the state level?

It is possible to register a mark with the state trademark agency, although the state registration does not offer the same level of protection provided by federal law. The main benefit of state registration is that it notifies anyone who checks the list that the mark is owned by the registrant. This fact will lead most would-be users of the same mark to choose another one rather than risk a legal dispute with the registered mark's owner. If the mark is also federally registered, this notice is presumed and the state registration isn't necessary. If, however, the mark is used only within the state and doesn't qualify for federal registration, state registration is a good idea.

How to Register Your Trademark

For most trademarks already in use, federal registration is a relatively straightforward process. You use a simple two-sided form provided by the PTO to:

- describe your mark

- state when it was first used
- describe the products or services on which the mark will be used, and
- suggest the classification under which the mark should be registered (there are approximately 40 classifications for goods and services; the PTO can help you figure out which one is right for your mark).

In addition, your form must be accompanied by:

- a "drawing" of your mark (for word marks, this simply involves setting the mark out in the middle of a page in capital letters)
- samples of how your proposed mark is being used, and
- the registration fee—currently $245.

On its Website, http://www.uspto.gov, the PTO offers two electronic registration options. PrinTEAS lets you fill in the form online but requires you to print out and mail in a hardcopy. ETEAS lets you both fill in and file the form online.

If you are applying to register your mark on the basis of its intended use (See *How can a business reserve a trademark for future use?*, above), then you needn't provide the samples or the date of first use, but you can't complete your registration until you put your mark into actual use and file some additional paperwork with the PTO.

The PTO offers a free booklet containing plain English instructions for filling out this form, and also provides help on its Website: www.uspto.com. For more information about registering your trademark, see the resource list at the end of this chapter.

How Trademarks Differ From Patents and Copyrights

Trademarks are often mentioned in the same breath as copyrights and patents. While they do sometimes apply to the same thing, they're more often defined by their differences. It's important to understand how trademark law differs from other laws protecting creative works (collectively called "intellectual property laws"); rules and benefits depend on the type of intellectual property at issue.

How does trademark differ from copyright?

Copyright protects original works of expression, such as novels, fine and graphic arts, music, phonorecords, photography, software, video, cinema and choreography by preventing people from copying or commercially exploiting them without the copyright owner's permission. But the copyright laws specifically do not protect names, titles or short phrases. That's where trademark law comes in. Trademark protects distinctive words, phrases, logos, symbols, slogans and any other devices used to identify and distinguish products or services in the marketplace.

There are, however, areas where both trademark and copyright law may be used to protect different aspects of the same product. For example, copyright laws may protect the artistic aspects of a graphic or logo used by a business to identify its goods or services, while trademark may protect the graphic or logo from use by others in a confusing manner in the marketplace. Similarly, trademark laws are often used in conjunction with copyright laws to protect advertising copy. The trademark laws protect the product or service name and any slogans used in the advertising, while the copyright laws protect the additional creative written expression contained in the ad.

For more information about copyright law, see Chapter 7, *Copyrights*.

What's the difference between patent and trademark?

Patents allow the creator of certain kinds of inventions that contain new ideas to keep others from making commercial use of those ideas without the creator's permission. For example, Tom invents a new type of hammer that makes it very difficult to miss the nail. Not only can Tom keep others from making, selling or using the precise type of hammer he invented, but he may also be able to apply his patent monopoly rights to prevent people from making commercial use of any similar type of hammer during the time the patent is in effect (20 years from the date the patent application is filed).

Generally, patent and trademark laws do not overlap. When it comes to a product design, however—say, jewelry or a distinctively shaped musical instrument—it may be possible to obtain a patent on a design aspect of the device while invoking trademark law to protect the design as a product identifier. For instance, an auto manufacturer might receive a design patent for the stylistic fins that are part of a car's rear fenders. Then, if the fins were intended to be—and actually are—used to distinguish the particular model car in the marketplace, trademark law may kick in to protect the appearance of the fins.

For more information about patent law, see Chapter 6, *Patents*.

More Information About Trademarks

Trademark: How to Name a Business and Product, by Kate McGrath and Stephen Elias (Nolo Press), shows you how to choose a legally strong business and product name, register the name with state and federal agencies and sort out any name disputes that arise.

Patent, Copyright and Trademark, by Stephen Elias (Nolo Press), provides concise definitions and examples of the important words and phrases commonly used in trademark law.

McCarthy on Trademarks and Unfair Competition, by J. Thomas McCarthy (Clark Boardman Callaghan), is a book intended for lawyers that provides an exhaustive treatment of trademark law.

Trademark Law—A Practitioners Guide, by Siegrun D. Kane (Practicing Law Institute), is a good overview of trademark law written for lawyers.

Trademark Registration Practice, by James E. Hawes (Clark Boardman Callaghan), a book for trademark lawyers, provides the ins and outs of registering a trademark with the U.S. Patent and Trademark Office.

The following associations of trademark lawyers offer a number of helpful publications. Write or call for a list of available materials.

International Trademark Association (INTA)
1133 Avenue of the Americas
New York, NY 10036
(212) 768-9887
http://www.inta.org/

American Intellectual Property Law Association (AIPLA)
2001 Jefferson Davis Highway, Suite 203
Arlington, VA 22202
(703) 415-0780
http://www.aipla.org/aipla

http://www.nolo.com

Nolo Press offers self-help information about a wide variety of legal topics, including trademarks.

http://www.findlaw.com

Findlaw offers an excellent collection of trademark-related materials on the Web, including trademark statutes, regulations, classification manuals and articles of general interest. Click the intellectual property link in the Legal Subjects area on the Findlaw homepage and then click the Trademarks WWW Sites and Resources link.

http://www.uspto.gov

The U.S. Patent and Trademark Office provides new trademark rules and regulations and, as of August 1998, is expected to put the federal registered trademark database online.

http://www.sci3.com

The Sunnyvale Center for Invention, Innovation and Ideas (a Patent and Trademark Depository Library), provides information about their excellent, low-cost trademark search service conducted by the Center's librarians.

http://www.ggmark.com/

This site, maintained by a trademark lawyer, provides basic trademark information and a fine collection of links to other trademark resources.

Your Money

Too many people spend money they haven't earned, to buy things they don't want, to impress people they don't like.

—WILL ROGERS

America's economy is driven by consumer spending. When we open any newspaper or magazine, turn on the radio or television, or take a drive across town, we're bombarded with ads urging us to spend our hard-earned dollars. And so we do. We pull out our cash, checks, credit cards, and increasingly, debit cards.

What the ads don't tell you is what to do when things go wrong—for example, when the item you buy is defective, when you lose your credit card, when you need extra time to pay or when you fall behind and the bill collectors start calling.

Fortunately, many federal (and some state) laws give you rights as a consumer; this chapter describes those that are most important. While no law substitutes for common sense, comparison shopping and avoiding offers that sound too good to be true, there are solutions to most of the problems you're likely to face as an American consumer.

Purchasing Goods and Services

I did not have three thousand pairs of shoes: I had one thousand and sixty.

—IMELDA MARCOS

While 19th century business relationships were governed by the doctrine "caveat emptor" or "let the buyer beware," the notion that a buyer-seller arrangement should be fair gained ground in the 20th century. As a result, you now have a right to receive nondefective goods—and services that meet a minimum standard.

When I buy something, is it covered by a warranty?

Generally, yes. A warranty (also called a guarantee) is an assurance about the quality of goods or services you buy, and is intended to give you recourse if something you purchase fails to live up to what you were promised.

Some warranties are implied and some are expressed. Virtually everything you buy comes with two implied warranties—one for "merchantability" and one for "fitness." The implied warranty of merchantability is an assurance that a new item will work if you use it for a reasonably expected purpose. For used items, the warranty of merchantability is a promise that the product will work as expected, given its age and condition. The implied warranty of fitness applies when you buy an item with a specific (even unusual) purpose in mind. If you related your specific needs to the seller, the implied warranty of fitness assures you that the item will fill your need.

Most expressed warranties state something such as "the product is warranted against defects in materials or workmanship" for a specified time. You are not automatically entitled to an expressed warranty. Most expressed warranties either come directly from the manufacturer or are included in the sales contract you sign with the seller. But an expressed warranty may be a feature in an advertisement or on a sign in the store ("all dresses 100% silk"), or it may even be an oral description of a product's features.

How long does a warranty last?

In most states, an implied warranty lasts forever. In a few states, however, the implied warranty lasts only as long as any expressed warranty that comes with a product. In these states, if there is no expressed warranty, the implied warranty lasts forever.

How do I enforce a warranty if something is wrong with what I bought?

Most of the time, a defect in an item will show up immediately and you can ask the seller or manufacturer to fix or replace it. If he won't, or if he tries only once and the fixed or replaced item is still defective, you can withhold payment (or refuse to pay a credit card charge). If you are uncomfortable doing this or have already paid for the item, call the seller and try to work out an arrangement. If he refuses, try to mediate the dispute through a community or Better Business Bureau mediation program. (For more information about mediation, see Chapter 17.)

If you can't get anywhere informally, you can sue. In most states, you must sue the seller or manufacturer within four years of when you discovered the defect, if the seller or manufacturer won't make good under a warranty.

Do I have any recourse if the item breaks after the warranty expires?

In most states, if the item gave you some trouble while it was under the warranty (and you had it repaired by someone authorized by the manufacturer to make repairs), the manufacturer must extend your original warranty for the amount of time the item sat in the shop. Call the manufacturer and ask to speak to the department that handles warranties.

If your product was trouble-free during the warranty period, the manufacturer may offer a free repair for a problem that arose after the warranty expired if the problem is a widespread one. Many manufacturers have secret "fix it" lists—items with defects that don't affect safety and therefore don't require a recall, but that the manufacturer will repair for free. It can't hurt to call and ask.

I just bought a stereo system and the salesclerk tried to sell me an extended warranty contract. Should I have bought it?

Probably not. Merchants encourage consumers to buy extended warranties (also called service contracts) when buying autos, appliances or electronic items because they are a source of big profits for stores, which pocket up to 50% of the amount you pay.

Rarely will you have the chance to exercise your rights under an extended warranty. Name-brand electronic equipment and appliances usually don't break down during the first few years (and if they do they're covered by the original warranty), and often have a lifespan well beyond the length of the extended warranty.

I think I was the victim of a scam. Can I get my money back?

Federal and state laws prohibit "unfair or deceptive trade acts or practices." If you think you've been cheated, *immediately* let the appropriate government offices know. Although any government investigation will take some time, these agencies often have the resources to go after unscrupulous merchants. Law enforcement in the consumer fraud area is not great in some parts of the country, but many hardworking investigators do their jobs superbly. The more agencies you notify, the more likely someone will take notice of your complaint and act on it.

Unfortunately, government agencies are rarely able to get you your money back. If the business is a reputable one, however, it may refund your money when a consumer fraud law enforcement investigator shows up. It certainly can't hurt you to complain.

How to File a Complaint for Fraud

The National Fraud Information Center, a project of the National Consumer's League, can help you if you've been defrauded. NFIC provides:

- assistance in filing a complaint with appropriate federal agencies
- recorded information on current fraud schemes
- tips on how to avoid becoming a fraud victim, and
- direct ordering of consumer publications in English or Spanish.

You can contact NFIC, National Consumer's League, 1701 K Street, NW, Suite 1200, Washington, DC 20005, 800-835-3323 (phone), 202-835-0747 (fax), 202-737-5084 (TTD), 202-347-3189 (electronic bulletin board), http://www.fraud.org (online).

If you want to contact a federal agency directly but aren't sure which one, call the U.S. Office of Consumer Affairs, 800-664-4435. Also contact your local prosecutor to find out if it investigates consumer fraud complaints. Finally, contact any local newspaper, radio station or television station "action line." Especially in metropolitan areas, these folks often have an army of volunteers ready to pursue every consumer complaint.

I received some unordered merchandise in the mail and now I'm getting billed. Do I have to pay?

You don't owe any money if you receive an item you never ordered—it's considered a gift. If you get bills or collection letters from a seller who sent you something you never ordered, write to the seller stating your intention to treat the item as a gift. If the bills continue, insist that the seller send you proof of your order. If this doesn't stop the bills, notify the state consumer protection agency in the state where the merchant is located.

If you sent for something in response to an advertisement claiming a "free" gift or "trial" period, but are now being billed, be sure to read the fine print of the ad. It may say something about charging shipping and handling; or worse, you may have inadvertently joined a club or subscribed to a magazine. Write the seller, offer to return the merchandise and state that you believe the ad was misleading.

I just signed a contract to have carpeting installed in my house and I changed my mind. Can I cancel?

Possibly. Under the Federal Trade Commission's "Cooling Off Rule," you have until midnight of the third busi-ness day after a contract was signed to cancel either of the following:
- door-to-door sales contracts for more than $25, or
- a contract for more than $25 made anywhere other than the seller's normal place of business—for instance, at a sales presentation at a hotel or restaurant, outdoor exhibit, computer show or trade show (other than public car auctions and craft fairs).

Do I have the right to cancel any other kinds of contracts?

A federal law called the Truth in Lending Act lets you cancel a home improvement loan, second mortgage or other loan where you pledge your home as security (except for a first mortgage) until midnight of the third business day after you signed the contract.

In addition, many states have laws that allow you to cancel written contracts covering the purchase of certain goods or services within a few days of signing, including contracts for dance or martial arts lessons, health club memberships, dating services, weight loss programs, time share properties and hearing aids. Call your state consumer protection agency (check directory assistance in your state capital) to find out what contracts, if any, are covered in your state.

I ordered some clothes through a catalogue and there's a delay in shipping. Can I cancel my order?

If you order goods by mail, phone, computer or fax (other than photo development, magazine subscriptions, seeds or plants), the Federal Trade Commission's "Mail or Telephone Order Rule" requires that the seller ship to you within the time promised or, if no time was stated, within 30 days.

If the seller cannot ship within those times, the seller must send you a notice with a new shipping date and offer you the option of canceling your order and getting a refund, or accepting the new date. If you opt for the second deadline, but the seller can't meet it, you must be sent a notice requesting your signature to agree to yet a third date. If you don't return the notice, your order must be automatically canceled and your money refunded. The seller must issue the refund promptly—within seven days if you paid by check or money order and within one billing cycle if you charged your purchase.

Do I have the right to a cash refund after I make a purchase?

Generally, no. A seller isn't required to offer refunds or exchanges, though many do.

Four states do have laws governing refund policies:

- *California.* Sellers who do not allow a full cash or credit refund (or an equal exchange) within seven days of purchase must post the store's refund-credit-exchange policy. If the seller fails to post the policy, you may return the goods, for a full refund, within 30 days of your purchase.
- *Florida.* If the seller has no refund policy, such a statement must be posted in the store. If a statement isn't posted, you may return unused and unopened goods within seven days for a full refund.
- *New York.* Sellers with a cash refund policy must post the policy and give the refund within 20 days. If a seller offers both refunds and exchanges, you may decide which you'd prefer.
- *Virginia.* Sellers must post their refund or exchange policies unless they give a full cash refund (or full credit) within 20 days after purchase.

More Information About Purchasing Goods and Services

Everybody's Guide to Small Claims Court, by Ralph Warner (Nolo Press), has extensive information on pursuing your rights in the event a seller or manufacturer won't make good on a warranty.

The Direct Marketing Association is a membership organization made up of mail-order companies and other direct marketers. If you have a complaint about a particular company, contact Mail-Order Action Line, c/o DMA, 1111 19th Street, NW, Suite 1100, Washington, DC 20036, 202-955-5030, 202-955-0085 (fax). DMA may contact the mail-order company and try to resolve your problem.

Using Credit and Charge Cards

American adults hold approximately two billion total credit and charge cards—an average of nine cards per person. Buying on credit has become a cornerstone of the American economy. But buying on credit can be very expensive—the interest rate on bank credit cards averages about 18%; on gasoline company and department store cards, it's over 20%. Only charge cards (also called travel and entertainment cards), such as American Express and Diners Club, don't generally impose interest.

My credit card debt is consuming my life. How can I cut credit card costs?

If you have more than one card, pay down the balances with the highest interest rates and then use (or obtain) a card with a low rate. Because there is great competition among credit card issuers (a record three billion solicita-

tions were mailed out in 1997), you might get a rate reduction simply by calling your current bank and asking.

Which Cards Should You Keep?

When you think about the costs of using your credit cards, you may decide that you're better off canceling most of them. If so, you'll have to choose which cards to keep. If you don't carry a monthly balance, keep a card with no annual fee, but make sure it has a grace period. If you carry a balance each month, get rid of the cards that come with the worst of the following features:

- High interest rates.
- Unfair interest calculations. Avoid cards that charge interest on the average daily balance, not the balance due. Here's why. Let's say you pay $1,200 of your $1,500 balance in January. A bank using the average daily balance will charge you in February interest on the $1,500 average daily balance from January, not on the $300 you still owe.
- No grace periods. This means you pay interest from the time of purchase until the time of payment even if you pay your balance in full.
- Nuisance fees. Get rid of cards with late payment fees, over-the-limit fees, inactivity fees, fees for not carrying a balance or for carrying a balance under a certain amount or a flat monthly fee that's a percentage of your credit limit.

I can't afford the minimum payment required on my statement. Can I pay less?

Most card companies insist that you make the monthly minimum payment, which is usually 2% to 2.5% of the outstanding balance. If you can convince the card issuer that your financial situation is desperate, the issuer may cut your payments in half. In some cases, the issuer may waive payments altogether for a few months. This courtesy is usually extended only to people who have never been late with payments.

Bear in mind that paying nothing or very little on your credit card should be only a temporary solution. The longer you pay only a small amount, the quicker your balance will increase due to interest charges.

My checking account and Visa card are from the same bank. Can the bank take money out of my checking account to cover my missed credit card payments?

No. A bank that takes money out of a deposit account to cover a missed credit card payment violates the federal Truth in Lending Act. You can sue for damages—the amount taken out of your account and any other damages you suffer, such as lost interest or bounced-check fees.

My wallet was stolen. Will I have to pay charges that the thief made using my credit cards?

No. Federal law limits your liability for unauthorized charges made on your credit or charge card after it has been lost or stolen. If you notify the card issuer within a reasonable time after you discover the loss or theft (usually 30 days), you're not responsible for any charges made after the notification, and are liable for only the first $50 of charges made before you notified the card issuer. In practice, card issuers rarely even charge the $50.

I purchased an item using my credit card and it fell apart. Can I refuse to pay?

Maybe. Under federal law, you must first attempt in good faith to resolve the dispute with the merchant. If that fails, you can withhold payment only if the purchase was for more than $50 and was made within your home state or within 100 miles of your home. (This limitation applies only if you used a card not issued by the seller, such as a MasterCard. There is no $50, 100-mile or in-state limitation if you use a seller's card, such as your Sears card.)

The 100-mile limitation is easy to calculate when purchases are made in person. But if you order through the mail, over the telephone or using your computer, the law is unclear as to where the purchase took place. Your best bet is to claim that the purchase was made in the state where you live (even if the catalogue company is on the other side of the country) because you placed the order.

My credit card billing statement contains an error. What should I do?

Immediately write a letter to the customer service department of the card issuer. Give your name, account number, an explanation of the error and the amount involved. Enclose copies of supporting documents, such as receipts showing the correct amount of the charge. You must act quickly—the issuer must receive your letter within 60 days after it mailed the bill to you.

Under the federal Fair Credit Billing Act, the issuer must acknowledge receipt of your letter within 30 days, unless it corrects the bill within that time. Furthermore, the issuer must, within two billing cycles (but in no event more than 90 days), correct the error or explain why it believes the amount to be correct. If the issuer does not comply with these time limits, you may deduct $50 from the disputed balance.

During the two-billing-cycle/90-day period, the issuer cannot report the amount to credit bureaus or other creditors as delinquent. The issuer can charge you interest on the amount you dispute during this period, but if it later agrees that you were correct, it must drop the interest accrued.

Must I give my phone number when I use a credit card?

Most often, no. Several states, including California, Delaware, Georgia, Kansas, Massachusetts, Minnesota, Nevada, New Jersey, New York, Oregon, Pennsylvania, Rhode Island and Wisconsin, bar merchants from recording personal information when you use a credit card. Furthermore, merchants agreements with Visa and MasterCard prohibit them from requiring a customer to furnish a phone number when paying with Visa or MasterCard.

I took out a cash advance using my credit card, and feel I was gouged. What are all those fees?

Cash advances usually come with the following fees:

- *Transaction fees.* Most banks charge a transaction fee of up to 4% for taking a cash advance.
- *Grace period.* Most banks charge interest from the date the cash advance is posted, even if you pay it back in full when your bill comes.
- *Interest rates.* The interest rate is often higher on cash advances than it is on ordinary credit card charges.

Using an ATM or Debit Card

A bank is a place where they lend you an umbrella in fair weather and ask for it back when it begins to rain.

—**ROBERT FROST**

Banks issue ATM cards to allow customers to withdraw money, make deposits, transfer money between accounts, find out their balances, get cash advances and even make loan payments at all hours of the day or night.

Debit cards combine the functions of ATM cards and checks. Debit cards are issued by banks, but can be used at stores. When you pay with a debit card, the money is automatically deducted from your checking account. Many merchants accept ATM cards as debit cards.

What are the advantages to using an ATM or debit card?

There are generally two advantages:

- You don't have to carry your checkbook and identification, but you can make purchases directly from your checking account.
- You pay immediately—without running up interest charges on a credit card bill.

Are there disadvantages?

Yes. You don't have the 20- to 25-day delay in paying the bill. Also, you don't have the right to withhold payment (the money is immediately removed from the account) in the event of a dispute with the merchant over the goods or services paid for. Finally, many banks charge transaction fees when you use an ATM or debit card at locations other than those owned by the bank.

Do I have to pay if there's a mistake on my statement or receipt?

Although ATM statements and debit receipts don't usually contain errors, mistakes do happen. If you find an error, you have 60 days from the date of the statement or receipt to notify the bank. Always call first and follow up with a letter. If you don't notify the bank within 60 days, it has no obligation to investigate the error and you're out of luck.

The bank has ten business days from the date of your notification to investigate the problem and tell you the result. If the bank needs more time, it can take up to 45 days, but only if it deposits the disputed amount of money into your account. If the bank later determines that there was no error, it can take the money back, but it must first send you a written explanation.

If Your ATM Card Is Lost or Stolen

If your ATM or debit card is lost or stolen (never, never, never keep your personal identification number—PIN—near your card), call your bank immediately, and follow up with a confirming letter. Under the federal Electronic Fund Transfers Act, your liability is:

- $0—after you report the card missing
- up to $50—if you notify the bank within two business days after you realize the card is missing (unless you were on extended travel or in the hospital)

- up to $500—if you fail to notify the bank within two business days after you realize the card is missing (unless you were on extended travel or in the hospital) , but do notify the bank within 60 days after your bank statement is mailed to you listing the unauthorized withdrawals
- unlimited—if you fail to notify the bank within 60 days after your bank statement is mailed to you listing the unauthorized withdrawals.

In response to consumer complaints about the possibility of unlimited liability, Visa and MasterCard now cap the liability on debit cards at $50. A few states (Iowa, Kansas, Massachusetts, Minnesota, New Mexico and Wisconsin) have capped the liability for unauthorized withdrawals on an ATM or debit card at $50 as well. And some large debit card issuers won't charge you anything if unauthorized withdrawals appear on your statement.

More Information About Credit, Charge, ATM and Debit Cards

Money Troubles: Legal Strategies to Cope With Your Debts, by Robin Leonard (Nolo Press), contains extensive information on credit, charge, ATM and debit card laws and practical usage tips.

The Federal Deposit Insurance Corporation, 1730 Pennsylvania Avenue, NW, Washington, DC 20429, 800-934-3342, 202-942-3427 (fax), 800-925-4618 (TDD), http://www.fdic.gov,

publishes free pamphlets, including *Fair Credit Billing*.

The Federal Trade Commission, 6th & Pennsylvania Avenue, NW, Washington, DC 20850, 202-326-2222, 202-326-2050 (fax), http://www.ftc.gov, publishes free pamphlets, including *Billing Errors, Fair Credit Billing, Lost or Stolen Credit and ATM Cards* and *Solving Credit Problems*.

Strategies for Repaying Debts

If you think nobody cares if you're alive, try missing a couple of car payments.

—EARL WILSON

If you're in debt, you probably feel very alone. But you shouldn't. Across all economic classes, disposable incomes are down, savings are evaporating, big businesses are merging (and laying people off), the military is downsizing and people are just generally struggling to get by. Here are some specific suggestions for dealing with debts.

I feel completely overwhelmed by my debts and don't know where to begin. What should I do?

Take a deep breath and realize that for the most part, your creditors want to help you. Whether you're behind on your bills or are afraid of getting be-hind, call your creditors. Let them know what's going on—job loss, re-duction in hours, medical problem or whatever—and ask for help. Suggest possible solutions such as a temporary reduction of your payments, skipping a few payments and tacking them on at the end of a loan, skipping a few payments and paying them off over a few months, dropping late fees and other charges or even rewriting a loan. If you need help negotiating with your creditors, consider contacting a non-profit credit advisor organization, such as Debt Counselors of America (http://www.dca.org) or a local Consumer Credit Counseling Service office.

I'm afraid I might miss a car payment—should I just let the lender repossess?

No. Before your car payment is due, call the lender and ask for extra time. If you're at least a few months into the loan and haven't missed any pay-ments, the lender will probably let you miss one or two months' pay-ments and tack them on at the end. If you don't pay or make arrangements with the lender, the lender can repos-sess without warning, although many will warn you to give you a chance to pay what's due.

If your car is repossessed, you can get it back by paying the entire bal-ance due and the cost of repossession or, in some cases, by paying the cost of the repossession and the missed payments, and then making payments under your contract. If you don't get the car back, the lender will sell it at an auction for far less than it's worth. You'll owe the lender the difference between the balance of your loan and what the sale brings in. The amount is usually in the thousands.

How soon after I miss a house payment will the bank begin foreclosure proceedings?

This varies from state to state and lender to lender, but most lenders don't start foreclosure proceedings until you've missed four or five pay-ments. Before taking back your house, a lender would rather rewrite the loan, suspend principal payments for a while (have you pay interest only), reduce your payments or even let you miss a few payments and spread them out over time.

If your loan is owned by one of the giant U.S. government mortgage holders, Fannie Mae or Freddie Mac, foreclosure could come even more slowly. Fannie Mae and Freddie Mac have been working with homeowners to avoid foreclosure when a loan is delinquent.

Might I be better off just selling my house?

You're certainly better off selling the house than having it go to foreclosure. If you can find a buyer who will offer to pay at least what you owe your lender, take the offer. If the offer is for less than what you owe your lender, your lender can block the sale. But many lenders will agree to a "short sale"—where the sale brings in less than you owe the lender and the lender agrees to forego the rest. Some lenders require documentation of any financial or medical hardship you are experiencing before agreeing to a short sale.

Can I just walk away from the house?

If you get no offers for your house or the lender won't approve a short sale, you can walk away from your house. Call the lender and ask if it will accept your deed in lieu of foreclosing. If the lender won't, prepare what's called a quitclaim deed—you "quit" your interest in the property—transferring ownership to your lender. You write DEED IN LIEU OF FORECLOSURE in block capital letters across the top of the deed, pay any transfer fee, record the quitclaim deed where you recorded your ownership deed and mail a copy of the recorded quitclaim deed to the lender. This means that you no longer own the house.

Beware of the IRS

IRS regulations could cost you money if you settle a debt or if a creditor writes off money you owe. The rules state that if a creditor agrees to forego a debt you owe, you must treat the amount you didn't pay as income. Similarly, if a creditor ceases collection efforts, declares the debt uncollectible and reports it as a tax loss to the IRS—including the amount owed after a house foreclosure or property repossession, or on a credit card bill—you must treat the write-off amount as income.

The rule applies to any bank, credit union, savings and loan or other financial institution that forgives or writes off a debt or part of a debt for $600 or more. The institution must send you and the IRS a Form 1099-C at the end of the tax year. These forms are for the report of income, which means that when you file your tax return for the tax year in which your debt was forgiven, the IRS will make sure that you report the amount on the Form 1099-C as income.

There are five exceptions stated in the Internal Revenue Code, three of which apply to consumers. So even if the financial institution issues a Form 1099-C or 1099-A, you do not have to report the income if:

- the cancellation of the debt is intended as a gift (this would be unusual)
- you discharge the debt in bankruptcy, or
- you were insolvent before the creditor agreed to waive the debt.

The Internal Revenue Code does not define what is meant by insolvent. Generally it means that your debts exceed the value of your assets. To figure out whether or not you are insolvent, you will have to total up your assets and your debts, including the debt that was forgiven or written off.

Let's say your assets are worth $35,000 and your debts total $45,000. You are insolvent to the tune of $10,000. If a creditor forgives or writes off debts up to that amount, you will not have to include the Form 1099-C income on your tax return.

On the other hand, let's say your assets and debts are the same, but your creditor forgives or writes off a $14,000 debt. Now, you can ignore $10,000 of the Form 1099-C income, but you will have to report $4,000 on your tax return.

My utility bill was huge because of a very cold winter. Do I have to pay it all at once?

Maybe not. Many utility companies offer customers an amortization program. This means that if your bills are higher in certain months than others, the company averages your yearly bills so you can spread out the large bills. Also, if you are elderly, disabled or low income, you may be eligible for reduced rates—ask your utility company.

I'm swamped with student loans and can't afford my payments. What can I do to avoid default?

First, know that you're right to do all you can to avoid default, rather than ignoring your loans and hoping they'll just go away. If you default, the amount you owe will probably skyrocket because the government can add a collections fee of up to 25% of the principle.

To avoid default, contact the companies that service your student loans and tell them why you can't make your payments. You may be eligible for a deferment or forbearance—ways of postponing repayment. In very limited circumstances, you may be able to cancel a loan. Also talk to your loan holders about flexible payment options—many now offer payments geared to borrowers' incomes.

In addition, consider consolidating your student loans. You can consolidate federal student loans through the government's direct lending program or through a private loan servicing company, such as Sallie Mae or USA Group. With loan consolidation, you can lower your monthly payments by extending your repayment period; you may also be able to lower your interest rate. Most loan consolidators offer flexible repayment options based on your income, and you may be able to consolidate even if one or more of your loans is in default. Types of loans eligible for consolidation, repayment options and interest rates vary slightly from lender to lender. Contact loan servicers for more information:

- Federal Direct Consolidation Loan Center: 800-557-7392, http://www.ed.gov/offices/OPE/DirectLoan/consolid.html
- Sallie Mae: 800-524-9100, http://www.Salliemae.com
- USA Group: 800-382-4506, http://www.usagroup.com.

I defaulted on a student loan a long time ago and I just received collection letters. I can't afford very much, but I can pay something. Any suggestions?

The Higher Education Amendments of 1992 require that the holder of a student loan accept "reasonable and affordable" payments based on your income and expenses. The holder cannot insist on a monthly minimum. If you make six consecutive reasonable and affordable monthly payments on time, you will become eligible to apply for new federal student loans or grants if you want to return to school. You must continue to make the monthly payments, however, until you make at least 12 consecutive payments. Only then will your loans come out of default. Once that happens, you can apply for an in-school deferment—that is, a postponement of your payments.

If you do not intend to return to school, the same rules apply: After you make 12 consecutive monthly payments, your loan will no longer be in default. When your loan comes out of default, the holder of your loan can—and probably will—sell it back to a regular loan servicing company. (This is called loan rehabilitation.) Your new loan servicer will put you on a standard ten-year repayment plan, which may cause your monthly payments to increase dramatically. If you can't afford them, you will need to apply for a deferment (if you are eligible) or request a flexible repayment option.

I paid off my student loan a long time ago, but the Department of Education recently wrote me saying I still owe it. Help!

You need documentation. First, contact your school and ask for its Department of Education report showing the loan's status. Then, think about ways you can show that you paid the loan: Do you have canceled checks or old bank statements? Can you get microfiche copies of checks from your bank or a government regulatory agency if your bank is out of business? Does an old roommate remember seeing you write a check every month? Can you get old credit reports (check with lenders from whom you've borrowed in years past) which may show a payment status on an old loan? Get old tax returns (from the IRS, if necessary) showing that you itemized the interest deduction on student loan payments back when that was permitted. The last holder of the loan might have a copy of the signed promissory note. Any of these things will help you prove to the Department of Education that you paid your loan.

When can a creditor garnish my wages, place a lien on my house, seize my bank account or take my tax refund?

For the most part, a creditor must sue you, obtain a court judgment and then solicit the help of a sheriff or other law enforcement officer to garnish wages. Even then, the maximum the creditor can take is 25% of your net pay—and you can protest that in court if you can't live on only 75% of your wages.

In three situations your wages may be garnished without your being sued:

- The IRS can take everything but about $100 a week.
- The Department of Education or a state guarantee agency can garnish up to 10% of your wages if you're in default on a student loan.
- Up to 50% of your wages can be garnished to pay child support or alimony.

To place a lien on your house or empty your bank account, almost all creditors must first sue you, get a judgment and then use a law enforcement officer. A few creditors, such as an unpaid contractor who worked on your house, can put a lien on your house without suing. And again, the IRS is an exception—it can place a lien or empty your bank account without suing first.

Your tax refund can never be taken unless the Treasury Department receives such a request from the IRS, the Department of Education or a child support collection agency.

If You Bounce a Check

In every state, writing a bad check is a crime. Aggressive district attorneys don't hesitate to prosecute, especially given that an estimated 450 million rubber checks are written each year. If you are prosecuted, you may be able to avoid a trial if your county has a "diversion" program where you attend classes for bad check writers. You must pay the tuition and make good on the bad checks you wrote.

Even if you escape criminal prosecution, you'll be charged a bad check "processing" fee by your bank. Many banks charge as much as $20 or $30. In addition, most creditors who receive a bad check can sue for damages. Before suing you, the creditor usually must first make a written demand that you make good on the bad check. If you don't pay up within approximately 30 days, the creditor can sue you. Damages recoverable by the merchant vary from state to state, but are often a minimum of $50, and more like a few hundred or a thousand dollars.

Can I go to jail for not paying my debts?

Debtor's prisons were eliminated in the U.S. around 1900. In a few unusual situations, however, you could be jailed: you willfully violate a court order, especially an order to pay child support; you are convicted of willfully refusing to pay income taxes; or you are about to conceal yourself or your property to avoid paying a debt for which a creditor has a judgment against you.

More Information About Repaying Debts

Money Troubles: Legal Strategies to Cope with Your Debts, by Robin Leonard (Nolo Press), explains your legal rights and offers practical strategies for dealing with debts and creditors.

Take Control of Your Student Loans, by Robin Leonard and Shae Irving (Nolo Press), provides strategies for repaying your loans, dealing with loan collectors and getting out of default.

The Ultimate Credit Handbook, by Gerri Detweiler (Penguin Books), provides tips on doubling your credit and cutting your debt.

Surviving Debt: A Guide for Consumers, by Jonathan Sheldon and Gary Klein (National Consumer Law Center), contains tips on dealing with debt collectors and repaying debts.

Debt Counselors of America, 800-680-3328, http://www.dca.org, offers free publications, recommended books, a forum for posting your debt questions, information on obtaining your audit report and special programs to help you get out of debt.

Consumer Credit Counseling Service, 800-388-2227, can put you in contact with the CCCS office located nearest you.

The Federal Student Aid Information Center, P.O. Box 84, Washington, DC 20044, 800-433-3243, http://www.ed.gov/prog_info/SFA/Student Guide provides information about federal student loan programs.

The Federal Trade Commission, 6th & Pennsylvania Avenue, NW, Washington, DC 20850, 202-326-2222, 202-326-2050 (fax), http://www.ftc.gov, publishes nearly 50 free pamphlets on debts and credit; call or write and ask for a complete list.

Dealing With the IRS

Of all debts men are least willing to pay the taxes.

—RALPH WALDO EMERSON

No three letters bring more fear to the average American than IRS. Yet, at one time or another in our lives, nearly everyone will owe a tax bill they can't pay, need extra time to file a tax return or even get audited. This section suggests several strategies for dealing with the government's largest bureaucracy.

How long should I keep my tax papers?

Keep anything related to your tax return—W-2 and 1099 forms, receipts and canceled checks for deductible items—for at least three years after you file. Three years is the amount of time the IRS usually has to audit you. For example, if you filed your 1997 tax return on April 15, 1998, keep those records until at least April 16, 2001. To be completely safe, you should keep your records for six years. The reason is that the IRS can audit up to six years after you file if the IRS believes you underreported your income by 25% or more.

One last caution: Keep records showing purchase costs and sales figures for real estate, stocks or other investments for at least three years after you sell these assets. This is because you must be able to show your taxable gain or loss to an auditor.

If I can't pay my taxes, should I file a return anyway?

Absolutely. If you don't file a tax return, the IRS will assess a penalty of up to 25% of the tax due. In addition, the IRS could (although it isn't likely to) criminally charge you for failing to file a return. Of course, filing a return without paying the taxes due will bring an IRS collector into your life, but a collector is easier to deal with if she doesn't have to hunt you down for nonfiling, too.

Who has access to my IRS files?

The federal Privacy Act of 1976 declares tax files to be "confidential." This was an attempt by Congress to correct the abuses of power uncovered in the Watergate scandal. Even IRS officials cannot rummage willy-nilly through your tax files unless they are involved in some kind of case involving you and your taxes. Consequently, individuals, businesses and credit reporting agencies do not have access to your tax information unless you authorize its release to the IRS in writing.

The privacy law has exceptions, however, and IRS security is sometimes lax. Your IRS files are shared with other federal and state agencies if they can demonstrate a "need to know." This usually means an investigation into your affairs by a law enforcement agency. In fairness to the IRS, most leakage of information is the result of sloppiness by other federal or state agencies granted access to IRS files. Furthermore, computer hackers have broken into IRS and government databases and retrieved private tax information. While violation of the Privacy Act is a crime, violators are rarely prosecuted.

Do many people cheat on their taxes? And what will happen to me if I cheat on mine?

No one really knows how many people cheat the IRS, but several years ago an independent poll found that 20% of Americans admitted to cheating. This is somewhat in line with government studies showing that 82% of us faithfully file and pay our taxes every year. The IRS claims that most cheating is by self-employed small business people who do not have taxes withheld by their employers. Arguably, cheating by the self-employed approaches 100% if you count small violations like mailing a personal letter with a business-bought stamp.

If you are caught in some major cheating, the government can (but rarely does) throw you in jail. Fewer than 1,500 individuals are jailed in the U.S. for tax crimes each year, many of whom also are charged with drug crimes. That is really not many people, considering there are about 180,000,000 American adults. The IRS would much prefer collecting money, not putting anyone in prison. More likely, you'll be assessed heavy penalties, and probably audited for several years.

I am faced with a tax bill that I can't pay. Am I completely at the IRS's mercy, or do I have some options?

There are six ways to deal with a tax bill you unquestionably owe:

- Borrow from a financial institution, family or friends and pay it in full.
- Negotiate a monthly payment plan with the IRS. (This will include interest and penalty charges.)
- File for Chapter 13 bankruptcy to set up a payment plan for your debts, including your taxes.
- Find out whether you can wipe out the debt in a Chapter 7 bankruptcy.
- Make an offer in compromise. (That is, ask the IRS to accept less than the full amount due.)
- Ask the IRS to designate your debt (temporarily) uncollectible if you are out of work or your income is very low. This will buy you time to get back on your feet before dealing with the IRS. Interest and penalties will continue to accrue.

Tax Avoidance Schemes Don't Work

Dozens of tax avoidance schemes emerge every decade. Some promoters are very persuasive, particularly if you are predisposed to believing that it's possible to opt out of the tax system. Sad to say, these promoters are all snake-oil salesmen, the most successful of whom make millions peddling their products at expensive "seminars" and through underground publications. One recent scheme involves holding your assets in multiple family trusts, limited partnerships and offshore banks. While these artifices may put your assets beyond the reach of your creditors, they won't beat the IRS.

I made a mistake on my tax return and am now being billed for the taxes, plus interest and penalties. Do I have to pay it all?

Maybe not. The IRS must charge you interest on your tax bill, but penalties are discretionary. The IRS abates (cancels) one-third of all penalties it charges. The trick is to convince the IRS that you had "reasonable cause" (a good excuse) for failing to observe the tax law. Examples that might work include:

- serious illness or a death in the family
- destruction of your records by a flood, fire or other catastrophe
- wrong advice from the IRS over the phone
- bookkeeper or accountant error, or
- your being in jail or out of the country at the time the tax return was due.

You can ask anyone at the IRS to cancel a penalty, in person or over the phone. And, you can ask for the penalty to be canceled even if you already paid it. The best way to get the IRS's attention is to use IRS Form 843, Claim for Refund and Request for Abatement.

Can the IRS take my house if I owe back taxes?

The IRS can seize just about anything you own—including your home and pension plans. There is a list of items exempt by federal law from IRS seizures, but it is hardly generous, and doesn't include your residence. Moreover, state homestead protection laws don't apply to the IRS. With that said, the good news is that the federal Taxpayer Bill of Rights discourages the IRS from taking homes of people who owe back taxes. In addition, the IRS doesn't like the negative publicity generated when it takes a home, unless of course it is the home of a notorious public enemy.

Nevertheless, if the IRS collection division has tried—and failed—to get any cooperation from a tax debtor (for example, if the debtor has not answered correspondence or returned phone calls, or has made threats, lied about her income or hidden her assets), the IRS may go after a residence as a last resort. A tax collector can't make the decision on his own—it must come from top IRS personnel.

If the IRS lets you know that it plans to take your house, your Congressperson may be able to intervene and put some pressure on the IRS to stop the seizure. And, if the seizure would add you and your family to the ranks of the homeless, you can contact your local IRS Problems Resolution Office to plead that the seizure would create a substantial hardship.

In the unhappy event the IRS does seize your home, all may not be lost.

The IRS must sell the home at public auction, usually held about 45 days after the seizure. Then, the high bidder at auction must wait 180 days to get clear title. In this interim period you have the right to redeem (buy back) the home by coming up with the bid price plus interest.

What are my chances of getting through an audit without owing additional taxes?

Although only about 1% of all tax returns are audited, the IRS has a pretty high success rate. Fewer than 15% of all IRS audit victims make a clean getaway. This is primarily because the IRS's sophisticated computer selection process makes it likely that the agency will audit returns in which "adjustments" are almost a certainty.

If you receive an audit notice, focus on limiting the damage rather than getting off scot-free. Most adjustments made following an audit result from poor taxpayer records, so make sure you have organized documentation to back up your deductions, exemptions and other claims. Ignore the tales about dumping a box of receipts on the auditor's desk in the hope that she will throw up her hands and let you off rather than go through the mess. It doesn't work like that. If you have any significant worries, get a tax pro to represent you or to help you navigate through the perilous audit waters.

Can I challenge the IRS if I get audited and don't agree with the result?

You do not have to accept any audit report. In most cases, you can appeal by sending a protest letter to the IRS within 30 days after receiving the audit report. If you request an appeals consideration, you will be granted a meeting with an Appeals Officer who is not part of the IRS division that performed your audit.

If your appeal fails, you still can file a petition in Tax Court. This is a fairly inexpensive and simple process if the audit bill is for less than $10,000. If it's for more, you will most likely need the help of a tax attorney.

Generally, it pays to contest an audit report by appealing and going to court. About half the people who challenge their audit report are partially successful in lowering their tax bill.

More Information
About Dealing With the IRS

Stand Up to the IRS, by Frederick W. Daily (Nolo Press), explains your legal rights and offers practical strategies for dealing with the IRS.

Debt Collections

Laws prohibit debt collectors from using abusive or deceptive tactics to collect a debt. Unfortunately, many collectors ignore the rules and don't play fair. In addition, creditors and debt collectors have powerful collection tools once they have won a lawsuit for the debt. Here are some frequently asked questions and answers to help you deal with debt collectors.

Collection agencies have been calling me all hours of the day and night. Can I get them to stop contacting me?

It's against the law for a bill collector who works for a collection agency (as opposed to working in the collections department of the creditor itself) to call you before 8 a.m. or after 9 p.m. The law, the federal Fair Debt Collection Practices Act (FDCPA), also bars collectors from calling you at work if you ask them not to, harassing you, using abusive language, making false or misleading statements, adding unauthorized charges and many other practices. Under the FDCPA, you can demand that the collection agency stop contacting you, except to tell you that collection efforts have ended or that the creditor or collection agency will sue you. You must put your request in writing.

I'm also getting calls from the collections department of a local merchant I did business with. Can I tell that collector to stop contacting me?

No. The FDCPA applies only to bill collectors who work for collection agencies. While many states have laws prohibiting all debt collectors—including those working for the creditor itself—from harassing, abusing or threatening you, these laws don't give you the right to demand that the collector stop contacting you. There is one exception: Residents of New York City can use a local consumer protection law to write any bill collector and say, "Leave me alone."

A bill collector insisted that I wire the money I owe through Western Union. Am I required to do so?

No, and it could add a lot to your debt if you do. Many collectors, especially when a debt is more than 90 days past due, will suggest several "urgency payment" options, including:

- *Sending money by express or overnight mail.* This will add at least $10 to your bill; a first class stamp is fine.
- *Wiring money through Western Union's Quick Collect or American Express's Moneygram.* This is another $10 waste.
- *Putting your payment on a credit card not charged to its maximum.* You'll never get out of debt if you do this.

You Can Run, But You Can't Hide

In this technological age, it's easy to run from collectors—but hard to hide. Collectors use many different resources to find debtors. They may contact relatives, friends, neighbors and employers, posing as long-lost friends to get these people to reveal your new whereabouts. In addition, collectors often get information from post office change of address forms, state motor vehicle registration information, voter registration records, former landlords and banks.

Can a collection agency add interest to my debt?

Not unless your original agreement calls for the addition of interest during collection proceedings or the addition of such interest is allowed under state law. Virtually all states do authorize the collection of such interest. In California, for example, collection agencies can add interest because a law permits a creditor to charge interest after default, even if the contract doesn't say anything about interest.

A collection agency sued me and won. Will I still be called and sent letters demanding payment?

Probably not. Before obtaining a court judgment, a bill collector generally has only one way of getting paid:

demand payment. This is done with calls and letters. You can ignore the phone calls and throw out your mail, and the collector can't do much else short of suing you. Once the collector (or creditor) sues and gets a judgment, however, you can expect more aggressive collections actions. If you have a job, the collector will try to garnish up to 25% of your net wages. The collector may also try to seize any bank or other deposit accounts you have. If you own real property, the collector will probably record a lien, which will have to be paid when you sell or refinance your property. Even if you're not currently working or have no property, you're not home free. Depending on the state, court judgments can last up to 20 years and, in many states, can be renewed.

What can I do if a bill collector violates the FDCPA?

If a bill collector violates the law, try to get him to repeat what he said. In most states, you can tape the conversation without the collector's knowledge. In about a dozen states (California, Connecticut, Delaware, Florida, Illinois, Maryland, Massachusetts, Montana, New Hampshire, Pennsylvania and Washington), you should try to get a third party to witness the collector's behavior. Invite the collector back to your home or have the witness listen on a phone extension while you and the collector talk. Say whatever you said the first time that caused the collector to make whatever illegal statement he made. After you have the conversation on tape or witnessed, you can make an official complaint.

File your complaint with the Federal Trade Commission (the adress and phone number are at the end of this section). Next, complain to your state consumer protection agency. Finally, send a copy of your complaint to the creditor who hired the collection agency. If the violations are severe enough, the creditor may stop the collection efforts.

Also, you can sue a collection agency (and the creditor that hired the agency) for up to $1,000 in small claims court for violating the FDCPA. You probably won't win if you can prove only a few minor violations. If the violations are outrageous, you can sue the collection agency and creditor in regular civil court. One Texas jury awarded a debtor $11 million when a debt collector made death and bomb threats against her and her husband that frightened them so much they moved out of the county.

More Information About Debt Collections

Money Troubles: Legal Strategies to Cope With Your Debts, by Robin Leonard (Nolo Press), explains your legal rights and offers practical strategies for dealing with debts and creditors.

The Federal Trade Commission, 6th & Pennsylvania Avenue, NW, Washington, DC 20850, 202-326-2222, 202-326-2050 (fax), http://www.ftc.gov/, publishes free pamphlets on debts and credit, including a couple on the Fair Debt Collections Practices Act. It also takes complaints about collection agencies.

Bankruptcy

Where everything is bad it must be good to know the worst.

—FRANCIS HERBERT BRADLEY

If you are seriously in debt, you might consider filing for bankruptcy. Here are some common questions and answers designed to help you understand the bankruptcy process and what bankruptcy can and cannot do for you.

What exactly is bankruptcy?

Bankruptcy is a federal court process designed to help consumers and businesses eliminate their debts or repay them under the protection of the bankruptcy court. Bankruptcy's roots can be traced to the Bible. (Deuteronomy 15:1-2 —"Every seventh year you shall practice remission of debts. This shall be the nature of the remission: Every creditor shall remit the due that he claims from his neighbor; he shall not dun his neighbor or kinsman.")

Aren't there different kinds of bankruptcy?

Yes. Bankruptcies can generally be described as "liquidation" or "reorganization."

Liquidation bankruptcy is called Chapter 7. Under Chapter 7 bankruptcy, a consumer or business asks the bankruptcy court to wipe out (discharge) the debts owed. Certain debts cannot be discharged—these are discussed below. In exchange for the discharge of debts, the business's assets or the consumer's nonexempt property is sold—that is, liquidated—and the proceeds are used to pay off creditors. The property a consumer might lose is discussed below.

There are several types of reorganization bankruptcy. Consumers with secured debts under $807,750 and unsecured debts under $269,250 can file for Chapter 13. Family farmers can file for Chapter 12. Consumers with debts in excess of the Chapter 13 debt limits or businesses can file for Chapter 11—a complex, time-consuming and expensive process. In any reorganization bankruptcy, you file a plan with the bankruptcy court proposing how you will repay your creditors. Some debts must be repaid in full; others you pay only a percentage; others aren't paid at all. Some debts you have to pay with interest; some are paid at the beginning of your plan and some at the end.

What generally happens in consumer bankruptcy cases?

In a Chapter 7 case, you file several forms with the bankruptcy court listing income and expenses, assets, debts and property transactions for the past two years. The cost to file is $175, which may be waived for people who receive public assistance or live below the poverty level. A court-appointed person, the trustee, is assigned to oversee your case. About a month after filing, you must attend a "meeting of creditors" where the trustee reviews your forms and asks any questions. Despite the name, creditors rarely attend. If you have any nonexempt property, you must give it (or its value in cash) to the trustee. The meeting lasts about five minutes. Three to six months later, you receive a notice from the court that "all debts that qualified for discharge were discharged." Then your case is over.

Chapter 13 is a little different. You file the same forms plus a proposed repayment plan, in which you describe how you intend to repay your debts over the next three, or in some cases five, years. The cost to file is $160 (it cannot be waived), and a trustee is assigned to oversee the case. Here, too, you attend the meeting of creditors, but often one or two creditors attend this meeting, especially if they don't like something in your plan. After the meeting of the creditors, you attend a hearing before a bankruptcy judge who either confirms or denies your plan. If your plan is confirmed, and you make all the payments called for under your plan, you often receive a discharge of any balance owed at the end of your case.

Nondischargeable Debts

The following debts are nondischargeable in both Chapter 7 and Chapter 13. If you file for Chapter 7, these will remain when your case is over. If you file for Chapter 13, these debts will have to be paid in full during your plan. If they are not, the balance will remain at the end of your case:

- debts you forget to list in your bankruptcy papers, unless the creditor learns of your bankruptcy case
- child support and alimony

- debts for personal injury or death caused by your intoxicated driving
- student loans for which the first payment became due within the past seven years (plus any time you were granted a deferment or forbearance or were in a previous bankruptcy case), unless it would be an undue hardship for you to repay
- fines and penalties imposed for violating the law, such as traffic tickets and criminal restitution, and
- recent income tax debts and all other tax debts.

In addition, the following debts may be declared nondischargeable by a bankruptcy judge in Chapter 7 if the creditor challenges your request to discharge them. These debts may be discharged in Chapter 13. You can include them in your plan—at the end of your case, the balance is wiped out:

- debts you incurred on the basis of fraud, such as lying on a credit application
- credit purchases of $1,075 of more for luxury goods or services made within 60 days of filing
- loans or cash advances of $1,075 or more taken within 60 days of filing
- debts from willful or malicious injury to another person or another person's property
- debts from embezzlement, larceny or breach of trust, and
- debts you owe under a divorce decree or settlement unless after bankruptcy you would still not be able to afford to pay them or the benefit you'd receive by the discharge outweighs any detriment to your ex-spouse (who would have to pay them if you discharge them in bankruptcy).

What property might I lose if I file for bankruptcy?

You lose no property in Chapter 13. In Chapter 7, you select property you are eligible to keep from either a list of state exemptions or exemptions provided in the federal Bankruptcy Code. Most debtors use the exemptions provided by their state.

Exemptions are generally as follows:

- *Equity in your home, called a homestead exemption.* Under the Bankruptcy Code, you can exempt up to $16,150. Some states have no homestead exemption; others allow debtors to protect all or most of the equity in their home.
- *Insurance.* You usually get to keep the cash value of your policies.
- *Retirement plans.* Pensions which qualify under the Employee Retirement Income Security Act (ERISA) are fully protected in bankruptcy. So are many other retirement benefits; often, however, IRAs and Keoghs are not.
- *Personal property.* You'll be able to keep most household goods, furniture, furnishings, clothing (other than furs), appliances, books and musical instruments. You may be limited up to $1,000 or so in how much jewelry you can keep. Most states let you keep a vehicle with more than $2,400 of equity. And many states give you a "wild card" amount of money—often $1,000 or more—that you can apply toward any property.
- *Public benefits.* All public benefits, such as welfare, Social Security and unemployment insurance, are fully protected.
- *Tools used on your job.* You'll probably be able to keep up to a few thousand dollars worth of the tools used in your trade or profession.
- *Wages.* In most states, you can protect at least 75% of earned but unpaid wages.

Why choose Chapter 13 over Chapter 7?

Although the overwhelming number of people who file for bankruptcy choose Chapter 7, there are several reasons why people select Chapter 13:

- You cannot file for Chapter 7 bankruptcy if you received a Chapter 7 or Chapter 13 discharge within the previous six years.
- You have valuable nonexempt property.
- You're behind on your mortgage or car loan. In Chapter 7, you'll have to give up the property or pay for it in full during your bankruptcy case. In Chapter 13, you can repay the arrears through your plan, and keep the property by making the payments required under the contract.
- You have debts that cannot be discharged in Chapter 7.
- You have codebtors on personal (nonbusiness) loans. In Chapter 7, the creditors will go after your codebtors for payment. In Chapter 13, the creditors may not seek payment from your codebtors for the duration of your case.
- You feel a moral obligation to repay your debts, you want to learn money management or you hope new creditors might be more inclined to grant you credit after a Chapter 13 than they would after a Chapter 7.

More Information About Bankruptcy

How to File for Chapter 7 Bankruptcy, by Stephen Elias, Albin Renauer and Robin Leonard (Nolo Press), is a complete guide to filing for Chapter 7 bankruptcy, including all the forms you need.

Nolo's Law Form Kit: Personal Bankruptcy, by Stephen Elias, Albin Renauer, Robin Leonard and Lisa Goldoftas (Nolo Press), contains all the forms and instructions necessary for filing a Chapter 7 bankruptcy.

Chapter 13 Bankruptcy: Repay Your Debts, by Robin Leonard (Nolo Press), contains the forms and instructions necessary to file your own Chapter 13 bankruptcy or successfully work with a lawyer.

Bankruptcy: Is It the Right Solution, by Robin Leonard (Nolo Press), provides tools to help you decide if filing for bankruptcy is for you and, if so, which type is best.

Rebuilding Credit

People who have been through a financial crisis—bankruptcy, repossession, foreclosure, history of late payments, IRS lien or levy or something similar—may think they won't ever get credit again. Not true. Following some simple steps, you can rebuild your credit in just a couple of years.

What's the first step in rebuilding credit?

To avoid getting into financial problems in the future, you must understand your flow of income and expenses. Some people call this making a budget. Others find the term budget too restrictive and use the term "spending plan." Whatever you call it, spend at least two months writing down every expenditure. At each month's end, compare your total expenses with your income. If you're overspending, you have to cut back or find more income. As best you can, plan how you'll spend your money each month. If you have trouble putting together your own budget, consider getting help from a nonprofit group, such as Debt Counselors of America or Consumer Credit Counseling Service, which provides budgeting help for free or at a low cost.

Okay, I've made my budget. What do I do next?

Now it's time to clean up your credit report. Credit reports are compiled by credit bureaus—private, for-profit companies that gather information about your credit history and sell it to banks, mortgage lenders, credit unions, credit card companies, department stores, insurance companies, landlords and even a few employers.

Credit bureaus get most of their data from creditors. They also search court records for lawsuits, judgments and bankruptcy filings. And they go through county records to find recorded liens (legal claims against property).

To create a credit file for a given person, a credit bureau searches its computer files until it finds entries that match the name, Social Security number and any other available identifying information. All matches are gathered together to make the report.

Noncredit data made part of a credit report usually includes names you previously used, past and present addresses, Social Security number, employment history, marriages and divorces. Your credit history includes the names of your creditors, type and number of each account, when each account was opened, your payment history for the previous 24–36 months, your credit limit or the original amount of a loan, and your current balance. The report will show if an account has been turned over to a collection agency or is in dispute.

How to Get Your Credit Report

There are three major credit bureaus— Equifax, Trans Union and Experian. The federal Fair Credit Reporting Act (FCRA) entitles you to a copy of your credit report, and you can get one for free if any of the following are true:

- you were denied credit because of information in your credit report and you request a copy within 60 days of being denied credit
- you receive public assistance
- you are unemployed and plan to apply for a job within 60 days, or
- you believe your file contains errors due to fraud.

Residents of Colorado, Georgia, Maryland, Massachusetts, New Jersey and Vermont are entitled to a free copy of their report once a year from each credit bureau.

If you don't qualify for a free report, you'll have to pay about $8 to obtain one. Write to Equifax (P.O. Box 740241, Atlanta, GA 30374), Trans Union (P.O. Box 390, Springfield, PA 19064) or Experian (P.O. Box 949, Allen, TX 75002-0949).

Send the following information:

- your full name (including generations such as Jr., Sr., III)
- your birth date
- your Social Security number
- your spouse's name (if relevant)
- your telephone number; and
- your current address and addresses for the previous five years.

What should I do if I find mistakes in my report?

As you read through your report, make a list of everything out of date:

- Lawsuits, paid tax liens, accounts sent out for collection, criminal records, late payments and any other adverse information older than seven years.
- Bankruptcies older than ten years from the discharge or dismissal. (Credit bureaus often list Chapter 13 bankruptcies for only seven years, but they can stay for as many as ten.)
- Credit inquiries (requests by companies for a copy of your report) older than two years.

Next, look for incorrect or misleading information, such as:

- incorrect or incomplete name, address, phone number, Social Security number or employment information
- bankruptcies not identified by their specific chapter number
- accounts not yours or lawsuits in which you were not involved
- incorrect account histories—such as late payments when you paid on time
- closed accounts listed as open—it may look as if you have too much open credit, and
- any account you closed that doesn't say "closed by consumer."

After reviewing your report, complete the "request for reinvestigation" form the credit bureau sent you or send a letter listing each incorrect item and explain exactly what is

wrong. Once the credit bureau receives your request, it must investigate the items you dispute and contact you within 30 days. If you don't hear back within 30 days, send a follow-up letter. If you let them know that you're trying to obtain a mortgage or car loan, they can do a "rush" investigation.

If you are right, or if the creditor who provided the information can no longer verify it, the credit bureau must remove the information from your report. Often credit bureaus will remove an item on request without an investigation if rechecking the item is more bother than it's worth.

If the credit bureau insists that the information is correct, call the bureau to discuss the problem:

- Experian: 800-392-1122
- Trans Union: 800-851-2674
- Equifax: 800-685-1111

If you don't get anywhere with the credit bureau, contact the creditor directly and ask that the information be removed. Write to the customer service department, vice president of marketing and president or CEO. If the information was reported by a collection agency, send the agency a copy of your letter, too.

If the creditor will not remove the information, remind the creditor that under the 1997 amendments to the Fair Credit Reporting Act, the creditor must do the following:

- refrain from reporting information they know is incorrect

- refrain from ignoring information they know contradicts what they have on file, and
- provide credit bureaus with correct information when that information becomes available.

If a credit bureau is including the wrong information in your report, or you want to explain a particular entry, you have the right to put a 100-word statement in your report. The credit bureau must give a copy of your statement—or a summary—to anyone who requests your report. Be clear and concise; use the fewest words possible.

I've been told that I need to use credit to rebuild my credit. Is this true?

Yes. The one type of positive information creditors like to see in credit reports is credit payment history. If you have a credit card, use it every month. (Make small purchases and pay them off to avoid interest charges.) If you don't have a credit card, apply for one. If your application is rejected, try to find a cosigner or apply for a secured card—where you deposit some money into a savings account and then get a credit card with a line of credit around the amount you deposited.

What else can I do to rebuild my credit?

After you've cleaned up your credit report, the key to rebuilding credit is to get positive information into your record. Here are two suggestions:

- If your credit report is missing accounts you pay on time, send the credit bureaus a recent account statement and copies of canceled checks showing your payment history. Ask that these be added to your report. The credit bureau doesn't have to add anything, but often will.
- Creditors like to see evidence of stability, so if any of the following information is not in your report, send it to the bureaus and ask that it be added: your current employment, your previous employment (especially if you've been at your current job fewer than two years), your current residence, your telephone number (especially if it's unlisted), your date of birth and your checking account number. Again, the credit bureau doesn't have to add these, but often will.

How long does it take to rebuild credit?

If you follow the steps outlined above, it will take about two years to rebuild your credit so that you won't be turned down for a major credit card or loan. After around four years, you may be able to qualify for a mortgage.

More Information About Rebuilding Your Credit

Credit Repair, by Robin Leonard (Nolo Press), is a quick and legal guide to rebuilding your credit. It contains several strategies for improving credit, sample credit reports with explanations on how to read them and the text of the federal and many state credit reporting laws.

Money Troubles: Legal Strategies to Cope With Your Debts, by Robin Leonard (Nolo Press), explains your legal rights and offers practical strategies for dealing with debts and creditors, including rebuilding your credit.

The Federal Trade Commission, 6th & Pennsylvania Avenue, NW, Washington, DC 20850, 202-326-2222, 202-326-2050 (fax), http://www.ftc.gov, publishes free pamphlets on debts and credit, including *Building a Better Credit Record, Cosigning a Loan, Fair Credit Reporting* and *Fix Your Own Credit Problems and Save Money.*

The Federal Deposit Insurance Corporation, 1730 Pennsylvania Avenue, NW, Washington, DC 20429, 800-934-3342, 202-942-3427 (fax), 800-925-4618 (TDD), http://www.fdic.gov, publishes free pamphlets about credit, including *Fair Credit Reporting.*

http://www.nolo.com

Nolo Press offers self-help information about a wide variety of legal topics, including advice about consumer law, debts and credit.

http://www.fraud.org

The National Fraud Information Center helps you file a complaint with federal agencies if you've benn defrauded. It also offers information on how to avoid becoming the victim of a scam.

http://www.dca.org

Debt Counselors of America is a nonprofit online resource dedicated to helping people get out of debt so they can resume a life of financial success. You'll find free publications, recommended books, a forum for posting your debt questions and special programs to help you get out of debt.

http://www.financenter.com/

The FinanCenter provides financial advice and includes a calculator to help you compare various financing alternatives when you're making a budget or considering a major purchase, such as a home or automobile. The cool graphics alone make visiting this site worthwhile.

http://www.bbb.org

The Better Business Bureau provides general information on their programs and services, including alerts, warnings and updates about businesses. You can also find information about filing a complaint against a business and using the BBB's dispute resolution program.

http://consumerlawpage.com

The Consumer Law Page, a service of a private law firm, has information on credit insurance, banking, fraud and defective products.

http://law.house.gov/

The U.S. House of Representatives Internet Law Library provides the texts of finance, economic and consumer protection laws including the federal bankruptcy code and bankruptcy rules, banking laws, Federal Trade Commission publications and selected state consumer protection laws.

http://www.pueblo.gsa.gov/

The Consumer Information Center provides the latest in consumer news as well as many publications of interest to consumers, including the Consumer Information Catalog.

http://www.fdic.gov
http://www.ftc.gov

Both the Federal Deposit Insurance Corporation and the Federal Trade Commission offer consumer protection rules, guides and publications.

http://www.irs.ustreas.gov/

The Internal Revenue Service provides tax information, forms and publications.

http://www.agin.com/lawfind/

This site provides an extensive list of online bankruptcy-related materials, including other online bankruptcy sites.

Cars and Driving

WHEN SOLOMON SAID THAT THERE WAS
A TIME AND A PLACE FOR EVERYTHING
HE HAD NOT ENCOUNTERED THE PROBLEM
OF PARKING AN AUTOMOBILE.

—BOB EDWARDS

Together, Americans own more than 137 million automobiles—that's at least one car for every 1.7 people in the country. It is not surprising that this average is well above that for the rest of the world, where there is approximately one car for every 12 people. Plainly, Americans love their cars—or at least the mobility they provide. For the privilege of owning and operating a vehicle, we pay an average of more than $3,000 per year. We also expend plenty of time and energy figuring out which cars to buy, how to insure and maintain them, and how keep out of trouble on the road. This chapter provides answers to many of your questions about owning a car and driving responsibly.

Buying a New Car

These days, the average new car costs almost $20,000. For that amount of money, you would hope for a hassle-free buying experience and a safe and reliable product. Unfortunately, new car buyers are frequently overwhelmed with the pressure to buy immediately or spend more than planned, and worse—the product you bring home might be plagued with problems ranging from annoying engine "pings," to frequent stalls, to safety hazards such as poor acceleration or carbon monoxide leaks.

I want to buy a new car, but I'm not sure how to finance my purchase. Do you have any general advice?

Clearly, if you can pay for the purchase outright you'll save money by not paying any interest charges. But if you don't happen to have $20,000 lying around and need to borrow money to buy your new car, consider the following sources:

- *The car dealer.* Many offer generous terms—for example, interest at 1.5% or 2%—especially in the early fall when dealers are anxious to clear out stock to make room for new models. Be careful that these low-interest loans don't require you to buy upgraded features—such as air conditioning or rust protection—or credit insurance.
- *Banks you do business with.* Dealer financing isn't your only option. Before you buy, contact the banks where you have your savings, checking, credit card or business accounts. Ask about the going rate for car loans. Also ask about discount rates for loans tied to your other accounts.
- *Credit union.* If you're a member of a credit union (or are eligible to join one), be sure to investigate its car loans. Historically, credit unions have offered some of the best loan terms.

Do you have any other suggestions for getting a good deal?

First, if you have an old car you're planning to get rid of, you'll probably get more selling it yourself than trading it in with the dealer. A dealer will give you the low *Kelley Blue Book* value at most. (The *Blue Book* is an annual publication listing wholesale and retail prices for cars by year and model. You can find it online at http://www.kbb.com.) Also, take a look at local classified ads to get an idea of how much your old car is likely to bring in if you sell it on your own.

Second, if you have a poor credit history, you'll need to put a substantial amount down (that is, finance very little) or get a cosigner to get a good interest rate.

Third, resist the urge to buy more car than you can afford—and don't talk yourself into a more expensive car by financing it for four or five years. You'll pay a bundle in interest that way. Know in advance what features you want and how much you're willing to pay. Stick to your guns. Hassling over the price of a new car can be quite unpleasant. If it's not something you enjoy, consider turning to a manufacturer or dealer whose price is nonnegotiable.

Comparing New Cars

There are several good sources to help you comparison shop when you're looking for a new car. Each year, *Consumer Reports* magazine publishes an annual car-buying issue, comparing price, features, service histories, resale values and reliability. Other helpful sources of information are *Motor Trend* magazine and *The Car Buyer's Art*, by Darrell Parrish (Book Express).

If I borrow money for the purchase, what should the lender tell me about my loan?

If you get a car loan from a bank, credit union or car dealer, the federal Truth in Lending Act requires that the lender disclose the following information, in writing:

- your right to a written itemization of the amount borrowed
- the total amount of the loan
- the monthly finance charge
- the annual interest rate
- the number, amount and due dates of all payments, and
- if any late payment fee or penalty may be imposed.

What other information do I need to know before I buy my new car?

Be sure you know the following before you sign any contract:
- what the warranty covers and how long it lasts
- how you might negate the warranty coverage (such as driving off-road)
- whether an extended warranty is available to you, and if so, the following:
  - what it will cost
  - what it covers
  - how long it lasts
  - whether it duplicates coverage provided by the manufacturer's warranty
  - how likely it is that you'll need it (whether the covered parts have a history of problems)
- the vehicle's estimated miles per gallon for city and highway driving, and
- the dealer's suggested maintenance schedule.

Don't Pick Up a New Car at Night

Never take delivery of a new vehicle at night. Even though it may be inconvenient to take time off during the day, you'll be able to look the car over carefully in the daylight. At night, even in good artificial light, it's hard to see nicks and dents. Also, you'll miss subtle changes in paint that may indicate that the car was damaged in transit and needed repainting.

If I change my mind after I buy a car, do I have the right to cancel the contract?

No. Unfortunately, many people think they have a right to change their mind, drive the car back to the dealer a day or two after buying, and cancel the contract. But the truth is, the dealer doesn't have to take the car back and probably won't, and you'll be stuck with a car you no longer want or cannot afford. Never buy a car unless you are absolutely certain you want it and can afford it.

This misunderstanding is so widespread that one state—California—requires the following to be included in new car contracts:

California law does not provide for a "cooling off" or other cancellation period for vehicle sales. Therefore, you cannot later cancel this contract simply because you change your mind, decide the vehicle costs too much, or wish you had acquired a different vehicle. After you sign below, you may only cancel this contract with the agreement of the seller or for legal cause, such as fraud.

I bought my car out of state. After I brought it home, I got a huge bill from the state taxing authority. What's it for?

Many people cross state lines to buy a car in a state that has no or a very low sales tax. When this happens, the state that lost the sale also loses sales tax revenue. To counterbalance the loss, that state will often impose a tax, called a "use" tax, on the purchaser of the vehicle. The use tax rate will be identical to your state's sales tax rate, and if you paid any sales tax in the state in which you purchased the vehicle, that amount will be deducted from the use tax bill before your state taxing authority sends it to you.

Soon after I brought my new car home, it started having problems. How do I know if it's a lemon?

An estimated 150,000 vehicles each year (or 1% of new cars) are lemons. To be considered a lemon, two things must be true:

- Your new car must have a "substantial defect" within a certain mileage period, usually 12,000 miles or one year, whichever comes first. (A few states extend this to two years.) A substantial defect is one that impairs the car's use, value or safety, such as brakes or turn signals which don't work. Unfortunately, minor defects, such as loose radio and door knobs—even several minor defects—don't qualify.
- The defect must remain unfixed after three or four repair attempts (depending on the state) or after the car has been in the shop for a cumulative total of 30 days.

What should I do if my new car is a lemon?

If your new car meets the lemon law requirements described above, every state gives you the right to take the manufacturer to arbitration and obtain a refund or replacement vehicle.

To get redress under a lemon law, you must notify the manufacturer of the defect. If you're not offered a satisfactory settlement, you can submit your dispute to arbitration, which is free and designed to take place without a lawyer. Automakers use the following types of arbitration programs:

- in-house programs run by the auto makers
- programs set up by the Better Business Bureau's Auto Line
- programs run by the American Automobile Association or the National Automobile Dealer's Association, and
- programs run through a state consumer protection agency.

You probably won't get to choose which program to use—the manufacturer selects it. If you do have a choice, however, know that consumers who appear before a state consumer protection agency usually fare much better than those who use a manufacturer's in-house program or a private arbitration program run by the BBB, AAA or NADA.

What happens at a lemon law arbitration?

At the arbitration hearing, the arbitrator hears both sides of the dispute. The arbitrator has approximately 60 days to decide if your car is a lemon and if you're entitled to a refund or a replacement. Consumers who bring substantial documentation to the hearing tend to do better than those with little evidence to back up their claims. The types of documentation that can help include:

- brochures and ads about the vehicle —an arbitration panel is likely to make the manufacturer live up to its claims, and
- vehicle service records showing how often you took the car into the shop.

"Secret Warranties"

Many automobile manufacturers have "secret warranty," or warranty adjustment, programs. Under these programs, a manufacturer makes repairs for free on vehicles with persistent problems after a warranty expires in order to avoid a recall and bad press. According to the Center for Auto Safety, at any given time there are a total of 500 secret warranty programs available through automobile manufacturers.

Unfortunately, consumers aren't told of these secret warranties unless they come forward after the warranty has expired, complain about a problem and demand that the manufacturer repair it.

A few states, including California, Connecticut, Virginia and Wisconsin, require manufacturers to tell eligible consumers when they adopt a secret warranty program, usually within 90 days of adopting the program.

What if I don't like the arbitrator's decision?

If you don't like the ruling, you can usually sue the manufacturer in court. You may want to do this if you have substantial "consequential" damages—that is, damages that resulted from owning the lemon, such as the cost of renting a car while your lemon was in the shop or time off from work every time your car broke down.

More Information About Lemons

If you think your new car is a lemon, an excellent book to help you sort out your rights and remedies is *The Lemon Book*, by Ralph Nader & Clarence Ditlow (Center for Auto Safety). It includes a state-by-state explanation of lemon laws.

Leasing a Car

More than one-third of new car owners lease, rather than purchase, their vehicles. Although leasing isn't for everyone, some people swear by it. Before you sign on the dotted line, be sure you know what you're getting into.

What are the advantages of leasing a new car?

There are three main reasons people lease, rather than buy, a new vehicle:

- People who like to drive a new car every few years will pay much less by leasing than if they buy. They also don't have to deal with getting rid of their old car—they just turn it in at the end of the lease period.
- Lease payments are lower than loan payments for any given car.
- Leasing gives people the opportunity to drive a more expensive car than they could afford to buy.

Are there any obvious disadvantages to leasing?

Yes—three in particular.

First, if you continually lease your cars, you will have never-ending car payments. If you look forward to paying off your car and owning it free and clear, don't lease.

Second, if you decide to buy the car at the lease-end, you'll pay several thousands of dollars more than if you had bought initially. For example, if you buy a car, paying $500 a month for four years, you'll pay a total of $24,000. You might be able to lease it for only $400 a month (total payments of $19,200), but you'll probably have to pay another $8,000 to keep it—and if you finance that $8,000, you'll pay even more.

Third, most leases charge you as much as 25¢ a mile if you exceed the annual mileage limit—usually between 12,000 and 15,000 miles. If you do or plan to do extensive driving, leasing probably isn't for you.

Are these costs disclosed up front?

Not necessarily. While the federal Consumer Leasing Act requires lease agreements to include a statement of costs (such as the number and amount of regular payments), terms such as insurance requirements and the penalty for defaulting, and whether you are obligated to pay only the monthly payments or whether you'll have a balloon payment at the end, many lease agreements are ambiguously drafted, with key provisions buried in the fine print.

Even the revised regulations— which strengthened the existing disclosures and added others—do not eliminate all of the abuses. For example, the revised law does not obligate a dealer to disclose the interest rate that's been built into your payments. If you want to lease, you'll have to be a diligent consumer willing to read all the fine print—ask a lot of questions and demand that the answers be put in writing.

Is there any way to find out the interest rate on a lease?

Yes. Ask the dealer for something called the "leasing factor." Multiply that factor by 24 and you'll get the approximate interest rate.

Are there any good leasing deals?

Yes—especially those heavily advertised by car manufacturers. Those deals usually offer low monthly payments or a high value for the vehicle at the end (so that you're not paying for a lot of depreciation during the lease term), and offer to lock-in the price you'd have to pay at lease-end if you want to keep the vehicle.

To get these good deals, you cannot deviate from the advertised terms. If you want air conditioning, a larger engine or any other feature that's not in the ad, the dealer will throw out the entire lease offer and you'll wind up paying a bundle.

Another way to get a good deal is to explore financing your lease through someone other than the dealer. A number of independent companies offer leases—look for these companies in your telephone Yellow Pages under "Automotive—Leasing." Also, if you belong to a credit union or AAA, ask about the possibility of financing your lease through them. Such deals are still in their infancy, but are catching on.

When buying a new car, I usually shop in the fall when dealers are trying to get rid of old inventory. Does this strategy work for leasing?

In general, no. Because dealers have lost money on cars sitting in their lots, they often increase the monthly lease payments to make up for lost revenue.

If I do lease a vehicle, who pays for maintenance and repairs?

Your lease agreement will specify who must pay. In addition, the agreement should come with a manufacturer's warranty. Ideally, it will cover the entire length of the lease and the number of miles you are likely to drive.

Most lease agreements obligate you to pay for "excessive wear and tear." This means that when you return the vehicle at lease-end, the dealer could charge you to fix anything deemed "excessive." You can avoid this by insisting that the dealer specify in writing exactly what is meant by "excessive" before you sign the lease contract.

Finally, look for a deal that includes "gap" insurance. If the vehicle is stolen or totaled, gap insurance will pay the difference between what you owe under the lease and what the dealer can recover on the vehicle (assuming it's not stolen)—a difference that could amount to thousands of dollars.

Can I cancel my lease agreement early?

Probably not, unless you're willing to pay a substantial penalty. If you want to cancel your lease, look carefully at the provision describing what happens if you default or want to terminate the lease early. The provision may include a claim that you'll owe an enormous sum of money, or may use a complex formula to calculate what you owe.

While the federal Consumer Leasing Act gives you the right to cancel the lease if the termination formula is so complex that you can't easily figure out how much you owe, this will be hard for you to assert with success. Lawyers for car manufacturers have rewritten lease contracts to avoid most of the ambiguities because of successful consumer lawsuits.

Even so, if you can't understand the formula, write to the dealer stating that you want to terminate the lease early but that the termination provision of the lease agreement is ambiguous. State further that you know you are entitled to sue for damages because of the dealer's failure to use a reasonable formula. Finally, state that you are willing to waive your right to sue if the dealer will waive the balance you owe. Because the dealer probably won't back off, consider hiring a lawyer to write some letters for you.

If you can't get the dealer to drop his claim that you owe money, you can try to negotiate to reduce your payments or to extend them over time.

Buying a Used Car

HORSEPOWER WAS A WONDERFUL

THING WHEN ONLY HORSES HAD IT.

—ANONYMOUS

While buying a used car might be the only way you can afford a new set of wheels, it's a transaction ripe with potential disaster. We probably all know someone who bought a used car—assured that "my grandmother drove it once a week for ten years to church and the grocery store"—only

to have it need $5,000 of work shortly after bringing it home.

How do I go about finding a used car?

It's best if you have some idea of the make, model and year that you're interested in. There are many good sources to help you compare cars. *Consumer Reports* magazine publishes an annual car-buying issue, comparing price, features, service histories, resale values and reliability. Other sources of information are *Motor Trend* magazine and *Used Cars,* by Darrell Parrish (Book Express). Once you've made this preliminary decision, look at the listings in your local newspaper. Don't forget weekly advertising papers or local automobile publications as well. Call any mechanics that you know and trust to see if they have any vehicles available or know of any. Finally, check with car dealers; they often have used cars that people have traded in to reduce the purchase price on their new cars.

How much should I spend on a used car?

Check the wholesale and retail values of the cars that interest you. Bookstores and libraries have copies of the *Kelley Blue Book,* or you can find it online at http://www.kbb.com. Lenders and insurance companies should be able to give you the same information.

You can also pay to get the information. For example, *Consumer Reports* (900-446-0500) will send or fax you price information on used cars.

Once you know the vehicle's wholesale and retail values, you'll want to pay wholesale (the lower number) and the seller will want to charge retail (the higher number). You'll probably settle somewhere in between. Your final price will depend on a number of factors, including the condition of the car and the person from whom you buy it.

Obviously, price isn't the only factor to consider when buying a used car. What else do I need to know?

With used cars, reliability is more important than price. Consider doing the following:

- Have the car checked out by a mechanic you trust.
- Have the car inspected by a diagnostic center. These businesses will check virtually every aspect and component of a car. They're more expensive—but more thorough— than a mechanic.

- Ask for copies of the maintenance records for the life of the car.
- Ask your state motor vehicles department to tell you who has owned the car, the mileage each time it has been sold and all states (other than where you live) where the car has been registered.
- Do your own visual inspection— you'll want to look for oddities that might indicate damage (such as scratches or new paint).

Also, look at the vehicle identification number (VIN) on the lower left-hand side of the front windshield. If it shows any signs of tampering, the car may be stolen. And finally, if you're buying the car from a private party (as opposed to a car dealer), make sure the person selling the car actually holds title. Ask to see the seller's driver's license (or other form of ID) and the title certificate for the vehicle.

Will a warranty protect me if I get a bad deal on a used car?

If you're buying a used car from a dealer, the dealer will probably offer you an extended warranty. Before buying, be sure you know exactly what is covered and what isn't, and for how long. You'll also need to know the type of problems the car has had in the past, and what types of problems that particular make of car is likely to have in the future. It makes no sense to buy an extended warranty that doesn't cover emissions, for example, if the type of car you're buying is likely to have emission problems in a year or so.

If you're buying a car from a private party, check to see if the car is still under a factory warranty or if the original owner purchased an extended warranty—and whether either of these warranties can be transferred to you as the new owner.

Used Car "Lemon Laws"

Connecticut, Massachusetts, New York and Rhode Island have lemon laws for used cars. If you're in one of these states and you buy a used car that turns out to be defective, contact your state attorney general or department of consumer affairs for the details of the law and how you can get redress under it.

Insuring Your Car

Certainly those so inclined can have lots of fun imagining possible needs for insurance.

—HAYDEN CURRY

Most states require that every registered vehicle or licensed driver have some vehicle liability insurance. But even where it's not required by law, most drivers have some liability coverage. Before you buy auto insurance, you must decide how much coverage you need and what types of coverage are appropriate for you. And of course, you'll want to find ways to cut your insurance costs.

Who is usually covered under an auto insurance liability policy?

An auto insurance liability policy usually covers the following people:

- *Named insured*—the person or people named in the policy, no matter what car they are driving.
- *Spouse*—even if the spouse of the named insured is not named on a policy, liability insurance almost always covers him or her, unless the couple does not live together.
- *Other relative*—anyone living in the household with the named insured who is related to the insured by blood, marriage or adoption, usually including a legal ward or foster child.
- *Anyone driving the insured vehicle with permission*—someone who steals the car is not covered.

Which vehicles are normally covered under an auto insurance liability policy?

- *Named vehicles*—an accident in a nonnamed vehicle is covered only if a named insured (see above) was driving.
- *Added vehicles*—any vehicle with which the named insured replaces the original named vehicle, and any additional vehicle the named insured owns during the policy period (you may be required to notify the company of the new or different

vehicle within 30 days after you acquire it).

- *Temporary vehicles*—any vehicle, including a rental vehicle, that substitutes for an insured vehicle that is out of use because it needs repair or service, or has been destroyed.

What kinds of damage are covered under an auto insurance liability policy?

Liability insurance covers medical costs for diagnosis and treatment of injuries, property damage, loss of use of damaged property, expenses incurred (such as the cost of renting a replacement vehicle) and lost income.

In addition, an injured person is entitled to a certain amount of "general damages," also referred to as pain and suffering.

What is uninsured motorist coverage?

If you have an accident with an uninsured vehicle or hit-and-run driver, the place to turn for compensation for your injuries is the uninsured motorist (UM) coverage of your own vehicle insurance policy. Normally, UM coverage does not include property damage to your own vehicle. Damage to your vehicle caused by an uninsured motorist would be covered by the collision coverage of your own policy.

Most UM coverage will pay up to your policy's UM limits for injuries caused to:

- you or a relative who lives with you, while a driver or passenger in the vehicle named in your UM insur-

ance policy or any other vehicle, or while a pedestrian
- anyone else driving your insured vehicle with your permission, and
- anyone else riding in the vehicle named in your insurance policy, or in any other vehicle you are driving but which you do not own.

What are the limits on my ability to collect under an uninsured motorist provision?

UM coverage usually limits your ability to collect—and the amount you receive—as follows:

- If your accident involves a hit-and-run driver, you must notify the police within 24 hours of the accident.
- If your accident involves a hit-and-run driver, the driver's car must have actually hit you—being forced off the road by a driver who disappears is not sufficient.
- Your UM coverage will be reduced by any amounts you receive under other insurance coverage, such as your personal medical insurance or any applicable workers' compensation coverage.
- If you or a relative are injured by an uninsured motorist while you are in someone else's car, your UM coverage will be secondary to the UM coverage of that other car's owner.

What is collision coverage?

Collision coverage pays for property damage to your vehicle resulting from a collision.

What is comprehensive coverage?

Comprehensive coverage pays for property damage to your vehicle resulting from anything other than a collision, such as a theft or a break-in.

What is no-fault automobile insurance?

No-fault coverage insurance eliminates injury liability claims and lawsuits in small accidents. It does so by requiring that each injured person's own insurance company pay for his or her medical bills and lost wages—up to certain dollar amounts—regardless of who was at fault.

About half the states have some form of no-fault law, often referred to in policies as Personal Injury Protection (PIP). The advantage of no-fault insurance is prompt payment of medical bills and lost wages without any arguments about who caused the accident. But most no-fault insurance provides extremely limited coverage:

- No-fault pays benefits for medical bills and lost income only. It provides no compensation for pain, suffering, emotional distress, inconvenience or lost opportunities.
- No-fault coverage does not pay for medical bills and lost income higher than the PIP limits of each person's policy. PIP benefits often fail to reimburse fully for medical bills and lost income.
- No-fault often does not apply to vehicle damage; those claims are paid under the liability insurance of the person at fault, or by your own collision insurance.

My auto insurance rates seem to keep going up. How can I cut some of the cost?

Here are a few suggestions for ways to reduce your premiums:

- Shop around for insurance. Just because your current company once offered you the best deal doesn't mean it's still competitive.
- Increase your deductibles.
- Reduce your collision or comprehensive coverage on older cars.
- Find out what discounts are available from your company (or from a different company). Discounts are often given to people who:
  - use public transit or carpool to work
  - take a class in defensive driving (especially if you are older)
  - own a car with safety features such as airbags or anti-lock brakes
  - install anti-theft devices
  - are students with good academic records
  - have no accidents or moving violations, or
  - have multiple insurance policies with the same company—such as automobile and homeowner's insurance.
- Find out which vehicles cost more to insure. If you're looking to buy a new car, call your insurance agent and find out which cars are expensive to repair, targeted by thieves or involved in a higher rate of accidents. These vehicles all have higher insurance rates.

• Consolidate your policies. Most of the time you will pay less if all owners or drivers who live in the same household are on one policy or at least are insured with the same company.

When No-Fault Benefits Aren't Enough

All no-fault laws permit an injured driver to file a liability claim, and lawsuit if necessary, against another driver who was at fault in an accident. The liability claim permits an injured driver to obtain compensation for medical and income losses above what the PIP benefits have paid, as well as compensation for pain, suffering and other general damages.

Whether and when you can file a liability claim for further damages against the person at fault in your accident depends on the specifics of the no-fault law in your state. Some states have "add-on" no-fault laws that put no restrictions on your right to file a liability claim in addition to your PIP claim. In these states, you can always file a liability claim against the person at fault for all damages in excess of your PIP benefits.

Other no-fault states have different types of thresholds that an injured person must reach before being permitted to file a claim for full compensation against those at fault for an accident. Some states have a monetary threshold only, some a serious injury threshold only, and still others have both. States with both requirements permit a liability claim if an injured person meets either one.

More Information About Insuring Your Car

How to Insure Your Car, by The Merritt Editors (Merritt Publishing), is a step-by-step guide to buying the right kind of auto insurance at a price you can afford.

Your Driver's License

To a teenager, a driver's license seems magical—a ticket to freedom. For the rest of us, driver's licenses aren't much more than scraps of paper or plastic bearing bad pictures. But every now and then a question may arise about a license: Is it still good if I move to another state? What if I take a trip to a foreign country? And how do I know if I'm in danger of losing my license?

State laws governing how you can get, use and lose your driver's license vary tremendously. We can't answer every question here, but we do discuss some of the bigger issues that arise in connection with driving privileges.

Is my driver's license good in every state?

If you have a valid license from one state, you may use it in other states that you visit. But if you make a permanent move to another state, you'll have to take a trip to the local department of motor vehicles to apply for a new license. Usually, you must do this within 30 days after moving to the new state. Most states will issue your new license without requiring tests, though some may ask you to take a vision test and a written exam covering basic driving rules.

In some situations, you may be unsure as to whether you need to apply for a new license. If you make frequent business trips to another state, or even if you attend school in a state away from home, there's no need to get another driver's license. But when you set up housekeeping in the new state and pay taxes there as well, it's time to apply.

Young Drivers Who Cross State Lines

Adults who visit another state may rely on their driver's licenses, but the same may not be true for young drivers. The driving age varies significantly from state to state (from 15 to 21), and a state that makes people wait longer to drive may not honor a license from a state that issues licenses to younger folks. For example, New Jersey issues licenses to 17-year-olds, and will recognize a license from any other state if the driver is at least 17. But a16-year-old who is legally permitted to drive in New York may not be allowed to drive in New Jersey. A young driver who plans to drive in another state where the legal limit is above his or her age should call that state's department of motor vehicles to find out what the rules are.

If I get a ticket in another state, will it affect my license?

Forty-five states belong to an agreement called the "Driver's License Compact." (The only states that don't belong are Georgia, Massachusetts, Michigan, Tennessee and Wisconsin.) When you get a ticket in one of these states, the department of motor vehicles will relay the information to your state—and the violation will add points to your driving record as if the ticket had been given at home.

Can I use my license in a foreign country?

Many countries, including the United States, have signed an international agreement allowing visitors to use their own licenses in other nations. Before traveling to another country, contact its consulate office or embassy to find out whether your license will be sufficient; you can find the phone number in your telephone book's white pages under the name of the country.

In addition, you may want to obtain an International Driver's Permit, issued by the American Automobile Association. This document translates the information on your driver's license into ten languages. Many countries require the permit, not because it meets their requirements for a license, but because it is a ready-made copy of the important information on your American license.

Finally, if you intend to stay in another country for an extended period of time, you should check with the consular office to find out whether you'll need to apply for a license in that country. Every country will have its own rules about when a "visit" turns into something more permanent.

When can my driver's license be suspended or revoked?

Driving a car is considered a privilege—and a state won't hesitate to take it away if a driver behaves irresponsibly on the road. A state may temporarily suspend your driving privileges for a number of reasons, including:
- driving under the influence of alcohol or drugs
- refusing to take a blood-alcohol test
- driving without liability insurance
- speeding
- reckless driving
- leaving the scene of an injury accident
- failing to pay a driving-related fine
- failing to answer a traffic summons, or
- failing to file an accident report.

In addition, many states use a "point" system to keep track of a driver's moving violations: Each moving violation is assigned a certain number of points. If a driver accumulates too many points within a given period of time, the department of motor vehicles suspends her license.

If you have too many serious problems as a driver, your state may take away (revoke) your license altogether. If this happens, you'll have to wait a certain period of time before you can apply for another license. Your state

may deny your application if you have a poor driving record or fail to pass any required tests.

Finally, a few states revoke or refuse to renew driver's licenses of parents who owe back child support. (See Chapter 16, *Parents and Children*, for more information.)

My elderly friend is becoming unsafe at the wheel. Will her license be taken away?

The number of drivers over 65 years old has more than doubled in the last 20 years. At present, there are 13 million older drivers; by the year 2020 there will be 30 million. Studies show that, as a group, older drivers drive less than younger drivers, but they have more accidents per mile.

Elderly, unsafe drivers who continue to drive despite the advice of family and friends often do not come to the attention of the state until the inevitable—the driver is stopped for erratic driving or, worse, he or she is involved in an accident. A few states try to screen out unsafe older drivers by requiring more frequent written tests. But the added tests are expensive and don't always identify unsafe driving habits.

All licensing departments accept information from police officers, families and physicians about a driver's abilities. If a licensing agency moves to cancel someone's license as the result of an officer's observations, an accident or the report of family members or a doctor, the driver usually has an opportunity to protest.

What will happen if I'm caught driving with a suspended or revoked license?

You'll probably be arrested. Driving with a suspended or revoked license is usually considered a crime that carries a heavy fine and possibly even jail time. At worst, it may be a felony; you'll end up in state prison or with an obligation to perform many hours of community service. The penalties will probably be heaviest if the suspension or revocation was the result of a conviction for driving under the influence of alcohol or drugs (DUI).

The Whole Truth and Nothing but the Truth

Many states will ask you specific questions regarding your health when you renew your driver's license. For example, you might receive a questionnaire that asks you whether you have ever had seizures, strokes, heart problems, dizziness, eyesight problems or other medical troubles. If you have medical problems and answer the questions truthfully, an examiner may question you further and may even deny you a license. If you don't tell the truth, you may get your license—but you're setting yourself up for big legal trouble if you are in an accident caused by one of these impairments. It's not that different from driving a car when you know the brakes are bad: If you go out on the road with defective

equipment that you know about (including the driver), you greatly increase the chance that you will be held responsible if the defect causes an accident.

If You're Stopped by the Police

You can lead a car to the highway, but you can't make it think.

—ANONYMOUS

Most of us know the fear of being pulled over by the police. An officer may stop your car for any number of reasons, including an equipment defect (such as a burned-out taillight), expired registration tags, a moving violation or your car's resemblance to a crime suspect's car. You may also have to stop if you encounter a police roadblock or sobriety checkpoint.

What should I do if a police officer pulls me over?

Remain as calm as possible, and pull over to the side of the road as quickly and safely as you can. Roll down your window, but stay in the car—don't get out unless the officer directs you to do so. It's a good idea to turn on the interior light, turn off the engine, put your keys on the dash and place your hands on top of the steering wheel. In short, make yourself visible and do nothing that can be mistaken for a dangerous move. For example, don't reach for a purse or backpack or open the glove box unless you've asked the officer's permission, even if you are just looking for your license and registration card. The officer may think you're reaching for a weapon.

When the officer approaches your window, you may want to ask (with all the politeness you can muster) why you were stopped. If you are at all concerned that the person who stopped you is not actually a police officer (for example, if the car that pulled you over is unmarked), you should ask to see the officer's photo identification along with her badge. If you still have doubts, you can ask that the officer call a supervisor to the scene or you can request that you be allowed to follow the officer to a police station.

If an officer pulls me over, can she search my car?

Yes, if the officer reasonably suspects criminal activity or if she fears for her safety. A solid hunch is all that's required, and the search may be valid even if the real reason behind the officer's decision to enforce a traffic law was her feeling that you were doing something illegal.

If the officer has reason to think that you pose a danger to her safety, she is allowed to search you and the immediate area around you (this may include the passenger compartment of your car and its contents—such as bags or a briefcase—and your glove compartment). For example, a driver who is belligerent and threatening might be asked to step out of the car for a pat-down while the passenger compartment, including a duffel bag, is searched for weapons.

If my car is towed and impounded, can the police search it?

Yes. If your car is impounded, the police are allowed to conduct a thorough search of it, including its trunk and any closed containers that they find inside. This is true even if your car was towed after you parked it illegally, or if the police recover your car after it is stolen.

The police are required, however, to follow fair and standardized procedures when they search your car, and may not stop you and impound your car simply to perform a search.

I was pulled over at a roadblock and asked to wait and answer an officer's questions. Is this legal?

Yes, as long as the police use a neutral policy when stopping cars (such as stopping all cars or stopping every third car) and minimize any inconvenience to you and the other drivers. The police can't single out your car unless they have good reason to believe that you've broken the law.

Drunk Driving

If you're caught while driving drunk or under the influence of drugs, you'll face serious legal penalties. Many states will put you in jail, even for a first offense, and almost all will impose hefty fines. If you're convicted more than once, you may also lose your driver's license.

How drunk or high does someone have to be before he can be convicted of driving under the influence?

In most states, it's illegal to drive a car while "impaired" by the effects of alcohol or drugs (including prescription drugs). This means that there must be enough alcohol or drugs in the driver's body to prevent him from thinking clearly or driving safely. Many people reach this level well before they'd be considered "drunk" or "stoned."

How can the police find out whether a driver is under the influence?

Police typically use three methods of determining whether a driver has had too much to be driving:

- *Observation.* A police officer will pull you over if he notices that you are driving erratically—swerving, speeding, failing to stop or even driving too slowly. Of course, you may have a good explanation for your driving (tiredness, for example), but an officer is unlikely to buy your story if he smells alcohol on your breath or notices slurred words or unsteady movements.
- *Sobriety tests.* If an officer suspects that you are under the influence, he will probably ask you to get out of the car and perform a series of balance and speech tests, such as standing on one leg, walking a straight line heel-to-toe or reciting a line of letters or numbers. The officer will look closely at your eyes, checking for pupil enlargement or constriction, which can be evidence of intoxication. If you fail these tests, the officer may arrest you or ask you to take a chemical test.
- *Blood-alcohol level.* The amount of alcohol in your body is understood by measuring the amount of alcohol in your blood. This measurement can be taken directly, by drawing a sample of your blood, or it can be calculated by applying a mathematical formula to the amount of alcohol in your breath or urine. Some states give you a choice of whether to take a breath, blood or urine test—others do not. If you test at or above the level of intoxication for your state (.08 to .10 percent blood-alcohol concentration, depending on the state), you are presumed to be driving under the influence unless you can convince a judge or jury that your judgment was not impaired and you were not driving dangerously. Defense attorneys often question the validity of the conversion formula when driver's alcohol levels are based on breath or urine tests.

Do I have to take a blood, breath or urine test if asked to do so by the police?

No, but it may be in your best interests to take the test. Many states will automatically suspend your license if you refuse to take a chemical test. And if your drunk driving case goes to trial, the prosecutor can tell the jury that you wouldn't take the test, which may lead the jury members to conclude that you refused because you were, in fact, drunk or stoned.

Am I entitled to talk to an attorney before I decide which chemical test to take?

The answer depends on where you live. In California, for example, you don't have the right to speak with an attorney first. But many other states, including Arizona and Kansas, allow you to talk to your lawyer before you take a chemical test.

On the way to the police station, the officer asked me how much I had to drink—without reading me my rights. Can my answers be used against me in court?

Yes, they can. In most situations, this type of questioning would be a violation of your constitutional rights. But the U.S. Supreme Court has held that drunk driving cases are different from most, and that officers may ask you questions while you're riding in the back of the police car—without reading you your rights (including the right to remain silent, the warning that anything you say may be used against you at trial and the right to have a lawyer).

When to Get a Lawyer

Defending against a charge of drunk driving is tricky business. Defenders need to understand scientific and medical concepts, and must be able to question tough witnesses, including scientists and police officers. If you want to fight your DUI charge, you're well advised to hire an attorney who specializes in these types of cases.

Traffic Accidents

Anyone who drives or rides in a car long enough is likely to be involved in at least a minor fender-bender. Anyone who rides a bicycle or motorcycle knows the roads are even more dangerous for two-wheelers. And on our crowded streets, pedestrians, too, are often involved in accidents with buses, cars and bikes. Knowing a few laws of the road, and the best steps to take when an accident occurs, can help ease the pain of any accident that occurs—and help make any claims process involved less painful, too.

What should I do if I'm involved in a traffic accident?

The most important thing you can do is to document the entire situation by taking careful notes soon after your accident. While this step is often overlooked, it can help make the entire claim process easier on you—and increase your chances of receiving all the compensation to which you are entitled. Having notes to remind you of all the details of what happened, and what you went through, is far easier and far more accurate than relying on your memory.

Write things down as soon as you can: begin with what you were doing and where you were going, the people you were with, the time and the weather. Include every detail of what you saw, heard and felt. Be sure to add anything you remember hearing anyone—a person involved in the accident or a witness—say about the accident.

Finally, make daily notes of the effects of your injuries. You may suffer pain, discomfort, anxiety, loss of sleep or other problems which are not as visible or serious as another injury, but for which you should demand additional compensation. These notes can be very useful two or six or ten months later, when you put together all the important facts into a final demand for compensation.

Reporting to the DMV

Many states have laws requiring that people involved in a vehicle accident resulting in physical injury or a certain amount of property damage report that accident in writing to the state's department of motor vehicles. Check with your insurance agent or your local department of motor vehicles to find out the time limits for filing this report; you often have just a few days. Be sure to ask whether you'll need any specific form for the report.

If you must file a report, and the report asks for a statement about how the accident occurred, give only a very brief statement—and admit no responsibility for the accident. Similarly, if the official form asks what your injuries are, list every injury and not just the most serious or obvious. An insurance company could later have access to the report, and if you have admitted some fault in it, or failed to mention an injury, you might run into some trouble explaining yourself.

What determines who is responsible for a traffic accident?

Figuring out who is at fault in a traffic accident is a matter of deciding who was careless. And for vehicle accidents, there is a set of official written rules telling people how they are supposed to drive and providing guidelines by which liability may be measured. These rules of the road are the traffic laws everyone must learn to pass the driver's license test. Complete rules are contained in each state's Vehicle Code, and they apply not only to automobiles but also to motorcycles, bicycles and pedestrians.

Sometimes a violation of one of these traffic rules is obvious and was clearly the cause of an accident—for example, when one driver runs a stop sign and crashes into another. In other situations, whether or not there was a violation will be less obvious—a common example is a crash that occurs when drivers merge into a single lane of traffic. And at other times, there may have been a traffic violation that had no part in causing the accident, and therefore should not affect who is liable.

What if the cause of the accident is not clear?

It is sometimes difficult to say that one particular act caused an accident. This is especially true if what you claim the other driver did is vague or seems minor. But if you can show that the other driver made several minor driving errors or committed several minor traffic violations, then you can argue that the combination of those actions caused the accident.

Special Rules for No-Fault Policyholders

Almost half the states have some form of no-fault auto insurance, also called Personal Injury Protection. (See *Insuring Your Car*, above.)

In general, no-fault coverage eliminates injury liability claims and lawsuits in smaller accidents in exchange for direct payment by the injured person's own insurance company of medical bills and lost wages—up to certain dollar amounts—regardless of who was at fault for the accident. No-fault often does not apply at all to vehicle damage; those

claims are still handled by filing a liability claim against the one who is responsible for the accident, or by looking to your own collision insurance.

How can I help prove to an insurance company that the other driver was at fault?

One place to look for support for your argument that the other driver was at fault is in the laws that govern driving in your state—the Vehicle Code. A simplified version of these laws, sometimes called "The Rules of the Road," is often available at your local department of motor vehicles office. The complete Vehicle Code is also available at many local department of motor vehicles offices, most public libraries and all law libraries; there is a law library at or near every courthouse and at all law schools.

In the index at the end of the last volume of the Vehicle Code are references to many rules of the road, one or more of which might apply to your accident. A librarian may be willing to help you with your search, so don't be afraid to ask. If you believe a rule might apply to your accident, copy not only its exact wording but also the Vehicle Code section number so that you can refer to it when you negotiate a settlement of your claim.

Can I be found liable if my car is rear-ended in a crash?

In some situations, both you and the car behind you will be stopped when a third car runs into the car behind you and pushes it into the rear of your car.

In that case, it is the driver of the third car who is at fault and against whose liability insurance you would file a claim.

Are there any other clear patterns of liability in traffic accidents?

A car making a left turn is almost always liable to a car coming straight in the other direction. Exceptions to this near-automatic liability can occur if:

- the car going straight was going too fast (this is usually difficult to prove)
- the car going straight went through a red light, or
- the left-turn car began its turn when it was safe but something unexpected happened which made it have to slow down or stop its turn.

Whatever the contributing factors, the law says the car making the left turn must wait until it can safely complete the turn before moving in front of oncoming traffic.

Also, as with a rear-end collision, the location of the damage on the cars sometimes makes it difficult for the other driver to argue that the accident happened in some way other than during a left turn. So, if you have had an accident in which you ran into someone who was making a left turn in front of you, almost all other considerations of fault go out the window and the other driver is nearly always liable.

Police Reports: Powerful Evidence

If the police responded to the scene of your accident, particularly if they were aware that anyone was injured, they probably made a written accident report.

Sometimes a police report will plainly state that a driver violated a specific Vehicle Code section and that the violation caused the accident. It may even indicate that the officer issued a citation. Other times, negligent driving is merely described or briefly mentioned somewhere in the report.

Regardless of how specific the report is, if you can find any mention in a police report of a Vehicle Code violation or other evidence of careless driving, it can serve as great support in showing that the other driver was at fault. Naturally, the clearer the officer's statement about fault, the easier your job will be.

http://www.nolo.com
Nolo Press offers self-help information about a wide variety of legal topics, including what to do if you're in an accident.

http://www.kbb.com
Kelley Blue Book can give you the resale and wholesale values of your vehicle, as well as new car prices.

http://www.edmunds.com
Edmund's offers information about buying a new car, including reviews, comparisons, prices and strategies.

http://www.bbb.org/library/ newcar.html
The Better Business Bureau offers tips on buying a new car, including financing suggestions.

http://www.bbb.org/library/ usedcar.html
The Better Business Bureau provides hints and checklists designed to help you through the process of buying a used car.

http://www.nhtsa.dot.gov/ problems
The National Highway Traffic Safety Administration provides recall notices, service bulletins, defect investigations, consumer complaints and other data about vehicle problems.

http://www.leaseguide.com
Automobile Leasing: The Art of the Deal offers information about leasing a car, including frequently asked questions, an auto consumer's lease kit and tips for getting a good deal.

http://www.insure.com
The Insurance News Network provides information about choosing auto insurance, including an interactive experts forum.

http://www.dui.com
The Driver Performance Institutes provide information about driving under the influence.

Traveling

Travel is the frivolous part of serious lives, and the serious part of frivolous ones.

—MADAME SWETCHINE

Each year, Americans spend billions of dollars on traveling. And though most of us fondly recall our annual vacations—the trip to Europe after graduating from college or our children's faces the first time they visited a Disney theme park—we often share with one another the horror stories: The plane that took off

16 hours late, the rental company that charged $1,000 for returning the car with a slight scratch or the tour company that went out of business the night before the trip. The questions and answers in this chapter are designed to help your travels go more smoothly—and to let you know your rights should you encounter troubles along the way.

Airlines

On any given day, over a million Americans take a trip by airplane. Major airlines have become some of the largest and most powerful businesses in the travel industry. Airline travel is subject to federal laws and regulations, although to a much lesser degree than 25 years ago. This deregulation has led to competition among airlines and a variety of benefits for passengers, including fare wars and frequent flyer programs.

How do airlines calculate fares?

The price of most airfares is determined by complicated computer programs which calculate how many passengers are likely to book seats on any given flight. But rather than fly with empty seats, an airline might offer discount fares. Ticket prices may also be affected by competition with other airlines that offer discounted prices. The result is that passengers on the same flight could be paying as many as a dozen different fares.

Electronic Tickets

Most airlines offer electronic tickets as an alternative to standard paper tickets. You are given a record locator number, sent a written receipt and must show your credit card and appropriate photo ID at the airport. Your rights and responsibilities are supposed to be the same with electronic and paper tickets, but new legal issues are sure to arise. For example, if you don't receive a written ticket before you fly and have no opportunity to read its terms, how can you be held to them? Or, if you purchase the ticket shortly before your trip and you don't receive the receipt before you depart, what happens if the airline loses your electronic ticket in its computer? To protect yourself in this situation, note the name of the ticketing agent, as well as the date and time you purchased the electronic ticket. Then ask the agent to fax you an itinerary indicating that you have purchased an electronic ticket.

What's all that fine print on the back of my airline ticket?

The back of all standard airline tickets has at least 11 paragraphs of fine print under the heading "Conditions of Contract." In Paragraph 3 you'll find a statement that various "applicable tariffs" and the "Carrier's Conditions of Carriage and Related Regulations" are incorporated into the contract. This means that each airline has filed with the U.S. Department of Transportation a series of statements about its obligations to its passengers and its limitations of liability. These tariffs and conditions are the terms of your contract with the airline.

The Conditions of Carriage cover everything from the number of bags you can check to the type of compensation you receive if your flight is delayed or canceled. Boarding priority, check-in requirements and most of the other fine-print terms that describe an airline's rights and responsibilities to its passengers are set forth in the Conditions of Carriage.

Conditions of Carriage vary from airline to airline. Although most airline tickets look identical, the subtle differences in the hidden terms can make a substantial difference in your rights as a passenger. You can obtain a summary of the hidden terms and conditions of most major airlines' contracts by requesting a copy of *United States Air Carriers, Conditions of Contract, Summary of Incorporated Terms (Domestic Air Transportation)* from the Air Transport Association, 1301 Pennsylvania Avenue, NW, Suite 1100, Washington, DC 20004, 800-497-3326. (Enclose a $55 check payable to ATAA.) In addition, your travel agent might have a copy.

Are there restrictions on my airline ticket?

Before the substantial deregulation of the airline industry in the 1980s, unused tickets were almost as good as cash—tickets could be cashed in, traded and even used on other airlines. This is still true for many full-fare, unrestricted tickets.

Most tickets, however, carry some sort of restrictions. Today, tickets usually have any or all of the following features:

- *Nontransferable.* A nontransferable ticket can be used only by the passenger whose name appears on the face of the ticket. If the names on the ID and the ticket do not match, the airline can confiscate the ticket. If a ticket is nontransferable but refundable, however, you may be able to cash in the old ticket and buy a new one with the new passenger's name.
- *Nonrefundable.* A nonrefundable ticket means you cannot get your money back if you decide not to travel. But each airline has exceptions. If you cannot make a flight for which you have a nonrefundable ticket, you may be able to apply the ticket toward a future flight or exchange it for credit toward future travel. If the fare has dropped on a flight for which you have a nonrefundable ticket, you

may be able to get "re-ticketed." In either situation, you will probably have to pay a fee to make the change.

- *Penalties.* Often, there are penalties for canceling or making changes.

Do airlines offer discounted tickets or let you change a ticket if you need to travel because of death or serious illness?

In certain exceptional cases, the airlines will allow nonrefundable tickets to be refunded if you need to cancel because of the illness or death of your traveling companion or a close relative. Similarly, an airline may offer a discounted fare (sometimes minor, sometimes generous) when a close relative becomes seriously ill or dies and you need to travel without any advanced planning. Who must be ill or have died for you to obtain a "bereavement fare" varies among airlines —for example, some airlines will give a discounted fare to attend the funeral of a parent, child, sibling, spouse or in-laws only, while other airlines include nonmarital partners and their immediate family members.

What should I do if I lose my ticket?

Contact the airline immediately. You will be required to fill out a lost-ticket application. The airline will either issue a replacement ticket (after you sign an agreement to reimburse it for the cost of the replacement ticket if someone uses your lost ticket) or force you to purchase a replacement ticket at the currently available fare

(often outrageously expensive because you don't get any advance purchase discounts). In addition, you usually have to pay some sort of service charge or penalty for issuing a replacement ticket.

After waiting three months to a year, the airline will issue you a refund for the price of your replacement ticket if your lost ticket was not used during that time.

Am I entitled to be compensated if the airline overbooks and I get bumped off the flight?

If a flight is overbooked, the airline is required to ask passengers to volunteer to take a later flight. Normally, the airline will offer some kind of incentive such as a free domestic or international round-trip ticket. Over 90% of U.S. passengers who are bumped are volunteers. If an insufficient number of passengers volunteer to be bumped from a flight, the airline must begin involuntary bumping. Generally, passengers with the most recent reservations or those who checked in the latest are the first to be bumped.

If you are bumped, you are entitled to compensation if you have a confirmed reservation (your ticket has an "ok" or "hk" in the Status column) and the scheduled plane has a seating capacity of more than 60 passengers. Even if you meet both of these requirements, the airline might refuse to compensate you if any of the following is true:

- You did not comply with the airline's ticketing, check-in and reconfirmation requirements.
- You are not acceptable for transportation under the airline's usual rules and practices—for example, you are drunk.
- The entire flight was canceled.
- A smaller aircraft was substituted for safety or operational reasons.
- You refuse an offer to take a seat in a different section (class) of the aircraft at no extra charge.
- The airline offers to place you on another flight or flights scheduled to reach your final destination within one hour of the scheduled arrival of the original flight.

Am I entitled to compensation if my flight is delayed, diverted or canceled?

A flight is considered on-time if it arrives at its destination within 15 minutes of the scheduled arrival time. Generally, a 15-minute delay will not affect your schedule very much. Longer delays can have serious consequences, particularly if you cannot make a connecting flight.

If your trip is delayed because of overbooking, the rules discussed in the previous question apply. If the delay is caused by any other reason, your rights depend on whether it's a domestic or international flight.

Domestic flights. Generally, airlines are not obliged to provide any compensation if the delay, diversion or cancellation was caused by factors outside of the airline's control, such as bad weather or air traffic congestion

at a particular airport. On the other hand, airlines are required to compensate you for problems deemed in their control, such as mechanical difficulties or late-arriving crew members. The offered compensation can vary substantially among airlines—full-service airlines are likely to offer more generous terms, such as meals, hotels, alternate transportation or even emergency toiletries in the event of an overnight delay, while budget or no-frills airlines may offer little, if any, compensation.

International flights. Recovering damages for an international flight delay is very difficult if the delay was caused by anything other than the airline's overbooking. Under an international treaty called the Warsaw Convention, an airline can escape liability for damages caused by flight delay if it can show that it took all necessary measures to avoid the damage or that it was impossible to take such measures.

If your international flight is delayed, you may be able to persuade the airline that it should cover direct costs caused by the delay, such as meal, hotel or telephone expenses. To back up your argument, you can quote Article 19 of the Warsaw Convention which states: "The Carrier shall be liable for damages occasioned by delay in the transportation by air of passengers, baggage or goods."

Compensation for Involuntarily Bumping
(Flights Within or Leaving U.S.)

Scheduled Arrival of New Flight	Domestic Flights	International Flights (Departing From the U.S.)
New flight scheduled to arrive less than one hour after original flight	No compensation	No compensation
New flight scheduled to arrive between one and two hours after original flight	Value of ticket segment, $200 maximum	Value of ticket segment, $200 maximum
New flight scheduled to arrive more than two hours after original flight (domestic only)	Twice the value of ticket segment, $400 maximum	N/A
New flight scheduled to arrive more than four hours after original flight (international only)	N/A	Twice the value of ticket segment, $400 maximum

Compensation for Involuntarily Bumping
(Flight Departing European Union Country)

Scheduled Duration or Distance of Original Flight	Arrival at Destination	Compensation
Less than two hours or 3,500 kilometers	Within two hours of originally scheduled arrival	75 ECUs (approximately $50)
Less than two hours or 3,500 kilometers	More than two hours late	150 ECUs (approximately $100)
Over two hours or over 3,500 kilometers	Within two hours of originally scheduled arrival	150 ECUs (approximately $100)
Over two hours or over 3,500 kilometers	More than two hours late	300 ECUs (approximately $200)

Am I entitled to compensation if my baggage is lost or damaged?

The airlines' treatment of baggage is a constant source of passenger complaints. At some point, nearly every airline passenger has waited for what seemed like an eternity for his or her baggage to show up on the baggage carousel. Many passengers can identify with the old suitcase commercial which showed a gorilla jumping up and down on the passenger's bags and throwing the passenger's suitcase around a room.

To be fair, most of the time baggage does arrive, in good shape, on the same flight you were on. When your luggage is damaged, delayed or lost, however, the results can be disastrous. The best way to protect yourself from the most serious losses is to follow one simple rule: *Never* put anything valuable or irreplaceable (such as jewelry), or that you might urgently need (such as medications), in checked baggage. Your compensation will rarely cover your actual loss.

Domestic flights. An airline can limit the amount it must pay if baggage is lost, damaged or delayed to $1,250 per passenger. You can get around this limit by declaring at check-in a higher value for the baggage, up to the airline's maximum, which is likely to be between $2,500 and $5,000. If you declare a higher value, the airline will charge you a fee based on a percentage of the declared value. The airline then becomes liable up to the declared value if it loses, damages or delays delivery of the baggage, unless the airline can prove that the actual loss was lower than the declared value.

International flights. The Warsaw Convention provides the rules under which liability for lost, delayed or damaged baggage is determined; these rules will not work to your advantage. Damages are calculated based on the weight of the baggage, regardless of the real value of the baggage or its contents. The Warsaw Convention states that the value for lost or damaged baggage is $9.07 per pound (or $20 per kilogram).

If your bag was weighed before the flight, then the value is determined by multiplying the weight of the bag times $9.07. For example, a 20-pound bag would be valued at $181.40. If your bags were not weighed, the airline will generally assume that all of your bags weighed a total of 70 pounds, and will reimburse you $634.90.

To add insult to injury, an airline can completely avoid responsibility for lost or damaged baggage if it can prove "that the damage was occasioned by error in piloting, in the handling of the aircraft or in navigation" and that, in all other respects, "the airline and its agents have taken all necessary measures to avoid the damage." It is difficult to understand why an airline should not be liable for your lost or damaged baggage if one of its pilots mishandles the airplane. On the other hand, if a pilot seriously mishandles the plane, your baggage may be the least of your concerns.

Are there any legal protections for the credits I earn in a frequent flyer program?

Originally designed as a way to encourage brand loyalty for air travelers, frequent flyer programs seem to have become a permanent fixture in the travel industry. Hotels, rental cars, credit cards and even telephone companies now offer frequent flyer points to entice customers with promises of free travel and other gifts. Airlines have been overwhelmed by the numbers of people who signed up—and by the millions of earned, but not yet claimed, frequent flier miles. As such, airlines are looking for ways to minimize the actual number of free trips they must give away.

While frequent flyer programs can provide you with some travel bargains, understand that there are few legal protections for the credits you earn. Under the rules of almost all frequent flyer programs, the airline can change award levels, have credits expire or even cancel the whole program without warning.

Does it pay to belong to more than one frequent flyer program?

Some travelers will pay more for their tickets if they receive frequent flyer credit or will take an indirect or inconvenient flight on an airline in order to get frequent flyer credit. One way to avoid this frequent flyer trap is to join more than one program. Although you can get travel awards faster by concentrating your travel on one airline, you may get better fares and connections if you don't restrict yourself in that way. When you compare tickets, keep in mind that frequent flyer miles are worth approximately 2¢ per mile; use that figure to help calculate which option is best. The 2¢ per mile estimate was calculated by dividing the average cost of a domestic round trip ticket (approximately $500) by the number of frequent flyer miles needed for such a ticket (25,000 miles).

Can I trade or sell my frequent flyer awards?

You can use your frequent flyer awards or give them to anyone you choose, but you cannot sell or trade them. Despite this clear limitation, frequent flyer awards are often bartered. Many of the deeply discounted tickets advertised in newspapers are actually tickets obtained by agents using purchased frequent flyer awards. Because airlines require you to present a photo ID when you check in and are traveling on a ticket obtained through a frequent flyer program, it is difficult to use these purchased coupons.

I have a ticket on an airline that seems headed for bankruptcy. What can I do?

When an airline goes bankrupt, you technically become one of the airline's creditors in bankruptcy. If you file a claim in the bankruptcy court, there is a chance you will recover some very small percentage of the value of the ticket, but more likely you will recover nothing at all.

In the past, most airlines would honor a bankrupt airline's ticket and allow you on a substitute flight. But these days, given the competitive nature of the airline industry, this is rarely done. Sometimes, as a gesture of good will (and a way of luring new customers), an airline will offer a special discounted fare for passengers holding tickets on a bankrupt airline. If you have a ticket on a bankrupt airline and are a frequent flyer on another airline, try to negotiate free or discounted travel using the bankrupt airline's ticket. Trip cancellation or trip interruption insurance can sometimes cover the cost of a replacement ticket.

Rental Cars

A TOURIST IS A FELLOW WHO TRAVELS

THOUSANDS OF MILES SO HE CAN BE

PHOTOGRAPHED STANDING IN FRONT

OF HIS CAR.

—EMILE GANEST

Whether on business or vacation, you may need to rent a car for at least part of your trip. This section outlines some of your basic rights as a renter. Most laws related to rental cars were enacted by state legislatures or derived from cases interpreting those state laws.

Do I have any recourse if the rental car company doesn't provide me with the type of car I reserved?

If you have guaranteed payment and the company does not have the car you reserved available for you, the company must do everything it can to find you a different car from its fleet. Theoretically, the company must find you a car from another rental car company if it has no suitable substitute, but in practice this rarely happens. If the alternate car found for you is more expensive, you should not have to pay the difference.

If you haven't put down a deposit or guarantee, the company is still required to have a car available. But rental car companies often overbook to cover no-shows, which means that the class of car you reserved won't be available. The rental car company will usually provide you with a larger, more expensive car and tell you it is giving you a "free upgrade." Most renters are happy to accept the upgrade to a larger, more expensive car. If you accept a smaller, cheaper car than the one you reserved, the rental company is obliged to charge you the lower rate. If you refuse to accept a substitute car, you will probably have difficulty getting compensation afterward—you had a duty to reduce your damages by accepting a car that was a reasonable substitute for the car you reserved.

What if the company fails to provide any car at all?

A company's overbooking may mean that no cars are available when you arrive. Your only real alternatives may be to find a substitute rental car at a different company or to take a taxi and seek reimbursement from the original car rental company. In addition, the rental car company may offer you future discounts.

My son was told he couldn't rent a car because he's only 20. Is that legal?

Yes. Most major companies refuse to rent a car to someone who is under 21, or in some cases 25, unless that person is an employee using a corporate account or is military personnel traveling on orders. Companies that do rent to people as young as 21 usually charge an additional fee for drivers between 21 and 24.

This discrimination is not illegal. Rental car companies can do business with whomever they choose, as long as they do not discriminate based on race, religion, national origin, sex or other categories protected under civil rights laws.

Do I need a credit card to rent a car?

Most rental car companies require a major credit card as a way to secure a deposit from you at the time of rental, although you can use the card or cash when you actually pay for the car. The company will check your credit limit and "freeze" an amount slightly greater than your estimated rental charges against your card, meaning that this amount is not available for you to charge. This freeze can last for several days after you return the car, even once the actual amount is charged or you pay with cash.

If you don't have a credit card, you can get a prepaid voucher through your travel agent by paying for the rental car first at the travel agency and bringing the voucher to the rental counter. The voucher may not cover taxes, surcharges, additional drivers, upgrades and other charges, so be sure to find out exactly what is included with the voucher before you pick up the car. Many companies require you to present a credit card or provide some other form of deposit even if you are using a voucher, so call ahead to find out.

Can a rental car company charge a penalty if I don't show up or if I cancel my reservation?

Nearly all rental car companies charge penalties for four-wheel drives, minivans, convertibles and other specialty rentals if you fail to cancel a reservation in advance or are a no-show. Some companies are testing similar policies on their standard rental cars.

Can a rental car company screen me based on my driving record?

Yes, and many companies now screen drivers when they rent in vacation-popular destinations such as Arizona, California, Florida, Nevada, New York, Virginia and Washington, DC.

Sales agents conduct screening checks by entering your license number into a computer program that calls up your driver's record as reported by your state department of motor vehicles. If your record doesn't meet the screening criteria of the rental company, the agent will refuse to rent you a car.

Instead of screening you, some rental car companies may require you to sign a statement that you have an acceptable driving record. This shifts the responsibility for providing accurate information away from the company and to you. If you have an accident and signed a statement that turns out to be incorrect, the rental car company could use it against you by claiming that you acted in violation of the rental agreement.

Screening Standards

Generally, a rental car company that screens drivers will deny you a vehicle if, during the past 36-month period, you:

- were caught driving with a suspended or invalid license
- had one instance of drunk driving, hit-and-run, driving a stolen car or other serious offense
- had three moving violations, or
- were at fault in two accidents.

The standards adopted by each rental car company vary and are subject to change, so you need to inquire about the specific rental screening standards of any company you are considering using.

If your driving record is questionable, do the following:

- Call your motor vehicle department to see if your state makes driver records available. If it doesn't, then relax and don't worry about being screened.
- If your state makes driver records available, when you call to reserve a rental car, ask if the company screens driving records and whether it maintains a nationwide blacklist.
- Get your driver record evaluated by a screening company. Several companies evaluate driving records to determine in advance whether drivers will be disqualified from renting. TML Information Services (800-388-9099), the leading evaluator of vehicle records for rental car companies, operates a program for drivers from states that make driver record data available online. For around $11 (less for AAA members), you can get an evaluation of your driving record against the criteria for screening risky drivers used by six major rental car companies.
- If you don't want to pay for an evaluation, get a copy of your driving record from the motor vehicle agency in your state (allow plenty of time), obtain the screening criteria of the rental car companies you are considering and make an evaluation on your own.
- If you are traveling for business, rent from a company that has a liability agreement with your employer—the screening company may overlook items that would otherwise disqualify you.

Finally, if you are disqualified by a screening system, have someone you are traveling with rent the car and do the driving.

How do rental car companies establish rental rates?

Car rental fees are set by each company and vary depending on the location of the rental office, time period the car will be rented, season, car model, special promotions or vacation packages, and your eligibility for discounts. In addition, because many rental car companies have franchises, the rates and policies of the central office may vary substantially from those of a local office. There is nothing illegal about these multiple prices, and there is nothing to stop you from asking about special fares when you rent or for a reduction after the rental if you learn that a better rate was available but was not offered to you. Although the company is not obligated to offer you the lower price, it may do so to maintain good customer relations.

Can the rental car company tack on other fees?

Yes, but the company must tell you about the fees before you rent. Here are the most common fees you're likely to encounter:

- *Mileage charges.* While many companies offer unlimited mileage, mileage charge policies change frequently, and you should ask each time you rent.
- *Fees for renting at an airport.* Renting at an airport may be more expensive than renting at an urban or suburban location because airports and local governments often add surcharges and taxes to rental car rates.
- *Additional driver fees.* Most rental car companies charge extra for anyone who drives the car other than the person who signs the rental agreement. Often, additional driver charges are waived for your spouse, immediate family member or business associate.
- *Young driver fees.* As indicated above, many rental car companies add a daily surcharge for any driver aged 21 to 24.
- *Child safety seat fees.* All states require children under a certain age to be placed in child car seats. If you don't bring your own seat, you will be required to rent one, usually at a cost of $3-$5 per day or $25 per week. You may be charged more for one-way rentals, and you may be required to make an extra deposit

for the seat if you are paying cash for the car rental.

- *Vehicle drop-off fees.* Many rental car companies charge high rates for dropping off a car at a location other than where you rented, unless the drop-off location is within the same metropolitan area as where you picked up the vehicle. Charges for picking up the car in one city and dropping it off in another can be as high as $1,000.
- *Refueling charges.* Most companies require you to return the rental car with a full tank of gas. If you can't or you forget, you'll be forced to pay the company's inflated price per gallon, as much as $2-$3 for onsite fill up.

Do I have to take the rental car insurance offered to me?

No, and chances are you shouldn't. Each year, travelers in the U.S. spend more than $1 billion on rental car insurance, much of it unneeded or unwanted. A few states, including California, Texas and Indiana, require rental car companies to inform you that the rental car insurance may duplicate your personal automobile policy. But still, rental car insurance options are complex, confusing and rife with potential rip-offs.

When faced with a rental car insurance policy, adopt this basic strategy:
- determine what coverage you already have through your automobile insurance or credit cards— many gold cards issued by Visa and

MasterCard provide rental car insurance coverage; American Express offers coverage as well
- find out what insurance options the rental car company offers, and
- don't fall prey to hardball sales tactics—buy only what you need.

What is loss damage waiver? Is it insurance?

Loss damage waiver, or LDW (also known as collision damage waiver, or CDW), has gotten substantial press in recent years due primarily to its high cost and to complaints by consumers of pressure from rental car companies to purchase unnecessary LDW.

Rental car companies claim that they are not selling insurance, and that LDW is simply a waiver of the company's right to collect from you if the rental car is damaged or stolen while under your control. In most rental contracts, the rental company shifts all responsibility for collision damage or other loss to you; the effect of purchasing LDW is to shift responsibility back to the rental car company. But three aspects of LDW make its value suspect:
- the high pressure or deceptive sales tactics used to sell LDW
- the high price for LDW—especially when you may already be protected by your own insurance or credit card, and
- the number of exclusions (loopholes) in LDW coverage that allow the company to charge you even if you purchased LDW to protect yourself.

Should You Purchase Loss Damage Waiver?

Purchasing loss damage waiver (LDW) may be a prudent choice for you if:

• You're in a foreign country and your auto insurance or credit card coverage does not include foreign rentals.

• You have no personal car insurance and do not want to rely on credit card coverage alone.

• Your personal auto insurance is insufficient to cover a rental vehicle.

• You can't afford to carry any credit charges until the credit card company reimburses you.

• Your rental car isn't covered under your insurance or your credit card coverage (this may be the case if you rent an antique or exotic car).

What should I know before I rent a car in a foreign country?

Although the laws governing car rentals differ in every country, here are some general rules.

First, most countries will accept your valid state driver's license with another form of photo ID. Some countries may also require an International Driver's Permit (available through AAA offices). Check with an AAA travel office before you travel. You don't need to take a test to get an International Driver's Permit; all it does is explain (in a number of languages) the type of license you have, any limitations that apply and when it will expire.

Second, your personal automobile insurance policy may have restrictions or limitations on driving in foreign countries. Check your coverage, including the terms of your credit card policy, before you rent in a foreign country.

Third, in some countries, the police will take your license if you are involved in an accident or stopped for a moving violation, and will not return it until you have paid any applicable fine. Get receipts for all payments you make, and report any mistreatment or apparent scams to the American embassy or consulate in that country.

Fourth, certain European countries track traffic violations with street cameras that photograph cars at intersections. The police trace the drivers using the license plate number of the car and request payment from the rental car company for the ticket. The rental car company is within its rights to collect the fine from you, even if the company is informed of the violation after you have returned and paid for the car.

More Information About Rental Cars

A Consumer's Guide to Renting a Car, Alamo Rental Car, Office of Public Affairs, P.O. Box 22776, Fort Lauderdale, FL 33335, 800-445-5664.

If you will be driving in Europe, the following publications have useful information:

Autorental Europe, by Bill Meier (Lansing Publications, Box 1887, Pleasanton, CA 94566), discusses the rental process and provides detailed specifications of European car models.

Exploring Europe by Car, by Patricia and Robert Foulke (Globe Pequot, Old Saybrook, CT, 800-243-0495), focuses on driving in Europe, with details on driving conditions and rules in different countries.

Motoeuropa, by Eric Bredesen (Seren Publishing), includes country-by-country specifics about renting cars and driving in Europe.

Hotels and Other Accommodations

When you travel, you have the choice of many different types of accommodations: hotels, motels, inns, bed and breakfasts, rental houses and other lodging. With some minor variations, the laws governing most types of accommodations are similar. To sim-plify matters, we use the term "hotel" to cover all types of accommodations.

Must a hotel provide me with a room, assuming there's a vacancy?

Generally, yes. The most basic legal principal concerning hotels is the "duty to receive." Created hundreds of years ago under the common law of England, the duty to receive required hotel keepers to accept and take care of any traveler who presented himself as a paying customer, as long as the inn had room. Although this basic duty to receive has been modified somewhat by state laws, it is still the basis for many of the fundamental obligations that a hotel has to its guests.

A hotel can say "no" only if it reasonably believes that you will:
- not pay for your room
- injure or annoy other guests, or
- physically damage or otherwise harm the hotel (including giving it a bad reputation).

If you arrive drunk and disorderly, threaten another guest or appear to want to use the room for prostitution, you'll probably be turned away.

Must a hotel honor my prepaid or guaranteed reservation?

A prepaid or guaranteed reservation is one where you give the hotel a credit card number and the hotel promises to have a room for you no matter when you show up, even if it's midnight or 3:00 a.m. If you have a guaranteed reservation and the hotel does not hold a room for you, the hotel has breached a contract and must do everything it can to find you a room—even if that means sending you to another hotel. If you guaranteed your reservation with a credit or debit card, the hotel may be required under the terms of its agreement with the card issuer to:

- pay for your first night's stay at an alternate hotel
- provide free transportation to the alternate hotel
- pay for a three-minute phone call to let your family or office know where you'll be staying, and
- forward all incoming calls to your new hotel.

Be sure to request these services. In all cases, if your alternate lodging is more expensive, the hotel should pay the difference.

Is a guaranteed reservation the same as a confirmed reservation?

If you have not paid for the reservation in advance or guaranteed it, but have received a "confirmed reservation" from the hotel, the hotel must keep a room for you unless you haven't met the conditions of the reservation. For example, it is common for a hotel to say, "We will hold the room for you until 6:00 p.m." or, "We will hold the room for you if we receive a written confirmation and deposit" by a certain date. If you do not fulfill these obligations, then the hotel does not have to hold the room for you. If you do meet your obligations and the hotel doesn't have a room for you, it must do its best to find you comparable lodging.

Do I have the right to a particular room?

Generally, no. A hotel manager can put you anywhere or move you from one room to another, as long as it is not done in a discriminatory way. The only exception is if you've reserved a certain room, like the honeymoon suite for your honeymoon.

If it's crucial for you to have a particular room, make sure the hotel management knows in advance and that you receive written confirmation for your reservation of that particular room. If the room you reserved is occupied by other guests, the management may, but is not obligated to, move those guests to another room. (A hotel can satisfy its obligation to you simply by providing a room comparable to the one you reserved.) If the room is uninhabitable (say, a water pipe breaks), then the hotel is excused from providing that particular room.

Do I have a right to privacy in my room?

If you are using your room in a normal way, not engaging in illegal acts or disturbing other guests, then you have a limited right of privacy in your room. But if the hotel management believes that you are carrying out illegal activities (such as dealing drugs), it is entitled to enter and search your room, even without your permission. The hotel management cannot, however, authorize the police to search your room without your permission or a search warrant.

The hotel management also has the right to enter your room to clean or perform needed maintenance, or if necessary, to stop you from disturbing other guests (for example, if you are playing the television very loudly) or destroying hotel property.

It is generally considered a violation of your privacy if the hotel tells an outside person the number of your room. The hotel can tell an inquirer whether you are a guest at the hotel and can connect any caller to your room. If you wish to maintain complete privacy, you must make it clear to the management that you are not to be contacted by anyone and that no one is to be told whether or not you are staying at the hotel.

Why do hotel room rates vary so much?

There is no set formula for determining what amount a hotel can charge, although rates must be "reasonable." Many states require hotels to post the maximum charge for a room in a conspicuous place in each room (usually on the back of the door). Although the hotel may not charge more than this maximum rate (often referred to as the "rack rate"), it certainly may rent the room for less.

Always check your hotel bill to see whether it matches the rate you were quoted when you reserved the room. Frequently, additional charges will be tacked on. Some, such as visitor fees or "bed taxes," may be mandated by local or state law and are probably legitimate.

Other fees, such as service charges or telephone charges, may not be legitimate. A hotel cannot legally charge

you more than the rate it quoted to you when you made your reservation, unless you approve the charges in advance. Many states have laws requiring that all additional charges be posted or approved in writing by guests.

Ask About Discount Rates

When you reserve a hotel room, you may be able to get a reduced price simply by asking about discounts available to the following people:

- corporate employees—many hotels have negotiated rates with large corporations that are 10%-30% lower than their standard rates and these rates are generally available to anyone who asks for them (although an occasional desk clerk will ask for a business card or other ID)
- seniors
- families with children
- AAA members
- members of certain professional associations (like the American Medical Association or American Bar Association)
- guests paying with certain credit cards, or
- members of frequent flyer or frequent guest programs.

I paid a lot for a room that fell way short of my expectations. Is there anything I can do?

Sometimes you may find yourself in a hotel room that looks nothing like the one described to you or pictured in an advertisement or brochure. If the advertisement or description was intentionally deceptive, the hotel may be guilty of fraud. The law generally allows a limited amount of exaggeration or "puffing" in advertisements, but it does not allow intentional deception. When you find yourself in such a situation, your best bet is to talk to the manager immediately—he may be able to reduce your room charge or move you to a better room. If the problem is with the entire hotel, however (for example, it's in a very dangerous neighborhood), you're better off requesting a refund and finding other accommodations.

If your hotel room is unclean or unsanitary, report it to the manager and the housekeeping department immediately. If they are unable to clean your room to your satisfaction, request a new room or a refund. Should you end up in a serious dispute over the cleanliness of a room, the health and safety codes for the city or state where the hotel is located may provide the best support for your argument. Report any serious violation to local health authorities, not only to bolster your claims, but as a service to future guests. Take photographs of the offending conditions if you can.

I fell and hurt myself on a hotel's premises. Do I have any recourse against the hotel?

A hotel may be liable if you slip or trip and fall on the hotel premises— for example, on spilled food or drink in a hotel bar or restaurant, on snow and ice that has not been cleared from a walkway, or on moist tile floors or other slick surfaces. You might also be hurt because of a design or building flaw (such as steps that are too steep) or the hotel's failing to light an area properly.

Does a hotel have any special obligation to protect its guests around the swimming pool?

Because swimming pools create a potentially dangerous situation, hotels must be especially vigilant in designing, maintaining and controlling access to them. Disclaimers such as "swim at your own risk" are unlikely to protect a hotel from liability if it didn't use sufficient care to protect its guests, such as failing to install a fence around a pool. This is true even if you are drunk. Most courts require hotels to anticipate that children, inebriated guests and others might find their ways into the pool if safeguards don't keep them out.

Is the hotel responsible if I am the victim of a crime at or near the hotel?

A hotel cannot be held liable for crimes committed on or near the hotel unless it should have anticipated the crime (for example, the hotel is in a very high crime area) and could have prevented it, either by providing sufficient warnings or taking better security measures. In such situations, the hotel's general duty to warn you about dangerous conditions may extend to a duty to warn about crime in or around the hotel. Furthermore, the hotel's actions—such as failure to install proper locks on windows and doors, provide adequate lighting in parking areas or take adequate measures to ensure that passkeys are not used by criminals—may make the hotel at least partially liable.

Is the hotel responsible if my belongings are stolen?

Traditionally, hotels were liable for virtually all loss or theft of a guest's property. Today, however, most states limit a hotel's liability if it takes certain steps to protect your belongings. For cash, jewelry and other valuables, a hotel is required to provide a safe. Most states require the hotel to tell you that the safe is available, that the hotel has limited liability for valuables left in the safe and that the hotel may have no liability if you do not place valuables in the safe.

The limitation of liability also includes a limitation for clothing and other personal goods you bring to the hotel. While you are not required to check expensive suits or mink stoles at the front desk as valuables, clothing and expensive luggage often exceed the amount of the hotel's maximum liability.

Generally, these limited liability laws were passed to protect hotels from forces beyond their control, such as fire or theft. If the hotel fails to use reasonable care to protect your valuables (for example, it leaves the safe unlocked), it will probably be liable for the full value of your loss.

Is the hotel liable if my car is damaged, broken into or stolen?

Traditionally, hotels were strictly liable for protecting your means of transportation. This meant caring for your horses, saddles, tack and the rest. These days, hotels are required to use reasonable care to protect your car. Many state laws set a monetary limit for loss or damage to a vehicle or its contents. But even in these states, negligence by the hotel—including the valet—could make the hotel liable for damage it should have foreseen.

Whether the contents of a car parked at a hotel are the hotel's responsibility is not clear. They do not fall into the traditional categories of goods within the hotel or transportation. The hotel is most likely to be liable when you pay for parking, a valet or other employee takes your car, retains the keys and is informed of the value of the contents of the car.

What if I don't check out when I say I will?

In most states, renting a hotel room gives you what is called a "revocable license" to use the room. This right is much more limited than the rights a tenant has when renting an apartment. Formal eviction proceedings don't have to be brought if you overstay your welcome. The hotel can simply change the lock (easy to do today because hotels often use preprogrammed entry cards, not keys) and pack up your items.

Travel Agents

One of the most common disruptions of marital bliss is the choice of where to spend a vacation. What this country needs is an ocean in the mountains.

—PAUL SWEENEY

At some point you're likely to rely on a travel agent—someone authorized to sell travel services to the public—to help you make decisions about where, when and how to travel. In the U.S., travel agents arrange 80% of all air travel, 95% of all cruise reservations, 30% of all car rentals and many hotel reservations. A travel agent's legal responsibilities vary depending on the role the agent plays in helping with your plans.

Does a travel agent work for me or for the travel industry?

A travel agent generally owes his highest duty to a travel supplier, such as an airline or tour operator, not you. This is because the travel supplier and the travel agent have an ongoing relationship—the agent represents the supplier and is compensated for providing business to the supplier.

You may feel that a travel agent should be "your" agent and should look out for your best interests, rather than the interests of travel suppliers. A good agent will take on this role, knowing that good customer service will lead to repeat business. In addition, the law is changing in this area, and sometimes a travel agent may be considered your agent as well. In most cases, however, the travel agent will owe you the normal duty owed by a salesperson to a customer, but no more.

Does a travel agent have any special responsibility when making a reservation for me?

If a travel agent fails to make a reservation for you—or delays in making a reservation for you—and you lose money because of it, the agent is responsible to you if the failure to make the reservation or the delay was his fault. For example, if the flight you want to take has seats available when you call your agent, but the agent delays in making your reservation, the flight sells out and you have to take a more expensive flight, the agent would be liable to you for the difference. On the other hand, if the flight was already sold out when you called the agent, the agent is not liable because his inability to make a reservation is not his fault.

When making a reservation, a travel agent must do his best to match the reservation to your specific requirements and limitations. If your travel agent makes the wrong reservation and you have a ticket on a plane destined for somewhere you don't want to go, the agent is probably responsible for paying the additional cost of getting you to your proper destination. If the agent books you into the wrong hotel or reserves the wrong type of rental car, he should compensate you for the difference between the value you would have received had the agent made the reservation properly and what you did receive as a result of the agent's mistake.

Is a travel agent responsible for confirming my reservation?

Generally, no. You must confirm your own reservations.

However, if your travel agent uses a tour operator or wholesaler who in turn makes your reservations, the agent probably has an obligation to verify your reservations with the various travel suppliers independently. The travel agent should not assume that a tour operator or wholesaler is reliable.

My travel agent charged me the wrong amount for my ticket. What should I do?

If you overpay because of a travel agent's mistake, the travel agent must reimburse you for the difference between the amount you paid and the actual fare. You must consider the proper fare at the time you reserved and paid for your ticket, not when a subsequent fare change was made.

If a travel agent charges you less than the actual cost of your ticket, you are not entitled to travel for less than the established fare. The travel supplier may require you to pay the additional amount due before you travel. Whether you can recover the difference from your travel agent depends on the circumstances. If you knew the correct price and agreed to it, and the travel agent simply hit the wrong key on the computer, you are not entitled to any compensation from the travel agent. On the other hand, if you didn't know the correct price and made your decision based upon what the agent told you, then you probably can recoup the difference if your reliance on the travel agent's statement was reasonable. (If you were told that a $999 flight was $799, your reliance would probably be reasonable. If, however, you were told that a $999 flight was $9.99, you'd be out of luck.)

Is a travel agent responsible for researching airlines, hotels and other suppliers?

Travel agents do not have to thoroughly investigate suppliers. In general, they are required only to stay current with reasonably available information, such as what is in trade journals and magazines. The most important types of information are often the supplier's reputation, track record and financial condition. A travel agent must provide this type of information, as well as any specific experience that the travel agent has had with that supplier, if it would likely affect your decision to use the supplier.

If a travel agent books you on a flight that has already been canceled or in a hotel that has not been built, you have a fairly strong argument that the agent was negligent and failed to undertake a basic investigation. If, however, a tour operator suddenly goes out of business or a hotel closes between the time you make your reservation and the time you arrive, the agent's responsibility is less clear.

Must a travel agent warn me of any travel risks?

If a travel agent knows of a substantial risk to you, such as an airline that is bankrupt but continuing to fly, the travel agent has an obligation to warn you of that risk, with the following limitations:

- A travel agent does not have to warn you about risks that are obvious and apparent, such as the risk that the car you rent from "Rent-a-Wreck" may not be in the best condition.
- A travel agent is not required to be a fortune teller, particularly concerning factors out of the agent's control. An agent might be liable for promoting a "sun and fun" vacation in India during monsoon season, but the agent does not have a duty to warn you about all possible conditions—such as unan-

nounced strikes, political conditions or bad weather—that could affect your enjoyment of the journey.
- A travel agent does not have to point out disclaimers or other legal elements of an agreement between you and the travel supplier, although a helpful travel agent might do so.

How are travel agents paid?

When a travel agent issues a ticket or makes other travel arrangements for you, he generally receives a commission from the travel supplier. This commission may range from 7% to 15% of the price you pay, but it is usually about 10%.

Do any professional associations regulate travel agents?

No. Travel agents have to meet very few formal requirements. Most travel agents do belong to one or more professional associations, however, and each association has a code of ethics that requires its members to remain knowledgeable of developments within the travel industry and to refrain from engaging in misleading sales practices. Membership in a professional association is voluntary, however, and if an agent violates the code of ethics, you have little recourse within the association.

If you have a complaint about a travel agent, ask someone in his office if he belongs to a professional association. If he does, contact the association as follows:

American Society of Travel Agents
(ASTA)
1101 King Street, Suite 200
Alexandria, VA 22314
703-739-2782
703-684-8319 (fax)
http://www.astanet.com (online)

Association of Retail Travel Agents
(ARTA)
845 Sir Thomas Court, Suite 3
Harrisburg, PA 17109
717-545-9548
606-264-0368 (fax)

International Airlines Travel Agent
Network (IATAN)
300 Garden City Plaza, Suite 342
Garden City, NY 11530
516-747-4716
516-747-4462 (fax)
http://www.iatan.org (online)

Institute of Certified Travel Agents
(ICTA)
148 Linden Street
Wellesley, MA 02181
617-237-0280
617-237-3860 (fax)

The association can tell you if the agent is a member in good standing. In some cases, an association may be able to help you if you have a complaint against one of their members. For example, ASTA has a mediation program to help resolve disputes between travel agents and their clients.

Travel Scams

Each year, fraud costs American consumers over $100 billion. One out of every seven cases of fraud involves travel, with most travel scams being carried out over the telephone or by mail. Travel fraud knows no socioeconomic boundaries—scam artists ply their wares in every travel market. This section describes some common travel scams to help you avoid becoming part of these grim statistics.

Are there any general rules to follow to avoid being the victim of a travel scam?

As with most things in life, if the offer sounds too good to be true, it probably is. That being said, here are some signs to watch out for:

- The solicitation says that you were "specially selected" or "awarded" a trip or prize, but you haven't entered any contest.
- You must make a payment to collect your prize.
- The salesperson uses high pressure sales tactics or insists on an immediate decision.
- You must disclose your income, Social Security number, bank account number or other private information.
- The company offers great bargains, but refuses to put the details in writing unless you pay first.
- The salesperson makes vague references to "all major airlines" or "all major hotels," without saying which ones you will use.
- You must wait more than 60 days before taking the trip or receiving the prize. (Most scam victims pay for their "prize" on their credit card;

scam artists know that you must dispute any credit card charge within 60 days. If they force you to wait more than 60 days, you can't challenge the charge.)

- The caller asks for your credit card number over the phone.
- The company requests a direct bank deposit or certified check, or offers to send a courier to your home to pick up your check.
- The deal cannot be booked through a travel agent.
- You must call a 900 number.
- The company cannot provide the names of references, or the references you call repeat nearly verbatim the claims of the travel provider.

Use a Credit Card Whenever Possible

Although using a credit card is not a surefire way to protect yourself, if you act quickly, you can dispute the charge and avoid paying for a scam. The Fair Credit Billing Act gives you 60 days from the date you receive your bill—not the date of your travel—to contest a charge. Some credit cards offer more extended coverage; a few even give members up to a year to contest a charge.

Some kids at my daughter's college lost money when they signed up for a trip that was canceled at the last minute. How can my daughter avoid becoming the next victim?

Many fly-by-night travel operations pitch specifically to students through telemarketing and other hard-sell tactics, hoping to take advantage of inexperienced travelers on a tight budget who are looking to save money.

Students should find out whether the tour company meets the standards set by the Council on Standards for International Educational Travel (CSIET). To qualify, tour operators must submit a review signed by an independent certified public accountant as well as extensive documentation concerning government regulations for student exchanges, promotions and student insurance.

Advisory List of International Educational Travel and Exchange Programs, an annually updated booklet listing companies that meet the standards, is available from CSIET, 3 Loudoun Street, SE, Leesburg, VA 22075, 703-739-9050. Be sure to call first for price information.

We just returned from Hawaii, where we were constantly solicited to buy a timeshare. Are these deals as good as they sound?

Probably not. An estimated 94% of all timeshare owners never intended to buy in the first place; they are swept away by high pressure sales pitches and cleverly disguised promotions.

The idea behind a timeshare is simple: For a one-time price plus an annual maintenance fee, you can buy the right to use a given vacation property for a certain amount of time (typically one week) each year. What you may not be told is the extent to which the annual maintenance fee will increase over time—one timeshare owner in Hawaii saw her annual maintenance fees climb 76% in six years. Timeshare operators also may force owners to pay unexpected "special assessment fees," sometimes as high as $1,000. While a timeshare has the potential to be a satisfactory arrangement, it often yields a variety of pitfalls and frustrations for the unwary purchaser.

A Typical Timeshare Sales Pitch

A new camera, a half-price parasail ride, a free day's rental car, a free gourmet meal—you name it, timeshare salespeople have offered it. Many timeshare developers lure tourists to sales presentations by selling tours and activities at highly discounted prices, but provide only vague disclosure of what is required to qualify for the discount deal.

In the usual scenario, the catch for the gift is that you must sit through a presentation about a timeshare vacation property. The presentations vary, but most include high-pressure sales pitches that drone on for hours and leave visitors desperate to get out. Timeshare salespeople frequently go over the advertised time allotted for their presentation and are not responsive if you complain. They sometimes refuse to give the promised gift or discount if you don't buy. Although it may be illegal to not give you the gift or discount, few consumers complain—they just want out.

I've been told that I shouldn't buy a timeshare because it will be hard to sell it later. Is this true?

Very likely, yes. Timeshare owners face a couple of traps when they try to sell. The first hurdle is the lack of a strong resale market. Although statistics vary, all studies show that there are many more timeshare owners wanting to sell than there are buyers.

Another problem is the likelihood that you will lose money on the sale of a timeshare. The original price of a timeshare may have included premiums of up to 40% to cover sales costs. As a result, a resale will yield as little as 60% of the original purchase price—plus you will have to pay a commission to the broker (often as high as 20%) who sells the property for you.

Is it possible to get out of a timeshare after signing a contract?

Maybe. Nearly 30 states have "cooling-off" laws; these let you get out of a timeshare contract if you act within a few days after signing (three to ten, depending on the state). If there is no cooling-off period, or you change your mind after the time has passed, your only recourse may be a formal lawsuit. Timeshare sellers are accustomed to handling claims from unhappy buyers and are unlikely to refund your money unless forced to do so.

Suing a Timeshare Operator

There are several types of claims you might bring against a slippery timeshare seller. The first, breach of contract, involves promises explicitly made and set forth in the sales agreements. If the size, location, condition or some other important fact about the timeshare is materially different from what you agreed to in the sales contract, you may have a basis for claiming breach of the contract. But beware: These contracts are carefully drawn up by the timeshare sellers' attorneys and are likely to cover almost any contingency—scrutinize carefully before signing.

You may also bring claims based on tactics used and promises made before you agreed to purchase your timeshare. These claims may be covered under state laws prohibiting unfair business practices or those designed to prevent fraudulent inducement. In both cases, the idea is that the seller used unfair sales tactics or lies to get you to buy the timeshare. You will have to show:

- what the seller said or did
- why it was misleading
- that you wouldn't have bought the timeshare if the seller hadn't used the misleading tactics or promises, and
- that you suffered some monetary loss because of the purchase.

Timeshare sales contracts usually include clauses that disclaim any promises made during the sales pitch. The contract you sign will ask you to agree that you are making the purchase only on the basis of the representations in that contract. Prospective purchasers who notice differences between what is in the contract and what was promised by the salesperson are likely to be told that the contract is only "legal jargon." This is *not* true. If a timeshare salesperson will not

put a promise in writing, don't go through with the sale. You will be forced to argue afterwards that you relied on that promise, even though you signed a contract that explicitly says you did not rely on any promises.

If you are the victim of a timeshare scam, you can ask for two things. First, you can ask to rescind the contract. You would get your money back, and the seller would regain title to the timeshare. If the seller (or court) refuses this, you must prove monetary damages, the largest of which is the difference between the amount you paid for the timeshare and its actual value. As you can imagine, it can be quite difficult to determine the actual value of a timeshare, although the amount you could obtain by reselling it is one possible indicator.

I received a vacation certificate in the mail. How can I figure out if it's legitimate?

First, review the tips at the beginning of this section. Then, if you note any of the following on a travel certificate, treat it with maximum skepticism and send it to the recycling bin:

- words such as "Certificate of Guarantee" and a spread-winged eagle or other prominent symbol designed to convey a sense of legitimacy
- a variety of possible vacation destinations, with no designated dates or price
- exciting descriptions of what you will do, such as "gala cruise," "glittering casino action," "moonlight dancing" or "resort accommodations," with no designated company names

- a phrase in the fine print indicating you were chosen "using credit and purchasing criteria to select individuals interested in the many benefits of travel," or
- fine print language stating that the receipt of one portion of the offer (for example, the airline ticket) is dependent on purchase of something else (such as hotel accommodations).

How can I find out if a cheap airfare offered by a charter airline is legitimate?

Although many charter companies provide legitimate low-cost travel options, their reliability is far from uniform. Over the past few years, many charter operations have collapsed, leaving consumers in the lurch—and some that are still in business pose financial risks for current customers.

The Department of Transportation (DOT) regulates the manner in which charter operators must handle consumer funds. Among other things, the regulations require charter operators to post a bond or deposit consumer funds in an escrow account. Nonetheless, charter operators have found ways to shirk the rules; they may fail to deposit passenger funds into escrow accounts or divert funds that have already been deposited.

DOT regulations require sellers of charter flights to file a prospectus with the DOT, explaining how their business is organized. To find out whether a low-fare carrier has at least done this, call DOT's Consumer Affairs Office at 202-366-5957 and ask for the carrier's prospectus number.

Where to Report a Travel Scam

If you are the victim of any kind of travel scam, contact one or more of the following agencies or associations:

STATE AND LOCAL GOVERNMENT AGENCIES

State consumer protection office. Call directory assistance in your state capital and ask for the number for your state attorney general, and the division or department of consumer affairs or consumer protection. *Local prosecutor.* Call the nearest district attorney or state attorney's office and ask whether there is a consumer fraud division. *State licensing board.* Some states are starting to license travel providers. Ask your state attorney general if travel providers are licensed in your state.

FEDERAL GOVERNMENT AGENCIES

National Fraud Information Center. NFIC can help you file a complaint with the appropriate federal agency, give you tips on how to avoid becoming the victim of a scam or send you consumer publications. You can reach NFIC as follows: 800-876-7060 (voice), 202-835-0767 (fax), 202-347-3189 (electronic bulletin board), 202-737-5084 (TTD) or http://www.fraud.org (online). Or you can write to NFIC, c/o National Consumer's League, 1701 K Street, NW, Suite 1200, Washington, DC 20005.

Federal Trade Commission. Although the FTC generally does not intervene in individual consumer disputes, any information you provide might lead to an FTC investigation. Also, the FTC has free consumer publications that could be helpful before or after you travel, including *Car Rental Guide, 900 Numbers, Telemarketing Travel Fraud, Timeshare Resales* and *Timeshare Tips.* Contact the FTC, 6th and Pennsylvania Avenue, NW, Washington, DC 20580, 202-326-2222, 202-326-2050 (fax), http://www.ftc.gov.

Department of Transportation (DOT) Consumer Affairs Office. DOT's "Fly Rights" guide contains information on federal regulations regarding delays, bankruptcy protection, overbooking, smoking and refunds. Copies cost $1.75 each and can be ordered by sending a check or money order to Superintendent of Documents, Consumer Information Center, Department 133-B, Pueblo, CO 81009. You can also register a complaint about an airline with DOT's Office of Consumer Affairs, 400 Seventh Street, SW, Room 10405, Washington, DC 20590, 202-366-2220, 202-366-7907 (fax), http://www.dot.gov.

Federal Communications Commission. If you were defrauded by a telemarketer or phone solicitor, or sucked in when a travel service provider aired a fraudulent ad on radio or television, contact the FCC, Office of Complaints, 1919 M Street, NW, Suite 6202, Washington, DC 20554, 202-418-0191, 202-418-0232 (fax), http://www.fcc.gov.

U.S. Postal Service. If you were cheated by anyone who used the U.S. mail, contact a postal inspector. Look in the government listing of your telephone book white pages for the local address or contact the federal office, USPS, Inspection Services, 475 L'Enfant Plaza, SW, Washington, DC 20260, 202-268-4267, 202-268-4563 (fax), http://www.usps.gov.

PRIVATE INDUSTRY

American Society of Travel Agents (ASTA). If you have a complaint concerning an ASTA member, contact ASTA, 1101 King Street, Alexandria, VA 22314, 703-739-2782, 703-684-8319 (fax), http://www.astanet.com. You can also request a free copy of *Avoiding Travel Problems.*

United States Tour Operators Association (USTOA). If you have a complaint concerning a USTOA member or a question about USTOA's consumer protection plan, contact USTOA, 342 Madison Avenue, Suite 1522, New York, NY 10173, 212-549-6599, 212-599-6744 (fax).

Better Business Bureau (BBB). You can provide a public service to other travelers by filing a complaint with all offices of the BBB where the scammer operates. In addition, the National Council of Better Business Bureaus operates a nationwide system for settling consumer disputes through mediation and arbitration. So, if you can find the company, you might be able to get some recourse through a BBB. Check http://www.bbb.org.

How can I tell whether a deeply discounted airfare is legitimate?

Deceptive airline advertising is so frequent that you may have already learned to read between the lines and scan the fine print to get the real picture. If you are not so savvy, watch out for the following:

- Deceptive two-for-one offers. The airline promises two tickets for the price of one, but then requires you to buy a ticket in a class that costs the same, if not more, than two tickets at some other published fare.
- Misleading discounts. Some airfare promotions advertise drastic price reductions in airfares without specifying the base fare from which the discounts are calculated. Furthermore, airlines usually advertise ticket prices at half their true cost. The fine print explains that the fare is "each way, based on round-trip purchase," despite the fact that you cannot buy a one-way ticket at the price shown.

- Phantom "sale" seats. The classic airline bait-and-switch tactic is to promote low airfares for a given route and then fail to disclose the strict limitations on the availability of seats. The airline may try to sell you a higher-priced seat or may offer a reasonable number of low-fare seats for the first few days of the promotion, and then retract the seats for the duration of the ad campaign.
- Frequent flyer deceptions. Airlines continue to severely limit the number of seats that they allocate to frequent flyers, especially for business and first class seats. As a result, frequent flyer customers may have a difficult time getting the seats they've earned.

More Information About Your Rights as a Traveler

Trouble-Free Travel ... and What to Do When Things Go Wrong, by Attorneys Stephen Colwell and Ann Shulman (Nolo Press), helps you anticipate and avoid hassles while traveling, and shows you how to deal with airlines, tour operators, rental car companies, hotels and other travel providers should problems arise.

http://www.nolo.com

Nolo Press offers self-help information about a wide variety of legal topics, including travel law.

http://www.dot.gov

The U.S. Department of Transportation offers information and tips for resolving travel problems.

http://www.travelocity.com

Travelocity can help you plan your entire trip, from finding the cheapest airfare to choosing your activities.

http://www.bbb.org/

The Better Business Bureau provides information on resolving disputes through mediation and arbitration.

http://www.air-transport.org

The Air Transport Association of America allows you to order most major airlines' conditions of contract, the hidden terms of your ticket.

http://travel.state.gov

The Bureau of Consular Affairs provides extensive information on travelers' security, applying for a passport, foreign countries' entry requirements, international adoptions and how U.S. consulates can help you overseas.

http://www.cdc.gov/travel/travel.html

The Centers for Disease Control and Prevention offers travel information on health risks in foreign countries and appropriate precautions to take.

http://www.faa.gov/apa

The Federal Aviation Administration provides information and tips on air travel, including a fact sheet called Fly Smart.

http://www.sath.org

The Society for the Advancement of Travel for the Handicapped offers information to assist disabled people preparing to take a trip.

http://www.customs.ustreas.gov

The U.S. Customs Service provides publications including guides for returning U.S. residents and import restrictions.

Wills and Estate Planning

It's not that I'm afraid to die. I just don't want to be there when it happens.

—WOODY ALLEN

The first thing that comes to many people's minds when they think of estate planning is property: Who gets what you own when you die? But estate planning encompasses much more—for example, minimizing probate court costs and estate taxes, deciding who will care for your minor children if you can't, appointing people to handle your medical and financial affairs if necessary, and expressing your wishes regarding memorial services and burial. While none of us relish the thought of thinking about these things, taking some time to do so now can save your loved ones a great deal of money, pain and confusion later on.

This chapter answers often-asked questions about estate planning, from basic wills to organ donation. Along the way we consider probate and the many ways to avoid it, methods for eliminating or reducing death taxes, and funeral planning. For information about arranging for someone to make your medical and financial decisions should you become unable to handle them yourself, see the next chapter, *Living Wills and Power of Attorney*.

Wills

Though most Americans are aware that they need a will, the majority—about 70% of us—don't have one. There are lots of reasons we put off making our wills, from fear of lawyers' fees to fear of death. But writing a will doesn't have to be expensive, or even terribly complicated. And once it's done, you can rest a little easier, knowing that your wishes are known and will be followed after your death.

What happens if I die without a will?

If you don't make a will or use some other legal method to transfer your property when you die, state law will determine what happens to your property. (This process is called "intestate succession.") Your property will be distributed to your spouse and children or, if you have neither, to other relatives according to a statutory formula. If no relatives can be found to inherit your property, it will go into your state's coffers. Also, in the absence of a will, a court will determine who will care for your young children and their property if the other parent is unavailable or unfit.

Do I need a lawyer to make my will?

Probably not. Making a will rarely involves complicated legal rules, and most people can draft their own will with the aid of a good self-help book or software program. If you know what you own and whom you care about, and you have a good self-help resource to guide you, it's hard to make a mistake.

But you shouldn't approach the task of will drafting absolutely determined not to consult a lawyer. If you have questions that aren't answered by the resource you're relying on, a lawyer's services are warranted. Even so, you don't have to turn over the whole project; you can simply ask your questions and then finish making your own will.

For example, you may want to consult a lawyer if:

- You have questions about your will or other options for leaving your property.
- You expect to leave a very large amount of assets—say, over $1 million—that will be subject to substantial estate taxes unless you engage in tax planning. (But first look at a good self-help resource that discusses tax-saving strategies.)
- You own a small business and have questions as to the rights of surviving owners or your ownership share.
- You must make arrangements for long-term care of a beneficiary—for example, a disabled child.
- You fear someone will contest your will on grounds of fraud, or claim that you were unduly influenced or weren't of sound mind when you signed it.
- You wish to leave no property, or very little property, to your spouse. It's usually not possible to do this unless you live in a community property state where your spouse already owns half of most assets acquired after marriage. (See *Can I disinherit relatives I don't like?*, below.) But a lawyer can explain exactly what your spouse is entitled to claim from your estate.

Also, some people simply feel more comfortable having a lawyer review their will, even though their situation has no apparent legal complications.

I don't have much property. Can't I just make a handwritten will?

Handwritten wills, called "holographic" wills, are legal in about 25 states. To be valid, a holographic will must be written, dated and signed in the handwriting of the person making the will. Some states allow will writers to use a fill-in-the-blanks form if the rest of the will is handwritten and the will is properly dated and signed.

If you have very little property, and you want to make just a few specific bequests, a holographic will is better than nothing if it's valid in your state. But generally, we don't recommend them. Unlike regular wills, holographic wills are not usually witnessed, so if your will goes before a probate court, the court may be unusually strict when examining it to be sure it's legitimate. It's better to take a little extra time to write a will that will easily pass muster when the time comes.

Making Your Will Legal

Any adult of sound mind is entitled to make a will. (And if you're reading this book, you're of sound mind.) Beyond that, there are just a few technical requirements:

- The will must be typewritten or computer generated (unless it is a valid handwritten will, as discussed above).
- The document must expressly state that it's your will.
- You must date and sign the will.
- The will must be signed by at least

two, or in some states three, witnesses. They must watch you sign the will, though they don't need to read it. Your witnesses must be people who won't inherit anything under the will.

You don't have to have your will notarized. In many states, though, if you and your witnesses sign an affidavit (sworn statement) before a notary public, you can help simplify the court procedures required to prove the validity of the will after you die.

Do I need to file my will with a court or in public records somewhere?

No. A will doesn't need to be recorded or filed with any government agency, although it can be in a few states. Just keep your will in a safe, accessible place and be sure the person in charge of winding up your affairs (your executor) knows where it is.

Can I use my will to name somebody to care for my young children, in case my spouse and I both die suddenly?

Yes. If both parents of a child die while the child is still a minor, another adult—called a "personal guardian"—must step in. You and the child's other parent can use your wills to nominate someone to fill this position. To avert conflicts, you should each name the same person. If a guardian is needed, a judge will appoint your nominee as long as he or she agrees that it is in the best interest of your children.

The personal guardian will be responsible for raising your children until they become legal adults. Of course, you should have complete confidence in the person you nominate, and you should be certain that your nominee is willing to accept the responsibility of raising your children should the need actually arise.

I'm raising a child on my own. Do I have to name the other biological parent as personal guardian, or can I name someone who I think will do a better job of caring for her?

If one parent dies, the other usually takes responsibility for raising the child. But if you and the other parent have parted ways, you may feel strongly that he or she shouldn't have custody if something happens to you. A judge will grant custody to someone else only if the surviving parent:

• has legally abandoned the child by not providing for or visiting the child for an extended period, or
• is clearly unfit as a parent.

In most cases, it is difficult to prove that a parent is unfit, absent serious problems such as chronic drug or alcohol use, mental illness or a history of child abuse.

If you honestly believe the other parent is incapable of caring for your child properly, or simply won't assume the responsibility, you should write a letter explaining why and attach it to your will. The judge will take it into account, and may appoint the person you choose as guardian instead of the other parent.

How to Leave Property to Young Children

Except for property of little value, the law requires that an adult manage property inherited by children until they turn 18. You can use your will to name someone to manage property inherited by minors, thus avoiding the need for a more complicated court-appointed guardianship. There are many ways to structure a property management arrangement. Here are four of the simplest and most useful:

Name a custodian under the Uniform Transfers to Minors Act

The Uniform Transfers to Minors Act (UTMA) is a law that has been adopted in almost the same form in every state except Michigan, South Carolina and Vermont. Under the UTMA, you can choose someone, called a custodian, to manage property you are leaving to a child. If you die when the child is under the age set by your state's law—18 in a few states, 21 in most, 25 in several others—the custodian will step in to manage the property. An UTMA custodianship must end by the age specified by your state's law (18, 21 or up to 25). At that time, your child receives what's left of the trust property outright. If, however, you want to extend property management beyond the age set by your state, you may want to use one of the next three methods.

Set up a trust for each child

You can use your will to name someone (called a trustee) who will handle any property the child inherits until the child reaches the age you specify. When the child reaches the age you specified, the trustee ends the trust and gives whatever is left of the trust property to the child.

Set up a pot trust for your children

If you have more than one child, you may want to set up just one trust for all of them. This arrangement is usually called a pot trust. In your will, you establish the trust and appoint a trustee. The trustee doesn't have to spend the same amount on each child; instead, the trustee decides what each child needs, and spends money accordingly. When the youngest child reaches a certain age, usually 18, the trust ends. At that time, any property left in the trust will be distributed as you direct in the trust document.

Name a property guardian

If you wish, you can simply use your will to name a property guardian for your child. Then, if at your death your child needs the guardian, the court will appoint the person you chose. The property guardian will manage whatever property the child inherits, from you or others, if there's no other mechanism (a trust, for example) to handle it.

Can I disinherit relatives I don't like?

It depends on whom you want to disinherit. If it's anyone other than your spouse or child, the rule is very simple: Don't mention that person in your will, and he or she won't receive any of your property. Rules for spouses and children are somewhat more complex.

Spouses. It is not usually possible to disinherit your spouse completely. If you live in a community property state (Arizona, California, Idaho, Louisiana, Nevada, New Mexico, Texas, Washington or Wisconsin), your spouse automatically owns half of all the property and earnings (with a few exceptions) acquired by either of you during your marriage. You can, however, leave your half of the community property, and your separate property (generally considered to be all property you owned before marriage or received via gift or inheritance during marriage), to anyone you choose.

In all other states, there is no rule that property acquired during marriage is owned by both spouses. To protect spouses from being disinherited, these states give your spouse a legal right to claim a portion of your estate, no matter what your will provides. But keep in mind that these provisions kick in only if your spouse challenges your will. If your will leaves your spouse less than the statutory share and he or she doesn't object, the document will be honored as written.

If you don't plan to leave at least half of your property to your spouse in your will and have not provided for him or her generously outside your will, you should consult a lawyer—unless your spouse willingly consents in writing to your plan.

Children. Generally, it's legal to disinherit a child. Some states, however, protect minor children against the loss of a family residence. For example, the Florida Constitution prohibits the head of a family from leaving his residence to anyone other than a spouse if he is survived by a spouse or minor child.

Most states have laws—called "pretermitted heir" statutes—to protect children of any age from being accidentally disinherited. If a child is neither named in your will–or specifically disinherited, these laws assume that you accidentally forgot to include that child. In many states, these laws apply only to children born after you made your will, but in a few states they apply to any child not mentioned in your will. The overlooked child has a right to the same share of your estate as he or she would have received if you'd left no will. The share usually depends on whether you leave a spouse and on how many other children you have, but it is likely to be a significant percentage of your property. In some states, these laws apply not only to your children, but also to any of your grandchildren by a child who has died.

To avoid any legal battles after your death, if you decide to disinherit a child, or the child of a deceased child, expressly state this in your will. And if you have a new child after you've made your will, remember to make a new will to include, or specifically disinherit, that child.

What happens to my will when I die?

After you die, your executor (the person you appointed in your will) is responsible for seeing that your wishes are carried out as directed by your will. He or she may hire an attorney to help wind up your affairs, especially if probate court proceedings are required. Probate and executors are discussed in more detail in the next three sets of questions.

Make Your Will and Records Accessible

Your executor's first task is to locate your will, and you can help by keeping the original in a fairly obvious place. Here are some suggestions:

- Store your will in an envelope on which you have typed your name and the word "Will."

- Place the envelope in a fireproof metal box, file cabinet or home safe. An alternative is to place the original in a safe deposit box. But before doing that, learn the bank's policy about access to the box after your death. If, for instance, the safe deposit box is in your name alone, the box can probably be opened only by a person authorized by a court, and then only in the presence of a bank employee. An inventory may even be required if any person enters the box or for state tax purposes. All of this takes time, and in the meantime, your document will be locked away from those who need access to it.

Finally, wherever you choose to keep your will, make sure your executor (and at least one other person you trust) knows where to find it.

What if someone challenges my will after I die?

Very few wills are ever challenged in court. When they are, it's usually by a close relative who feels somehow cheated out of his or her rightful share of the deceased person's property.

Generally speaking, only spouses are legally entitled to a share of your property. Your children aren't entitled to anything unless you unintentionally overlooked them in your will. (See *Can I disinherit relatives I don't like?*, above.)

To get an entire will thrown out as invalid, someone must go to court and prove that it suffers from a fatal flaw: the signature was forged, you weren't of sound mind when you made the will or you were unduly influenced by someone.

More Information About Wills

WillMaker (Nolo Press) (software for Windows or Macintosh), lets you create a valid will, durable power of attorney for finances, healthcare directives and final arrangements document using your computer.

The Quick and Legal Will Book, by Denis Clifford (Nolo Press), contains forms and instructions for creating a basic will.

Nolo's Will Book, by Denis Clifford (Nolo Press), contains a detailed discussion of wills and all the forms you need to create one.

Nolo's Law Form Kit: Wills (Nolo Press), contains a simple fill-in-the-blanks will.

Probate

THERE IS ONLY ONE WAY YOU CAN

BEAT A LAWYER IN A DEATH CASE.

THAT IS TO DIE WITH NOTHING.

THEN YOU CAN'T GET A LAWYER

WITHIN TEN MILES OF YOUR HOUSE.

—WILL ROGERS

When a person dies, someone must step in to wind up the deceased person's affairs. Bills must be paid, property must be accounted for and items must be passed on to the people chosen by the deceased person. If state law requires that all this be handled through court proceedings, the process can take many months.

What is probate?

Probate is a legal process that includes:

- proving in court that a deceased person's will is valid (usually a routine matter)
- identifying and inventorying the deceased person's property
- having the property appraised
- paying debts and taxes, and
- distributing the remaining property as the will directs.

Typically, probate involves paperwork and court appearances by lawyers, who are paid from estate property that would otherwise go to the people who inherit the deceased person's property. Property left by the will cannot be distributed to beneficiaries until the process is complete.

Probate rarely benefits your beneficiaries, and it certainly costs them money and time. Probate makes sense only if your estate will have complicated problems, such as many debts that can't easily be paid from the property you leave.

Property That Avoids Probate

Not all property has to go through probate. Most states allow a certain amount of property to pass free of probate, or through a simplified probate procedure. In California, for example, you can pass up to $100,000 of property without probate, and there's a simple transfer procedure for any property left to a surviving spouse.

In addition, property that passes outside of your will—say, through joint tenancy or a living trust—is not subject to probate. For a discussion of the most popular probate-avoidance methods, see *Avoiding Probate,* below.

Who is responsible for handling probate?

In most circumstances, the executor named in the will takes this job. If there isn't any will, or if the will maker fails to name an executor, the probate court names someone (called an administrator) to handle the process—most often the closest capable relative, or the person who inherits the bulk of the deceased person's assets.

If no formal probate proceeding is necessary, the court does not appoint an estate administrator. Instead, a close relative or friend serves as an informal estate representative. Normally, families and friends choose this person, and it is not uncommon for several people to share the responsibilities of paying debts, filing a final income tax return and distributing property to the people who are supposed to get it.

Executors

An executor is the person you name in your will to handle your property after death. The executor must be prepared to carry out a long list of tasks, prudently and promptly.

How do I choose an executor?

The most important factor in naming an executor is trust. The person you choose should be honest, with good organizational skills and the ability to keep track of details. If possible, name someone who lives nearby and who is familiar with your financial matters; that will make it easier to do chores like collecting mail and locating important records and papers.

Many people select someone who will inherit a substantial amount of their property. This makes sense, because a person with an interest in how your property is distributed is likely to do a conscientious job of managing your affairs after your death. He or she may also come equipped with knowledge of where your records are kept and an understanding of why you want your property left as you have directed.

Whomever you select, make sure the person is willing to do the job. Discuss the position with the person you've chosen before you make your will.

Are there restrictions on whom I may choose as my executor?

Your state may impose some restrictions on who can act as executor. You can't name a minor, a convicted felon

12.9

or someone who is not a U.S. citizen. Most states allow you to name someone who lives in another state, but some require that out-of-state executors be a relative or a primary beneficiary under your will. Some states also require that nonresident executors obtain a bond (an insurance policy that protects your beneficiaries in the event of the executor's wrongful use of your estate's property) or an in-state resident to act as the executor's representative. These complexities underscore the benefits of naming someone who lives nearby. If you feel strongly about naming an executor who lives out of state, be sure to familiarize yourself with your state's rules.

BOND

Is it difficult to serve as executor?

Serving as an executor can be a tedious job, but it doesn't require special financial or legal knowledge. Common sense, conscientiousness and honesty are the main requirements. An executor who needs help can hire lawyers, accountants or other experts and pay them from the assets of the deceased person's estate.

Essentially, the executor's job is to protect the deceased person's property until all debts and taxes have been paid, and see that what's left is transferred to the people who are entitled to it. The law does not require an executor to be a legal or financial expert or to display more than reasonable prudence and judgment, but it does require the highest degree of honesty, impartiality and diligence. This is called a "fiduciary duty"—the

FIDUCIARY DUTY!

NO CONFLICT OF INTEREST

↓

IMPARTIALITY

duty to act with scrupulous good faith and candor on behalf of someone else.

Does the person named in a will as executor have to serve?

No. When it comes time, an executor can accept or decline this responsibility. And someone who agrees to serve can resign at any time. That's why many wills name an alternate executor, who takes over if necessary. If no one is available, the court will appoint someone to step in.

Does the executor get paid?

Obviously, the main reason for serving as an executor is to honor the deceased person's request. But the executor is also entitled to payment. The exact amount is regulated by state law and is affected by factors such as the value of the deceased person's property and what the probate court decides is reasonable under the circumstances. Commonly, close relatives and close friends (especially those who are inheriting a substantial amount anyway) don't charge the estate for their services.

Is a lawyer necessary?

Not always. An executor should definitely consider handling the paperwork without a lawyer if he or she is the main beneficiary, the deceased person's property consists of common kinds of assets (house, bank accounts, insurance), the will seems straightforward and good self-help materials are at hand. Essentially, shepherding a case through probate court requires shuffling a lot of papers. In the vast majority of cases, there are no disputes that require a decision by a judge. So the executor may never see the inside of a courtroom, but will certainly become familiar with the court clerk's office. The executor may even be able to do everything by mail. Doing a good job requires persistence and attention to tedious detail, but not necessarily a law degree.

If, however, the estate has many types of property, significant tax liability or potential disputes among inheritors, an executor may want some help.

There are two ways for an executor to get help from a lawyer:

- Hire a lawyer to act as a "coach," answering legal questions as they come up. The lawyer might also do some research, look over documents before the executor files them or prepare an estate tax return.
- Turn the probate over to the lawyer. If the executor just doesn't want to deal with the probate process, a lawyer can do everything. The lawyer will be paid out of the estate. In most states, lawyers charge by the hour ($150–$200 is common) or charge a lump sum. But in a few places, including Arkansas, California, Delaware, Hawaii, Iowa, Missouri, Montana and Wyoming, state law authorizes the lawyer to take a certain percentage of the gross value of the deceased person's estate unless the executor makes a written agreement calling for less. An executor can probably find a competent lawyer who will agree to a lower fee.

If an executor doesn't want to hire a lawyer, is there any other way to get help?

Lawyers aren't the only source of information and assistance. Here are some others:

- *The court*. Probate court clerks will probably answer basic questions about court procedure, but they staunchly avoid saying anything that could possibly be construed as "legal advice." Some courts, however, have lawyers on staff who look over probate documents; they may point out errors in the papers and explain how to fix them.
- *Other professionals*. For certain tasks, an executor may be better off hiring an accountant or appraiser than a lawyer. For example, a CPA may be a big help on some estate tax matters.
- *Paralegals*. In many law offices, lawyers delegate all the probate paperwork to paralegals (nonlawyers who have training or experience in preparing legal documents). Now, in some areas of the country, experienced paralegals have set up shop to help people directly with probate paperwork. These paralegals don't offer legal advice; they just prepare documents as the executor instructs them, and file them with the court. To find a probate paralegal, an executor can look in the Yellow Pages under "Typing Services" or "Attorney Services." The executor should hire someone only if that person has substantial experience in this field and provides references that check out.

An Executor's Duties

Executors have a number of duties, depending on the complexity of the deceased person's estate. Typically, an executor must:

Decide whether or not probate court proceedings are needed. If the deceased person's property is worth less than a certain amount (it depends on state law), formal probate may not be required.

Figure out who inherits property. If the deceased person left a will, the executor will read it to determine who gets what. If there's no will, the administrator will have to look at state law (called "intestate succession" statutes) to find out who the deceased person's heirs are.

Decide whether or not it's legally permissible to transfer certain items immediately to the people named to inherit them, even if probate is required for other property.

If probate is required, file the will (if any) and all required legal papers in the local probate court.

Find the deceased person's assets and manage them during the probate process, which may take up to a year. This may involve deciding whether to sell real estate or securities owned by the deceased person.

Handle day-to-day details, such as terminating leases and credit cards, and notifying banks and government agencies—such as Social Security, the post office, Medicare and the Veterans Administration—of the death.

Set up an estate bank account to hold money that is owed to the deceased person—for example, paychecks or stock dividends.

Pay continuing expenses—for example, mortgage payments, utility bills and homeowner's insurance premiums.

Pay debts. As part of this process, the executor must officially notify creditors of the probate proceeding, following the procedure set out by state law.

Pay taxes. A final income tax return must be filed, covering the period from the beginning of the tax year to the date of death. State and federal estate tax returns may also be required, depending on how much property the deceased person owned at death and to whom the property was left.

Supervise the distribution of the deceased person's property to the people or organizations named in the will.

More Information About Executors and Probate

The Executor's Handbook, by Theodore E. Hughes and David Klein (Facts On File), is a general but useful guide to an executor's duties. It's not a how-to book, but it discusses many aspects of the executor's job, including funerals, wills, the probate court process, simplified procedures for small estates and managing assets.

Social Security, Medicare and Pensions, by Joseph Matthews (Nolo Press), explains how to make claims for survivors benefits from the Social Security Administration, Federal Civil Service and the Veterans Administration.

How to Probate an Estate in California, by Julia Nissley (Nolo Press), leads you through the California probate process step by step. It contains tear-out copies of all necessary court forms, and instructions for filling them out. Although the forms are used only in California, the book contains much information that would be valuable background in any state.

Avoiding Probate

Because probate is time consuming, expensive and usually unnecessary, many people plan in advance to avoid it. There are a number of ways to pass property to your inheritors without probate. Some of these probate-avoidance methods are quite simple to set up; others take more time and effort.

Should I plan to avoid probate?

Whether to spend your time and effort planning to avoid probate depends on a number of factors, most notably your age, your health and your wealth. If you're young and in good health, a simple will may be all you need —adopting a complex probate avoidance plan now may mean you'll have to redo it as your life situation changes. And if you have very little property, you might not want to spend your time planning to avoid probate. Your property may even fall under your state's probate exemption; most states have laws that allow a certain amount of property to pass free of probate, or through a simplified probate procedure.

But if you're older (say, over 50), in ill health or own a significant amount of property, you'll probably want to do some planning to avoid probate.

How to Avoid Probate

No one probate-avoidance method is right for all people. Which methods, if any, you should use depends on your personal and financial situation. Here are some common techniques to consider:

Pay-on-death designations

Designating a pay-on-death beneficiary is a simple way to avoid probate for bank accounts, government bonds, individual retirement accounts and, in many states, stocks and other securities. In a few states, you can even transfer your car through such an arrangement. All you need to do is name someone to inherit the property at your death. You retain complete control of your property when you are alive, and you can change the beneficiary if you choose. When you die, the property is transferred to the person you named, free of probate.

Joint tenancy

Joint tenancy is a form of shared ownership where the surviving owner(s) automatically inherits the share of the owner who dies. Joint tenancy is often a good choice for couples who purchase property together and want the survivor to inherit. (Some states also have a very similar type of ownership, called "ten-ancy by the entirety," just for married couples.) Adding another owner to property you already own, however, can create problems. The new co-owner can sell or borrow against his or her share. Also, there are negative tax consequences of giving appreciated property to a joint tenant shortly before death.

A living trust

A revocable living trust is a popular probate-avoidance device. You create the trust by preparing and signing a trust document. Once the trust is created, you can transfer property to it, without giving up any control over the trust property. When you die, the trust property can be distributed directly to the beneficiaries you named in the trust document, without the blessing of the probate court. Living trusts are discussed in more detail in the next set of questions.

Insurance

If you buy life insurance, you can designate a specific beneficiary in your policy. The proceeds of the policy won't go through probate unless you name your own estate as the beneficiary.

Gifts

Anything you give away during your life doesn't have to go through probate. Making nontaxable gifts (up to $10,000 per recipient per year, or to a tax-exempt entity) can also reduce eventual federal estate taxes. So if you can afford it, a gift-giving program can save on both probate costs and estate taxes.

*More Information
About Avoiding Probate*

8 Ways to Avoid Probate, by Mary Randolph (Nolo Press), explains eight simple and inexpensive methods of sparing your family the hassle and expense of probate after your death.

Plan Your Estate, by Denis Clifford and Cora Jordan (Nolo Press), offers an in-depth discussion of almost all aspects of estate planning, including probate avoidance.

Living Trusts

If you're considering setting up a living trust to avoid probate, there's no shortage of advice out there—much of it contradictory. Personal finance columnists, lawyers, your Uncle Harry—everybody's got an opinion.

Whether or not a living trust is right for you depends on exactly what you want to accomplish and how much paperwork you're willing to put up with. Living trusts work wonderfully for many people, but not everyone needs one.

What is a living trust?

A trust, like a corporation, is an entity that exists only on paper but is legally capable of owning property. A flesh-and-blood person, however, must actually be in charge of the property; that person is called the trustee. You can be the trustee of your own living trust, keeping full control over all property legally owned by the trust.

There are many kinds of trusts. A "living trust" (also called an "inter vivos" trust by lawyers who can't give up Latin) is simply a trust you create while you're alive, rather than one that is created at your death under the terms of your will.

All living trusts are designed to avoid probate. Some also help you save on death taxes, and others let you set up long-term property management.

Why do I need a living trust?

If you don't take steps to avoid probate, after your death your property will probably have to detour through probate court before it reaches the people you want to inherit it. In a nutshell, probate is the court-supervised process of paying your debts and distributing your property to the people who inherit it. (For more information see *Probate* and *Executors*, above.)

The average probate drags on for months before the inheritors get anything. And by that time, there's less for them to get: In many cases, about 5% of the property has been eaten up by lawyer and court fees. The exact amount depends on state law and the rates of the lawyer hired by the executor.

Don't Forget Your Will!

Even if you make a living trust, you still need a will. Here's why:

A will is an essential back-up device for property that you don't transfer to your living trust. For example, if you acquire property shortly before you die, you may not think to transfer ownership of it to your trust—which means that it won't pass under the terms of the trust document. But in your back-up will, you can include a clause that names someone to get any property that you don't leave to a particular person or entity.

If you don't have a will, any property that isn't transferred by your living trust or other probate-avoidance device (such as joint tenancy) will go to your closest relatives in an order determined by state law. These laws may not distribute property in the way you would have chosen.

How does a living trust avoid probate?

Property you transfer into a living trust before your death doesn't go through probate. The successor trustee—the person you appointed to handle the trust after your death—simply transfers ownership to the beneficiaries you named in the trust. In many cases, the whole process takes only a few weeks, and there are no lawyer or court fees to pay. When the property has all been transferred to the beneficiaries, the living trust ceases to exist.

Is it expensive to create a living trust?

The expense of a living trust comes up front. Lawyers have figured out that they can charge high fees—much higher than for wills, documents usually of comparable complexity—for living trusts. They commonly charge upwards of $1,000 to draw up a simple trust. If you're going to hire a lawyer to draw up your living trust, you might pay as much now as your heirs would have to pay for probate after your death—which means the trust offers no net savings.

But you don't have to pay a lawyer to create a living trust. With a good self-help book or software program, you can create a valid Declaration of Trust (the document that creates a trust) yourself. If you run into questions that a self-help publication doesn't answer, you may need to consult a lawyer, but you probably won't need to turn the whole job over to an expensive expert.

Isn't it a hassle to own property in a trust?

Making a living trust work for you does require some crucial paperwork. For example, if you want to leave your house through the trust, you must sign a new deed showing that you now own the house as trustee of your living trust. And in a few states, you may need to use special language in your trust document to avoid wrinkles in your state's income tax laws. This paperwork can be tedious, but the hassles are fewer these days because living trusts are becoming quite commonplace.

Is a trust document ever made public, like a will?

A will becomes a matter of public record when it is submitted to a probate court, as do all the other documents associated with probate—inventories of the deceased person's assets and debts, for example. The terms of a living trust, however, need not be made public.

Does a trust protect property from creditors?

Holding assets in a revocable trust doesn't shelter them from creditors. A creditor who wins a lawsuit against you can go after the trust property just as if you still owned it in your own name.

After your death, however, property in a living trust can be quickly and quietly distributed to the beneficiaries (unlike property that must go through probate). That complicates matters for creditors; by the time they find out about your death, your property may already be dispersed, and the creditors have no way of knowing exactly what you owned (except for real estate, which is always a matter of public record). It may not be worth the creditor's time and effort to try to track down the property and demand that the new owners use it to pay your debts.

On the other hand, probate can offer a kind of protection from creditors. During probate, known creditors must be notified of the death and given a chance to file claims. If they miss the deadline to file, they're out of luck forever.

I'm young and healthy. Do I really need a trust now?

Probably not. At this stage in your life, your main estate planning goals are probably making sure that in the unlikely event of your early death, your property is distributed how you want it to be and, if you have young children, that they are cared for. You don't need a trust to accomplish those ends; writing a will, and perhaps buying some life insurance, would be simpler.

Can a living trust save on estate taxes?

A simple probate-avoidance living trust has no effect on taxes. More complicated living trusts, however, can greatly reduce your federal estate tax bill. Federal estate taxes are collected from large estates—those worth $625,000 to $1 million, depending on the year of death.

One tax-saving living trust is designed primarily for married couples with children. It's commonly called an AB trust, though it goes by many other names. This type of trust can save up to hundreds of thousands of dollars in estate taxes, money that will be passed on to the couple's final inheritors. For more information about how an AB trust works, see the next set of questions, *Estate and Gift Taxes.*

More Information About Living Trusts

Living Trust Maker (Nolo Press) (software for Windows or Macintosh), lets you make a simple revocable probate-avoidance trust using your computer.

Make Your Own Living Trust, by Denis Clifford (Nolo Press), contains forms and instructions for preparing two kinds of living trusts: a basic probate avoidance trust and a tax-saving AB trust.

Plan Your Estate, by Denis Clifford and Cora Jordan (Nolo Press), is a detailed guide to estate planning, including information about living trusts.

Estate and Gift Taxes

In this world nothing can be said to be certain, except death and taxes.

—BENJAMIN FRANKLIN

It's a universal truth that you can't take it with you. But will your inheritors have to pay for what you leave behind? Most people who consider estate planning are understandably concerned with death taxes (also called estate and inheritance taxes). The good news is that most people's estates won't have to pay any death taxes—federal or state.

Will my estate have to pay taxes after I die?

It depends. The federal government imposes estate taxes only if your property is worth more than a certain amount—$625,000 in 1998—at your death. But there are a couple of important exceptions to the general rule. All property left to a spouse is exempt from the tax, as long as the spouse is a U.S. citizen. And estate taxes won't be assessed on any property you leave to a tax-exempt charity.

THE PERSONAL ESTATE TAX EXEMPTION

YEAR	AMOUNT
1998	$625,000
1999	$650,000
2000-2001	$675,000
2002-2003	$700,000
2004	$850,000
2005	$950,000
2006 and after	$1 million

As of 1998, special rules apply to family businesses and farms. An estate worth up to $1.3 million can be transferred free of estate tax if it consists largely of a family business. Many restrictions apply to this tax break, however. Here are a few of them: the value of the business must exceed 50% of the gross estate; the business must be left to certain family members or long-time employees; and the deceased owner must have participated in the business. And if the new owners sell within ten years, some or all of the tax saved must be repaid to the IRS.

Don't some states also impose death taxes?

A handful of states impose death taxes. These taxes are of two types: inheritance taxes and estate taxes.

Inheritance taxes are paid by your inheritors, not your estate. Typically, how much they pay depends on their relationship to you. For example, Nebraska imposes a 15% tax if you leave $25,000 to a friend, but only 1% if you leave the money to your child. But tax rates vary from state to state. If you live in Connecticut, your child wouldn't owe any taxes on a $25,000 inheritance, but your friend would owe 9%.

States That Impose Inheritance Taxes

Connecticut	Montana
Delaware	Nebraska
Indiana	New Hampshire
Iowa	New Jersey
Kansas	North Carolina
Kentucky	Oklahoma
Louisiana	Pennsylvania
Maryland	South Dakota
Michigan	Tennessee

State estate taxes are similar to the estate tax imposed by the federal government. Your estate must pay this tax no matter who your beneficiaries are. The good news is that every state except Massachusetts, Mississippi, New York and Ohio has abolished these taxes, at least in effect. In the rest, the state takes part of the money that you owe to the feds; it's a matter for accountants and tax preparers, but doesn't increase the tax bill.

You can find a listing of your state's death tax laws in Nolo's *Plan Your Estate*, by Denis Clifford and Cora Jordan.

What are the rates for federal estate taxes?

The estate tax rate starts at 37% for property worth between $600,000 and $750,000. The maximum is 55% for property worth over $3 million.

Are there ways to avoid federal estate taxes?

Yes, although there are fewer ways than many people think, or hope, there are.

The most popular method is frequently used by married couples with grown children. It's called an AB trust, though it's sometimes known as a "credit shelter trust," "exemption trust," "marital life estate trust" or "marital bypass trust." Spouses put their property in the trust, and then, when one spouse dies, his or her half of the property goes to the children—with the crucial condition that the surviving spouse gets the right to use it for life and is entitled to any income it generates. When the second spouse dies, the property goes to the children outright. Using this kind of trust keeps the second spouse's taxable estate half the size it would be if the property were left entirely to the spouse, which means that estate taxes may be avoided altogether.

Unlike a probate-avoidance revocable living trust, an AB trust controls what happens to property for years after the first spouse's death. A couple who makes one must be sure that the surviving spouse will be financially and emotionally comfortable receiving only the income from the money or property placed in trust, with the children as the actual owners of the property.

How an AB Trust Works: An Example

Ellen and Jack have been married for nearly 50 years. They have one grown son, Robert, who is 39. Ellen and Jack create an AB trust and transfer all their major items of property to it. They name each other as life beneficiaries, and Robert as the final beneficiary.

Ellen dies first. The trust automatically splits into two parts: Trust A, which is irrevocable, contains Ellen's share of the property. Trust B is Jack's trust, and it stays revocable as long as he is alive.

The property in Trust A legally belongs to Robert, but with one very important condition: His father, Jack, is entitled to use the property, and collect any income it generates, for the rest of his life. When Jack dies, the property will go to Robert free and clear.

Now let's take a look at the tax savings: Ellen's half of the trust property is worth $600,000 when she dies.

At Ellen's death

Taxable estate $600,000

Estate tax $0

(because of the personal exemption)

At Jack's death

Taxable estate $600,000

Estate tax $0

If Ellen had left all her property to Jack outright, his estate would have been worth $1.2 million at his death—which would have resulted in thousands of dollars of estate tax.

Are there other ways to save on estate taxes?

Yes. Common ones include what's called a "QTIP" trust, which enables a surviving spouse to postpone estate taxes that would otherwise be due when the other spouse dies. And there are many different types of charitable trusts, which involve making a sizable gift to a tax-exempt charity. Some of them provide both income tax and estate tax advantages.

Can I avoid paying state death taxes?

If your state imposes death taxes, there probably isn't much you can do. But if you live in two states—winter here, summer there—your inheritors may save on death taxes if you can make your legal residence in the state with lower, or no, death taxes.

Can't I just give all my property away before I die and avoid estate taxes?

No. The government long anticipated this one. If you give away more than $10,000 per year to any one person or noncharitable institution, you are assessed federal "gift tax," which applies at the same rate as the estate tax. There are, however, a few exceptions to this rule. You can give an unlimited amount of property to your spouse, unless your spouse is not a U.S. citizen, in which case you can give away up to $100,000 per year free of gift tax. Any property given to a tax-exempt charity avoids federal gift taxes. And money spent directly for someone's medical bills or school tuition is exempt as well.

But I've heard that people save on estate taxes by making gifts. How?

You can achieve substantial estate tax savings by making use of the $10,000 annual gift tax exclusion for gifts to people and nonexempt organizations. If you give away $10,000 for four years, you've removed $40,000 from your taxable estate. And each member of a couple has a separate $10,000 exclusion. So a couple can give $20,000 a year to a child free of gift tax. If you have a few children, or other people you want to make gifts to (such as your sons- or daughters-in-

law), you can use this method to significantly reduce the size of your taxable estate over a few years.

Consider a couple with combined assets worth $1.2 million and three children. Each year they give each child $20,000 tax free, for a total of $60,000 per year. In seven years, the couple has given away $420,000 and has reduced their estate to $600,000, below the federal estate tax threshold.

Of course, there are risks with this kind of gift-giving program. The most obvious is that you are legally transferring your wealth. Gift giving to reduce eventual estate taxes must be carefully evaluated to see if you can comfortably afford to give away your property during your lifetime.

More Information About Estate and Gift Taxes

9 Ways to Avoid Estate Taxes, by Mary Randolph and Denis Clifford (Nolo Press), presents the nine major methods you can use to avoid, or reduce, federal estate taxes.

Plan Your Estate, by Denis Clifford and Cora Jordan (Nolo Press), is a detailed guide to estate planning, including all major methods of reducing or avoiding estate and gift taxes.

Funeral Planning and Other Final Arrangements

Many of us are squeamish when it comes to thinking and talking about death, particularly our own. But there are many good reasons to spend some time considering what you want to have happen to your body after death, including any ceremonies and observances you'd like.

Why should I leave written instructions about my final ceremonies and the disposition of my body?

Letting your survivors know your wishes saves them the difficulties of making these decisions at a painful time. And many family members and friends find that discussing these matters ahead of time is great relief— especially if a person is elderly or in poor health and death is expected soon.

Planning some of these details in advance can also help save money. For many people, death goods and services cost more than anything they bought during their lives except homes and cars. Some wise comparison shopping in advance can help ensure that costs will be controlled or kept to a minimum.

Why not leave these instructions in my will?

A will is not a good place to express your death and burial preferences for one simple reason: Your will probably won't be located and read until several weeks after you die—long after decisions must be made.

A will should be reserved for directions on how to divide and distribute your property and, if applicable, who should get care and custody of your children if you die while they're still young.

What happens if I don't leave written instructions?

If you die without leaving written instructions about your preferences, state law will determine who will have the right to decide how your remains will be handled. In most states, the right—and the responsibility to pay for the reasonable costs of disposing of remains—rests with the following people, in order:

- spouse
- child or children
- parent or parents
- the next of kin, or
- a public administrator, who is appointed by a court.

Disputes may arise if two or more people—the deceased person's children, for example—share responsibility for a fundamental decision, such as whether the body of a parent should be buried or cremated. But such disputes can be avoided if you are willing to do some planning and to put your wishes in writing.

What details should I include in a final arrangements document?

What you choose to include is a personal matter, likely to be dictated by custom, religious preference or simply your own whims. A typical final arrangements document might include:

- the name of the mortuary or other institution that will handle burial or cremation
- whether or not you wish to be embalmed
- the type of casket or container in which your remains will be buried or cremated, including whether you want it present at any after-death ceremony
- the details of any ceremony you want before the burial or cremation
- who your pallbearers will be if you wish to have some
- how your remains will be transported to the cemetery and gravesite
- where your remains will be buried, stored or scattered
- the details of any ceremony you want to accompany your burial, interment or scattering, and
- the details of any marker you want to show where your remains are buried or interred.

What services can I expect from a mortuary?

Most mortuaries or funeral homes are equipped to handle many of the details related to disposing of a person's remains. These include:

- collecting the body from the place of death
- storing the body until it is buried or cremated

- making burial arrangements with a cemetery
- conducting ceremonies related to the burial
- preparing the body for burial, and
- arranging to have the body transported for burial.

Where can I turn for help in making final arrangements?

From an economic standpoint, choosing the institution to handle your burial is probably the most important final arrangement that you can make. For this reason, many people join memorial or funeral societies, which help them find local mortuaries that will deal honestly with their survivors and charge reasonable prices.

Society members are free to choose whatever final arrangements they wish. Most societies, however, emphasize simple arrangements over the costly services often promoted by the funeral industry. The services offered by each society differ, but most societies distribute information on options and explain the legal rules that apply to final arrangements.

If you join a society, you will receive a form that allows you to plan for the goods and services you want—and to get them for a predetermined cost. Many societies also serve as watchdogs, making sure that you get and pay for only the services you choose.

The cost for joining these organizations is low—usually from $20 to $40 for a lifetime membership, although some societies periodically charge a small renewal fee.

To find a funeral or memorial society near you, look in the YellowPages of your telephone book under Funeral Information and Advisory Services, or contact the Funeral and Memorial Societies of America, 800-458-5563, http://vbiweb.champlain.edu/famsa (online).

If you don't want to join a society, you can look for a mortuary or funeral home on your own. You'll have to shop around to find the institution that best meets your needs in terms of style, proximity and cost.

Beware of Prepayment Plans

Shopping around for the most suitable and affordable funeral goods and services is a wise idea. Be extremely cautious, however, about paying in advance—often called prepaying—for them.

Although there are a number of legal controls on how the funeral industry can handle and invest funds earmarked for future services, there are many reported instances of mismanaged or stolen funds. A great many other abuses go unreported by family members too embarrassed or too grief-stricken to complain.

There are additional pitfalls. When mortuaries go out of business, the consumer who has prepaid is often left without funds and without recourse. Also, many individuals who move to a new locale during their lifetimes are dismayed to find that their prepayment funds are nonrefundable or that there is a substan-

tial financial penalty for withdrawing or transferring them. In addition, money paid now may not cover inflated costs of the future, meaning that survivors will be left to cover the substantially higher costs.

If you are interested in setting aside a fund of money to pay for your final arrangements, a more prudent approach for most people is to set up a trust or savings account earmarked to pay for your final arrangements. Most banks and savings institutions will do so for a very slight charge. You can easily withdraw or transfer the funds during your life, if need be. At your death, the trusted individual or institution you name in the bank documents can take over and spend the money as you have directed.

More Information About Final Arrangements

Funeral and Memorial Societies of America can help you locate a funeral or memorial society near you. Call 800-458-5563 or reach Famsa online at http://vbiweb.champlain.edu/famsa.

WillMaker (software for Windows or Macintosh) (Nolo Press), lets you use your computer to create a final arrangements document, in addition to a valid will, healthcare directives and a durable power of attorney for finances.

Body and Organ Donations

In addition to making other arrangements for your funeral and burial or cremation, you may want to arrange to donate some or all of your body organs. You must make these arrangements separately and document your wishes on a special form.

How can I arrange to donate my body for scientific research or study after my death?

Arrangements for whole body donations must usually be made while you are alive, although some medical schools will accept a cadaver through arrangements made after death.

The best place to contact to arrange a whole body donation is the nearest medical school. If you live in a state with no medical school or one that has very strict requirements for whole body donations, you may wish to find out more about your body donation options from the National Anatomical Service at 800-727-0700.

How can I arrange to donate my body organs for others to use after my death?

The principal method for donating organs is by indicating your intent to do so on a uniform donor card. Once signed, this card identifies you to medical personnel as a potential organ donor. You can get a donor card or form from most hospitals, the county or state office of the National Kidney Foundation or a community eye bank.

In most states, you can also obtain an organ donation card from the department of motor vehicles. Depending on where you live, you can check a box, affix a stamp or seal or attach a separate card to your license, indicating your wish to donate one or more organs.

Even if you have not signed a card or other document indicating your intent to donate your organs, your next of kin can approve a donation after you die. If you fill out an organ donor card, make sure you tell family members you have done so. Even if you have indicated an intent to donate your organs, an objection by your next of kin will often defeat your intention; medical personnel usually do not proceed in the face of an objection from relatives. The best safeguard is to discuss your wishes with close friends and relatives, emphasizing your strong feelings about donating your body for research or teaching.

http://www.nolo.com
Nolo Press offers self-help information about a wide variety of legal topics, including wills and estate planning.

http://www.netplanning.com
The National Association of Estate Planning Attorneys offers question and answer databases on numerous estate planning topics.

http://www.law.cornell.edu/topics/estate_gift_tax.htm
The Legal Information Institute at Cornell Law School provides information about estate and gift taxes, as well as referrals to other tax and estate planning resources on the World Wide Web.

http://www.investorguide.com/Retirement.htm *Investor Guide: Retirement includes articles covering basic estate planning information, plus links to other good estate planning sites on the Web.*

Living Wills and Powers of Attorney

There is no mortal whom sorrow and disease do not touch.

—EURIPIDES

Many of us fear that we may someday become seriously ill and unable to handle our own affairs. Who would act on our behalf to pay bills, make bank deposits, watch over investments and deal with the paperwork that accompanies collecting insurance and government benefits? Who would make arrangements for our medical care and see that our wishes for treatment are carried out?

Preparing a few simple documents—healthcare directives and a durable power of attorney for finances—can ease these worries by ensuring that your affairs will stay in the hands of trusted people whom you choose. This chapter answers your questions about these documents and how they work, as well as what happens if a court appoints a conservator—that is, the person who will manage your affairs if you haven't drafted legally valid instructions naming someone to take over.

Healthcare Directives

Nearly 80% of Americans die in a hospital or other care facility. The doctors who work in these facilities are generally charged with preserving a patient's life through whatever means are available. This may or may not be what you would like in the way of treatment. Healthcare directives give you the opportunity to write out your wishes in advance and ensure some legal respect for them if ever you are unable to speak for yourself.

What is a living will?

A living will, known in some states as a directive to physicians or healthcare directive, sets out your wishes about what medical treatment should be withheld or provided if you become unable to communicate those wishes. The directive creates a contract with the attending doctor. Once the doctor receives a properly signed and witnessed directive, she is under a duty either to honor its instructions or to make sure you are transferred to the care of another doctor who will.

Many people mistakenly believe that healthcare directives are used only to instruct doctors to withhold life-prolonging treatments. In fact, some people want to reinforce that they would like to receive all medical treatment that is available—and a healthcare directive is the proper place to say so.

What is a durable power of attorney for healthcare? Doesn't that do the same thing as a living will?

A durable power of attorney for healthcare—called a healthcare proxy in some states—gives another person authority to make medical decisions for you if you are unable to make them for yourself. Unlike a healthcare directive, this document doesn't necessarily state what type of treatment you want to receive. You can leave those decisions to your proxy if you feel comfortable doing so. Depending on the requirements imposed by your state law, you may need to make one or two documents to express your wishes for medical care. For example, your healthcare directive may contain a clause appointing a proxy (sometimes called an attorney-in-fact, agent or representative) to be certain your wishes are carried out as you've directed. On the other hand, you may need to create two separate documents: a directive explaining the treatment you wish to receive, and a durable power of attorney appointing someone to oversee your directive.

What happens if I don't have any healthcare documents?

If you have not completed a formal document such as a healthcare directive to express your wishes or a durable power of attorney to appoint someone to make healthcare decisions on your behalf, the doctors who attend you will use their own discretion in deciding what kind of medical care you will receive.

When a question arises about whether surgery or some other serious procedure is authorized, doctors may turn for consent to a close relative—spouse, parent or adult child. Friends and unmarried partners, although they may be most familiar with your wishes for your medical treatment, are rarely consulted, or are purposefully left out of the decision-making process.

Problems arise when partners and family members disagree about what treatment is proper. In the most complicated case scenarios, these battles over medical care wind up in court, where a judge, who usually has little medical knowledge and no familiarity with you, is called upon to decide the future of your treatment. Such legal battles—which are costly, time consuming and usually painful to those involved—are unnecessary if you have the care and foresight to use a formal document to express your wishes for your healthcare.

When Your Healthcare Directive Takes Effect

Your healthcare directive becomes effective when three things happen:

- you are diagnosed as close to death from a terminal condition or permanently comatose—or, in a few states, if you have a number of other serious conditions

- you cannot communicate your own wishes for your medical care—orally, in writing or through gestures, and

- the medical personnel attending you are notified of your written directions for your medical care.

In most instances, your directive becomes part of your medical record when you are admitted to a hospital or other care facility. But to ensure that your wishes will be followed if your need for care arises unexpectedly or while you are out of your home state or country, it is best to give copies of your completed documents to several people, including your regular physician, your healthcare proxy (if you have appointed one) and another trusted friend.

Whom should I choose as a healthcare proxy?

The person you name as your healthcare proxy should be someone you trust—and someone with whom you feel confident discussing your wishes. While your proxy need not agree with your wishes for your medical care, you should believe that he respects your right to get the kind of medical care you want.

The person you appoint to oversee your healthcare wishes could be a spouse or partner, relative or close friend. Keep in mind that your proxy may have to fight to assert your wishes in the face of a stubborn medical establishment—and against the wishes of family members who may be driven by their own beliefs and interests, rather than yours. If you foresee the possibility of a conflict in enforcing your wishes, be sure to choose a proxy who is strong willed and assertive.

While you need not name someone who lives in the same state as you do, proximity may be an important factor. The reality is that the person you name may be called upon to spend weeks or months near your bedside, making sure medical personnel abide by your wishes for your healthcare. If you name someone who lives far away, make sure that person is willing to travel and stay with you a while. The job of proxy may demand it.

You should not choose your doctor or an employee of a hospital or nursing home where you receive treatment. In fact, the laws in many states prevent you from naming such a person. In a few instances, this legal constraint may frustrate your wishes. For example, you may wish to name your spouse or partner as your representative, but if he works as a hospital employee, you may be barred from naming that person. If the law in your state bans your first choice, you will have to name another person to serve.

What if I really don't know anyone I trust to supervise my medical care?

Naming a healthcare proxy is an optional part of completing your healthcare directive. It is better not to name anyone than to name someone who is not comfortable with the directions you leave—or who is not likely to assert your wishes strongly.

Medical personnel are still technically bound to follow your written wishes for your healthcare—or to find someone who will care for you in the way you have directed. It is far better to put your wishes for final healthcare in writing than to let the lack of a representative stand in the way.

What types of medical care should I consider when completing my healthcare documents?

Technological advances mean that currently unfathomable procedures and treatments will become available, and treatments that are now common will become obsolete. Also, the treatments that are available vary drastically with region, depending on the sophistication and funding levels of local medical facilities.

While putting together your healthcare directive, the best that you can do is to become familiar with the kinds of medical procedures that are most commonly administered to patients who are seriously ill. These include:

- blood and blood products
- cardiopulmonary resuscitation (CPR)
- diagnostic tests
- dialysis
- drugs
- respirators, and
- surgery.

Can I leave instructions about pain medication, or about food and water?

The laws of most states assume that people want relief from pain and discomfort and specifically exclude pain-relieving procedures from definitions of life-prolonging treatments that may be withheld. Some states also exclude food and water (commonly called nutrition and hydration) from their definitions of life-prolonging treatments. But there is some controversy about whether providing food and water, or drugs to make a person comfortable, will also have the effect of prolonging life. Some people are so adamant about not having their lives prolonged when they are comatose or likely to die soon that they choose to direct that all food, water and pain relief be withheld, even if the doctor thinks those procedures are necessary. Under the U.S. Constitution, you are allowed to leave these instructions even if your state's law is restrictive—your doctors should be bound to follow your wishes.

On the other hand, some people feel concerned about how much pain or discomfort they may experience during a final illness; these people are willing to have their lives prolonged rather than face the possibility that discomfort or pain would go untreated. Obviously, it's a very personal choice—you're free to leave the instructions that feel right for you.

Where can I get a healthcare directive—and who can help complete it?

Many people first realize the need for healthcare documents when they're being admitted to a hospital. But hospital admission time is probably not the best time to learn about your options in directing healthcare or to reflect on your wishes—it's better to get information and complete your documents when you're under less stress.

Local senior centers may be good resources for help. Many of them have trained healthcare staff on hand who will be willing to discuss your healthcare options. The patient representative at a local hospital may also be a good person to contact for help. And if you have a regular physician, you can discuss your concerns with him or her.

Local special interest groups and clinics may provide help in obtaining and filling out healthcare directives—particularly organizations set up to meet the needs of the severely ill, such as AIDS groups or cancer organizations. Check your telephone book for a local listing—or call one of the group's hotlines for more information or a possible referral.

There are also a number of seminars offered to help people with their healthcare documents. Beware of groups that offer such seminars for a hefty fee, however. Hospitals and senior centers often provide them free of charge.

More Information About Healthcare Directives

WillMaker (Nolo Press) (software for Windows and Macintosh), walks you step by step through the process of writing your own will, durable power of attorney for finances, healthcare documents and a document setting out your final arrangements.

Make Your Documents Legal

There are a few requirements you must meet in order to make a valid healthcare directive. In most states, you must be 18 years old, though a few states allow parents to make healthcare directives for their minor children. All states require that the person making a healthcare directive be able to understand what the document means, what it contains and how it works.

Also, every state requires that you sign your documents. If you are physically unable to sign them yourself, you can direct another person to sign them for you.

You must sign your documents, or have them signed for you, in the presence of witnesses or a notary public—sometimes both (this depends on your state's law). The purpose of this additional formality is so that there is at least one other person who can confirm that you were of sound mind and of legal age when you made the documents.

Durable Powers of Attorney for Finances

A durable power of attorney for finances is a simple, inexpensive and reliable way to arrange for someone to make your financial decisions should you become unable to do so yourself. It's also a wonderful thing to do for your family members. If you do become incapacitated, the durable power of attorney will likely appear as a minor miracle to those close to you.

How does a durable power of attorney work?

When you create and sign a power of attorney, you give another person legal authority to act on your behalf. The person who is given this authority is called your attorney-in-fact or, sometimes, your agent. The word attorney here means anyone authorized to act on another's behalf; it's most definitely not restricted to lawyers.

A "durable" power of attorney stays valid even if you become unable to handle your own affairs (incapacitated). If you don't specify that you want your power of attorney to continue if you become incapacitated, it will automatically end if you later become unable to take care of yourself.

When does a durable power of attorney take effect?

A durable power of attorney can be drafted so that it goes into effect as soon as you sign it. That is appropriate if you face a serious operation or incapacitating illness—or even if you're not incapacitated but want your attorney-in-fact to start helping with financial tasks right away.

You can also specify that the durable power of attorney does not go into effect unless a doctor certifies that you have become incapacitated. This is called a "springing" durable power of attorney. It allows you to keep control over your financial matters unless and until you become incapacitated, when it springs into effect.

How do I create a durable power of attorney for finances?

To create a legally valid durable power of attorney, all you need to do is properly complete and sign a fill-in-the-blanks form that's a few pages long. Some states have their own forms.

After you fill out the form, you must sign it in front of a notary public. In some states, witnesses must also watch you sign the document. If your attorney-in-fact will have authority to deal with your real estate, you must put a copy on file at the local land records office. (In just two states, North and South Carolina, you must record your power of attorney for it to be durable.)

Some banks, title companies, insurance companies, brokerage companies and other financial institutions have their own durable power of attorney forms. If you want your attorney-in-fact to have an easy time with these institutions, you may need to prepare two (or more) durable powers of attorney: your own form and forms provided by the institutions with which you do business.

What happens if I don't have a durable power of attorney for finances?

If you become incapacitated and you haven't prepared a durable power of attorney for finances, a court proceeding is probably inescapable. Your spouse, closest relatives or companion will have to ask a court for authority over at least some of your financial affairs.

If you are married, your spouse does have some authority over property you own together—to pay bills from a joint bank account, for example. There are significant limits, however, on your spouse's right to sell property owned by both of you.

If your relatives go to court to get someone appointed to manage your financial affairs, they must ask a judge to rule that you cannot take care of your own affairs—a public airing of a very private matter. And like any court proceeding, it can be expensive if your relatives must hire a lawyer. Depending on where you live, the person appointed is called a conservator, guardian of the estate, committee or curator. When this person is appointed, you lose the right to control your own money and property.

The appointment of a conservator is usually just the beginning of court proceedings. Often the conservator must:

- post a bond—a kind of insurance policy that pays if the conservator steals or misuses property
- prepare (or hire a lawyer or accountant to prepare) detailed financial reports and periodically file them with the court, and
- get court approval for certain transactions, such as selling real estate or making slightly risky investments.

A conservatorship isn't necessarily permanent, but it may be ended only by the court. Conservatorships are discussed in more detail in the next set of questions.

The Attorney-in-Fact's Duties

Commonly, people give an attorney-in-fact broad power over their finances. But you can give your attorney-in-fact as much or as little power as you wish. You may want to give your attorney-in-fact authority to do some or all of the following:

- use your assets to pay your everyday expenses and those of your family

- buy, sell, maintain, pay taxes on and mortgage real estate and other property
- collect benefits from Social Security, Medicare or other government programs or civil or military service
- invest your money in stocks, bonds and mutual funds
- handle transactions with banks and other financial institutions
- buy and sell insurance policies and annuities for you
- file and pay your taxes
- operate your small business
- claim property you inherit or are otherwise entitled to
- represent you in court or hire someone to represent you, and
- manage your retirement accounts.

Whatever powers you give the attorney-in-fact, the attorney-in-fact must act in your best interests, keep accurate records, keep your property separate from his or hers and avoid conflicts of interest.

I have a living trust. Do I still need a durable power of attorney for finances?

A revocable living trust can be useful if you become incapable of taking care of your financial affairs. That's because the person who will distribute trust property after your death (the successor trustee) can also, in most cases, take over management of the trust property if you become incapacitated.

Few people, however, transfer all their property to a living trust, and the successor trustee has no authority over property that the trust doesn't own. So a living trust isn't a complete substitute for a durable power of attorney for finances.

Can my attorney-in-fact make medical decisions on my behalf?

No. A durable power of attorney for finances does not give your attorney-in-fact legal authority to make medical decisions for you.

You can, however, prepare a durable power of attorney for healthcare, a document that lets you choose someone to make medical decisions on your behalf if you can't. In most states, you'll also want to write out your wishes in a "living will" (also called a healthcare directive or directive to physicians), which will tell your doctors your preferences about certain kinds of medical treatment and life-sustaining procedures if you can't communicate your wishes.

Healthcare documents are discussed in more detail in the previous section of this chapter.

When does the durable power of attorney end?

It ends at your death. That means that you can't give your attorney-in-fact authority to handle things after your death, such as paying your debts, making funeral or burial arrangements or transferring your property to the people who inherit it. If you want your attorney-in-fact to have authority to wind up your affairs after your death, use a will to name that person as your executor.

Your durable power of attorney also ends if:

- You revoke it. (As long as you are mentally competent, you can revoke a durable power of attorney at any time.)
- A court invalidates your document. (This happens rarely, but a court may declare your document invalid if it concludes that you were not mentally competent when you signed it, or that you were the victim of fraud or undue influence.)
- You get a divorce. (In a few states, including California, Illinois, Indiana and Missouri, if your spouse is your attorney-in-fact and you divorce, your ex-spouse's authority is automatically terminated. In any state, however, it is wise to revoke your durable power of attorney after a divorce and make a new one.)
- No attorney-in-fact is available. (A durable power of attorney must end if there's no one to serve as attorney-in-fact. To avoid this problem, you can name alternate attorneys-in-fact in your document.)

More Information About Durable Powers of Attorney for Finances

Willmaker (Nolo Press)(software for Windows and Macintosh), walks you step by step through the process of writing your own will, durable power of attorney for finances, healthcare documents and a document setting out your final arrangements. About a dozen states (Alaska, California, Colorado, Connecticut, Illinois, Indiana, Minnesota, Montana, New Mexico, New York, North Carolina Texas and Wisconsin) have their own fill-in-the-blank forms, published in their statute books. You can find your state's form by going to a law library and looking up "Durable Power of Attorney" in the index to the state statutes. Then type out a document, following the model form eaclty.

Conservatorships

A conservatorship is a legal arrange-ment in which an adult has the court-ordered authority and responsibility to manage another adult's financial affairs. Many states use the terms "conservator" and "guardian" inter-changeably, or use other terms such as "custodian" or "curator." In this book, we use the term "guardian" for a per-son who makes personal decisions for a child, and "conservator" for someone who takes care of financial matters for an incapacitated adult. The adult who needs help is called the "conservatee."

If you need information about guardianships for children, see Chapter 16, *Parents and Children*.

When is a conservatorship necessary?

A conservatorship is permitted only when someone is so incapacitated that he cannot manage his own financial affairs. Generally, conservatorships are established for people who are in comas, suffer from advanced stages of Alzheimer's disease or have other serious illnesses or injuries.

Conservatorships are rarely needed for people who have made—or can knowingly sign—financial documents, such as a durable power of attorney for finances. (See the previous section of this chapter.)

What are the advantages of a conservatorship?

Conservatorships are subject to court supervision, which provides a powerful safeguard for an incapacitated adult's property. To prevent a conservator from mismanaging the property of the person she is helping (the conservatee), most courts require the conservator to provide periodic reports and accountings that give details about the conservatee's assets and how the conservatee's money was spent. Many courts also require the conservator to seek permission before making major decisions about the conservatee's property, such as whether to sell his real estate.

What are the downsides to a conservatorship?

Conservatorships are time consuming and expensive; they often require court hearings and the ongoing assistance of a lawyer. The paperwork can also be a hassle because, as mentioned above, the conservator must keep detailed records and file court papers on a regular basis.

In addition, a conservator must usually post a bond (a kind of insurance policy that protects the conservatee's estate from mishandling). The bond premiums are paid by the conservatee's estate—and are an unnecessary expense if the conservator is competent and trustworthy.

Occasionally, however, a conservator will mismanage a conservatee's assets. Common abuses range from reckless handling of the conservatee's assets to outright theft. Although each state has rules and procedures designed to prevent mishandling of assets, few have the resources to keep an eye on conservators and follow through if they spot trouble. Many cases of incompetence or abuse go unnoticed.

Finally, a conservatorship can be emotionally trying for the conservatee. All court proceedings and documents are public records, which can be embarrassing for someone who values independence and privacy.

How are conservators compensated for their services?

The conservatee's estate must reimburse the conservator for necessary expenses and pay for the conservator's services—if these payments are "reasonable" in the eyes of a court. Generally, payments are made to professional or public conservators, but a family member who has been appointed conservator may also seek compensation by making a request to the court.

Are there ways to block a conservatorship?

Before a court approves a conservatorship, notice must be given to the proposed conservatee and his close family members. Anyone—including the proposed conservatee, family members and friends—may object to the conservatorship in general, or to the specific choice of conservator. The person who wants to block the conservatorship must file papers with the court, inform all interested parties (the proposed conservatee, family members and possibly close friends) and attend a legal hearing. The final decision is up to a judge.

The best way to avoid a conservatorship is to prepare a durable power of attorney for finances before a health crisis occurs. That way, someone you've hand-picked will be able to step in and make decisions for you if necessary. (For information about preparing this document, see the previous section of this chapter.)

How does a judge choose a conservator?

When a conservatorship petition is filed in court, a judge must decide whom to appoint. Often, just one person is interested in taking on the role of conservator—but sometimes several family members or friends vie for the task. If no one suitable is available to serve as conservator, the judge may appoint a public or other professional conservator.

When appointing a conservator, a judge follows certain preferences established by state law: Most states give preference to the conservatee's spouse, adult children, adult siblings or other blood relatives. But a judge has some flexibility; he may use his discretion to pick the person he thinks is best for the job. Without strong evidence of what the conservatee would have wanted, however, it is unlikely that a nonrelative would be appointed over a relative. Because of this, conservatorship proceedings may cause great heartache if an estranged relative is chosen as conservator over the conservatee's partner or close friend.

Who financially supports someone under a conservatorship?

If the conservatee has the means, money for his support will come from his own assets. But a conservator should seek all financial benefits and coverage for which the conservatee may qualify. These benefits may include Social Security, medical insurance, Veterans Administration benefits, pension and retirement benefits, disability benefits, public assistance and Supplemental Security Income. When needed, close family members (including the conservator) often contribute their own money to help support a conservatee.

When does a conservatorship end?

A conservator must care for the conservatee's finances until the court issues an order relieving her from responsibility. This ordinarily happens when:

- the conservatee dies
- the conservatorship estate is used up
- the conservatee regains the ability to handle her own finances, or
- the conservator becomes unable or unwilling to handle the responsibilities. In this situation, the conservatorship itself does not end, but someone else takes over the conservator's duties.

More Information About Conservatorships

The Conservatorship Book, by Lisa Goldoftas & Carolyn Farren (Nolo Press), contains forms and instructions for getting a conservator appointed in California, without a lawyer. For information about conservatorships in other states, visit your local law library.

http://www.nolo.com

Nolo Press offers self-help information on a wide variety of legal topics, including healthcare directives, powers of attorney and conservatorships.

http://www.choices.org/

Choice In Dying offers information and publications about healthcare directives, as well as state-specific forms that you can download.

Many sites offer state-specific information about durable powers of attorney for finances and conservatorships. If you need more information about your state's laws, you can use an online search engine to hunt for a site that will help you. Chapter 19 of this book contains instructions for conducting searches online—see the Legal Research *section.*

Older Americans

To be seventy years young is sometimes far more cheerful and hopeful than to be forty years old.

—OLIVER WENDELL HOLMES, JR.

For many older Americans, the final years are no longer the Golden Years. Worries over limited incomes—and the real threat of being financially ruined by any extended bout with the medical system—crowd out thoughts of leisure and fulfillment.

There is help available for supplementing limited incomes and covering medical care in your later years, but you have to take some initiative to find it. It also helps if you have the good fortune and foresight to do some early planning.

Social Security

Social Security is the general term that describes a number of related programs —retirement, disability, dependents and survivors benefits. These programs together provide workers and their families with some money when their normal flow of income shrinks because of retirement, disability or death.

Unfortunately, the government's original goal of providing financial security through these programs is becoming increasingly remote. The combination of rapidly rising living costs, stagnating benefit amounts and penalties for older people who continue to work make the amount of support offered by Social Security less adequate with each passing year. This shrinking of the Social Security safety net makes it that much more important that you know how to get the maximum benefits to which you are entitled.

How much can I expect to get in Social Security benefits?

There is no easy answer to this question. The amount of benefits to which you are entitled under any Social Security program is not related to need, but is based on the income you have earned through years of working. In most jobs, both you and your employer have paid Social Security taxes on the amounts you earned. Since 1951, Social Security taxes have also been paid on reported self-employment income. Social Security keeps a record of these earnings over your working lifetime, and pays benefits based upon the average amount earned.

Who is eligible to collect benefits?

The specific requirements vary depending on the type of benefits, the age of the person filing the claim and, if you are claiming as a dependent or survivor, the age of the worker. There is a general requirement, however, that everyone must meet to receive one of these Social Security benefits: The worker on whose earnings record the benefit is to be paid must have worked in "covered employment" for a sufficient number of years —that is, earned what Social Security calls work credits—by the time he or she claims retirement benefits, becomes disabled or dies. To find out about your eligibility, call the Social Security Administration, 800-772-1213.

Note that Social Security eligibility rules have recently changed for some specific types of workers, including federal, state and local government workers; workers for nonprofit organizations; members of the military; household workers; and farm workers. If you have been employed for some time as one of these types of workers, check with the Social Security Administration for special rules that may affect your eligibility.

Social Security Benefits: A Guide to the Basics

Four basic categories of Social Security benefits are paid based upon the record of your earnings: retirement, disability, dependents and survivors benefits.

Retirement benefits. You may choose to begin receiving retirement benefits at any time after you reach age 62; the amount of benefits will increase for each year you wait until age 70. The increase in delayed benefits varies from 2% to 8%, depending on the year in which you were born. But no matter how long you wait to begin collecting benefits, the amount you receive will probably be only a small percentage of what you were earning.

Because so many variables are thrown into the mix in computing benefit amounts—some of them based on your individual work record and retirement plans, some of them based on changes and convolutions in Social Security rules—it is impossible to give you what you want most: a solid estimate of the amount that will appear on your retirement benefit check. For a single person first claiming retirement benefits in 1998, the average monthly benefit is about $765; $1,290 for a couple. But these numbers are just averages. Benefits change yearly as the cost of living changes.

Disability benefits. If you are under 65 but have met the work requirements and are considered disabled under the program's medical guidelines, you can receive benefits roughly equal to what your retirement benefits would be.

Dependents benefits. If you are the spouse of a retired or disabled worker who qualifies for retirement or disability benefits, you and your minor or disabled children may be entitled to benefits based on the worker's earning record. This is true whether or not you actually depend on your spouse for your support.

Survivors benefits. If you are the surviving spouse of a worker who qualified for retirement or disability benefits, you and your minor or disabled children may be entitled to benefits based on your deceased spouse's earnings record.

How are my benefit amounts calculated?

The amount of any benefit is determined by a formula based on the average of your yearly reported earnings in covered employment since you began working. To further complicate matters, Social Security computes the average of earnings differently depending on your age. If you reached age 62 or became disabled on or before December 31, 1978, the computation is simple: Social Security averages the actual dollar value of your total past earnings—and bases the amount of your monthly benefits on that amount.

If you turned 62 or became disabled on or after January 1, 1979, Social Security divides your earnings into two categories: earnings from before 1951 are credited with their actual dollar amount, up to a maximum of $3,000 per year; and from 1951 on, yearly limits are placed on earnings credits, no matter how much you actually earned in those years.

How can I find out what I've earned so far?

The Social Security Administration keeps a running computer account of your earnings record and work credits, tracking both through your Social Security number. The Administration mails out copies of individual Social Security records on a Personal Earnings and Benefit Estimate Statement. The statement is mailed to everyone age 60 and over who is not currently receiving Social Security benefits.

If you are age 60 or over but have not received your statement, or you are under age 60 and want to check your statement now, you can request a copy by filing out a simple form, SSA 7004, called a Request for Earnings and Benefit Estimate Statement, available at your local Social Security office. If you cannot easily get to your local office, you can request a copy of the form, in either Spanish or English, by calling 800-772-1213.

Request Your Earnings and Benefit Statement Online

You can request your Personal Earnings and Benefits Estimate Statement through the Social Security Administration's Website, without having to fill out and request a written form. The Administration reportedly responds to online requests much more quickly than it does to mailed requests, so using this format may shave weeks off the time it takes to get your estimate.

If you have access to the Internet, you can find the Social Security Administration's site at www.ssa.gov. Once you get to the site, look for the headings listed under Online Direct Service. Click *Request a Personal Earnings and Benefits Statement*.

If You Find an Error

Some government-watchers estimate that the Social Security Administration makes mistakes on at least 3% of the total official earnings records it keeps. It is always wise for you to check the SSA's work. Make sure that the Social Security number noted on your earnings statement is your own. Also make sure the earned income amounts listed on the agency's records mesh with your own records of earnings as listed on your income tax forms or pay stubs.

When you have evidence of your covered earnings in the year or years for which you think Social Security has made an error, call Social Security's helpline at 800-772-1213, Monday through Friday from 7 a.m. to 7 p.m. This is the line that takes all kinds of Social Security questions and it is often swamped, so be patient. It is best to call early in the morning or late in the afternoon, late in the week or late in the month. Have all your documents handy when you speak with a representative.

If you would rather speak with someone in person, call your local Social Security office and make an appointment to see someone there, or drop into the office during regular business hours. If you drop in, be prepared to wait, perhaps as long as an hour or two, before you get to see a representative. Bring with you two copies of your benefits statement and the evidence that supports your claim of higher income. That way, you can leave one copy with the Social Security worker. Write down the name of the person with whom you speak so that you can reach the same person when you follow up.

The process to correct errors is slow. It may take several months to have the changes made in your record. And once Social Security confirms that it has corrected your record, go through the process of requesting another benefits

statement to make sure the correct information is in your file.

Can I collect more than one type of benefit at a time?

No. You may qualify for more than one type of Social Security benefit, but you can collect just one. For example, you might be eligible for both retirement and disability, or you might be entitled to benefits based on your own retirement as well as on that of your retired spouse. You can collect whichever one of these benefits is higher, but not both.

Can I claim spousal benefits if I'm divorced?

You are eligible for dependents benefits if both you and your former spouse have reached age 62, your marriage lasted at least ten years and you have been divorced for at least two years. This two-year waiting period does not apply if your former spouse was already collecting retirement benefits before the divorce.

You can collect benefits as soon as your former spouse is eligible for retirement benefits. He or she does not actually have to be collecting those benefits for you to collect your dependents benefits.

If you are collecting dependents benefits on your former spouse's work record and then marry someone else, you lose your right to those benefits. You may, however, be eligible to collect dependents benefits based on your new spouse's work record. If you divorce again, you can return to collecting benefits on your first spouse's record, or on your second spouse's record if you were married for at least ten years the second time around.

Can I keep a job even after I start collecting retirement benefits?

Yes—and many people do just that. But if you plan on working after retirement, be aware that the money you earn may cause a reduction in the amount of your Social Security benefits. Until you reach age 70, Social Security will subtract money from your retirement check if you exceed a specific amount of earned income for the year.

The amount of earned income you are permitted without loss of Social Security retirement benefits depends on your age—and the amount also changes each year. In 1998, for example, the limits on earned income are $9,120 per year if you were age 62 to 64; $14,500 if age 65 to 69. Once you turn age 70, there is no limit at all on the amount you can earn and still receive your full Social Security retirement benefit.

If you are age 62 to 64 and you earn income over the year's limit, your Social Security retirement benefits are reduced by one dollar for every two dollars over the limit. If you are 65 to 69, you lose one dollar in benefits for every three dollars of earned income over the limit.

How do I claim my Social Security benefits?

Start by contacting your local Social Security office. Most sizable cities have at least one Social Security office; in major urban areas, there will be several. You can find the address and telephone number of the office closest to you in your telephone directory under the listing for United States Government, Social Security Administration, or sometimes under United States Government, Department of Health and Human Services, Social Security Administration. If you have trouble finding an office nearby, call the Social Security Administration at 800-772-1213.

Social Security workers should be able to answer general questions about benefits and rules over the phone—including what type of paperwork must be completed and what documentation is required to claim each kind of benefit. It is generally best to get the benefit application process started by paying a personal visit to the nearest office. If illness or disability prevents this, however, call for accommodations. The most important thing is to act promptly and apply for the benefits to which you are entitled.

What do I do if I feel I've been wrongly denied my benefits?

If your application for benefits is denied, you may not be completely out of luck. A substantial percentage of decisions are changed on appeal. For example, almost half of all disability appeals, which are by far the most common, are favorably changed during the appeal process.

There are four possible levels of appeal following any Social Security decision. The first is called reconsideration; it is an informal review that takes place in the local Social Security office where your claim was filed. The second level is a hearing before an administrative law judge; this is an independent review of what the local Social Security office has decided, made by someone outside the local office. The third level is an appeal to the Social Security national appeals council in Washington, DC. And the final level is filing a lawsuit in federal court.

Appealing a Social Security claim need not be terribly difficult. In many situations, the appeal will require little more from you than taking another opportunity to explain why the information you already presented should qualify you for a benefit. In other cases, it will simply involve presenting one or two more pieces of information that better explain your situation to Social Security personnel.

Begin your appeal by completing a simple, one-page form you can get from the Social Security office. It is called a Request for Reconsideration. Most of the form is easy to fill out; you'll be asked for basic information such as your name and Social Security number. Then you will need to state, very briefly, the reasons why you think you were unfairly denied benefits or were allotted lower benefits than you believe you earned. When you submit your form, you can attach other material you want the administrators to consider, such as recent medical records or a letter from a doctor or employer about your ability to work. You must send in the completed Re-

quest for Reconsideration within 60 days after you of receive written notice of Social Security's decision denying you benefits.

Sign Up Three Months Before Your Birthday

If you need to receive benefit payments at the youngest eligibility age, file your claim three months before the birthday on which you will become eligible. This will give Social Security time to process your claim so that you will receive the benefits on time. If you file a claim later, you cannot get benefits retroactively for months during which you were eligible but before you applied.

Anyone who is eligible for Social Security benefits is also eligible for Medicare coverage at age 65. (For more information about Medicare, see the next series of questions.) Even if you are not going to claim Social Security benefits at age 65—because your benefit amount will be higher if you wait—you should sign up for Medicare coverage three months before your 65th birthday. There is no reason to delay signing up for Medicare, and waiting until after your 65th birthday will delay coverage.

**More Information
About Social Security**

Social Security, Medicare and Pensions,
by Joseph Matthews with Dorothy
Matthews Berman (Nolo Press), explains

Social Security rules and offers strategies for dealing with the Social Security system.

The Social Security Administration, 800-772-1213, answers general questions about eligibility and applications over the phone. It also operates a helpful Website that provides information about Social Security benefits and regulations. You can reach it at http://www.ssa.gov.

In every state, there is a department or commission on aging that gives information and provides advice about problems with Social Security claims. Check the phone book under Aging or Elderly for the service in your state.

Medicare

Give me health and a day and I will make the pomp of emperors ridiculous.

—RALPH WALDO EMERSON

Over the last several decades, Medicare has been carving an inroad into the mountain of consumer health care costs. At present, the Medicare system provides some coverage for almost 40 million people, most of them seniors. Medicare pays for most of the cost of hospitalization and much other medical care for older Americans—about half of all medical costs for people over 65.

Despite its broad coverage, Medicare does not pay for many types of medical services, and pays only a portion of the costs of other services. And with attacks on Medicare gaining political momentum, the chunk of medical care costs Medicare will continue to cover is likely to become even smaller. To take maximum advantage of the benefits Medicare does provide, to protect yourself against the gaps in Medicare coverage and to understand the current political debate about the program's future, you must become well informed about how the Medicare system works.

What is Medicare?

Medicare is a federal government program that helps older and some disabled people pay their medical bills. The program is divided into two parts: Part A and Part B. Part A is called hospital insurance and covers most of the costs of a stay in the hospital, as well as some follow-up costs after time in the hospital. Part B, medical insurance, pays some of the cost of doctors and outpatient medical care.

Medicare, Medicaid: What's the Difference?

People are sometimes confused about the differences between Medicare and Medicaid. Medicare was created in an attempt to address the fact that older citizens have medical bills significantly higher than the rest of the population, while it is much more difficult for most seniors to continue to earn enough money to cover those bills. Eligibility for

Medicare is not tied to individual need. Rather, it is an entitlement program; you are entitled to it because you or your spouse paid for it through Social Security taxes.

Medicaid, on the other hand, is a federal program for low-income, financially needy people, set up by the federal government and administered differently in each state.

Although you may qualify and receive coverage from both Medicare and Medicaid, there are separate eligibility requirements for each program; being eligible for one program does not necessarily mean you are eligible for the other. Also, Medicaid pays for some services for which Medicare does not.

Who is eligible for Medicare Part A coverage?

There are two types of eligibility for Medicare Part A hospital insurance. Most people age 65 and over are covered for free, based on their work records or on their spouse's work records. People over 65 who are not eligible for free Medicare Part A coverage can enroll in it and pay a monthly fee for the same coverage—at least $170 per month according to current rules. The premium increases by 10% for each year after your 65th birthday during which you are not enrolled. You will also have to pay an initial hospital insurance deductible, about $764 in 1998, which increases every year.

If you enroll in paid Part A hospital insurance, you must also enroll in Part B medical insurance, for which you pay an additional monthly premium.

Inpatient Care Generally Covered by Part A

The following list gives you an idea of what Medicare Part A does, and does not, cover during your stay in a participating hospital or skilled nursing facility. Remember, though, even when Part A pays for something, there are significant financial limitations on its coverage.

Medicare Part A hospital insurance covers:

- a semi-private room (two to four beds per room); a private room if medically necessary
- all meals, including special, medically-required diets
- regular nursing services
- special care units, such as intensive care and coronary care
- drugs, medical supplies and appliances furnished by the facility, such as casts, splints or a wheelchair; also, outpatient drugs and medical supplies if they permit you to leave the hospital or nursing facility sooner
- hospital lab tests, X-rays and radiation treatment billed by the hospital
- operating and recovery room costs
- blood transfusions; you pay for the first three pints of blood, unless you arrange to have them replaced by an outside donation of blood to the hospital, and
- rehabilitation services, such as physical therapy, occupational therapy and speech pathology provided while

you are in the hospital or nursing facility.

Medicare Part A hospital insurance does not cover:

- personal convenience items such as television, radio or telephone
- private duty nurses, or
- a private room, unless medically necessary.

How much of my bill will Medicare Part A pay?

All rules about how much Medicare Part A pays depend on how many days of inpatient care you have during what is called a benefit period or spell of illness. The benefit period begins the day you enter the hospital or skilled nursing facility as an inpatient—and continues until you have been out for 60 consecutive days. If you are in and out of the hospital or nursing facility several times but have

not stayed out completely for 60 consecutive days, all your inpatient bills for that time will be figured as part of the same benefit period. Medicare Part A pays only certain amounts of a hospital bill for any one benefit period—and the rules are slightly different depending on whether the care facility is a hospital, psychiatric hospital, skilled nursing facility or care received at home or through a hospice.

What kinds of costs does Medicare Part B cover?

Part B is medical insurance. It is intended to help pay doctor bills for treatment in or out of the hospital. It also covers many other medical expenses you incur when you are not in the hospital, such as the costs of necessary medical equipment and tests.

The rules of eligibility for Part B medical insurance are much simpler than for Part A: If you are age 65 or over and a citizen of the United States, or you are a resident of the United States who has been here lawfully for five consecutive years, you are eligible to enroll in Medicare Part B medical insurance. This is true whether or not you are eligible for Part A hospital insurance.

Types of Services Covered by Medicare Part B

Part B medical insurance is intended to cover basic medical services provided by doctors, clinics and laboratories. The lists of services specifically covered and not covered are long, and do not always make a lot of common sense. Making the effort to learn what is and is not covered can be important—you may get the most benefits by fitting your medical treatments into the covered categories whenever possible.

Part B insurance pays for:

- doctors' services (including surgery) provided at a hospital, doctor's office or your home
- some screening tests, such as colorectal cancer screening, mammograms and PAP smears
- medical services provided by nurses, surgical assistants or laboratory or X-ray technicians
- services provided by pathologists or radiologists while you're an inpatient at a hospital
- outpatient hospital treatment, such as emergency room or clinic charges, X-rays and injections
- an ambulance, if required for a trip to or from a hospital or skilled nursing facility
- drugs or other medicine administered to you at a hospital or doctor's office
- medical equipment and supplies, such as splints, casts, prosthetic devices, body braces, heart pacemakers, corrective lenses after a cataract operation, oxygen equipment, wheelchairs and hospital beds
- some kinds of oral surgery
- some of the cost of outpatient physical and speech therapy
- manual manipulation of out-of-place vertebrae by a chiropractor, and
- part-time skilled nursing care, physical therapy and speech therapy provided in your home.

How much of my bill will Medicare Part B pay?

When all your medical bills are added up, you will see that Medicare pays, on average, for only about half the total. There are three major reasons why Part B medical insurance pays for so little.

First, Medicare does not cover a number of major medical expenses, such as routine physical examinations, medications, glasses, hearing aids, dentures and a number of other costly medical services.

Second, Medicare only pays a portion of what it decides is the proper amount—called the approved charges—for medical services. When Medicare decides that a particular service is covered and determines the approved charges for it, Part B medical insurance usually pays only 80% of those approved charges; you are responsible for the remaining 20%.

Finally, the approved amount may seem reasonable to Medicare, but it is often considerably less than what doctors actually charge. If your doctor or other medical provider does not accept assignment of the Medicare charges, you are personally responsible for the difference.

Free Prescription Drugs

You may be able to avoid the outrageous cost of prescription drugs by asking your doctor for samples of the drugs. Pharmaceutical companies, in an effort to push their particular brand of drugs, send free samples to doctors, and many doctors are willing to dispense those drugs to you free of charge instead of forcing you to buy the drugs on your own.

But many doctors forget what they have in the way of samples, or simply do not offer samples unless asked. It will usually help if you ask your doctor if he or she has samples of the drug you need, explaining that it will be very hard on your pocketbook if you have to purchase them.

States With Limits on Billing

Several states—Connecticut, Massachusetts, Minnesota, New York, Ohio, Pennsylvania, Rhode Island and Vermont—have passed balance billing or charge-limit laws. These laws forbid a doctor from billing patients for the balance of the bill above the amount Medicare approves. The patient is still responsible for the 20% of the approved charge not paid by Medicare Part B.

The specifics of these patient protection laws vary from state to state: Some forbid balance billing to any Medicare patient, others apply the restriction only to patients with limited incomes or assets. To find out the rules in your state, call the following agencies:

Connecticut Medical Assignment Program: 800-443-9946

Massachusetts Office of Elder Affairs: 800-882-2003

Minnesota Board of Aging, Ombudsman: 800-657-3591

New York State Office for the Aging: 800-342-9871

Ohio State Department of Health: 800-899-7127

Pennsylvania State Department of Aging: 717-783-8975

Rhode Island Department of Elderly Affairs: 800-322-2880

Vermont Department of Aging and Disabilities: 800-642-5119

More Information About Medicare

Social Security, Medicare and Pensions by Joseph Matthews with Dorothy Matthews Berman (Nolo Press), further explains Medicare rules and offers strategies for dealing with the Medicare system.

The Medicare Handbook, available from the Social Security Administration, 800-772-1213, provides a complete list of Medicare benefits.

Pensions

Some employers set up pension plans for employees as part of compensation for work. Although no law requires employers to offer these retirement funds, they are a crucial part of many labor negotiations and individual job decisions.

Since the 1980s, however, the number and scope of pension plans— and the number of workers covered by them—have been steadily shrinking. Workers are far more frequently laid off or let go, and as they lose their jobs, they also lose the pension benefits that go with longtime employment. Also, with jobs now scarce and decent jobs even more scarce, employers no longer have to offer a pension plan to attract most workers.

What is a pension plan?

A pension is an agreement between you, your employer and, sometimes, your union. Under the agreement, your employer contributes a certain amount of money to a retirement fund during the years you work. With some plans, you must contribute as well. Then, when you retire, you begin to receive money from the fund. Most people begin to collect retirement money at age 65, but many pension plans pay a smaller amount at younger ages.

Pensions come in several shapes and sizes, but most plans can be divided into two basic categories: defined benefit and defined contribution plans.

What's the difference between "defined benefit" and "defined contribution" plans?

Under a defined benefit plan, you receive a definite, predetermined amount of money when you retire or become disabled. The amount you receive is based on your years of service with a particular employer. Most often, your monthly benefit is a fixed amount of money for each year of service. For example, a plan may pay $20 per month for each year of service. If you worked 20 years for that company, your pension would be $400 per month until you die or payments end, as specified in your individual plan.

Payments under a defined benefit plan may also be calculated on a percentage of your salary over the years. In such plans, the benefit is figured by taking your average salary over all the years you worked, multiplying that average by the fixed percentage established by the pension plan, and then multiplying that total by the number of years you worked for the company.

EXAMPLE

Bob's average salary over 20 years' employment with one employer was $20,000 per year. The company's pension plan used 1% of yearly salary as the pension base. Bob's pension would be calculated by taking 1% of his average salary of $20,000, which is $200. That amount would then be multiplied by Bob's 20 years of service, for a yearly pension of $4,000.

Defined contribution plans, on the other hand, do not guarantee any particular pension amount upon retirement. They guarantee only that the employer will pay into the pension fund a certain amount every month, or every year, for each employee. The employer usually pays a fixed percentage of an employee's wages or salary, although sometimes the amount is a fraction of the company's profits, with the size of each employee's pension share depending on the amount of wage or salary. Payments end at the employee's death, or as specified in the individual plan. Some plans, for example, pay benefit amounts to survivors for a specified number of years.

Are 401(k) plans another type of pension?

Not exactly. At some companies, pension plans have been replaced with 401(k) deferred compensation plans. These plans are not so much pension plans as controlled savings and investment plans—financial structures into which employees can place a certain amount of their wages and defer the taxes on them until retirement. Employers have lower administrative costs for these plans than for traditional pension plans, have no obligation to contribute any set amount per year to the employees' accounts and in many plans, do not contribute at all.

Who is entitled to pension benefits?

If your employer offers a pension, you must be permitted to participate in that plan if you are age 21 or older and have worked for the company for at least one year. One year means a total of 1,000 hours at work in a 12-month period beginning your first day of work; that is an average of 20 hours a week for 50 weeks.

To participate in a plan simply means that your time at the job will be counted toward qualifying for retirement benefits, and the employer must begin paying into your pension account if the plan requires ongoing employer contributions. But this does not necessarily mean that you will receive a pension; that question is governed by a different set of rules.

The Tax Advantages of Retirement Plans

Many people are interested in doing some fancier footwork with their retirement dollars to take advantage of possible tax breaks. A common choice is the Individual Retirement Account, or IRA, which allows people to set up a fund of money that functions as a personal retirement account—with a few more strings and a few more potential benefits attached.

Traditional IRAs and 401K Plans. The money you deposit each year is tax-deductible. So at income tax time, you can reduce your taxable income by the amount of your contribution.

Also, the income and profits that come from investing the money you save are not taxed now, either. You are free to reinvest that money and earn income on it, too.

However, you must start making withdrawals eventually. When you do, the money you take out will be subject to income tax. By then, though, you are likely to be retired and in a lower tax bracket.

Roth IRAs. The Roth IRA, created by the 1997 Taxpayer Relief Act, is a whole different animal. Contributions are not tax-deductible. Income accumulates tax-free, however, as long as the contributions stay in the account at least five years. Most important, withdrawals are not taxed.

There are no mandatory withdrawals. As a result, a Roth IRA could contain a much larger amount at your death than a comparable traditional IRA or 401(k), meaning that you can pass that larger amount on without probate fees.

What does it mean to have "vested" pension benefits?

Every pension plan establishes a level of accumulated benefits—years of employment—after which you have a legal right to receive a pension at retirement. This is true whether or not you continue to work for that employer up to retirement age. When your accumulated benefits reach this level, they are called vested benefits.

There are good reasons to understand how and when your benefits become vested. Before retiring or changing jobs, you will want to know whether your pension rights have vested. Also, in many pension plans there are different levels of vesting, so you must learn what those levels are to know how much of a pension to count on, and when is the best time to leave the job.

Can I collect a private pension and Social Security retirement benefits at the same time?

Not always. Some pension plans— known as integrated plans—are de- pendent on Social Security retirement benefits. In these plans, the pension benefit is reduced by all, or some per- centage of, the retiree's Social Security check. Since 1988, however, the law has required that the plan leave you with at least half of your pension. Un- fortunately, Social Security benefits can wipe out your entire integrated pension plan earnings for pensions earned before 1988, if those benefits are greater than the pension amount.

Integrated pension plans work in one of two ways:

Benefit goals. Some integrated plans set up what is called a benefit goal for your retirement—the amount of money you should have from a combi- nation of pension and Social Security retirement income. The plan's benefit goal is usually a percentage of your average pre-retirement income. Your pension amount is then only what is needed to make up the difference between your Social Security benefits and this predetermined benefit goal.

EXAMPLE

Roberto worked for a company that had an integrated pension plan that set a benefit goal of 40% of the retiree's final salary. Roberto was making $28,000 a year when he re- tired, so his benefit goal was $11,200 (40% of $28,000) a year, or $933 a month.

Based on his years of service, the company's plan would have owed him $500 a month, without integration. But Roberto also received $650 a month in Social Secu- rity retirement benefits, bringing his total Social Security and pension benefits to $1,150 a month. This is $217 more than the benefit goal of $933 a month. So Roberto's pension would be reduced by $217, from $500 to $283 a month.

Offset plans. Another common vari- ety of integrated pension is the offset plan, which reduces or offsets pension benefits by a certain percentage of Social Security benefits. For example, an offset plan might reduce your pen- sion benefits by 50% of your Social Security benefits. If you had earned $250 monthly in pension benefits before the offset, but you receive $400 a month from Social Security, your pension would be reduced by $200— 50% of the $400 Social Security ben- efit. In the end, you would only receive $50 a month from the pension fund.

The Envelope, Please: Will I Get All the Money at Once?

Pension plans pay retirement benefits in a number of different ways. Frequently, a single plan will offer several payment options. The form of payment not only determines when you receive benefits, but also how much in total you receive and whether your spouse or other survivor can continue to get benefits after you die.

Lump-sum payment. Many defined contribution plans offer to pay you the entire amount accumulated in your pension account at retirement. If you need the money immediately to meet living expenses, this is an obvious choice. Also, this entire pension amount can serve as, or add to, an investment in a business, home or other property. Or, if you are investment savvy, you may feel that you can get a greater return on the money than the alternatives offered by your pension plan.

Simple life annuity. Annuities pay a fixed amount of benefits every year (although most annuities actually pay monthly) for the life of the person who is entitled to them. In a simple life annuity, when the person receiving the annuity dies, the benefits stop. There is no final lump sum payment and no provision to pay benefits to a spouse or other survivor. If you are relatively healthy when you claim your retirement, a simple life annuity may pay you more over the years than a lump sum pension plan.

Continuous annuity. Some plans offer an annuity that pays monthly installments for the life of the retired worker, and also provide a smaller continuing annuity for the worker's spouse or other survivor after the worker's death. If the worker dies within a specified time after retiring—usually five or ten years—the annuity will be paid to the surviving spouse or other beneficiary for the rest of the period set out in the annuity plan. A retiring worker who chooses this option will receive less in monthly pension benefits—usually about 10% less—than would be paid under a simple life annuity.

Joint and survivor annuity. A pension plan that pays benefits in any annuity form is required to offer a worker the choice of a joint and survivor annuity in addition to whatever other form of annuity is offered. This form of annuity pays monthly benefits as long as the retired worker is alive, and then continues to pay the worker's spouse for life. Some pension plans also permit a survivor annuity to be paid to a nonspouse beneficiary, but the law does not require that such a benefit be offered. A worker who chooses the joint and survivor annuity will receive slightly less in pension benefits than under a simple annuity plan; how much less is determined by the age of the worker's spouse or other named beneficiary. The younger the beneficiary—that is, the longer the pension is likely to be paid—the lower the benefits. The amount the survivor receives is usually half of the retired worker's pension amount, although a few plans provide for larger survivor payments.

Do I sacrifice my pension rights if I take early retirement?

Many pension plans allow you to choose reduced benefits if you have not quite reached retirement age. Full retirement benefits are usually offered at age 65, although a very few plans still offer full benefits earlier. Early retirement age is usually between 60 and 65.

If your pension plan offers early retirement, it must also offer an early retirement survivor annuity. The annuity gives your spouse, or in some plans another named survivor, a right to collect pension money if you die before normal retirement age. For your survivor to collect this annuity, you must have reached either the company's early retirement age, or have reached an age ten years before the plan's normal retirement age, whichever is later. In practical terms, this means you must have reached at least age 55.

Can I lose pension benefits if the company I work for changes hands?

When a company is sold or reorganized, it often changes the rules of its pension plan. But if your pension benefits have vested under an existing plan, you cannot legally be deprived of any of those benefits when the plan's rules change. The law does not protect you, however, if your pension rights have not yet vested at the time of the change.

Under federal law, if the company you work for is taken over by a new company which keeps the existing pension plan, your years of service continue to accumulate and the benefits you receive must at least equal the benefits you would have received under the old plan. The law does not, however, obligate a new company to continue paying into the existing pension plan. If the existing plan is discontinued, your benefits under that plan will not increase even though you continue to work. If the new company institutes its own pension plan, however, your continued work may accumulate credits under that plan, eventually entitling you to a second pension. These rules do not protect you from changes in a pension plan which occurred prior to 1974.

Know Your Rights

Your employer must provide a Summary Plan Description that explains how your pension plan works and describes your benefit choices. You must receive this information within 90 days after qualifying as a participant in the plan, usually one year after the first day as a full-time employee. Your plan description should explain rules regarding participation, benefit accrual, vesting, pay-out options, retirement ages and claim procedures. If the plan changes, you are entitled to an updated Summary Plan Description from the personnel or pension plan administrator's office where you work, or from your union's pension office.

In addition to the general plan description, you are entitled to a statement of your personal benefit account that explains the benefits you have accrued and tells you what benefits have vested, or when they will vest. Not all employers provide this statement regularly; you may have to make a written request for it. You are also entitled to a copy of your benefit statement if you leave your job.

Each pension plan must make a yearly report to the federal government about the investments of the money in the plan fund. You should be able to see a copy of the latest annual report or to obtain a copy at minimal expense from your pension plan administrator's office.

And any time you have a question about your pension plan, you may make a written request for clarification to the plan administrator. If the administrator's office does not give you a satisfactory answer, direct your questions to the local area office of the federal government's Labor-Management Services Administration. You can find its number in the government listings of the white pages of the telephone book under United States Government, Department of Labor.

Do I have any rights to a spouse's pension if we divorce?

The answer depends on what state you live in and what agreement you and your spouse reach. Because pension benefits are deferred compensation for work already done, in community property states (Arizona, California, Idaho, Louisiana, Nevada, New Mexico, Texas, Washington and Wisconsin) and many other states, the portion of the pension earned during marriage is considered marital property and is subject to division at divorce.

Valuing a pension in order to divide it before the pension holder

retires is not easy. Pensions are evaluated by people called actuaries, who figure out what a pension is worth by estimating the following:

- when the pension holder will retire
- when the pension holder will die
- what salary the pension holder will have at retirement, and
- what inflation and interest rates are likely to do between now and when the pension holder retires.

Divorcing couples have several options when dividing pension rights. You can:

- *Agree to keep rights to your own pension plans.* This eliminates the need to value the pensions and minimizes your future financial ties.
- *Give up your individual interest in your spouse's pension plan in exchange for receiving money or some other property of equal value.* This requires that you value the pension, but minimizes your future financial ties.
- *Divide the value of your pension rights so that each takes a future share.* This requires that you value the pension. Furthermore, you stay financially tied to your ex-spouse because you won't get your share of the benefits until your ex-spouse is eligible to retire. You run the risk of your ex-spouse leaving the job before vesting or before the pension builds up.

Do I have any legal protection if my pension fund is mismanaged?

Since 1974, when the Employee Retirement Income Security Act (ERISA) was passed, at least some of the worst sorts of disappearing pension acts have been halted. To protect pension rights, ERISA:

- sets minimum standards for pension plans, guaranteeing that pension rights cannot be unfairly denied or taken from a worker
- provides some protection for workers in the event certain types of pension plans cannot pay the benefits to which workers are entitled, and
- requires that employers provide full and clear information about employees' pension rights, including the way pension benefits accumulate, how the company invests pension funds and when and how pension benefits can be collected.

What if the pension fund simply runs out of money?

Under ERISA, there is some protection against such pension fund collapse. The Pension Benefit Guaranty Corporation (PBGC), a public, non-profit insurance fund, provides some limited coverage against bankrupt pension funds. Should a pension fund be unable to pay all its obligations to its retirees, the PBGC may pay some of the pension fund's unfulfilled obligations.

If you have a question about termination of benefits because of failure of your pension plan or the sale or end of your employer's company, write or call the Pension Benefit Guaranty Corporation, 1200 K Street, NW, Washington, DC 20005-4026, 202-326-4010, 202-326-4179 (TDD), 202-326-4016 (fax).

How do I claim my pension benefits?

Although ERISA does not spell out one uniform claim procedure for all pension plans, it does establish some rules which must be followed when you retire and want to claim your benefits. All pension plans must have an established claim procedure and all participants in the plan must be given a summary of the plan which explains that procedure. When your claim is filed, you must receive a decision on the claim, in writing, within a "reasonable time." The decision must state specific reasons for the denial of any claimed benefits and must explain the basis for determining the benefits which are granted.

What do I do if my claim is denied or if I disagree with the amount I receive?

If you disagree with either the amount of your benefits or the method in which they are to be paid, you have 60 days from the date you receive a written notice of the amount and method to file a written appeal. Your plan summary explains where and how to file the appeal. If you are considering an appeal, or have filed one, you have the right to examine the pension plan's files and records regarding your pension account, and you can present written materials that correct or contradict information in those files.

Within 60 days of filing your appeal, the pension plan administrators must file a written response to your claim. If your appeal is denied, you have a legal right to press your claim in either state or federal court.

More Information About Pension Plans

Social Security, Medicare and Pensions, by Joseph L. Matthews with Dorothy Matthews Berman (Nolo Press), contains detailed information about pension plans and shows you how to maximize your pension benefits.

Get a Life: You Don't Need a Million to Retire Well, by Ralph Warner (Nolo Press), discusses strategies for creating a satisfying and enjoyable retirement, including pension plans.

Divorce and Money, by Violet Woodhouse & Victoria F. Collins with M.C. Blakeman (Nolo Press), guides you through the difficult process of dividing retirement funds in the event of a divorce.

You can also get information and assistance regarding your rights under pension plans from the independent, non-government Pension Rights Center, 918 16th Street, NW, Suite 704, Washington, DC 20006-2902, 202-296-3778, 202-833-2472 (fax).

http://www.nolo.com
Nolo Press offers self-help information about a wide variety of legal topics, including issues affecting older Americans.

http://www.seniorlaw.com
This site provides information about healthcare coverage for estate planning and the rights of the elderly and disabled.

http://www.aarp.org
The American Association of Retired Persons offers helpful information on a range of issues for older people—including family, health, money matters, housing and crime prevention.

http://www.aoa.dhhs.gov/ elderpage.html
The Administration on Aging's ElderPage provides directories of resources that can help with aging isssues—along with a host of articles covering topics such as retirement planning, housing alterations and Medicare fraud.

http://www.pbgc.gov/
The Pension Benefit Guaranty Corporation (PBGC) was established to protect pension benefits, primarily by giving financial assistance to some types of plans that have become insolvent. Its site provides information on pension rights and benefits, including what to expect if your pension plan changes hands and how to appeal an adverse pension decision.

15

Spouses and Partners

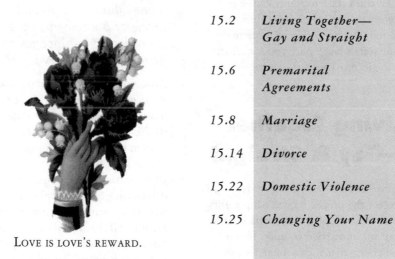

LOVE IS LOVE'S REWARD.

—JOHN DRYDEN

We all know the stories: Boy meets girl, boy and girl fall in love, get married and live happily ever after. And sometimes boy meets boy or girl meets girl—but the fairy tale hopes remain largely unchanged.

What we often don't see are the details: Where do boy and girl get a marriage license, and do they need blood tests first? What should girl and girl do if they can't get married, but they want to buy a house together? And what if the fairy tale turns into a nightmare, and one partner wants to end it?

Our intimate relationships aren't always the stuff of childhood tales, and there are a lot of real-world concerns—emotional and practical—that need attention every day. The questions and answers in this chapter are designed to help you with some of the legal tasks and troubles that may surface during the course of your relationship. Keep in mind that the laws in this area vary, sometimes dramatically, from state to state. We've put together a good overview to get you started, but be certain to confirm your state's law before you act on any of the information given here.

Living Together —Gay & Straight

Many laws are designed to govern and protect the property ownership rights of married couples. But no such laws exist for unmarried couples. If you and your partner are unmarried, you must take steps to protect your relationship and define your property rights. You will also face special concerns if you are raising children together.

My partner and I don't own much property. Do we really need a written contract covering who owns what?

If you haven't been together long and don't own much, it's really not necessary. But the longer you live together, the more important it is to prepare a written contract making it clear who owns what—especially if you begin to accumulate a lot of property. Otherwise, you might face a serious (and potentially expensive) battle if you split up and can't agree on how to divide what you've acquired. And when things are good, taking the time to draft a well-thought-out contract helps you clarify your intentions.

My partner makes a lot more money than I do. Should our property agreements cover who is entitled to her income and the items we purchase with it?

Absolutely. Although each person starts out owning all of his or her job-related income, many states allow this to be changed by an oral contract or even by a contract implied from the circumstances of how you live. These types of contracts are ripe for misunderstanding. For example, absent a written agreement stating whether income will be shared or kept separate, one partner might falsely claim the other promised to split his income 50-50. Although this can be tough to prove in court, the very fact that a lawsuit can be brought creates a huge problem. For obvious reasons, it's an especially good idea to make a written agreement if a person with a big income is living with and supporting someone with little or no income.

What is palimony? And should we make any agreements about it?

Palimony is a phrase coined by journalists—not a legal concept—to describe the division of property or alimony-like support paid to one partner in an unmarried couple by the other after a break up. Members of unmarried couples are not legally entitled to such payments unless they have an agreement. To avoid a cry for palimony, it's best to include in a written agreement whether or not one person will make payments to the other.

Buying a House? Make an Agreement

It's particularly important to make a written property agreement if you buy a house together; the large financial and emotional commitments involved are good reasons to take extra care with your plans.

Your contract should cover at least four major areas:

How is title (ownership) to be listed on the deed? One choice is as "joint tenants with rights of survivorship," meaning that when one of you dies, the other automatically inherits the whole house. Another option is "tenants in common," meaning that when one of you dies, that share of the house goes to whomever is named in a will or trust, or goes to blood relatives if the deceased partner left no estate plan.

How much of the house does each of you own? If it's not 50-50, is there a way for the person who owns less than half to increase his share—for example,

by fixing up the house or making a larger share of the mortgage payment?

What happens to the house if you break up? Will one of you have the first right to stay in the house (perhaps to care for a young child) and buy the other out, or will the house be sold and the proceeds divided?

If one of you has a buyout right, how will the house be appraised and how long will the buyout take? Most people agree to use the realtor they used to buy the house to appraise it, and then give the buying partner one to five years to pay off the other.

My partner and I have a young son, and I'm thinking of giving up my job to become a full-time parent. How might I be compensated for my loss of income?

This is a personal—not a legal—question. If you and your partner decide that compensation is fair, there are many ways to arrange it. For example, you could make an agreement stating that if you break up while you're still providing childcare, your partner will pay an agreed-upon amount to help you make the transition to a new situation. Or, you might agree in writing that your partner will pay you a salary during the time you stay at home, including Social Security and other required benefits.

Am I liable for the debts of my partner?

Not unless you have specifically undertaken responsibility to pay a particular debt—for example, as a cosigner or if the debt is charged to a joint account. By contrast, husbands and wives are generally liable for all debts incurred during marriage, even those incurred by the other person. The one exception for unmarried couples applies if you have registered as domestic partners in a city where the domestic partner ordinance states that you agree to pay for each other's "basic living expenses" (food, shelter and clothing).

If one of us dies, how much property will the survivor inherit?

Nothing, unless the deceased partner made a will or used another estate planning device such as a living trust or joint tenancy agreement, or, if under the terms of a contract (such as a contract to purchase household furnishings together), the survivor already owns part of the property. This is unlike the legal situation married couples enjoy, where a surviving spouse automatically inherits a major portion of a deceased spouse's property. The bottom line is simple: To protect the person you live with, you must specifically leave her property using a will, living trust or other legal document.

If I am injured or incapacitated, can my partner make medical or financial decisions on my behalf?

Not unless you have executed a document called a "durable power of attorney" giving your partner the specific authority to make those

decisions. Without a durable power of attorney, huge emotional and practical problems can result. For example, the fate of a severely ill or injured person could be in the hands of a biological relative who disapproves of the relationship and who makes medical decisions contrary to what the ill or injured person wants. It is far better to prepare the necessary paperwork so the loving and knowing partner will be the primary decision-maker. For more information about durable powers of attorney, see Chapter 13, *Living Wills and Powers of Attorney.*

If my partner and I live together long enough, won't we have a common law marriage?

Probably not. A common law marriage can occur only when:
- a straight couple (common law marriages don't apply to same-sex couples) lives together in one of the few states that still recognize common law marriages
- for a significant period of time (not defined in any state)
- holding themselves out as a married couple—typically this means using the same last name, referring to the other as "my husband" or "my wife" and filing a joint tax return, and
- intending to be married.

Unless all four are true, there is no common law marriage. When one exists, the couple must go through a formal divorce to end the relationship.

Parenting Concerns of Unmarried Couples

All unmarried couples face unique concerns when they raise children together.

- Straight couples who have children together need to take steps to ensure that both are recognized as the legal parents. Both parents should be listed on the birth certificate, and at a minimum the father should sign a statement of paternity. Even better, both parents should sign a statement of parentage acknowledging the father's paternity.

- All unmarried couples face potential obstacles when adopting together. All states favor married couples as adoptive parents. Two states (New Hampshire and Florida) expressly prohibit lesbians and gay men from adopting. This doesn't mean the other states welcome same-sex couples or that any state reaches out to help straight unmarried couples adopt.

In fact, all unmarried couples must work extra hard with local social workers to obtain favorable recommendations. During the past ten years or so, unmarried (mostly lesbian and gay, but some straight) couples have been granted adoptions in over a dozen states. Many of those states have also granted "second parent" adoptions to the partner of the biological parent, without the biological parent's rights being terminated. For more information about Adoption, see Chapter 16, *Parents and Children*.

- Members of unmarried couples who have children from former marriages face the potential prejudice of an ex-spouse or a judge called on to make a custody determination. In most states, this is a much greater concern for lesbian and gay parents than for straight ones, as judges (with the exception of a few states which also come down hard on any unmarried couple) tend to be more tolerant of opposite-sex cohabitation than same-sex cohabitation. Many judges prefer to place children with a parent who is heterosexual and married, if that's an option.

States That Recognize Common Law Marriage

Alabama
Colorado
District of Columbia
Iowa
Kansas
Montana
New Hampshire*

Oklahoma
Pennsylvania
Rhode Island
South Carolina
Texas
Utah

*For inheritance purposes only.

More Information About Living Together

The Living Together Kit, by Ralph Warner and Toni Ihara (Nolo Press), explains the legal rules that apply to unmarried couples and includes sample contracts governing jointly owned property.

A Legal Guide for Lesbian and Gay Couples, by Hayden Curry, Denis Clifford and Robin Leonard (Nolo Press), sets out the law and contains sample agreements for same-sex couples.

Premarital Agreements

Love reasons without reason.
—WILLIAM SHAKESPEARE

Before a couple marries, the parties may make an agreement concerning certain aspects of their relationship. This agreement might cover their responsibilities and property rights during marriage—for example, how the mortgage gets paid and who will stay home to take care of the kids. But more likely it will determine how property will be divided, and whether alimony will be paid, in the event the couple later divorces. These agreements are also called antenuptial or prenuptial agreements.

Are premarital agreements legal?

Courts usually uphold premarital agreements unless one person shows that the agreement:

- promotes divorce (for example, by providing for a large award of alimony in the event of divorce),
- was written and signed with the intention of divorcing, or
- was created unfairly (for example, one spouse giving up all of the rights in his spouse's future earnings without the advice of an attorney).

Nor will courts uphold agreements of a nonmonetary nature. For example, you can't sue your spouse for failure to take out the garbage, even if your premarital agreement says that he or she must do so every Tuesday night.

Should my fiancé and I make a premarital agreement?

Whether you should make a premarital agreement depends on your circumstances and on the two of you as individuals. Some couples choose to make a premarital agreement as a way of clarifying their intentions and expectations, as well as their rights should they later split up.

On the other hand, some couples make premarital agreements to circumvent what a court might decide in the event of a divorce. Often this happens when one partner has property that he or she wishes to keep if the marriage ends—for example, a considerable income or a family business. Perhaps most frequently, premarital agreements are made by individuals who have children or grandchildren from prior marriages. In this case, a partner may use a premarital agreement to ensure that the bulk of his or her property passes to the children or grandchildren, rather than the current spouse.

Are there rules about what can or cannot be included in a premarital agreement?

A law called the Uniform Pre-Marital Agreement Act provides legal guidelines for people who wish to make agreements prior to marriage regarding ownership, management and control of property; property disposition

on separation, divorce and death; alimony; wills; and life insurance beneficiaries.

States that haven't adopted the Act (or which have made some changes to it) have other laws, which often differ from the Act in minor ways. One important difference is that a few states, including California, do not allow premarital agreements to modify or eliminate the right of a spouse to receive court-ordered alimony at divorce. Other states have their own quirky laws—Maine, for example, voids all premarital agreements one and one-half years after the parties to the contract become parents, unless the agreement is renewed.

In every state, whether covered by the Act or not, couples are prohibited from making binding provisions about child support payments.

States That Have Adopted the Uniform Pre-Marital Agreement Act

Arizona	Nevada
Arkansas	New Jersey
California	North Carolina
Hawaii	North Dakota
Illinois	Oregon
Iowa	Rhode Island
Kansas	South Dakota
Maine	Texas
Montana	

Can my fiancé and I make our premarital agreement without a lawyer?

You can look up the laws for your state and write your agreement yourselves. Unfortunately, however, there's no good self-help resource for writing premarital agreements, and if you make a mistake, a court may find your agreement unenforceable. If you'd like to draft a contract on your own, we recommend that you have an attorney look it over to make sure you've followed the law to the letter.

I've been living with someone for several years and we've decided to get married. Will our existing property agreement be enforceable even after we are married?

Probably not. To be enforceable, contracts made before marriage must be made in contemplation of marriage. This means that unless your living together contract is made shortly before your marriage, when you both plan to be married, a court will disregard it.

If you want to convert your living together contract into a premarital agreement, follow these steps:

- Use your upcoming marriage as an opportunity to take another look at your agreement, and make any agreed-upon updates and changes.
- Rewrite your agreement. Call it a premarital or prenuptial agreement, and state that it is made in contemplation of marriage and does not take effect until you marry.

- Because there is no good self-help resource in this area, and because even a small mistake can result in your agreement later being held unenforceable, have your agreement checked out by a lawyer.
- Sign the document in front of a notary.

Marriage

THERE IS MORE OF GOOD NATURE

THAN OF GOOD SENSE AT THE BOTTOM

OF MOST MARRIAGES.

—HENRY DAVID THOREAU

Marriage is the legal union of two people. When you are married, your responsibilities and rights toward your spouse concerning property and support are defined by the laws of the state in which you live. The two of you may be able to modify the rules set up by your state, however, if you desire to do so.

Your marriage can only be terminated by a court granting a divorce or an annulment.

What are the legal rights and benefits conferred by marriage?

Marriage entails many rights and benefits, including the rights to:

- file joint income tax returns with the IRS and state taxing authorities
- create a "family partnership" under federal tax laws, which allows you to divide business income among

family members (this will often lower the total tax on the income)

- create a marital life estate trust (this type of trust is discussed in Chapter 12—see *Estate and Gift Taxes*)
- receive spouse's and dependent's Social Security, disability, unemployment, veterans', pension and public assistance benefits
- receive a share of your deceased spouse's estate under intestate succession laws
- claim an estate tax marital deduction
- sue a third person for wrongful death and loss of consortium
- sue a third person for offenses that interfere with the success of your marriage, such as alienation of affection and criminal conversation (these lawsuits are available in only a few states)
- receive family rates for insurance
- avoid the deportation of a noncitizen spouse
- enter hospital intensive care units, jails and other places where visitors are restricted to immediate family
- live in neighborhoods zoned for "families only"
- make medical decisions about your spouse in the event of disability, and
- claim the marital communications privilege, which means a court can't force you to disclose the contents of confidential communications between you and your spouse during your marriage.

Requirements for Marriage

You must meet certain requirements in order to marry. These vary slightly from state to state, but often include:

- being at least the age of consent (usually 18, though sometimes you may marry younger with your parents' consent)
- not being too closely related to your intended spouse
- having mental capacity—that is, you must understand what you are doing and what consequences your actions may have
- being sober at the time of the marriage
- not being married to anyone else
- getting a blood test, and
- obtaining a marriage license.

What's the difference between a "marriage license" and a "marriage certificate"?

A marriage license is the piece of paper that authorizes you to get married and a marriage certificate is the document that proves you are married.

Typically, couples obtain a marriage license, have the wedding ceremony and then have the person who performed the ceremony file a marriage certificate in the appropriate county office within a few days. (This may be the office of the county clerk, recorder or registrar, depending on where you live.) The married couple will be sent a certified copy of the marriage certificate within a few weeks after the marriage ceremony.

Most states require both spouses, the person who officiated and one or two witnesses to sign the marriage certificate; often this is done just after the ceremony.

Where can we get a marriage license?

Usually, you may apply for a marriage license at any county clerk's office in the state where you want to be married. (In some circumstances, you must apply in the county or town where you intend to be married—this depends on state law.) You'll probably have to pay a small fee for your license, and you may also have to wait a few days before it is issued.

In some states, even after you get your license you'll have to wait a short period of time—one to three days—before you tie the knot. But if you wait too long, your license will expire. Licenses are good for 30 days to one year, depending on the state. If your license expires before you get married, you can apply for a new one.

For more specific information about marriage license laws in your state, see *Marriage Licenses and Blood Tests*, below.

Do all states require blood tests? And why are they required?

Many states—but not all—require blood tests for couples planning to marry (see the chart below). These tests are to find out whether either partner has a venereal disease or rubella (measles). The tests may also disclose the presence of genetic disorders such as sickle-cell anemia or Tay-Sachs disease. You will not be tested for HIV, but in some states, the person who tests you will provide you with information about HIV and AIDS.

If either partner tests positive for a venereal disease, what happens depends on the state where you are marrying. Some states may refuse to issue you a marriage license. Other states may allow you to marry as long as you both know that the disease is present.

MARRIAGE LICENSES AND BLOOD TESTS

State	Blood tests required	Waiting period between applying for and receiving license	How soon you can marry after receiving license	When license expires
Alabama	Yes	None	Immediately	30 days
Alaska	No	3 days	Immediately	90 days
Arizona	No	None	Immediately	1 year
Arkansas	No	None	Immediately	No provision
California	No	None	Immediately	90 days
Colorado	No	None	Immediately	30 days
Connecticut	Yes	4 days	Immediately	65 days
Delaware	No	None	1 day; 4 days if both spouses are nonresidents	30 days
District of Columbia	Yes	3 days	Immediately	No provision
Florida	No	None	Immediately	30 days
Georgia	Yes	None	Immediately	No provision
Hawaii	Yes	None	Immediately	30 days
Idaho	Yes	None	Immediately	No provision
Illinois	Yes	None	1 day	60 days
Indiana	Yes	None	Immediately	60 days
Iowa	No	3 days	Immediately	20 days
Kansas	No	3 days	Immediately	No provision
Kentucky	No	3 days	Immediately	30 days
Louisiana	Yes	None	3 days	30 days
Maine	No	3 days	Immediately	90 days
Maryland	No	2 days	Immediately	6 months
Massachusetts	Yes	3 days	Immediately	60 days
Michigan	No	3 days	Immediately	33 days
Minnesota	No	5 days	Immediately	6 months
Mississippi	Yes	3 days	Immediately	No provision
Missouri	No	None	Immediately	No provision

MARRIAGE LICENSES AND BLOOD TESTS

State	Blood tests required	Waiting period between applying for and receiving license	How soon you can marry after receiving license	When license expires
Montana	Yes	None	Immediately	6 months
Nebraska	Yes	None	Immediately	1 year
Nevada	No	None	Immediately	1 year
New Hampshire	No	3 days	Immediately	90 days
New Jersey	Yes	3 days	Immediately	30 days
New Mexico	Yes	None	Immediately	No provision
New York	Yes	None	1 day	60 days
North Carolina	No	None	Immediately	No provision
North Dakota	No	None	Immediately	60 days
Ohio	No	5 days	Immediately	60 days
Oklahoma	Yes	3 days if either spouse is under 18	Immediately	30 days
Oregon	No	3 days	Immediately	60 days
Pennsylvania	Yes	3 days	Immediately	60 days
Rhode Island	No	None	Immediately	3 months
South Carolina	No	1 day	Immediately	No provision
South Dakota	No	None	Immediately	20 days
Tennessee	No	3 days if either spouse is under 18	Immediately	30 days
Texas	No	None	3 days	30 days
Utah	No	None	Immediately	30 days
Vermont	Yes	None	1 day	60 days
Virginia	No	None	Immediately	60 days
Washington	No	3 days	Immediately	60 days
West Virginia	Yes	3 days	Immediately	60 days
Wisconsin	No	5 days	Immediately	30 days
Wyoming	No	None	Immediately	No provision

Who can perform a marriage ceremony?

Nonreligious ceremonies—called civil ceremonies—must be performed by a judge, justice of the peace or court clerk who has legal authority to perform marriages, or by a person given temporary authority by a judge or court clerk to conduct a marriage ceremony. Religious ceremonies must be conducted by a clergy member—for example, a priest, minister or rabbi. Native American weddings may be performed by a tribal chief or by another official, as designated by the tribe.

Are there requirements about what the ceremony must include?

Usually, no special words are required as long as the spouses acknowledge their intention to marry each other. Keeping that in mind, you can design whatever type of ceremony you desire.

It is customary to have witnesses to the marriage, although they are not required in all states.

What is a common law marriage?

In sixteen states, heterosexual couples can become legally married if they:
• live together for a long period of time
• hold themselves out to others as husband and wife, and
• intend to be married.

These marriages are called common law marriages. Contrary to popular belief, even if two people cohabit for a certain number of years, if they don't intend to be married and hold themselves out as married, there is no common law marriage.

When a common law marriage exists, the spouses receive the same legal treatment given to other married couples, including the requirement that they go through a formal divorce to end the marriage.

To find out whether your state recognizes common law marriages, see the list on page 15.6.

Does any state yet recognize same-sex marriages?

As of July 1998, lesbian and gay couples cannot legally marry in any state. This may change, however, as a case is presently working its way through the Hawaii courts that could legalize same-sex marriages in that state. A Hawaii circuit court ruled in December 1996 that denying lesbian or gay couples the freedom to marry is unconstitutional. However, the state will not begin issuing marriage licenses to lesbian or gay couples while the case is being appealed to the Hawaii Supreme Court. A decision is expected sometime in 1998.

Even if same-sex marriages are eventually recognized in Hawaii, same-sex couples will be fighting an uphill battle to have their unions honored in the other 49 states. Several states, including Georgia, South Dakota, Texas and Utah have already passed laws designed to thwart same-sex marriages—and others are sure to follow. In addition, the Defense of Marriage Act was signed into law in 1996 barring the federal government from recognizing same-sex marriages and permitting states to ignore same-sex marriages performed in other states.

For more information about same-sex marriage, you can contact the Forum on the Right to Marriage (FORM), 617-868-3676. You may also want to contact the Marriage Project of the Lambda Legal Defense and Education Fund, 212-809-8585.

Divorce

THERE IS NO DISPARITY

IN MARRIAGE LIKE UNSUITABLILITY

OF MIND AND PURPOSE.

—CHARLES DICKENS

Divorce is the legal termination of a marriage. In some states, divorce is called dissolution or dissolution of marriage. A divorce usually includes division of marital property and, if necessary, arrangements for child custody and support. It leaves both people free to marry again.

How does an annulment differ from a divorce?

Like a divorce, an annulment is a court procedure that dissolves a marriage. But an annulment treats the marriage as though it never happened. For some people, divorce carries a stigma, and they would rather their marriage be annulled. Others prefer an annulment because it may be easier to remarry in their church if they go through an annulment rather than a divorce.

Grounds for annulment vary slightly from state to state. Generally, an annulment may be obtained for one of the following reasons:

- *misrepresentation or fraud*—for example, a spouse lied about the capacity to have children, stated that she had reached the age of consent or failed to say that she was still married to someone else

- *concealment*—for example, concealing an addiction to alcohol or drugs, conviction of a felony, children from a prior relationship, a sexually transmitted disease or impotency

- *refusal or inability to consummate the marriage*—that is, refusal or inability of a spouse to have sexual intercourse with the other spouse, or

- *misunderstanding*—for example, one person wanted children and the other did not.

These are the grounds for civil annulments; within the Roman Catholic church, a couple may obtain a religious annulment after obtaining a civil divorce, in order for one or both spouses to remarry.

Most annulments take place after a marriage of a very short duration—a few weeks or months, so there are usually no assets or debts to divide or children for whom custody, visitation and child support are a concern. When a long-term marriage is annulled, however, most states have provisions for dividing property and debts, as well as determining custody, visitation, child support and alimony. Children of an annulled marriage are *not* considered illegitimate.

When are married people considered separated?

Many people are confused about what is meant by "separated"—and it's no wonder, given that there are four different kinds of separations:

Trial separation. When a couple lives apart for a test period, to decide whether or not to separate permanently, it's called a trial separation. Even if they don't get back together, the assets they accumulate and debts they incur during the trial period are usually considered jointly owned.

Living apart. Spouses who no longer reside in the same dwelling are said to be living apart. In some states, living apart without intending to reunite changes the spouses' property rights. For example, some states consider property accumulated and debts incurred between living apart and divorce to be the separate property or debt of the person who accumulated or incurred it.

Permanent separation. When a couple decides to split up, it's often called a permanent separation. It may follow a trial separation, or may begin immediately when the couple starts living apart. In most states, all assets received and most debts incurred after permanent separation are the separate property or responsibility of the spouse incurring them.

Legal separation. A legal separation results when the parties separate and a court rules on the division of property, alimony, child support, custody and visitation—but does not grant a divorce. The money awarded for support of the spouse and children under these circumstances is often called separate maintenance (as opposed to alimony and child support).

What is a "no-fault" divorce?

"No-fault" divorce describes any divorce where the spouse suing for divorce does not have to prove that the other spouse did something wrong. All states allow divorces regardless of who is at "fault."

To get a no-fault divorce, one spouse must simply state a reason recognized by the state. In most states, it's enough to declare that the couple cannot get along (this goes by such names as "incompatibility," "irreconcilable differences" or "irremediable breakdown of the marriage"). In nearly a dozen states, however, the couple must live apart for a period of months or even years in order to obtain a no-fault divorce.

Is a no-fault divorce the only option even when there has been substantial wrongdoing?

In 18 states, yes. The other states allow a spouse to select either a no-fault divorce or a fault divorce. Why choose a fault divorce? Some people don't want to wait out the period of separation required by their state's law for a no-fault divorce. And in some states, a spouse who proves the other's fault may receive a greater share of the marital property or more alimony.

The traditional fault grounds are:
- cruelty (inflicting unnecessary emotional or physical pain)—this is the most frequently used ground
- adultery
- desertion for a specified length of time

- confinement in prison for a set number of years, and
- physical inability to engage in sexual intercourse, if it was not disclosed before marriage.

What happens in a fault divorce if both spouses are at fault?

Under a doctrine called "comparative rectitude," a court will grant the spouse least at fault a divorce when both parties have shown grounds for divorce. Years ago, when both parties were at fault, neither was entitled to a divorce. The absurdity of this result gave rise to the concept of comparative rectitude.

Can a spouse successfully prevent a court from granting a divorce?

One spouse cannot stop a no-fault divorce. Objecting to the other spouse's request for divorce is itself an irreconcilable difference that would justify the divorce.

A spouse can prevent a fault divorce, however, by convincing the court that he or she is not at fault. In addition, several other defenses to a divorce may be possible:

- *Collusion.* If the only no-fault divorce available in a state requires that the couple separate for a long time and the couple doesn't want to wait, they might pretend that one of them was at fault in order to manufacture a ground for divorce. This is collusion because they are cooperating in order to mislead the judge. If, before the divorce, one spouse no

longer wants a divorce, he could raise the collusion as a defense.

- *Condonation.* Condonation is someone's approval of another's activities. For example, a wife who does not object to her husband's adultery may be said to condone it. If the wife sues her husband for divorce, claiming he has committed adultery, the husband may argue as a defense that she condoned his behavior.

- *Connivance.* Connivance is the setting up of a situation so that the other person commits a wrongdoing. For example, a wife who invites her husband's lover to the house and then leaves for the weekend may be said to have connived his adultery. If the wife sues her husband for divorce, claiming he has committed adultery, the husband may argue as a defense that she connived—that is, set up—his actions.

- *Provocation.* Provocation is the inciting of another to do a certain act. If a spouse suing for divorce claims that the other spouse abandoned her, her spouse might defend the suit on the ground that she provoked the abandonment.

GROUNDS FOR DIVORCE

State	Fault grounds	No-fault grounds (other than separation)	Separation	Length of separation
Alabama	x	x	x	2 years
Alaska	x	x		
Arizona		x		
Arkansas	x		x	18 months
California		x		
Colorado		x		
Connecticut	x	x	x[1]	18 months
Delaware	x	x		
District of Columbia			x	6 months
Florida		x		
Georgia	x	x		
Hawaii		x	x	2 years
Idaho	x	x	x	5 years
Illinois	x	x[2]	x[2]	2 years
Indiana		x		
Iowa		x		
Kansas		x		
Kentucky		x		
Louisiana	x		x	180 days
Maine	x	x		
Maryland	x		x	1 year
Massachusetts	x	x		
Michigan		x		
Minnesota		x	x	180 days
Mississippi	x	x		
Missouri		x		
Montana		x		
Nebraska		x		
Nevada		x	x	1 year
New Hampshire	x	x		

State	Fault grounds	No-fault grounds (other than separation)	Separation	Length of separation
New Jersey	x		x	18 months
New Mexico	x	x		
New York	x		x	1 year
North Carolina	x		x	1 year
North Dakota	x	x		
Ohio	x	x[3]	x	1 year
Oklahoma	x	x		
Oregon		x		
Pennsylvania	x	x	x	2 years
Rhode Island	x	x	x	3 years
South Carolina	x		x	1 year
South Dakota	x	x		
Tennessee	x	x	x[4]	2 years
Texas	x	x	x	3 years
Utah	x	x	x	3 years
Vermont	x		x	6 months
Virginia	x		x[5]	1 year
Washington		x		
West Virginia	x	x	x	1 year
Wisconsin		x		
Wyoming		x		

[1] Separation-based divorce must also allege incompatibility.

[2] Must allege irretrievable breakdown and separation for no-fault; if parties consent, two years may be reduced to six months.

[3] Divorce will be denied if one party contests ground of incompatibility.

[4] Separation-based divorce allowed only if there are no children.

[5] May be reduced to six months if there are no children.

Do you have to live in a state to get a divorce there?

All states except South Dakota and Washington require a spouse to be a resident of the state for a certain length of time (30 days to one year, depending on the state) before filing for a divorce there. Someone who files for divorce must offer proof that he has resided there for the required length of time.

Can one spouse move to a different state or country to get a divorce?

If one spouse meets the residency requirement of a state or country, a divorce obtained there is valid, even if the other spouse lives somewhere else. The courts of all states will recognize the divorce.

Any decisions the court makes regarding property division, alimony, custody and child support, however, may not be valid unless the nonresident spouse consented to the jurisdiction of the court or later acts as if the foreign divorce was valid—for example, by paying court-ordered child support.

I'M A GREAT HOUSEKEEPER.

I GET DIVORCED. I KEEP THE HOUSE.

—ZSA ZSA GABOR

How is property divided at divorce?

It is common for a divorcing couple to decide about dividing their property and debts themselves, rather than leave it to the judge. But if a couple cannot agree, they can submit their property dispute to the court, which will use state law to divide the property.

Division of property does not necessarily mean a physical division. Rather, the court awards each spouse a percentage of the total value of the property. Each spouse gets items whose worth adds up to his or her percentage.

Courts divide property under one of two schemes: equitable distribution or community property.

- *Equitable distribution.* Assets and earnings accumulated during marriage are divided equitably (fairly). In practice, often two-thirds of the assets go to the higher wage earner and one-third to the other spouse. Equitable distribution principles are followed everywhere except the community property states listed just below.
- *Community property.* In Arizona, California, Idaho, Louisiana, Nevada, New Mexico, Texas, Washington and Wisconsin, all property of a married person is classified as either community property, owned equally by both spouses, or the separate property of one spouse. At divorce, community property is generally divided equally between the spouses, while each spouse keeps his or her separate property.

DURATIONAL RESIDENCY REQUIREMENTS FOR DIVORCE

The durational residency requirement is the length of time a person filing for divorce must live in that state before he or she can file court papers.

State	No Statutory Provision	30 days	6 Weeks	60 Days	3 Months or 90 Days	6 Months or 180 Days	12 Months or 1 year
Alabama						x	
Alaska		x					
Arizona					x		
Arkansas				x			
California						x	
Colorado					x		
Connecticut							x
Delaware						x	
District of Columbia						x	
Florida						x	
Georgia					x		
Hawaii					x		
Idaho			x				
Illinois					x		
Indiana						x	
Iowa							x
Kansas				x			
Kentucky						x	
Louisiana						x	
Maine						x	
Maryland							x
Massachusetts							x
Michigan						x	
Minnesota						x	
Mississippi						x	
Missouri					x		
Montana					x		
Nebraska							x
Nevada			x				
New Hampshire							x
New Jersey							x
New Mexico						x	
New York							x

State	No Statutory Provision	30 days	6 Weeks	60 Days	3 Months or 90 Days	6 Months or 180 Days	12 Months or 1 year
North Carolina						x	
North Dakota							
Ohio						x	x
Oklahoma						x	
Oregon						x	
Pennsylvania						x	
Rhode Island							x
South Carolina[1]					x		
South Dakota	x						
Tennessee						x	
Texas						x	
Utah					x		
Vermont						x	
Virginia						x	
Washington	x						
West Virginia							x
Wisconsin						x	
Wyoming				x			

[1]If only one spouse is a resident of South Carolina, the requirement is one year.

Very generally, here are the rules for determining what's community property and what isn't:

Community property includes all earnings during marriage and everything acquired with those earnings. All debts incurred during marriage, unless the creditor was specifically looking to the separate property of one spouse for payment, are community property debts.

Separate property of one spouse includes gifts and inheritances given just to that spouse, personal injury awards received by that spouse and the proceeds of a pension that vested (that is, the pensioner became legally entitled to receive it) before marriage. Property purchased with the separate funds of a spouse remain that spouse's separate property. A business owned by one spouse before the marriage remains his or her separate property during the marriage, although a portion of it may be considered community property if the business increased in value during the marriage or both spouses worked at it.

Property purchased with a combination of separate and community funds is part community and part separate property, so long as a spouse is able to show that some separate funds were used. Separate property mixed together with community property generally becomes community property.

More Information About Divorce

How to Do Your Own Divorce in California, by Charles Sherman (Nolo Press Occidental), contains step-by-step instructions for obtaining a California divorce without a lawyer.

How to Do Your Own Divorce in Texas, by Charles Sherman (Nolo Press Occidental), contains step-by-step instructions for obtaining a Texas divorce without a lawyer.

Divorce and Money: How to Make the Best Financial Decisions During Divorce, by Violet Woodhouse and Victoria F. Collins with M.C. Blakeman (Nolo Press), explains the financial aspects of divorce and how to divide property fairly.

Nolo's Pocket Guide to Family Law, by Robin Leonard and Stephen Elias (Nolo Press), explains legal concepts you may run across if you're involved in a divorce, adoption or other family law matter.

Annulment: Your Chance to Remarry Within the Catholic Church, by Joseph P. Zwack (Harper & Row), explains how to get a religious annulment.

Domestic Violence

Domestic violence occurs more often than most of us realize. Those who are abused range in age from children to the elderly, and come from all backgrounds and income levels. The majority of those subjected to domestic violence are women abused by men, but women also abuse other women, men abuse men and women abuse men. If you're being hurt at home, the first rule of advice is to get away from the abuser and go to a safe place where he or she cannot find you. Then, find out about your options for getting help.

What kind of behavior is considered domestic violence?

Domestic violence can take a number of forms, including:
- physical behavior such as slapping, punching, pulling hair or shoving
- forced or coerced sexual acts or behavior such as unwanted fondling or intercourse, or jokes and insults aimed at sexuality
- threats of abuse—threatening to hit, harm or use a weapon on another, or to tell others confidential information, and
- psychological abuse—attacks on self-esteem, controlling or limiting another's behavior, repeated insults and interrogation.

Typically, many kinds of abuse go on at the same time in a household.

Finding a Safe Place

Many communities have temporary homes called battered women's shelters where women and their children who are victims of domestic violence may stay until the crisis passes or until they are able to find a permanent place to relocate. The best way to find these shelters is to consult the local police, welfare department, neighborhood resource center or women's center. You can also look in your phone book under Crisis Intervention Services, Human Service Organizations, Social Service Organizations, Family Services, Shelters or Women's Organizations. In some states, the police are required to provide an apparent battering victim a list of referrals for emergency housing, legal services and counseling services.

If you're having trouble finding resources in your area, you can contact the National Battered Women's Hotline, 800-799-SAFE (7233).

If I leave, how can I make sure the abuser won't come near me again?

The most powerful legal tool for stopping domestic violence is the temporary restraining order (TRO). A TRO is a decree issued by a court that requires the perpetrator to stop abusing you. The order may require, for example, that the perpetrator stay away from the family home, where you work or go to school, your children's school and other places you frequent (such as a particular church). The order will also prohibit further acts of violence.

Many states make it relatively easy for you to obtain a TRO. In New York, California and some other states, for example, the court clerk will hand you a package of forms and will even assist you in filling them out. In other areas, nonlawyers may be available to help you complete the forms. When you've completed your forms, you'll go before a judge to show evidence of the abuse, such as hospital or police records. Judges are often available to issue TROs after normal business hours because violence certainly occurs at times other than between 9 a.m. and 5 p.m.

Programs for Abusive Men

A number of programs have been established to help abusive men change their behavior. You can get more information from the following organizations:

Men Overcoming Violence (MOVE)
54 Mint Street, Suite 300
San Francisco, CA 94103
415-777-4496

Abusive Men Exploring New Directions (AMEND)
789 Sherman Street, Suite 580
Denver, CO 80203
303-832-6363

EMERGE: Counseling and Education to Stop Male Violence
18 Hurley Street, Suite 100
Cambridge, MA 02141
617-422-1550

In my community, judges don't issue TROs after 5 p.m. How can I get protection?

Contact your local police department. In many communities, the police can issue something called an emergency protective order when court is out of session. An emergency protective order usually lasts only for a brief period of time, such as a weekend or a holiday, but otherwise it is the same as a temporary restraining order. On the next business day, you will need to go to court to obtain a TRO.

Are TROs and emergency protective orders only available when the abuser is a spouse?

No, in most states, the victim of an abusive live-in lover can obtain a TRO or emergency protective order. In a few states, the victim of any adult relative, an abusive lover (non-live-in) or even a roommate can obtain such an order. To learn about your state's rule, contact a local crisis intervention center, social service organization or battered women's shelter.

Help for Abused Gay Men and Lesbians

The following organizations provide information and support for battered gay men and lesbians:

Community United Against Violence (CUAV)
973 Market Street, Suite 500
San Francisco, CA 94103
415-777-5500
415-333-4357 (Crisis Hotline)

Lesbian Battering Intervention Project
Minnesota Coalition for Battered Women
450 N. Syndicate Street, #122
St. Paul, MN 55104
612-646-6177
612-646-0994 (Crisis Hotline)

What should I do once I have a TRO?

Register it with the police located in the communities in which the abuser has been ordered to stay away from you—where you live, work, attend school or church and where your children go to school. Call the appropriate police stations for information about how to register your order.

What if the abuse continues even if I have a TRO?

Obviously, a piece of paper cannot stop an enraged spouse or lover from acting violent, although many times it is all the deterrent the person needs.

If the violence continues, contact the police. They can take immediate action and are far more willing to intervene when you have a TRO than when you don't. Of course, if you don't have a TRO or it has expired, you should also call the police—in all states, domestic violence is a crime and you don't have to have a TRO for the police to investigate.

The police should respond to your call by sending out officers. In the past, police officers were reluctant to arrest abusers, but this has changed in many communities where victims' support groups have worked with police departments to increase the number of arrests. You can press criminal charges at the police department, and ask for criminal prosecution. Documentation is crucial if you want to go this route. Be sure to insist that the officer responding to your call makes an official report. Also, get the report's prospective number before the officer leaves the premises.

If you do press charges, keep in mind that only the district attorney decides whether or not to prosecute. If you don't press charges, however, the chance is extremely low that the district attorney will pursue the matter.

Getting Legal Help

If you want to take legal action against your abuser or you need other legal help related to domestic abuse, the following organizations can refer you to assistance programs in your area:

The National Coalition Against Domestic Violence (NCADV), 303-839-1852.

The National Battered Women's Hotline, 800-799-SAFE (7233).

Changing Your Name

You may be thinking of changing your name for any number of reasons —perhaps you're getting married or divorced, or maybe you just don't like the name you've got and you want one that suits you better. Whatever the reason, you'll be glad to know that name changes are common—and usually fairly easy to carry out.

I'm a woman who is planning to be married soon. Do I have to take my husband's name?

No. When you marry, you are free to keep your own name, take your husband's name or adopt a completely different name. Your husband can even adopt your name, if that's what you both prefer. Give some careful thought to what name feels best for you. You can save yourself considerable time and trouble by making sure you are happy with your choice of name before you change any records.

Can my husband and I both change our names—to a hyphenated version of our two names or to a brand new name?

Yes. Some couples want to be known by a hyphenated combination of their last names, and some make up new names that combine elements of each. For example, Ellen Berman and Jack Gendler might become Ellen and Jack Berman-Gendler or, perhaps, Ellen and Jack Bergen. You can also pick a name that's entirely different from the names you have now, just because you like it better.

What if I do want to take my husband's name? How do I make the change?

If you want to take your husband's name, simply start using the name as soon as you are married. Use your new name consistently, and be sure to change your name on all of your identification, accounts and important documents. To change some of your identification papers—your Social Security card, for example—you'll need a certified copy of your marriage certificate, which you should receive within a few weeks after the marriage ceremony.

For a list of people and institutions to contact about your name change, see *Changing Identification and Records*, below.

I took my husband's name when I married, but now we're getting divorced and I'd like to return to my former name. How do I do that?

In most states, you can request that the judge handling your divorce make a formal order restoring your former or birth name. If your divorce decree contains such an order, that's all the paperwork you'll need. You'll probably want to get certified copies of the order as proof of the name change— check with the court clerk for details. Once you have the necessary docu

mentation, you can use it to have your name changed on your identification and personal records.

If your divorce papers don't show your name change, you can still resume your former name without much fuss. In most states, you can simply begin using your former name consistently, and have it changed on all your personal records (see *Changing Identification and Records*, below). If you're returning to a name you had before marriage, you're not likely to be hassled about the change. A few states have more stringent laws, however, and you'll have apply to a court for an order approving your name change. Contact your local clerk of court to find out whether you'll need a court order.

After my husband and I are divorced and I return to my former name, can I change the last name of my children as well?

Traditionally, courts ruled that a father had an automatic right to have his child keep his last name if he continued to actively perform his parental role. But this is no longer true. Now a child's name may be changed by court petition when it is in the best interest of the child to do so. When deciding to grant a name change, courts consider many factors, such as the length of time the father's name has been used, the strength of the mother-child relationship and the need of the child to identify with a new family unit (if the change involves remarriage). The courts must balance these factors against the strength and importance of the father-child relationship. What this all boils down to is that it's up to a judge to decide which name is in the child's best interest.

Keep in mind that even if you do change your children's last name, you won't be changing the legally recognized identity of their father. Nor will a name change affect the rights or duties of either parent regarding visitation, child support or rights of inheritance. Changes such as these occur only if the parental roles are altered by court order—for example, a new custody decree or a legal adoption.

I just don't like my birth name and I want to change it. Can I choose any name I want?

There are some restrictions on what you may choose as your new name. Generally, the limits are as follows:

- You cannot choose a name with fraudulent intent—meaning you intend to do something illegal. For example, you cannot legally change your name to avoid paying debts, keep from getting sued or get away with a crime.
- You cannot interfere with the rights of others, which generally means capitalizing on the name of a famous person.
- You cannot use a name that would be intentionally confusing. This might be a number or punctuation—for example, "10," "III" or "?".
- You cannot choose a name that is a racial slur.
- You cannot choose a name that could be considered a "fighting

word," which includes threatening or obscene words, or words likely to incite violence.

That's "Mr. Three" to You

Minnesota's Supreme Court once ruled that a man who wanted to change his name to the number "1069" could not legally do so, but suggested that "Ten Sixty-Nine" might be acceptable (*Application of Dengler* 287 NW2d 637 (1979)).

Do I have to file forms in court to change my birth name?

Maybe not. In all but a handful of states, you can legally change your name by usage only. A name change by usage is accomplished by simply using a new name in all aspects of your personal, social and business life. No court action is necessary, it costs nothing and it is legally valid. (Minors and prison inmates are generally exceptions to this rule.)

Practically speaking, however, an official court document may make it much easier to get everyone to accept your new name. Because many people and agencies do not know that a usage name change is legal, they may want to see something in writing signed by a judge. Also, certain types of identification—such as a new passport or a birth certificate attachment—are not readily available if you change your name by the usage method.

If it's available in your state, you may want to try the usage method and see how it goes. If you run into too many problems, you can always file a court petition later.

You can find out whether your state requires a court order by contacting your local clerk of court. Or, if the court clerk doesn't give you enough information, you can look at your state's statutes in a local law library—start in the index under "Name" or "Change of Name," or ask the reference librarian for help.

How do I implement my name change?

Whether you have changed your name by usage or by court order, the most important part of accomplishing your name change is to let others know you've taken a new name. Although it may take a little time to contact government agencies and businesses, don't be intimidated by the task—it's a common procedure.

The practical steps of implementing a name change are:

• *Advise officials and businesses.* Contact the various government and business agencies with which you deal and have your name changed on their records. See *Changing Identification and Records*, below.

• *Enlist help of family and friends.* Tell your friends and family that you've changed your name and you now want them to use only your new one. It may take those close to you a while to get used to associating you with a new sound. Some of them might even object to using the new name, perhaps fearing the person they know so well is becoming

someone else. Be patient and persistent.

• *Use only your new name.* If you are employed or in school, go by your new name there. Introduce yourself to new acquaintances and business contacts with your new name.

If you've made a will or other estate planning document (such as a living trust), it's best to replace it with a new document using your new name. Your beneficiaries won't lose their inheritances if you don't, but changing the document now will avoid confusion later.

Finally, remember to change your name on other important legal papers—for example, powers of attorney, living wills, trusts and contracts.

Changing Identification and Records

To complete your name change, you'll need to tell others about it. Contact the people and institutions you deal with and ask what type of documentation they require to make your name change official in their records. Different institutions may have very different rules; some may need only your phone call, others may require special forms or a copy of a court document.

It's generally recommended that you first acquire a driver's license, then a Social Security card in your new name. Once you have those pieces of identification, it's usually fairly simple to acquire others or have records changed to reflect your new name.

Here are the people and institutions to notify of your name change:

- friends and family
- employers
- schools
- post office
- Department of Motor Vehicles
- Social Security Administration
- Department of Records or Vital Statistics (issuers of birth certificates)
- banks and other financial institutions
- creditors and debtors
- telephone and utility companies
- state taxing authority
- insurance agencies
- registrar of Voters
- passport office
- Public Assistance (welfare) office
- Veterans Administration.

What should I do if I have a hard time getting my new name accepted?

Some people and institutions may be reluctant to accept your new name—particularly if you've changed it without a court order. If you live in a state where no court order is required, however, you should be able to persuade them to make the change.

Start by providing documentation that shows both the old and new names. If you've recently obtained a passport, it may be helpful because it can show your old name as well as the new name as an AKA ("also known as").

If you're stonewalled, you may want to gently but forcefully give a rundown of state law that supports your position. (You can research the law for your state at your local law library or on the Internet. See Chapter 19, *Legal Research*.) If the person with whom you are dealing remains uncooperative, ask to speak to his or her supervisor. Be confident that you have the legal right to change your name, even if the people you're dealing with don't know your rights. Keep going up the ladder until you get results. If you have trouble at the local office of a government agency, contact the main office. If you come up against a seemingly impossible situation, get the help of your local elected official.

Finally, if you run into more trouble than you're prepared to deal with, consider going to court and getting a signed order from a judge. It costs more and will take a little time, but an official document will certainly make it easier to handle people and institutions who refuse to accept your new name.

More Information About Changing Your Name

How to Change Your Name (California Edition), by David Ventura Loeb and David W. Brown (Nolo Press), provides complete information on how to change your name in California.

Local law libraries are good sources of information for name changes. Look under "Name" or "Change of Name" in the index of your state's statutes, or ask the reference librarian for help. You can also research state laws on the Internet. See Chapter 19, *Legal Research*, for more information.

http://www.nolo.com

Nolo Press offers self-help information about a wide variety of legal topics, including relationships between spouses and partners.

http://www.qrd.com

Queer Legal Resources provides information about lesbian and gay rights, including issues affecting couples.

http://www.inter-law.com/ tfam.html

The 'Lectric Law Library's Lawcopedia on Family Law offers articles and other information on a wide variety of family law issues, including articles about living together.

http://divorce-online.com

The American Divorce Information Network provides FAQs, articles and information on a wide range of divorce issues.

http://www.abanet.org/ textonly/domviol/home.html

The American Bar Association offers help and information for those affected by domestic violence.

16

Parents and Children

*A child of five could understand this.
Fetch me a child of five.*

—GROUCHO MARX

Raising children is a big job, and an emotional subject even
when family relationships are well established and running
smoothly. An adoption, divorce or guardianship proceeding adds
extra stress, requiring us to juggle law, economics and our highly

charged feelings. Be reassured, however, that there are many people who
can help you find your way through
family law proceedings, including
knowledgeable lawyers, mediators,
counselors and therapists. In this chapter, we get you started by answering
many of your questions about the laws
that affect parents and their children.

Adopting a Child

Adoption is a court procedure by
which an adult legally becomes the
parent of someone who is not his or her
biological child. Adoption creates a
parent-child relationship recognized
for all purposes—including child support obligations, inheritance rights and
custody. The birthparents' legal relationship to the child is terminated,
unless a legal contract allows them to
retain or share some rights or the adoption is a stepparent adoption, in which
case only the parent without custody
loses parental rights.

This section discusses the general
legal procedures and issues involved in
adopting a child, including the advantages and disadvantages of various
types of adoption and some of the special concerns of single people or unmarried couples (gay and straight) who
want to adopt a child. Stepparent adoptions and the rights of relatives are discussed a little later in this chapter.

Who can adopt a child?

As a general rule, any adult who is
found to be a "fit parent" may adopt a
child. Married or unmarried couples
may adopt jointly, and unmarried
people may adopt a child through a
procedure known as a single-parent
adoption.

Some states have special requirements for adoptive parents. A few of
these require an adoptive parent to be
a certain number of years older than
the child. For example, California requires adoptive parents to be at least
ten years older than the adoptee,
while Idaho requires a difference of 15
years. And some states require the
adoptive parent to live in the state for
a certain length of time before they
are allowed to adopt. For instance, an
adoptive parent in Georgia must have
been a state resident for at least six
months, and Minnesota has a one-year
residency requirement. You will need
to check the laws of your state to see
whether any special requirements apply to you. And keep in mind that if
you're adopting through an agency,
you may have to meet strict agency
requirements in addition to any requirements under state law.

Even if you find no state or agency
barriers to adopting a child, remember that some people or couples are
likely to have a harder time adopting
than others. A single man or a lesbian
couple may not legally be prohibited
from adopting, but may have a harder
time finding a placement than would
a married couple. This is because all
states look to the "best interests of the
child" as their bottom line, and will
judge the various characteristics of the
parent or couple—often factoring in
biases about who makes a good par-

ent—when making a placement determination.

I'm single, but I'd like to adopt a child. What special concerns will I face?

As a single person, you may have to wait longer to adopt a child, or be flexible about the child you adopt. Agencies often "reserve" healthy infants and younger children for two-parent families, putting single people at the bottom of their waiting lists. And birthparents themselves often want their children to be placed in a two-parent home.

If you're a single person wishing to adopt, you should be prepared to make a good case for your fitness as a parent. You can expect questions from case workers about why you haven't married, how you plan to support and care for the child on your own, what will happen if you do marry and other questions that will put you in the position of defending your status as a single person. To many single adoptive parents, such rigorous screening doesn't seem fair, but it is common.

Agencies serving children with special needs may be a good option for singles, as such agencies often cast a wider net when considering adoptive parents. Of course, you shouldn't take a child unless you feel truly comfortable with the idea of raising him or her—but being flexible will make the obstacles to single-parent adoptions easier to overcome.

My long-term partner and I prefer not to get married, but we'd like to adopt a child together. Will we run into trouble?

There is no specific prohibition against unmarried couples adopting children—sometimes called two-parent adoptions. Like singles, however, you may find that agencies are biased towards married couples. You may have a longer wait for a child, or you may have to expand your ideas about what kind of child you want.

Is it still very difficult for lesbians and gay men to adopt children?

Only Florida and New Hampshire specifically prohibit lesbians and gay men from adopting children. But that doesn't mean it's easy to adopt in other states. Connecticut, for example, allows judges to consider the sexual orientation of the adoptive parent in determining whether an adoption should take place. The same is true in other states—even if a state adoption statute does not specifically mention sexual orientation, it may become an issue in court, and some judges will use it to find a prospective adoptive parent to be unfit.

On the other hand, many gay men and lesbians have been able to adopt children, and an increasing number of states are allowing gay and lesbian couples to adopt jointly. Beginning in Alaska in 1985, joint adoptions by gay and lesbian couples have been granted in California, Colorado, the District of Columbia, Illinois, Indiana, Massachusetts, Michigan, Minnesota,

New Jersey, New York, Oregon, Pennsylvania, Texas, Vermont and Washington.

Keep in mind that the legal landscape in all areas affecting gays and lesbians is changing rapidly. Just as a legislature might make it easier for gays and lesbians to adopt, a court decision to the contrary might provide quite a different result. Lesbians and gay men will need an experienced attorney to handle an adoption. But you can do your own homework: The National Center for Lesbian Rights (address and phone number listed below) provides information for gay men and lesbians who want to adopt.

Can I adopt a child whose race or ethnic background is different from mine?

Usually, yes. You do not need to be the same race as the child you want to adopt, although some states do give preference to prospective adoptive parents of the same race or ethnic background as the child. Adoptions of Native American children are governed by federal law—the Indian Child Welfare Act—which outlines specific rules and procedures that must be followed when adopting a Native American child.

Whose consent is needed for an adoption to take place?

For any adoption to be legal, the birthparents must consent to the adoption unless their parental rights have been legally terminated for some other reason. All states prohibit birthparents from giving their consent

to an adoption until after the child's birth, and some states require even more time—typically three to four days after the birth—before the parents are allowed to consent. This means that birthparents can legally change their minds about putting their child up for adoption at any point before the child is born.

Types of Adoption

Agency Adoptions. Agency adoptions involve the placement of a child with adoptive parents by a public agency, or by a private agency licensed or regulated by the state. Public agencies generally place children who have become wards of the state because they were orphaned, abandoned or abused. Private agencies are often run by charities or social service organizations. Children placed through private agencies are usually brought to an agency by parents that have or are expecting a child that they want to give up for adoption.

Independent Adoptions. In an independent or private adoption, a child is placed with adoptive parents without the assistance of an agency. Some independent adoptions consist of direct arrangement between the birthparents and the adoptive parents, while others are arranged through an intermediary such as a lawyer, doctor or clergyperson. Whether or not an intermediary is used, a lawyer is essential because of the legal complexities involved. Most states allow independent adoptions, though many regulate them quite carefully. Independent adoptions are not allowed in Connecticut, Delaware, Massachusetts or Minnesota.

Identified Adoptions. An identified, or designated, adoption is one in which the adopting parents locate a birthmother (or the other way around) and then ask an adoption agency to handle the rest of the adoption process. In this way, an identified adoption is a hybrid of an independent and an agency adoption. Prospective parents are spared the waiting lists of agencies by finding the birthparents themselves, but reap the other benefits of agencies, such as their experience with legal issues and their counseling services. Identified adoptions provide an alternative to parents in states that ban independent adoptions.

International Adoptions. In an international adoption, the adoptive parents take responsibility for a child who is a citizen of a foreign country. In addition to satisfying the adoption requirements of both the foreign country and the parents' home state in the U.S., the parents must obtain an immigrant visa for the child through the U.S. Immigration and Naturalization Service. The INS has its own rules for international adoptions, such as the requirement that the adoptive parents be either married or, if single, at least 25 years old. The INS also requires adoptive parents to complete several forms and submit a favorable home study report. Finally, you must apply for U.S. citizenship for the child; it is not granted automatically.

Relative Adoptions. When a child is related to the adoptive parent by blood or marriage, the adoption is a relative adoption. The most common example of this type of adoption is a stepparent

adoption, in which a parent's new spouse adopts a child from a previous partner. Grandparents often adopt their grandchildren if the parents die while the children are minors. These adoptions are usually easier and simpler than nonrelative adoptions.

What are some of the advantages and disadvantages of an agency adoption?

Using an agency to manage your adoption can be helpful for a number of reasons. Agencies are experienced in finding children, matching them with parents and satisfying the necessary legal requirements. Agencies will do most of the legwork of an adoption, from finding a birthparent to finalizing the papers, and they'll walk adoptive parents through many of the crucial steps in between, such as conducting the home study, obtaining the necessary consents and advising parents on the state's specific legal requirements.

One key advantage of an agency adoption is the extensive counseling that agencies provide throughout the process. Typically, counseling is available for adoptive parents, birthparents and the children (if they are older). Careful counseling can help everyone involved weather the emotional, practical and legal complexities that are likely to arise during the adoption.

Finally, many agencies specialize in certain kinds of children; this may be helpful if you want, for example, to adopt an infant, a child of a different race from yours or a child with special medical needs. Some agencies also offer international adoption services.

On the down side, private agencies are often extremely selective when choosing adoptive parents. This is because they have a surplus of people who want to adopt and a limited number of available children. Most agencies have long waiting lists of prospective parents, especially for healthy, white infants. Agencies weed out parents using criteria such as age limits, marital status, income, health, religion, family size, personal history (including criminal conduct) and residency requirements.

Additionally, agencies often wait to place the child in the adoptive home until all necessary consents have been given and become final. Because of this, a child may be placed in foster care for a few days or weeks, depend-

ing on the situation and the state's law. The lag-time concerns many adoptive parents who want the child to have a secure, stable home as soon as possible. Some agencies get around this by placing infants immediately through a type of adoption known as a "legal risk placement": If the birthmother decides she wants her child back before her rights have been legally terminated, the adoptive parents must let the child go.

Public agencies often have many children ready to be adopted, but they often specialize in older or special-needs children. If you want a newborn, a public agency might not be able to help you. Also, public agencies often do not provide many other services such as the much-needed counseling that private agencies offer. Generally, they don't have as many resources as private agencies.

How do I find an adoption agency?

There are an estimated 3,000 adoption agencies in the United States, public and private. If you live in a state like California or New York, you'll have more options than if you live in a less populated state. But wherever you live, you'll probably have to do some searching to find an agency that meets your needs and is able to work with you. You can call a national adoption organization for referrals to get you started. The addresses and phone numbers of several organizations are listed at the end of this section.

Be persistent with the agencies you contact. If they tell you that there are no children, ask whether there is a waiting list. Then ask other questions such as: Is the waiting list for child placement or a home study? How do they determine who may file an application? Can you fill out an application now? If not, when can you? Do they hold orientation meetings? If so, when will the next one be held? Ask if you can speak with other parents in circumstances similar to yours who have adopted through the agency. These parents may provide valuable information about the service they received from the agency, how long the process took and whether they were ultimately happy with the outcome. Screen the agencies as much as they screen you.

How can I check on the reputation of an adoption agency?

As discussed above, you can and should speak with other parents who have adopted through the agency. In addition, you should check out the agency's accreditation. Start with the licensing department of your state. It can tell you whether the agency has been cited for licensing violations, or whether the licensing office has received any complaints about the agency. You can also request a copy of the state's rules governing agencies so that you understand the standards to which your agency is held.

The staff at your state's department of social services may also be able to give you information about the agency. Finally, you can check your state or local department of consumer affairs to see if it handles complaints about adoption agencies.

Are agency adoptions very expensive?

They can be. Agencies charge fees to cover the birthmother's expenses as allowed by state law; these expenses may include medical costs, living expenses during the pregnancy and costs for counseling. Add to this the agency's staff salaries and overhead—and charges can mount up quickly.

Many agencies charge a flat fee for adoptions, while others add the birthmother's expenses to a fixed rate for the agency's services. Some agencies use a sliding scale that varies with adoptive parents' income levels, usually with a set minimum and maximum fee. You can expect to pay between $1,000 and $6,000 to adopt a young child, and $10,000 or more to adopt a newborn. Some agencies charge a lower rate for handling special needs adoptions.

Public agencies generally do not charge fees for placing children in adoptive homes.

What are the costs involved in an independent adoption?

Because each situation is unique, fees for independent adoptions vary widely. Prospective parents must generally cover the costs of finding a birthmother, all costs related to the pregnancy and birth, and the legal costs involved in the adoption process. Some states also include the birthmother's living expenses during the pregnancy. Expenses such as hospital bills, travel costs, phone bills, home study fees, attorney fees and court costs can often surpass $10,000.

You Can't Buy a Baby

It is illegal in all states to buy or sell a baby. All states, however, allow adoptive parents to pay certain "reasonable" costs that are specifically related to the adoption process. Each state has its own laws defining the expenses that may be paid by adoptive parents in any kind of adoption proceeding—agency or independent. If you pursue an independent adoption, you must adhere to these laws when you give any money to the birthmother. And agencies are regulated to make sure that they charge adoptive parents only for the costs that the state allows.

Most states allow the adoptive parents to pay the birthmother's medical expenses, counseling costs and attorney fees. Some states allow payments to cover the birthmother's living expenses such as food, housing and transportation during pregnancy. Most states require all payments to be itemized and approved by a court before the adoption is finalized. Be sure to know and understand your state's laws, because providing or accepting prohibited financial support may subject you to criminal charges. And the adoption itself may be jeopardized if you make improper payments.

What should I keep in mind when deciding whether to pursue an independent adoption?

Birth and adoptive parents are sometimes attracted to independent adoptions because they allow control over the entire adoption process. Rather than relying on an agency as a go-between, the birthparent and adoptive parents can meet, get to know each other and decide for themselves whether the adoption should take place. Independent adoptions also avoid the long waiting lists and restrictive qualifying criteria that are often involved in agency adoptions. And independent adoptions usually happen much faster than agency adoptions, often within a year of beginning the search for a child.

One major drawback to independent adoptions is that they are illegal in some states, currently Connecticut, Delaware, Massachusetts and Minnesota. States that do allow independent adoptions sometimes regulate them in other ways—for example, by prohibiting adoptive parents from advertising for birthmothers. Be sure to check your state's laws before you proceed.

Another concern is that birthparents might not receive adequate counseling during the adoption process. This may leave your agreement more vulnerable to unraveling. Furthermore, some states extend the period in which birthparents may revoke their consent for independent adoptions; this places your agreement at additional risk.

Finally, independent adoptions are a lot of work. Adoptive parents often spend enormous amounts of time—and money—just finding a birthmother, not to mention the efforts required to follow through and bring the adoption to a close. Some parents decide afterwards that the energy and expense needed to adopt independently are just too much, and they hire an agency to do the work for their next adoption.

Open Adoptions

An open adoption is one in which there is some degree of contact between the birthparents and the adoptive parents—often this includes contact with the child as well. There is no one standard for open adoptions; each family works out the arrangement that works best for them. Some adoptive parents consider meeting the birthparents just once before the birth of the child, while others form ongoing relationships which may include written correspondence or visits.

Open adoptions often help reduce stress and worry by eliminating the power of the unknown: Rather than fearing the day that a stranger will come knocking on their door to ask for the child back, adoptive parents are reassured by knowing the birthparents personally and dealing with them directly. This openness can be beneficial to the child as well, who will grow up with fewer questions—and misconceptions—than might a child of a "closed" adoption.

If you want your adoption to be open and decide to use an agency, be sure to find out their policies on open placements. Some agencies offer only closed or "semi-open" adoptions, and will not provide identifying information about birth or adoptive parents even if both families want the adoption to be open. On the other hand, independent adoptions—where allowed—permit any degree of openness desired by the birth and adoptive families.

What's a home study?

All states require adoptive parents to undergo an investigation to make sure that they are fit to raise a child. Typically, the study is conducted by a state agency or a licensed social worker who examines the adoptive parents' home life and prepares a report that the court will review before allowing the adoption to take place. Some states do not require a report to be submitted to a court, however; these states allow the agency or social worker to decide whether the prospective parents are fit to adopt. Common areas of inquiry include:

- financial stability
- marital stability
- lifestyles
- other children
- career obligations
- physical and mental health, and
- criminal history.

In recent years, the home study has become more than just a method of investigating prospective parents: It serves to educate and inform them as well. The social worker helps to prepare the adoptive parents by discussing issues such as how and when to talk with the child about being adopted, and how to deal with the reaction that friends and family might have to the adoption.

Can I adopt a child from another country?

You can adopt a foreign child through an American agency which specializes in intercountry adoptions—or you can adopt directly. If you prefer a direct adoption, you will have to adhere not only to the adoption laws of your state, but also to U.S. immigration laws and the laws of the country where the child is born. It will be a complex process, so be prepared for some tangles. Do as much research as you can before you fly off to find a child; the more you know about the chosen country's adoption system ahead of time, the better off you'll be when you get there.

U.S. immigration laws require that prospective adoptive parents be married or, if single, at least 25 years old. The adoptive parents must file an Orphan Petition (INS form I-600) with the Immigration and Naturalization Service which shows either that the child's parents have died, disappeared or have abandoned the child, or that one remaining parent is not able to care for the child and consents to the child's adoption and immigration to the U.S. If there are two known parents, the child will not qualify as an orphan under any circumstances.

Along with the Orphan Petition, you will need to submit a number of other documents, including a favorable home study report. If the INS approves the petition, and there are no disqualifying factors such as a communicable disease, the child can be issued an immigrant visa.

Much of the paperwork for an intercountry adoption can be completed even before you have identified a specific child to adopt. Advance preparation is a valuable option because the INS paperwork often takes a long time to process, and may hold up the child's arrival in the U.S. even after all foreign requirements have been met.

Finally, be sure to check your own state laws for any preadoption requirements. Some states, for instance, require you to submit the written consent of the birthmother before they approve the entry of the child into the state. Some experts recommend that parents who adopt overseas readopt the child in their own state in order to make sure that the adoption fully conforms to state law.

For more information about intercountry adoptions, see the resource list at the end of this section.

What should my adoption petition say?

A standard adoption petition will generally include five pieces of information:

1) the names, ages and address of the adoptive parents

2) the relationship between the adoptive parents and the child to be adopted

3) the legal reason that the birthparents' rights are being terminated (usually that they consented to the termination)

4) a statement that the adoptive parents are the appropriate people to adopt the child, and

5) a statement that the adoption is in the child's best interests.

Typically, the written consent of the birthparents or the court order terminating their parental rights is also filed along with the petition. Adoptive parents also often include a request for an official name change for the child.

Do I need an attorney to handle the adoption of my child?

If you do not use an agency, yes. And even if you do use an agency, you will probably need to hire a lawyer to draft the adoption petition and to represent you at the hearing. Although there is no legal requirement that a lawyer be involved in an adoption, the process can be quite complex and should be handled by someone with experience and expertise. When seeking a lawyer, find out how many adoptions he or she has handled, and whether any of them were contested or developed other complications.

When is an adoption considered final?

All adoptions—agency or independent—must be approved by a court. The adoptive parents must file a petition to finalize the adoption proceeding; there will also be an adoption hearing.

Before the hearing, anyone who is required to consent to the adoption must receive notice. Usually this includes the biological parents, the adoption agency, the child's legal representative if a court has appointed one and the child himself if he is old enough (12 to 14 years in most states).

At the hearing, if the court determines that the adoption is in the child's best interest, the judge will issue an order approving and finalizing the adoption. This order, often called a final decree of adoption, legalizes the new parent-child relationship and usually changes the child's name to the name the adoptive parents have chosen.

Stepparent Adoptions

The majority of adoptions in the United States are stepparent adoptions, in which the biological child of one parent is formally adopted by that parent's new spouse. This type of adoption may occur when one biological parent has died or has left the family after a divorce, and the remaining parent remarries. While most stepparents do not formally adopt their stepchildren, if they do, they obtain the same parental rights as biological parents. This section discusses some of the issues that arise when a stepparent adopts a stepchild.

My new spouse wants to adopt my son from a previous marriage. Are there special adoption rules for stepparents?

Generally speaking, a stepparent adoption is much easier to complete than a nonrelative adoption. The procedure is generally the same as for any adoption, but specific steps are sometimes waived or streamlined. For instance, waiting periods, home studies and even the adoption hearing are sometimes dispensed with in a stepparent adoption.

In all stepparent adoptions, however, your ex-spouse will need to consent to the adoption because she is the other legally recognized parent of the child. If your former spouse refuses to consent, the adoption will not be allowed unless his or her parental rights are terminated for some other reason—abandonment or unfitness, for example.

My new husband has a great relationship with my 10-year-old son, and wants to adopt him. My son communicates about once or twice a year with his real father, who will consent to the adoption. Is adoption the right thing to do?

Stepparent adoptions can be complicated when the noncustodial biological parent is still alive and in contact with the child. There may be no legal reason why the adoption cannot take place, but the emotional impact of the adoption also needs to be considered.

If an adoption will bring stability to your new family and help your son feel more secure, it may be the right choice. But no matter how well your son gets along with your new husband, he may feel conflicting loyalties between his adoptive father and his real father, and this may be hard for him to handle. Generally speaking, the less contact your son has with his real father, the more sense it makes for an adoption to take place.

Besides the impact on the child (which should be of primary importance), also make sure your ex-husband understands that giving consent to the adoption means giving up all parental rights to his son, including any right to visit him or make decisions for him regarding issues such as medical treatment or education. In addition, he would no longer be responsible for child support once his parental rights were terminated.

I had my daughter when I was unmarried, and we haven't heard from her father for several years. I'm now married to another man, and he wants to adopt my daughter. Do I have to find her biological father and get his consent to the adoption before it can take place?

As in any adoption, the adoption cannot take place until the absent parent either gives consent or has his parental rights terminated for some other reason. That being said, there are a few specific ways to proceed with an adoption when one biological parent is out of the picture.

First, it is possible to go forward without a biological parent's consent if you can prove that the absent parent has not exercised any parental rights and convince the court that it's appropriate to legally terminate that parent-child relationship. Most states' laws allow parental rights to be terminated when a parent has willfully failed to support the child or has abandoned the child for a period of time, usually a year. Generally, abandonment means that the absent parent hasn't communicated with the child or supported the child financially.

If the absent parent is a father, another common way to terminate his parental rights is to show that he is not, legally speaking, the presumed father of the child. Most states have statutes establishing who the presumed father of a child is in certain situations. In this case, you won't have to prove that the father has abandoned the child. You simply must show that he does not meet the legal definition of presumed father. For instance, in all states, a man who is married to a woman at the time she gives birth is legally presumed to be the child's father. Another way of establishing presumed fatherhood in many states is by marrying the mother after the child has been born and being named as the father on the child's birth certificate.

If you can show that the father doesn't meet any of the tests in your state for presumed fatherhood, the court may terminate his rights and allow you to proceed without his consent. If, however, the father meets one of the state's tests for presumed fatherhood, you'll need either to obtain the father's consent to the adoption, or to have his rights terminated by proving abandonment, willful failure to support the child or parental unfitness.

Adoption Rights: Birthparents, Grandparents and Children

The rights of parents to raise and care for their children have traditionally received strong legal protection. Courts have long recognized that the bond between parents and children is a profound one, and the law will not interfere with that bond except in the most carefully defined circumstances.

Since adoption generally involves creating a parent-child relationship where there previously was none—and sometimes negating someone's parental rights in the process—balancing the legal rights of the parties involved can sometimes be difficult. This section discusses how the legal rights of birthparents, grandparents and children can be affected by the adoption process.

Are birthparents allowed to change their minds and take children back even after they've been placed in the adoptive parents' home?

Even after the birthparents have consented to an adoption and the child is living in the adoptive home, many states set aside a period of time during which the birthparents can change their minds. Depending on the state, the birthparents have the right to withdraw consent weeks or even months after the placement. Though it can be nervewracking—and sometimes devastating—for the adoptive parents who have begun to care for the child, it's important that they understand that birthparents have this right. Adoptive parents should find out how long their state allows for birthparents to legally withdraw consent.

The birthmother of the baby we were going to adopt just decided she wants to keep her child. She's eight months pregnant, and we've paid all of her medical bills during her pregnancy. Can we get our money back?

Unless the mother agrees to pay you back, you're probably out of luck. Especially with independent adoptions, paying a birthmother's allowable costs is a risk for adoptive parents. Birthparents often change their minds, and courts will not force them to pay back the expenses paid by the adoptive parents.

My girlfriend is pregnant and I'm the father. I want to keep the baby, but she wants to give it up for adoption. Can she do that?

No. If you acknowledge that you're the father of the child, your consent is needed before the baby can be adopted. The rights of fathers have gotten much more attention in recent years and are now more strongly protected by the law. Some court rulings have held that father's homes must be strongly considered as best for the child. It's important to understand, however, that fathers' rights vary greatly from state to state, and the law in this area is far from settled. If you don't want to see your baby adopted, you should be sure to acknowledge paternity and make it clear to the mother that you won't allow your parental rights to be terminated.

My husband and I found an expectant mother who wants us to adopt her baby. But her mother is trying to talk her out of giving up the child. Can a grandparent legally object to an adoption?

No. The parents of a birthmother don't have any legal right to stop her from giving up the baby. Also, grandparents won't necessarily be favored as adoptive parents over nonrelative parents. (One big exception to this rule is the adoption of Native American children, where a special federal law applies.)

That said, however, grandparents often hold a lot of sway over birthparents, and in many cases have convinced them at the last minute not to give up their babies. If you know that the grandparents are actively trying to talk the birthmother out of the adoption, you should know that there's an increased risk that the adoption might fall through. In this situation, it's especially important to keep in close touch with the birthmother and make extra efforts to encourage open communication. You'll have to judge for yourself how confident you feel about proceeding with a birthmother whose family is opposed to the adoption.

I was adopted as a baby. Now I'm 25 and I want to find my birthparents. Do I have a legal right to obtain my birth records?

In most adoptions, the original birth records and other case documents are "sealed" by the court that finalizes the adoption, which means that no one can see them without the court's permission. But as attitudes toward adoption have become more open, states have adopted a variety of ways for adopted children to find their birthparents, some of which do not require the unsealing of records.

Only a few states offer adult adopted children open access to original birth certificates. More popular is a system called "search and consent," in which an adopted child has an agency contact the birthparent, who then indicates whether or not he or she agrees to be identified. If the birthparent consents, then the agency provides the information to the child. The most common system is a mutual consent registry, used in about 25 states, in which birthparents and adopted children provide identifying information about themselves to the registry. If a birthparent and his or her adopted child both appear within a register, the agency in charge of the register will share the information with each of them, enabling them to contact each other.

If one of these options isn't available or doesn't work for you, it may be possible to obtain your birth records. Generally, a court will unseal a record for "good cause," such as a need for medical or genetic information.

The best way to start your search is to contact a local adoption agency that knows your state's laws and procedures for contacting birthparents.

The National Adoption Information Clearinghouse and the North American Council on Adoptable Children are good sources for referrals to local agencies. (See the end of this section for contact information.)

Another useful tool in searching for birthparents is the Internet. Dozens of organizations and services designed to help adopted children find their birth families have cropped up on the Web. A good place to start is Yahoo!'s adoption category, located at http://www.yahoo.com/Society_and_Culture/Families/Parenting/Adoption/. You'll find numerous links to sites that not only explain how to use your local state agencies to pursue your search, but also how to take advantage of the oceans of personal information online and search on your own.

More Information About Adopting a Child

The Adoption Resource Book, by Lois Gilman (HarperPerennial), is a comprehensive guide for anyone considering adoption.

The Committee for Single Adoptive Parents, P.O. Box 15084, Chevy Chase, MD 20815, is a clearinghouse for single people seeking information about adoption. The Committee publishes *The Handbook for Single Adoptive Parents*.

The National Adoption Information Clearinghouse, P.O. Box 1182, Washington, DC 20012-1182, 703-352-3488, 888-251-0075 (toll-free), naic@calib.com (e-mail), http://www.calib.com/naic (Website). NAIC provides free information about adoption as well as referrals to local agencies and support groups.

The National Center for Lesbian Rights, Adoption & Foster Parenting Project, 870 Market Street, Suite 570, San Francisco, CA 94102, 415-392-6257, provides help to gay men and lesbians who want to adopt.

The National Federation for Open Adoption Education, c/o The Independent Adoption Center, 391 Taylor Boulevard, Pleasant Hill, CA 94523, 510-827-2229, can refer you to agencies with expertise in open adoptions.

The North American Council on Adoptable Children (NACAC), 1821 University Avenue, St. Paul, MN 55104, 612-644-3036, can provide you with information about adoption resources in your local area.

Adopt International: Everything You Need to Know to Adopt a Child from Abroad, by O. Robin Sweet & Patty Bryan (Noonday Press), is a good source of information for prospective parents considering an international adoption.

The United States Immigration and Naturalization Service, 425 I Street, Washington, DC 20536, publishes a pamphlet called *The Immigration of Adopted and Prospective Adoptive Children*, as well as other forms you will need for an international adoption.

U.S. Immigration Made Easy, by Laurence Canter & Martha Siegel (Nolo Press), contains a chapter on international adoptions, including the necessary INS forms.

Child Custody and Visitation

YOU CAN'T SHAKE HANDS

WITH A CLENCHED FIST.

—INDIRA GHANDI

When parents separate or divorce, the term "custody" often serves as shorthand for "who gets the children" under the divorce decree or judgment. In 20 states, custody is split into two types: physical custody and legal custody. Physical custody refers to the responsibility of taking care of the children, while legal custody involves making decisions that affect their interests (such as medical, educational and religious decisions). In states that don't distinguish between physical and legal custody, the term "custody" implies both types of responsibilities.

Legal v. Physical Custody

In the states listed below, a court may make different awards for legal and physical custody. In all other states, a custody award encompasses both legal and physical custody.

Alabama	Mississippi
Arizona	Missouri
California	New Hampshire
Colorado	New Jersey
Connecticut	Ohio
Georgia	Pennsylvania
Hawaii	Texas
Idaho	Utah
Indiana	Virginia
Iowa	West Virginia
Minnesota	Wisconsin

Does custody always go to just one parent?

No. Courts frequently award at least some aspects of custody to both parents, called "joint custody." Joint custody usually takes at least one of three forms:
- joint physical custody (children spend a relatively equal amount of time with each parent)
- joint legal custody (medical, educational, religious and other decisions about the children are shared), or
- both joint legal and joint physical custody.

In every state, courts are willing to order joint legal custody, but about half the states are reluctant to order joint physical custody unless both parents agree to it and they appear to be sufficiently able to communicate and cooperate with each other. In New Hampshire and New Mexico, courts are required to award joint custody except where the children's best interests—or a parent's health or safety—would be compromised. Many other states expressly allow their courts to order joint custody even if one parent objects to such an arrangement.

Can someone other than the parents have physical or legal custody?

Sometimes neither parent can suitably assume custody of the children, perhaps because of substance abuse or a mental health problem. In these situations, others may be granted custody of the children or be given a temporary guardianship or foster-care arrangement by a court.

Joint Custody

Only Arkansas, New York, North Dakota, Rhode Island and Virginia have no statutes relating to joint custody. In these states, joint custody may be allowed under court decisions.

Joint custody required unless the children's best interests—or a parent's health or safety—would be compromised:

New Hampshire	New Mexico

Joint custody permitted even when one parent objects to the arrangement:

Alabama	Minnesota
Alaska	Mississippi
Arizona	Missouri
California	Montana
Colorado	Nebraska
Florida	New Jersey
Idaho	Ohio
Illinois	Oklahoma
Indiana	South Dakota (possibly)
Iowa	Utah (possibly)
Massachusetts	Wisconsin
Michigan	

Joint custody available if both parents agree:

Connecticut	North Carolina
Delaware	Oregon
District of Columbia	Pennsylvania
Georgia	South Carolina
Hawaii	Tennessee
Kansas	Texas
Kentucky	Vermont
Louisiana	Washington
Maine	West Virginia
Maryland	Wyoming
Nevada	

What factors do courts take into account when deciding who gets custody of the children?

A court gives the "best interests of the child" the highest priority when deciding custody issues. What the best interests of a child are in a given situation depends upon many factors, including:

- the child's age, gender, mental and physical health
- the mental and physical health of the parents
- the lifestyle and other social factors of the parents, including whether the child is exposed to secondhand smoke and whether there is any history of child abuse
- the love and emotional ties between the parent and the child, as well as the parent's ability to give the child guidance
- the parent's ability to provide the child with food, shelter, clothing and medical care
- the child's established living pattern (school, home, community, religious institution)
- the quality of the schools attended by the children
- the child's preference, if the child is above a certain age (usually about 12), and
- the ability and willingness of the parent to foster healthy communication and contact between the child and the other parent.

Assuming that none of these factors clearly favors one parent over the other, most courts tend to focus on which parent is likely to provide the children a stable environment. With younger children, this may mean awarding custody to the parent who has been the child's primary caregiver. With older children, this may mean giving custody to the parent who is best able to foster continuity in education, neighborhood life, religious institutions and peer relationships.

Are mothers more likely to be awarded custody over fathers?

In the past, most states provided that custody of children of "tender years" (about five and under) had to be awarded to the mother when parents divorced. This rule is now rejected in most states, or relegated to the role of tie-breaker if two fit parents request custody of their preschool children. Most states require their courts to determine custody on the basis of what's in the children's best interests without regard to the sex of the parent.

As it turns out, most divorcing parents agree that the mother will have custody after a separation or divorce and that the father will exercise reasonable visitation. This sometimes happens because fathers presume that mothers will be awarded custody or because the mother is more tenacious in seeking custody. In still other situations, the parents agree that the mother has more time, a greater inclination or a better understanding of the children's daily needs.

Are there special issues if a gay or lesbian parent is seeking custody or visitation rights?

In a few states, including Alaska, California, District of Columbia, New Mexico and Pennsylvania, a parent's sexual orientation cannot in and of itself prevent a parent from being given custody of or visitation with his or her child. As a practical matter, however, lesbian and gay parents— even in those states—may be denied custody or visitation. This is because judges, when considering the best interests of the child, may be motivated by their own or community prejudices, and may find reasons other than the lesbian or gay parent's sexual orientation to deny custody or appropriate visitation.

Is race ever an issue in custody or visitation decisions?

The U.S. Supreme Court has ruled it unconstitutional for a court to consider race when a noncustodial parent petitions for a change of custody. In that case, a white couple had divorced, and the mother had been awarded custody of their son. She remarried an African-American man and moved to a predominantly African-American neighborhood. The father filed a request for modification of custody based on the changed circumstances. A Florida court granted the modification, but the U.S. Supreme Court reversed, ruling that societal stigma, especially a racial one, cannot be the basis for a custody decision. (*Palmore v. Sidoti*, 466 U.S. 429 (1984)).

When a court awards physical custody to one parent and "visitation at reasonable times and places" to the other, who determines what's reasonable?

The parent with physical custody is generally in the driver's seat regarding what is reasonable. This need not be bad if the parents cooperate to see that the kids spend a maximum amount of time with each parent. Unfortunately, it all too often translates into very little visitation time with the noncustodial parent, and lots of bitter disputes over missed visits and inconvenience. To avoid such problems, many courts now prefer for the parties to work out a fairly detailed parenting plan (known as a parenting agreement) which sets the visitation schedule and outlines who has responsibility for decisions affecting the children.

I have sole custody of my children. My ex-spouse, who lives in another state, has threatened to go to court in his state and get the custody order changed. Can he do that?

All states and the District of Columbia have enacted a statute called the Uniform Child Custody Jurisdiction Act (UCCJA), which sets standards for when a court may make a custody determination and when a court must defer to an existing determination from another state. Having the same law in all states helps standardize how custody decrees are treated. It also helps solve many problems created by kidnapping or disagreements over custody between parents living in different states.

In general, a state may make a custody decision about a child only if it meets one of these tests (in order of preference):

• The state is the child's home state. This means the child has resided in the state for the six previous months, or was residing in the state but is absent because a parent took the child to another state. (A parent who wrongfully removed or retained a child in order to create a "home state" will be denied custody.)

• The child has significant connections in the state with people such as teachers, doctors and grandparents and, in the words of the UCCJA, "substantial evidence in the state concerning the child's care, protection, training and personal relationships." (A parent who wrongfully removed or retained a child in order to create "significant connections" will be denied custody.)

• The child is in the state and either has been abandoned or is in danger of being abused or neglected if sent back to the other state.

• No other state can meet one of the above three tests, or a state that can meet at least one test has declined to make a custody decision.

If a state cannot meet one of these tests, the courts of that state cannot make a custody award, even if the child is present in the state. In the event more than one state meets the above standards, the law specifies that only one state may make custody decisions. This means that once a state makes a custody award, any other state must keep its hands off the matter.

Custodial Interference

In most states, it's a crime to take a child from his or her parent with the intent to interfere with that parent's physical custody of the child (even if the taker also has custody rights). This crime is commonly referred to as "custodial interference." In most states, the parent deprived of custody may sue the taker for damages, as well as get help from the police to have the child returned.

If a parent without physical custody (who may or may not have visitation rights) removes a child from—or refuses to return a child to—the parent with physical custody, it is considered kidnapping or child concealment in addition to custodial interference. Federal and state laws have been passed to prosecute and punish parents guilty of this type of kidnapping, which is a felony in over 40 states.

In many states, interfering with a parent's custody is a felony if the child is taken out of state. Many states, however, recognize good-cause defenses, such as where the taker acted to prevent imminent bodily harm to herself or himself, or to the child. In addition, some states let a parent take a child out of state if the parent is requesting custody in court and has notified the court or police of the child's location.

I've heard that mediation is the best approach to solving disagreements about child custody. Is this true?

Mediation is a nonadversarial process where a neutral person (a mediator) meets with disputing persons to help them settle a dispute. The mediator does not have power to impose a solution on the parties, but assists them in creating an agreement of their own. (In Alaska, California, Delaware, Michigan, New Mexico and South Dakota, however, the mediator may be asked by the court to make a recommendation if the parties cannot reach an agreement.)

There are several important reasons why mediation is a superior method to litigation for resolving custody and visitation disputes:

- Mediation usually does not involve lawyers or expert witnesses (or their astronomical fees).
- Mediation usually produces a settlement after five to ten hours of mediation over a week or two. (Child custody litigation can drag on for months or even years.)
- Mediation enhances communication between the couple and makes it much more likely that they will be able to cooperate after the divorce or separation when it comes to raising their children. Experts who have studied the effects of divorce on children universally conclude that when divorcing or separating parents can cooperate, the children suffer far less.

How to Find a Family Law Mediator

Several states require mediation in custody and visitation disputes and a number of others allow courts to order mediation. In these situations, the court will direct the parents to the mediator and will pay for the services. Parents can also find and pay for the mediator themselves. With increasing frequency, family law attorneys are offering mediation services for child custody and other divorce-related disputes, as are a number of nonlawyer community mediators. Two resources for finding a family law mediator in your area are:

Academy of Family Mediators
4 Militia Drive
Lexington, MA 02173
617-674-2663

Society of Professionals in Dispute Resolution (SPIDR)
815 15th Street, NW, Suite 530
Washington, DC 20005
202-783-7277

Things are so bitter between my ex and me that it's hard to see us sitting down together to work things out. How can mediation possibly work?

Mediators are very skilled at getting parents who are bitter enemies to cooperate for the sake of their children. The more parents can agree on the details of separate parenting, the better it will be for them and their children. And mediators are skilled at getting the parents to recognize this fact and then move forward towards negotiating a sensible parenting agreement. If there is a history of abuse or if the parents initially cannot stand to be in the same room with each other, the mediator can meet with each parent separately and ferry messages back and forth until agreement on at least some issues is reached. At this point, the parties may be willing to meet face to face.

Under what circumstances can custody and visitation orders be changed within the state where they were obtained?

After a final decree of divorce or other order establishing custody and visitation (such as a paternity decree) is filed with a court, parents may agree to modify the custody or visitation terms. This modified agreement (also called a "stipulated modification") may be made without court approval. If one parent later reneges on the agreement, however, the other person may not be able to enforce it unless the court has approved the modification. Thus, it is generally advisable to obtain a court's blessing before relying on such agreements. Courts usually approve modification agreements unless it appears that they are not in the best interests of the child.

If a parent wants to change an existing court order and the other parent won't agree to the change, he or she must file a motion (a written request) asking the court that issued the order to modify it. Usually, courts will modify an existing order only if the parent asking for the change can show a "substantial change in circumstances." This requirement encourages stability of arrangements and helps prevent the court from becoming overburdened with frequent and repetitive modification requests. Here are some examples of a substantial change in circumstances:

• *Geographic move.* If a custodial parent makes a significant move, or the move will seriously disrupt the stability of the child's life, the move may constitute a changed circumstance that justifies the court's modification of a custody or visitation order. Some courts switch custody from one parent to the other, although the increasingly common approach is to ask the parents to work out a plan under which both parents may continue to have significant contact with their children. If no agreement is reached, what the court will do depends on where you live. Courts in some states will permit the move unless it is shown that the child will be adversely affected. In other states,

the court will carefully examine the best interests of the child and make a decision about which parent should have custody.

• *Change in lifestyle.* Changes in custody or visitation orders may be obtained if substantial changes in a parent's lifestyle threatens or harms the child. If, for example, a custodial parent begins working at night and leaving a nine-year-old child alone, the other parent may request a change in custody. Similarly, if a noncustodial parent begins drinking heavily or taking drugs, the custodial parent may file a request for modification of the visitation order (asking, for example, that visits occur when the parent is sober, or in the presence of another adult). What constitutes a lifestyle sufficiently detrimental to warrant a change in custody or visitation rights varies tremendously depending on the state and the particular judge deciding the case.

More Information About Child Custody

Child Custody: Building Parenting Agreements That Work, by Mimi Lyster (Nolo Press), shows separating or divorcing parents how to create a win-win custody agreement.

National Center for Lesbian Rights, 870 Market Street, Suite 570, San Francisco, CA 94102, 415-392-6257, provides legal information, referrals and assistance to lesbian and gay parents.

National Congress for Fathers and Children, 9454 Wilshire Boulevard, Suite 207, Beverly Hills, CA 90212, 800-733-3237 or 310-247-6051, provides information and assistance for fathers.

Joint Custody Association, 10606 Wilkins Avenue, Los Angeles, CA 90024, 310-475-5352, provides assistance to joint custodial parents.

Child Support

Children have more need of models than of critics.

—JOSEPH JOUBERT

Child support is an emotional subject. Parents who are supposed to receive it on behalf of their children often do not. Parents who are supposed to pay it often cannot, or choose not to for a variety of reasons that are not legally recognized. It is the children who suffer the most when child support levels are inadequate or obligations are not met. Therefore, the trend in all states is to increase child support levels and the ways child support obligations can be enforced.

How long must parents support their children?

Biological parents and adoptive parents must support a child until:
- the child reaches the age of majority (and sometimes longer if the child has special needs or is in college)

- the child is on active military duty
- the parents' rights and responsibilities are terminated (for example, when a child is adopted), or
- the child has been declared emancipated by a court. (Emancipation can occur when a minor has demonstrated freedom from parental control or support and an ability to be self-supporting.)

How are child support obligations affected by a divorce or separation?

When one parent is awarded sole custody of a child, the other parent typically is required to fulfill his or her child support obligation by making payments to the custodial parent. The custodial parent, however, meets his or her support obligation through the custody itself. When parents are awarded joint physical custody in a divorce, the support obligation of each is often based on the ratio of each parent's income to their combined incomes, and the percentage of time the child spends with each parent.

Are fathers who never married the mother still required to pay child support?

The short answer to this question is yes. When a mother is not married, however, it's not always clear who the father is. An "acknowledged father" is any biological father of a child born to unmarried parents for whom paternity has been established by either the admission of the father or the agreement of the parents. Acknowledged fathers are required to pay child support.

Additionally, a man who never married may be presumed to be the father of a child if he welcomes the child into his home and openly holds the child out as his own. In some states, the presumption of paternity is considered conclusive, which means it cannot be disproved, even with contradictory blood tests.

The obligation to pay child support does not depend on whether a court ordered it. Where most unmarried fathers encounter this principle is when the mother seeks public assistance. Sooner or later the welfare department will ask the court to order the father to reimburse it, based on his support obligation and income during the period in question. Sometimes this happens many years later, and the father is required to pay thousands of dollars in back support that he never knew he owed.

Is a stepparent obligated to support the children of the person to whom he or she is married?

No, unless the stepparent legally adopts the children.

Calculating Child Support

Under the federal Child Support Enforcement Act of 1984, each state must develop guidelines to calculate a range of child support to be paid, based on the parents' incomes and expenses. These guidelines vary considerably from state to state, which means that in virtually identical situations the child support

ordered in one state may be far more or less than that ordered in another state. Some states allow their judges considerable leeway in setting the actual amount, as long as the general state guidelines are followed. But an increasing number of states do not trust their judges to be consistent and therefore impose very strict guidelines that leave the judges very little latitude.

Regardless of how much latitude judges are given, the guidelines in effect in most states specify factors which must be considered in determining who pays child support, and how much. These factors usually include:

- the needs of the child—including health insurance, education, day care and special needs
- the income and needs of the custodial parent
- the paying parent's ability to pay, and
- the standard of living of the child before divorce or separation.

Can the court base its child support order on what I am able to earn as opposed to what I'm actually earning?

In most states, the judge is authorized to examine a parent's ability to earn as well as what she is actually earning, and order higher child support if there is a discrepancy. Actual earnings are an important factor in determining a person's ability to earn, but are not conclusive where there is evidence that a person could earn more if she chose to do so.

For example, assume a parent with an obligation to pay child support leaves his current job and enrolls in medical or law school, takes a job with lower pay but good potential for higher pay in the future or takes a lower-paying job that provides better job satisfaction. In each of these situations, a court may base the child support award on the income from the original job (ability to earn) rather than on the new income level (ability to pay). The basis for this decision would be that the children's current needs take priority over the parent's career plans and desires.

On the other hand, several courts have ruled that a parent's imprisonment entitles the parent to a reduction or suspension of child support where there is no showing that the imprisonment resulted from an attempt to avoid paying the support.

What happens if a parent falls behind on his or her child support payments?

Each installment of court-ordered child support is to be paid according to the date set out in the order. When a person does not comply with the order, the overdue payments are called arrearages or arrears. Judges have become very strict about enforcing child support orders and collecting arrearages. While the person with arrears can ask a judge for a downward modification of future payments, the judge will usually insist that the arrearage be paid in full, either immediately or in installments. In fact, judges in most states are prohibited

by law from retroactively modifying a child support obligation.

EXAMPLE

Joe has a child support obligation of $300 per month. Joe is laid off of his job, and six months pass before he finds another one with comparable pay. Although Joe could seek a temporary decrease on the grounds of diminished income, he lets the matter slide and fails to pay any support during the six-month period. Joe's ex-wife later brings Joe into court to collect the $1,800 arrearage; Joe cannot obtain a retroactive ruling excusing him from making the earlier payments.

In addition, back child support cannot be cancelled in a bankruptcy proceeding. This means that once it is owed, it will always be owed, until paid.

My ex-spouse is refusing to pay court-ordered child support. How can I see to it that the order is enforced?

Under the Child Support Enforcement Act of 1984, the district attorneys (or state's attorneys) of every state must help you collect the child support owed by your ex. Sometimes this means that the D.A. will serve your ex with papers requiring him to meet with the D.A. and arrange a payment schedule, and telling him that if he refuses to meet or pay, he could go to jail. If your ex has moved out of state, you or the D.A. can use legal procedures to locate him and seek payment. Federal and state parent locator services can also assist in locating missing parents.

Federal laws permit the interception of tax refunds to enforce child support orders. Other methods of enforcement include wage attachments, seizing property, suspending the business or occupational license of a payer who is behind on child support or—in some states—revoking the payer's driver's license. Your state's D.A. may employ any one of these methods in an attempt to help you collect from your ex.

If you and your ex live in different states, you may use the Revised Uniform Reciprocal Enforcement of Support Act (RURESA) to seek payment. Under that law, the court in the state where you live contacts a court in your ex-spouse's state, which in turn requires him to pay. This procedure will be provided to you free of charge. Unfortunately, however, it often falls short of its stated goals due to the complexity of the process and the low priority frequently assigned to these cases by the courts and law enforcement officers which are involved.

In 1992, Congress passed the Child Support Recovery Act (CSRA) which makes it a federal crime for a parent to willfully refuse to make support payments to a parent who lives in another state. This statute has been challenged on constitutional grounds (beyond the authority of Congress), and its enforcement is spotty.

As a last resort, the court that has issued the child support order can hold your ex in contempt and, in the absence of a reasonable explanation for the delinquency, impose a jail term.

This contempt power is exercised sparingly in most states, primarily because most judges would rather keep the payer out of jail where he has a chance of earning the income necessary to pay the support.

I think our existing child support order is unfair. How can I change it?

You and your child's other parent may agree to modify the child support terms, but even an agreed-upon modification for child support must be approved by a judge to be legally enforceable.

If you and your ex can't agree on a change, you must request the court to hold a hearing in which each of you can argue the pros and cons of the proposed modification. As a general rule, the court will not modify an existing order unless the parent proposing the modification can show changed circumstances. This rule encourages stability of arrangements and helps prevent the court from becoming overburdened with frequent and repetitive modification requests.

Depending on the circumstances, a modification may be temporary or permanent. Examples of the types of changes that frequently support temporary modification orders are:
- a child's medical emergency
- the payer's temporary inability to pay (for instance, because of illness or an additional financial burden such as a medical emergency or job loss), or
- temporary economic or medical hardship on the part of the recipient parent.

A permanent modification may be awarded under one of the following circumstances:
- either parent receives additional income from remarriage
- changes in the child support laws
- job change of either parent
- cost of living increase
- disability of either parent, or
- needs of the child.

A permanent modification of a child support order will remain in effect until support is no longer required or the order is modified at a later time—again, because of changed circumstances.

Do I have to pay child support if my ex keeps me away from my kids?

Yes. Child support should not be confused with custody and visitation. Every parent has an obligation to support his or her children. With one narrow exception, no state allows a parent to withhold support because of disputes over visitation. The exception? If the custodial parent disappears for a lengthy period so that no visitation is possible, a few courts have ruled that the noncustodial parent's duty to pay child support may be considered temporarily suspended.

No matter what the circumstances, if you believe that your ex is interfering with your visitation rights, the appropriate remedy is to go back to court to have your rights enforced rather than stop making support payments.

More Information About Child Support

How to Raise or Lower Child Support in California, by Roderic Duncan and Warren Siegel (Nolo Press), contains forms and instructions for going to court to get an existing order changed to the appropriate level.

Nolo's Pocket Guide to Family Law, by Robin Leonard and Stephen Elias (Nolo Press), explains legal concepts you may run across if you're involved in a divorce, custody dispute, adoption or other family law matter.

In addition, the following organizations can give you information about enforcing child support orders:

National Child Support
Enforcement Association
Hall of the States
400 N. Capitol Street, Suite 414
Washington, DC 20001-1512
202-624-8180

Administration for Children and Families
Child Support Enforcement
Mail Stop: OCSE/DCS/NRC
370 L'Enfant Promenade, SW
Washington, DC 20447
202-401-9383

Guardianship of Children

A guardianship is a legal arrangement in which an adult has the court-ordered authority and responsibility to care for a child (someone under 18 in most states) or an incapacitated adult. This section focuses on guardianships of children.

A guardianship may be necessary if a child's parents die, or if the child has been abandoned, is not receiving adequate care or is being abused in some way.

What does a guardian do?

Typically, a guardian takes care of a child's personal needs, including shelter, education and medical care. A guardian may also provide financial management for a child, though sometimes a second person (often called a "conservator" or "guardian of the estate") is appointed for this purpose.

What is the difference between a guardianship and an adoption?

An adoption permanently changes the relationship between the adults and child involved. The adopting adults legally become the child's parent. The biological parent (if living) gives up all parental rights and obligations to the child, including the responsibility to pay child support. If a biological parent dies without a will, the child has no right to inherit.

Although a guardianship establishes a legal relationship between a child and adult, it does not sever the legal relationship between the biological parents and the child. For example, the biological parents are legally required to provide financial support for the child. And if a biological parent dies without a will, the child has certain automatic inheritance rights.

May I be appointed guardian if the child's parents object?

It depends on how a judge sees the situation. You'll need to start by filing guardianship papers in court. A court investigator will likely interview you, the child and his or her parents and make a recommendation to the judge. The judge will then review the case and decide whether to appoint you. As a general rule, guardianships are not granted unless:
- the parents voluntarily consent
- the parents have abandoned the child, or
- a judge finds that it would be detrimental to the child for his or her parents to have custody.

If a child lives with me, do I need a guardianship?

You won't need a guardianship if the child is only staying with you for a few weeks or months. But anyone who anticipates caring for a child for a period of years will probably need a legal guardianship. Without this legal arrangement, you may have trouble registering the child in school, arranging for medical care and obtaining benefits on the child's behalf. In addition, you'll have no right to keep the child if his parents want him back—even if you think they're not capable of caring for him properly.

If You Want to Avoid a Formal Guardianship

An adult who has physical custody of a child may have strong reasons to avoid becoming a legal guardian—for example:

- The caretaker expects that the child's parents will not consent to a legal guardianship.
- Dynamics between family members are such that filing for a guardianship might set off a battle for legal custody. (This would be especially likely where a stepparent and one natural parent care for a child.)
- The caretaker doesn't want his or her personal life scrutinized in court or by a court-appointed investigator.

Some adults try to slide by and raise children (often grandchildren or other relatives) without any legal court authorization. If you go this route, you could run into problems with institutions that want authority from a parent or court-appointed legal guardian. Some communities and institutions are, however, very accommodating of people who are bringing up someone else's children. Califor-

nia, for example, has created a form that gives a nonparent permission to enroll a child in school and make medical decisions on his or her behalf without going to court. Research the laws for your state, or talk to a knowledgeable family law attorney, to find out whether there are ways for you to care for a child short of becoming a legal guardian.

When does a guardianship end?

A guardianship ordinarily lasts until the earliest of these events:

- the child reaches legal age
- the child dies
- the child's assets are used up—if the guardianship was set up solely for the purpose of handling the child's finances, or
- a judge determines that a guardianship is no longer necessary.

Even if a guardianship remains in force, a guardian may step down from his or her role with permission from the court. In that case, a judge will appoint a replacement guardian.

Who financially supports a child under a guardianship?

Unless a court terminates the biological parents' rights (uncommon in most guardianship situations), the parents are responsible for supporting their child. In practice, however, financial support often becomes the guardian's responsibility. The guardian may choose to pursue financial benefits on the child's behalf, such as public assistance and Social Security.

Any funds the guardian receives for the child must be used for that child's benefit. Depending on the amount of money involved, the guardian may be required to file periodic reports with a court showing how much money was received for the child and how it was spent.

Are You Prepared to Be a Guardian?

An obvious but important question to ask yourself before you take any steps to establish a guardianship is whether you're truly prepared for the job.

- Do you want the ongoing responsibilities of a legal guardianship—including potential liability for the child's actions?
- If you're managing the child's finances, are you willing to keep careful records, provide a court with periodic accountings and go to court when you need permission to handle certain financial matters?
- What kind of personal relationship do you have with the child? Do you want to act as the legal parent of this child for the duration of the guardianship?
- Will the guardianship adversely affect you or your family because of your own children, health situation, job, age or other factors?
- Do you have the time and energy to raise a child?
- What is the financial situation? If the child will receive income from Social Security, public assistance programs, welfare, a parent or the estate of a deceased parent, will this be enough to provide a decent level of support? If not, are you able and willing to spend your own money to raise the child?
- Do you anticipate problems with the child's relatives—including parents—who may suddenly reappear and contest the guardianship? (This is rare, but it can happen.)
- What kind of relationship do you have with the child's parents? Will they support the guardianship, or will they more likely be hostile, antagonistic or interfering?

It's smart to consider your options carefully before initiating a guardianship proceeding. After honestly answering the questions above, you may need to rethink your plans.

Is it true that parents may need a guardianship of their own child?

It's strange but true: Sometimes parents need to establish a particular type of guardianship—called a "guardianship of the estate"—to handle their own child's finances—even if the child lives with them. This situation usually arises when significant amounts of property (at least $5,000 in most states) are given directly to a child.

Understandably, institutions and lawyers are reluctant to turn assets over to parents when they were intended for a child. A guardianship of the estate relieves the institution from liability, and the parents are directly accountable to a court to show how funds are spent and invested.

EXAMPLE

The Thompsons lived next door to an elderly widow, who was extremely fond of their small daughter. When the widow died, she left her house to little Suzy Thompson. The lawyer handling the widow's estate suggests that Suzy's parents go to court to establish a guardianship of their child's estate. The house is then transferred into the name of Suzy's guardianship estate, which her parents manage until she reaches adulthood.

While this system is effective in protecting children's assets from unscrupulous parents, setting up a formal guardianship of the estate involves time and money that well-meaning parents sometimes find burdensome. For this reason, all states have passed laws to make it easier to give money or property to children. These laws provide simple, inexpensive procedures by which gifts to minors (typically up to $10,000) can be managed by their parents without setting up a formal guardianship of the estate. The gift-giver must simply name, in his or her will or in a trust document, someone to manage the gift until the child reaches adulthood. No court involvement is required. (For more information about leaving property to children, see Chapter 12, *Wills and Estate Planning*.)

I have young children, and I'm worried about who will care for them if something happens to me. How can I name a guardian?

You can use your will to name a guardian for your children. The specifics are discussed in Chapter 12 of this book, *Wills and Estate Planning*.

More Information About Guardianships

The Guardianship Book, by Lisa Goldoftas and David Brown (Nolo Press), contains all forms and instructions necessary to become a child's guardian in California.

For information about guardianships in other states, visit your local law library.

online help
help online help online help

http://www.nolo.com
Nolo Press offers self-help information about a wide variety of legal topics, including laws that affect parents and their children.

http://www.calib.com/naic
The National Adoption Information Clearinghouse provides information about adoption as well as referrals to local agencies and support groups.

http://www.adoption.com/
This site provides information about adoption agencies, international adoption and many other adoption issues.

http://www.divorce-online.com/
Divorce Online provides general information, including articles about mediation and child custody. The site also gives answers to frequently asked family law questions.

**http://www.law.cornell.edu/
topics/topic2.html#family#law**
The Legal Information Institute at Cornell Law School provides links to many of the family laws available on the Web, including laws governing adoption, child custody and children's rights. As of August 1996, it contained state-specific links to statutes for Arizona, California, Colorado, Florida, Indiana, Minnesota, New York, Texas, Utah, Washington and Wyoming.

Courts and Mediation

NINETY PERCENT OF OUR LAWYERS SERVE

TEN PERCENT OF OUR PEOPLE. WE ARE

OVER-LAWYERED AND UNDER-REPRESENTED.

—JIMMY CARTER

The average citizen's ability to gain access to the American justice system has long been determined by economic status. The wealthy can afford experienced lawyers—the legal system's gatekeepers—while most others are frozen out. Fortunately, a number of initiatives are being developed to level the legal playing field. Although still too few, and often too limited in terms of the size and types of disputes they can consider, mediation, expanded small claims courts and the reconfiguration of formal courts to make nonlawyers welcome are all part of the changing landscape. Together they give hope that all Americans will have access to our legal system in the years ahead.

Representing Yourself in Court

In the spring of 1988, a man was arrested in New York for impersonating a lawyer over a lengthy period of time. Assistant Manhattan District Attorney Brian Rosner said one judge told him:

"I should have suspected he wasn't a lawyer. He was always so punctual and polite."

With lawyers' fees typically running in excess of $200 an hour, it often makes sense to represent yourself in a small civil (noncriminal) lawsuit. The task may seem daunting, but if you have a good self-help resource to guide you and perhaps even someone who knows the ropes to coach you when you need help, you really can act as your own lawyer—safely and efficiently.

Is it ever truly sensible to appear in court without a lawyer?

When it comes to small claims court, which is designed to be accessible to nonlawyers—yes, of course. But sometimes it's also a good idea to represent yourself in a more formal court pro-ceeding. Hiring a lawyer is almost always unaffordable for disputes that involve less than $25,000 and often unaffordable for disputes in the $50,000–$100,000 range. In these cases, representing yourself may be your only reasonable option.

Are you saying that for small cases, the cost of hiring a lawyer is too high, given the amount at stake?

With lawyers charging $150–$250 per hour, and any contested court case racking up dozens of hours of attorney time, it is obvious that attorney fees can quickly dwarf what is at stake in many disputes. But the problem is really much larger: No matter what the size of the case, most people don't have the kind of money it takes to hire a lawyer in the first place. This means that unless the dispute is the type that lawyers will take for a contingency fee—a percentage of the total recovery—the person will either have to go it alone or give up the lawsuit altogether.

Free Legal Services

Before you decide to represent yourself, you may want to explore the possibility of getting help at no cost to you. Here are several situations in which you may be able to get an attorney to represent you for free.

If you face criminal charges.

If you've been charged with a crime and cannot afford to hire your own lawyer, you have a constitutional right to an attorney at government expense. At your request, an attorney, often from a public defender's office, can be appointed to represent you when you are formally charged in court with a criminal offense.

If you've been injured.

If you have been severely injured and wish to sue, a lawyer may agree to represent you on a "contingency fee" basis. This means that you pay attorney's fees only when and if the attorney recovers money for you; the attorney takes an agreed-upon percentage of that money as fees. Be aware, however, that even if a lawyer takes your case on a contingency fee basis, you still have to pay costs, which can add up to several thousand dollars. Costs include court filing fees, court reporters' fees, expert witnesses and jury fees. The good news is that if you win your case, the judge will usually order your adversary to pay you back for these costs.

If you qualify for legal aid.

If you can't afford an attorney, you may qualify for legal aid. Legal aid lawyers are government lawyers who represent people with low incomes in a variety of legal situations, including eviction defense, denial of unemployment compensation or other benefits, and consumer credit problems. If you think you might qualify, look in your telephone directory or ask a local attorney, lawyer referral service or elected representative for the nearest legal aid office.

If your claim involves an issue of social justice.

If your dispute involves a social justice issue, an attorney with an interest in that issue may represent you on a "pro bono" (no fee or reduced fee) basis. For example, if your claim involves sexual harassment by an employer, abuse by a spouse or partner, discrimination in housing or employment, freedom of speech or religion or environmental pollution, you may find an attorney or organization willing to represent you pro bono. Call a local bar association or a private organization that deals with the kind of problem you face, such as the American Civil Liberties Union, the NAACP Legal Defense Fund, the Natural Resources Defense Council, the National Women's Law Center or the Lambda Legal Defense and Education Fund (gay and lesbian rights).

If I do decide to represent myself, how can I possibly cope with all the picky procedural rules and complex legal language?

Essentially, you have two choices. Get the dispute diverted to mediation (see *Mediation*, below), where things are done in plain English and procedural rules are kept to a minimum, or take the time to learn how to navigate a formal court proceeding. As with learning any other bureaucratic process, doing this will take some effort, but it is not impossible.

Will I really be able to learn everything I need to know to represent myself competently?

Again, the basics of how to bring or defend a case aren't difficult. But trying to get on top of every nuance of procedure and strategy isn't easy. That's why Nolo suggests a two-pronged approach: learn how to handle routine representation tasks yourself while hiring a lawyer as a self-help law coach to provide advice on strategy and tactics as needed. In many situations, hiring a lawyer to coach your self-help efforts will cost only about 10%–20% of what it would cost to hire the lawyer to do the entire job.

How to Find a Lawyer Coach

Ten years ago, trying to find a lawyer who would help you find your own way through the legal system was next to impossible. Today, given the surplus of lawyers and a gradual change in the profession's attitude towards self-helpers, it's much easier. Because law is an increasingly specialized field, however, you'll want to find someone who is knowledgeable about your type of problem—not just any lawyer. Try to get a referral from someone else who has recently worked with lawyers in the area of your legal concern. For example, if you're opening a small business and want to find an appropriate lawyer to provide occasional guidance, you might talk to the owners of excellent local businesses to see whom they work with. Once you have a few names, make and pay for a first appointment (lawyers will respect you less if you ask for a free consultation). Come right out and ask the lawyer if she is prepared to help you help yourself. Be persistent, and you're likely to find a lawyer who meets your needs.

If I'm trying to decide whether to sue someone—for example, a contractor who goofed up my expensive remodeling project. What are my first steps?

You need to answer two fundamental questions as part of deciding whether it's worthwhile to go forward:
• Do I have a good case?
• Assuming I do, can I collect when I win?

If the answer to either question is no, you probably won't want to sue.

How hard is it to collect a court judgment?

That depends on your opponent. Most reputable businesses and individuals will pay you what they owe. But if your opponent tries to stiff you, you may be in for a struggle. Unfortunately, the court won't collect your money for you or even provide much help; it will be up to you to identify the assets you can grab.

Normally, if an individual is working or owns valuable property—such as land or investments—collection isn't difficult; you can instruct your local law enforcement agency (usually the sheriff, marshal or constable) to garnish her wages or attach her non-exempt property. The same is true of a successful business, especially one which receives cash directly from customers; you can authorize your local sheriff or marshal to collect your judgment right out of the cash register. And in many states, if you are suing a contractor or other business person with a state license, you can apply

to have the license suspended until the judgment is paid.

But if you can't identify any collection source—for example, you're dealing with an unlicensed contractor of highly doubtful solvency—think twice before suing. A judgment will be of no value to you if the business or individual is insolvent, goes bankrupt or disappears.

I think I can collect if I win. But how do I decide if I have a good case?

Lawyers break each type of lawsuit ("cause of action," in attorney-speak) into a short list of required elements. As long as you know what the elements are for your type of lawsuit, it's usually fairly easy to determine whether your case is legally sound. For example, a lawsuit against a contractor for doing substandard construction would be for breach of contract (the contractor agreed either orally or in writing to do the job properly). The legal elements for this type of lawsuit are:

Contract formation. You must show that you have a legally binding contract with the other party. If you have a written agreement, this element is especially easy to prove. Without a written contract, you will have to show that you had an enforceable oral (spoken) contract, or that an enforceable contract can be implied from the circumstances of your situation.

Performance. You must prove that you did what was required of you under the terms of the contract. Assuming you have agreed upon your payments and otherwise cooperated, you'll have no problems with this element.

Breach. You must show that the party you plan to sue failed to meet her contractual obligations. This is usually the heart of the case—you'll need to prove that the contractor failed to do agreed-upon work or did work of poor quality.

Damages. You must show that you suffered an economic loss as a result of the other party's breach of contract. Assuming the work must be redone or finished, this element is also easy to prove.

The legal elements for other types of lawsuits are different. You can find outlines for most in Nolo's *Represent Yourself in Court.*

Is it difficult to prepare the paperwork to initiate a lawsuit?

Actually, it's often fairly easy—especially if you learn how to do the necessary legal research and prepare drafts of the papers, restricting your lawyer's role to that of checking your work. Initiating a lawsuit is especially straightforward in states such as California and Michigan, where court clerks provide preprinted fill-in-the-blanks forms for many types of lawsuits. But even in states where lawsuits are filed the old-fashioned way, using paragraphs of appropriate legal jargon on numbered legal paper, the actual wording is almost always available word for word from lawyer "forms books" or CD-ROMs. These information sources, which are routinely used by lawyers, are available at all law libraries and are usually fairly easy for the nonlawyer to understand.

I've filed my lawsuit. What do I need to do next?

Before a case gets scheduled for trial, a number of things need to happen. Information about most of these—for example, whether and when a settlement conference must take place, when papers must be filed and how to place a case on the court's trial calendar—are available from the court clerk. Unfortunately, how to accomplish other pre-trial tasks—which often come under the broad title "discovery"—is left largely up to you and the other parties to the lawsuit. For example, one type of discovery consists of your taking the deposition (oral statement) of the other party or one or more witnesses to find out what he or she is likely to say at trial. Other types of discovery consist of interrogatories (written questions to the other party), a request to produce documents or a request that the other party admit certain facts (stipulations). Books such as *Represent Yourself in Court,* by Paul Bergman and Sara J. Berman-Barrett (Nolo Press), will provide you with some basic information about pre-trial discovery; check with your local law library. And *Represent Yourself in Court* will also help you develop a trial strategy. Nevertheless, this is an area where it will usually be a good idea to regularly consult your self-help law coach.

What are the advantages and disadvantages of taking a deposition?

Depositions, which normally consist of face-to-face questioning of the other party or a witness before trial, have several big advantages as compared to the other types of discovery mentioned above:

- You can offer a deposition transcript into evidence at trial if the deponent (the person questioned) is unavailable to give live testimony. This rule explains why you might consider deposing a helpful witness who may not be available to testify at the time of trial.
- If an adversary's witness whose deposition you have taken testifies significantly differently at trial than at the deposition, you can read the inconsistent deposition testimony into the trial record to impeach (attack) the deponent's credibility.

EXAMPLE

You have sued your former employer for violating state law by firing you for missing work because you served on a jury in a lengthy trial. Before trial you take the deposition of your former supervisor, Paul Chepick. At the deposition, Chepick testified that your work performance had been satisfactory before you went on the jury. At trial, Chepick testifies that you were fired not because of your jury service, but because of a number of work-related problems. Because Chepick's deposition testimony contradicts his trial testimony, you could read the deposition testimony into the record at trial to call his believability into question.

- As compared to conducting discovery by asking written questions (interrogatories), depositions allow for more flexibility in questioning because you hear a deponent's answer before you ask the next question. For example, assume that a deponent unexpectedly refers to an important business meeting that you had no idea had taken place. In a deposition, you can immediately follow up the remark with questions about what took place during this meeting.
- You can take anyone's deposition. You can depose your adversary, an employee who works for your adversary or an ordinary or expert witness hired by your opponent—even your opponent's attorney! By contrast, you can send written questions (interrogatories) only to your opponent, not to an ordinary or expert witness.
- You elicit the testimony of an individual deponent. While your adversary's lawyer will probably attend the deposition and can consult with the deponent during recesses (breaks in the testimony), it is the deponent who has to answer the questions. By contrast, attorneys often play a major role in preparing the answers to written interrogatories and usually advise clients how to answer them in a way that provides you with as little information as possible.
- You can use a deposition to learn and ask about documents (or other tangible items) by simply using a Notice of Deposition (for your opponent) or a subpoena duces tecum (for a nonparty witness) to list items

you want the deponent to bring to the deposition.

Unfortunately, deposing an adversary or a witness who supports your adversary also has considerable disadvantages. Weigh these considerations very carefully before you decide to take a deposition:

- Depositions are the most expensive discovery tool. Even if you are representing yourself (and therefore not paying an attorney to take or attend a deposition), you must pay a court reporter to transcribe the testimony and prepare a written transcript. While costs vary somewhat by locality, it's not unusual for a court reporter to charge up to $5.00 per page of transcript. A day of deposition testimony fills up about 150 pages, meaning that a day-long deposition may cost you around $750. If you win your case, however, the judge may order your adversary to pay your deposition costs.

- If you haven't investigated a case thoroughly enough to know which witnesses are most likely to have important information, you may end up paying dearly to depose a witness whose main answers are, "I don't know." By contrast, written interrogatories give you access to "corporate knowledge." When you send interrogatories to an adversary that is a business or other entity, any employee with knowledge has to contribute to the answers.

- Effective deposition questioning is a difficult skill, even for many attor- neys. You have to pose questions carefully in order to be confident that you know how adverse wit- nesses will testify at trial. If ques- tions are vague or you forget to cover a topic, you won't be prepared for your opponent's evidence at trial or to show that a witness has changed a story and therefore should not be believed.

- Your adversary's lawyer can be present at a deposition. The attorney may throw you off track by object- ing to your questions. Also, an adversary's attorney can help wit- nesses "refresh their recollections" during recesses. Finally, seeing you in action will allow the attorney to estimate your own credibility, and by listening to your questions learn more about your case than you learn about the adversary's.

- If you depose an adverse witness who becomes unavailable for trial, you enable the adversary to offer the deposition transcript into evidence at trial.

How do I take a deposition?

Start by checking your local court rules. Pay particular attention to the time window for taking depositions and know how to notify a person whose deposition you want to take. Under all rules, you'll need to select a date and location for the deposition, arrange and pay for a court reporter's presence (many are listed in phone books) and give the deponent and opposing counsel (or your self-repre- sented adversary) at least ten days' written notice. Even better, as a courtesy, talk to all the necessary people ahead of time and arrange a mutually convenient date and location.

If you want to depose a "non-party witness" (someone other than your adversary), you'll probably have to serve the witness with an official court form called a "Subpoena re Deposition." If you want the non-party witness to bring documents to the deposition, use instead a form carrying the fancy title "Subpoena Duces Tecum re Deposition." (These forms should be available from a court clerk.) List the documents you want the witness to bring along, and state briefly how they pertain to the case.

Once the deposition has been scheduled, follow these tips to learn as much information as you can:

• Prepare a list of questions before you take a witness's deposition. You need not slavishly follow the list, but having one to refer to should prevent you from forgetting important topics.

• Bring (or subpoena) copies of any written statements about the case that the deponent has previously given. For example, bring the police report if the witness gave a statement to a police officer who included it in the report, or the witness's own affidavit if one was attached to a pleading filed in court. Ask the deponent to amplify on and fill any holes in a statement's contents, then check to see if the deponent in any way contradicts a prior

statement. If so, you might ask the witness to repeat the contradictory statement. That way, if you impeach (attack the credibility of) the witness at trial, the witness cannot easily wriggle out by saying, "I made a careless mistake during my deposition."

• Bring copies of any other documents about which you want to question the witness, regardless of whether the witness wrote the document or has any connection to it. For example, you may want to know whether the witness ever saw a document, the date on which the witness saw it or whether the witness is aware of the information in the document.

• Review and bring along all paperwork relating to the case organized chronologically, including the complaint, answer and any motions or court rulings. These documents can help if an issue arises concerning the relevance of your questions.

When my case finally makes it to the courtroom, I'm afraid I won't know what to say, when to say it or even where to stand. How can I learn what to do?

It's not hard to learn how to conduct yourself in court. This is especially true if your trial is before a judge without a jury, because many judges make an effort to simplify jargon and procedure. And there are several practical steps you can take to learn the ropes:

- Attend a few trials involving similar issues. You'll see that it won't be that difficult to present your story and evidence to a judge.
- Carefully read a self-help book such as Nolo's *Represent Yourself in Court*, which explains what you'll need to do in great detail. For example, you'll want to prepare a brief but thorough opening statement to tell the judge what your case is about.
- Prepare a Trial Notebook which outlines each major aspect of your trial and what you need to do and say at each point. For example, based on taking the other side's deposition or asking written questions (interrogatories), you probably have a pretty good idea what she will say when she testifies. Clearly, it's a good idea to use your Trial Notebook to prepare a carefully crafted outline of what you plan to ask her in court. Similarly, because you will know before trial who else will testify for the other side, your Trial Notebook should contain a well-organized list of points you want to cover when you have a chance to question (cross-examine) them.

A Typical Trial

Allowing for many possible variations, most trials begin with each side making an opening statement—each party presents an overview of his case, including what he expects to prove. The next stage is the direct examination during which the plaintiff (the person who filed the suit) presents her testimony as to what happened and supports it with witnesses' statements and other relevant evidence. After each of the plaintiff's witnesses testifies, the defendant gets a chance to cross-examine them. In doing so, the defendant attempts to produce testimony favorable to his version of events and to cast doubt on the reliability or credibility of the plaintiff's witnesses. Finally, each side gets to make a closing argument explaining to the judge or jury why they should win.

What about presenting witnesses? I'm more than a little intimidated by having to act like Perry Mason.

And well you should be. It's not easy being an actor. But fortunately, appearing in a routine court proceeding isn't that difficult, as long as you know the basic rules. For instance, when you present eyewitnesses, you do so by asking a series of questions. First you need to establish that your witness has personal knowledge of the event in question. This normally means you must show that your witness personally observed, heard, smelled, touched or tasted whatever he is testifying to—for example, that your witness was on the spot and overheard the contractor you are suing talking to someone about the details of your garage job. Second, you must learn to ask questions that allow that person to explain whatever it is he knows that supports your case without putting words into his mouth (called leading the witness). You can learn the basic techniques of how to question a witness and how to object to any improper questions asked by reading a good self-help book.

You've said a lot about trials before judges. Don't I have a right to have my civil case heard by a jury?

For some types of cases, such as those involving child support or custody, or a request for an injunction (to stop the city from cutting down a tree, for example), you are not entitled to a jury. And in some courts, the parties in all small civil cases must first try mediation before initiating any type of trial. But in most civil cases, including those involving personal injury, breach of contract, professional malpractice, libel or slander, you are entitled to a jury trial if you want one.

You may, however, want to think twice before you request a jury trial; it will be more complicated and harder to handle a case before a jury on your own than it would be to represent yourself before a judge. It can be tricky, for example, to participate in the jury selection process. Most who go it alone are better off avoiding this added level of complexity by trying their case in front of a judge. But, of course, the other party has a say, too, and if that person demands a jury, so be it.

More Information About Representing Yourself in Court

Represent Yourself in Court: How to Prepare and Try a Winning Case, by Paul Bergman and Sara J. Berman-Barrett (Nolo Press), explains all aspects of a civil court trial including how to determine if you have a good case, line up persuasive witnesses, present effective testimony in court, cross-examine opponents and even pick a jury.

The Criminal Law Handbook, by Paul Bergman and Sara J. Berman-Barrett (Nolo Press), tells you what you'll want to know if you or someone you love has been charged with a crime.

Small Claims Court

Small claims court judges resolve disputes involving relatively modest amounts of money. The people or businesses involved normally present their cases to a judge or court commissioner under rules that encourage a minimum of legal and procedural formality. The judge then makes a decision (a judgment) reasonably promptly. Although procedural rules dealing with when and where to file and serve papers are established by each state's laws and differ in detail, the basic approach to properly preparing and presenting a small claims case is remarkably similar everywhere.

How much can I sue for in small claims court?

The limit is normally between $3,000 and $7,500, depending on your state. For instance, the maximum is $3,000 in New York, $5,000 in California, $7,500 in Minnesota and $3,500 in Vermont. Recently, there has been a trend toward increasing small claims court limits.

Can any kind of case be resolved in small claims court?

No. Small claims courts primarily resolve small monetary disputes. In a few states, however, small claims courts may also rule on a limited range of other types of legal disputes, such as evictions or requests for the return of an item of property (restitution). You cannot use small claims court to file a divorce, guardianship, name change or bankruptcy, or to ask for emergency relief (such as an injunction to stop someone from doing an illegal act).

When it comes to disputes involving money, you can usually file in small claims court based on any legal theory that would be allowed in any other court—for example, breach of contract, personal injury, intentional harm or breach of warranty. A few states do, however, limit or prohibit small claims suits based on libel, slander, false arrest and a few other legal theories.

Finally, suits against the federal government or a federal agency, or even against a federal employee for actions relating to his or her employment cannot be brought in small claims court. Suits against the federal government normally must be filed in a federal District Court or other federal court, such as Tax Court or the Court of Claims. Unfortunately, there are no federal small claims procedures available except in federal Tax Court.

Are there time limits in which a small claims court case must be filed?

Yes. States establish rules called "statutes of limitations" which dictate how long you may wait to initiate a lawsuit after the key event giving rise to the lawsuit occurs or, in some instances, is discovered. Statutes of limitations rules apply to all courts, including small claims.

You'll almost always have at least one year to sue (measured from the event or, sometimes, from its discovery). Often, you'll have much longer. If you're planning to sue a state or local government agency, however, you'll usually need to file a formal claim with that agency within three to six months of the incident. Only after your initial timely complaint is denied are you eligible to file in small claims court.

SMALL CLAIMS COURT LIMITS FOR THE 50 STATES

Alabama	$3,000
Alaska	$7,500
Arizona	Small Claims Division, $2,500; regular Justice Court, $5,000
Arkansas	$5,000
California	$5,000, except that a plaintiff may not file a claim over $2,500 more than twice a year. $2,500 is also the limit for suits involving a surety company
Colorado	$5,000
Connecticut	$2,500
Delaware	$15,000
District of Columbia	$5,000
Florida	$5,000 (Small Claims Court); $15,000 (County Court)
Georgia	$5,000
Hawaii	$3,500; no limit in landlord-tenant residential deposit cases; for return of leased/rented personal property, the property must be worth more than $3,500; counterclaims up to $20,000
Idaho	$3,000
Illinois	$5,000 (Small Claims); $2,500 (Cook County "Pro Se").
Indiana	$3,000 ($6,000 in Marion County)
Iowa	$4,000
Kansas	$1,800
Kentucky	$1,500
Louisana	$2,000
Maine	$4,500
Maryland	$2,500
Massachussetts	$2,000; no limit for action for property damage caused by a motor vehicle
Michigan	$1,750
Minnesota	$7,500 ($4,000 in cases involving a commercial plaintiff)
Mississippi	$2,500
Missouri	$3,000
Montana	$3,000
Nebraska	$2,100
Nevada	$3,500
New Hampshire	$5,000
New Jersey	$2,000 in Small Claims; $10,000 in Regular Special Civil Court
New Mexico	$5,000 (Magistrate's Court); $5,000 (Metropolitan Court)
New York	$3,000
North Carolina	$3,000
North Dakota	$5,000

Ohio	$3,000 in small claims (municipal); $5,000 in small claims (County Court); $15,000 in regular County Court with simplified mediation procedure
Oklahoma	$4,500
Oregon	$3,500
Pennsylvania	$5,000 (Municipal Court); $8,000 (District or Justice Court)
Rhode Island	$1,500
South Carolina	$5,000
South Dakota	$4,000
Tennessee	$15,000; $25,000 in counties where population is over 700,000; $25,000 in a suit to recover personal property
Texas	$5,000
Utah	$5,000
Vermont	$3,500
Virginia	$3,000; up to $15,000 in regular district court (check with County Court clerk); $15,000 in District Court
Washington	$2,500
West Virginia	$5,000
Wisconsin	$5,000; no limit on eviction suits
Wyoming	$4,000; County Court, $7,000

If some time has passed since the incident giving rise to your lawsuit occurred—for example, after the breach of a written contract or a personal injury—you may need to do a little research to determine whether you can still file your claim. Check your state's legal code under the index heading "statute of limitations."

Where should I file my small claims lawsuit?

Assuming the other party lives or does business in your state, rules normally require that you sue in the small claims court district closest to that person's residence or headquarters. In some instances, you also may be able to sue in the location (court district) where a contract was signed or a personal injury occurred (such as

an auto accident). Check with your small claims clerk for detailed rules.

If a defendant has no contact with your state, you'll generally have to sue in the state where the defendant lives or does business. Because of the distance involved, out-of-state small claims lawsuits tend to be expensive and unwieldy.

If You Want to Avoid Going to Court

If you want what's owed to you, but you don't want to take on the trouble of bringing a lawsuit, you have a couple of options to consider. First, even if you've been rudely turned down in the past, ask for your money at least once more. This time, make your demand in the form of a straightforward letter, concluding with the statement that you'll file in small claims court in ten days unless payment is promptly received. Unlike a conversation, where the other party may assume you'll never follow up, a demand letter is like a slap in the face that lets the person know you're serious about getting paid. Because many individuals and small business people have a strong aversion to the idea of a public trial (including the time and inconvenience), making it clear you are prepared to file a lawsuit can be an effective catalyst to getting the other party to talk settlement.

In addition, many states offer, and a few require, community- or court-based mediation designed to help the parties arrive at their own compromise settlement with the help of a neutral third party. Mediation works best where the parties have an interest in staying on good terms, as is generally the case with neighbors, family members or small business people who have done business together for many years. This type of dispute resolution can be remarkably successful. In Maine, for example, where mediation is required before a small claims suit may be brought, over half of the cases are settled voluntarily, without a court fight. For more information about mediation, see the next series of questions.

Will I get paid if I win the lawsuit?

Not necessarily. The court may decide in your favor, but it won't handle collection for you. So before you sue, always ask, "Can I collect if I win?" If not, think twice before suing.

Worrying about whether or not you can get paid is reasonable, because some people and businesses are "judgment proof"—that is, they have little money or assets and aren't likely to acquire much in the foreseeable future. If they don't pay voluntarily, you may be out of luck. Ask yourself whether the person you're suing has a steady job, valuable real property or investments. If so, it should be reasonably easy to collect by garnishing his wages if you win. If not, try to identify another collection source, such as a bank account, before going forward. For people who seem to have no job or assets, ask whether they are likely to be more solvent in the future, since court judgments are good for 10 to 20 years in many states and can usually be renewed for longer periods. You'll want to consider now whether the person might inherit money, graduate from college and get a good job, or otherwise have an economic turn-around sometime down the road.

If I'm sued in small claims court but the other party is really at fault, can I countersue?

In some states, you can and must countersue as long as your claim arises out of the same event or transaction. In other states, "counterclaims" are not mandatory and you can sue separately later. No matter what the technical rules, you'll normally want to countersue promptly.

If the amount you sue for is under the small claims limit, your case will probably remain in that court. If, however, you want to sue for more, check with your small claims clerk for applicable rules. Often, you'll need to have the case transferred to a different court which has the power to handle cases where more money is at stake.

What should I do to prepare my small claims case?

Whether you are a plaintiff (the person suing) or the defendant (person being sued), the key is to realize that it's usually what you bring with you to court to back up your story—not what you say—that determines whether you'll win or lose. This makes sense if you understand that the judge has no idea who you are and whether your oral (spoken) testimony is reliable. After all, your opponent is likely to claim that the "true story" is exactly the reverse of your version.

In short, your chances of winning will greatly increase if you carefully collect and prepare your evidence. Depending on the facts of your case, a few of the evidentiary tools you can use to convince the judge you are right include eyewitnesses, photographs, letters from experts, advertisements falsely hyping a product or service and written contracts.

What's the best way to present my case to a judge?

First, understand that the judge is busy and has heard dozens of stories like yours. To keep the judge's attention, get to the point fast by describing the event that gave rise to your claim. Immediately follow up by stating how much money you are requesting. To be able to do this efficiently, it's best to practice in advance. Here is an example of a good start: "Your

Honor, my car was damaged on January 10, 1998, when the defendant ran a red light at Rose and Hyacinth Streets in the town of Saginaw and hit my front fender. I have a canceled check to show it cost me $427 to fix the fender."

After you have clearly stated the key event, double back and tell the judge the events that led up to your loss. For example, you might now explain that you were driving below the speed limit and had entered the intersection when the light was green, and when the defendant came barreling through the red light, you did your best to avoid the defendant's car.

A Court Without Lawyers?

In a handful of states, including California, Michigan and Nebraska, you must appear in small claims court on your own. In most states, however, you can be represented by a lawyer if you like. But even where it's allowed, hiring a lawyer is rarely cost-efficient. Most lawyers charge too much given the relatively modest amounts of money involved in small claims disputes. Happily, several studies show that people who represent themselves in small claims cases usually do just as well as those who have a lawyer.

Will witnesses need to testify in person?

If possible, it's best to have key witnesses present in court. But if this isn't convenient, a clearly written memo or letter will be allowed under the rules of most small claims courts. (Be sure to check your state's rules.) Have the witness start the statement by establishing who he or she is. ("My name is John Lomox. I've owned and managed Reo's Toyota Repair Service for the last 17 years.") In clear, unemotional language, the witness should explain what he or she observed or heard. ("I carefully checked Mary Wilson's engine and found that it has been rebuilt improperly, using worn-out parts.") Finally, the witness should try to anticipate any questions a reasonable person might ask and provide the answers. ("Although it can take a few days to get new parts for older engines, such as the one Mary Wilson owned, it is easy and common practice to do so.")

If I lose my case in small claims court, can I appeal?

The answer depends on the state in which you live. Many states allow either party to appeal within a certain period of time, usually between 10 and 30 days, and obtain a new trial.

In many states, appeals must be based solely on the contention that the judge made a legal mistake, and not on the facts of the case. Other states have their own unique rules. In California, for example, a defendant may appeal to the Superior Court within 30 days. A plaintiff may not appeal at all, although she can make a motion to correct clerical errors or to correct a decision based on a legal mistake.

To find the law for your state, call your local small claims court clerk.

More Information About Small Claims Court

Everybody's Guide to Small Claims Court (Nolo Press) (National and California Editions), by Ralph Warner, explains how to evaluate your case, prepare for court and convince a judge you're right. It also contains a useful section on trying to negotiate or mediate a compromise with the other party without going to court.

Collect Your Court Judgment, by Gini Graham Scott, Stephen Elias and Lisa Goldoftas (Nolo Press), explains 19 legal ways to collect after you win a lawsuit in California. It also shows you how to locate debtors and their assets.

Mediation

I'd rather jaw, jaw, jaw, than war, war, war.

—WINSTON CHURCHILL

If you're involved in a legal dispute, you may be able to settle it without going to court. One way to do this is to work out a solution with the help of a mediator—a neutral third person. Unlike a judge or an arbitrator, a mediator will not take sides or make decisions, but will help each party evaluate goals and options in order to find a solution that works for everyone. The only exception to this rule is made for certain types of child custody mediations; in those cases, a mediator may have the power to recommend a solution to a judge if the parties cannot agree.

When you reach an agreement with an opposing party through mediation, you can make it legally binding by writing down your decisions in the form of an enforceable contract.

What kinds of cases can be mediated?

Most civil (noncriminal) disputes can be mediated, including those involving contracts, leases, small business ownership, employment and divorce. For example, a divorcing couple might mediate to work out a mutually agreeable child custody agreement, or estranged business partners might choose mediation to work out

an agreement to divide their business. Nonviolent criminal matters, such as claims of verbal or other personal harassment, can also be successfully mediated.

Finally, you may want to consider mediation if you get into a scrape with a neighbor, roommate, spouse, partner or co-worker. Mediation can be particularly useful in these areas because it is designed to identify and cope with divisive interpersonal issues not originally thought to be part of the dispute. For example, if one neighbor sues another for making outrageous amounts of noise, the court will usually deal with only that issue—and by declaring one neighbor a winner and the other a loser, may worsen long-term tensions. In mediation, however, each neighbor will be invited to present all issues in dispute. It may turn out that the overly loud neighbor was being obnoxious in part because his neighbor's dog constantly pooped on his lawn or his son's pickup blocked a shared driveway. In short, since mediation is designed to surface and solve all problems, it's a far better way to restore long-term peace to the neighborhood, home or workplace.

How long does mediation take?

Typical cases such as consumer claims, small business disputes or auto accident claims are usually resolved after a half day or, at most, a full day of mediation. Cases with multiple parties often last longer: Add at least an hour of mediation time for each additional party. Major business disputes—those involving lots of money, complex contracts or ending a partnership—may last several days or more.

Private divorce mediation, where a couple aims to settle all the issues in their divorce—property division and alimony, as well as child custody, visitation and support—generally requires half a dozen or more mediation sessions spread over several weeks or a couple of months.

How is mediation different from arbitration?

A mediator normally has no authority to render a decision; it's up to the parties themselves—with the mediator's help—to work informally toward their own agreement. An arbitrator, on the other hand, conducts a contested hearing between the parties and then, acting as a judge, rends a legally binding decision. The arbitrator's decision-making power may, however, be limited based on a written agreement between the parties. For example, the parties may agree that damages will be awarded in an amount between $200,000 and $500,000. Arbitration, which has long been used to resolve commercial and labor disputes, resembles a court hearing—with witnesses called and evidence taken.

The 6 Stages of Mediation

While mediation is not as formal as going to court, the process is more structured than many people imagine. A typical mediation involves six distinct stages.

Mediator's Opening Statement

After the disputants are seated at a table, the mediator introduces everyone, explains the goals and rules of the mediation and encourages each side to work cooperatively toward a settlement.

Disputants' Opening Statements

Each party is invited to tell, in his or her own words, what the dispute is about and how he or she has been affected by it, and to present some general ideas about resolving it. While one person is speaking, the other is not allowed to interrupt.

Joint Discussion

The mediator may try to get the parties talking directly about what was said in the opening statements. This is the time to determine what issues need to be addressed.

Private Caucuses

Often considered the guts of mediation, the private caucus is a chance for each party to meet privately with the mediator (usually in a nearby room) to discuss the strengths and weaknesses of his or her position, and new ideas for settlement. The mediator may caucus with each side just once, or several times, as needed.

Joint Negotiation

After caucuses, the mediator may bring the parties back together to negotiate directly.

Closure

This is the end of the mediation. If an agreement has been reached, the mediator may put its main provisions in writing as the parties listen. The mediator may ask each side to sign the written summary of agreement or suggest they take it to lawyers for review. If the parties want to, they can write up and sign a legally binding contract. If no agreement was reached, the mediator will review whatever progress has been made and advise everyone of their options, such as meeting again later, going to arbitration or going to court.

Why should I consider having my case mediated?

If you've given up on negotiating a settlement of your dispute directly with the other party, mediation may be the most painless and efficient way to solve it. Compared to a lawsuit, mediation is swift, confidential, fair and low cost.

Mediation sessions are usually scheduled within a few weeks or, at most, a couple of months from the time of a request—and most sessions last only a few hours or a day, depending on the type of case. In contrast, lawsuits often take many months, or even years, to resolve.

Another advantage of mediation is confidentiality. With very few exceptions (for example, where a criminal act or child abuse is involved), what you say during mediation cannot legally be revealed outside the mediation proceedings or used later in a court of law.

And mediation will nearly always save you money. In many parts of the country, nonprofit community mediation centers handle relatively minor consumer, neighborhood, workplace and similar disputes for free or for a nominal charge. Private dispute resolution companies tackle more complex cases for a fraction of the cost of bringing a lawsuit. A half-day mediation of a personal injury claim, for example, may cost each side about $500. By comparison, a full-scale court battle could cost $50,000 or more, sometimes much more.

Finally, consider that agreements reached through mediation are more likely to be carried out than those imposed by a judge. When folks go to court, the losing party is almost always angry and often prone to look for ways to violate the letter or spirit of any judgment. In contrast, a number of studies show that people who have freely arrived at their own solutions through mediation are significantly more likely to follow through.

What Will It Cost?

In nearly all cases, mediating is far less expensive than going to court. Actual fees will vary depending on the type of case and who does the mediating. Here are some examples to consider.

Neighborhood dispute Three neighbors are involved in a dispute over disruptive children. Mediation is provided by any of 400 nonprofit community mediation centers in the United States.
Typical length of mediation: full day
Typical fees per party: $10 filing fee (waived for financial hardship)

Personal injury claim A passenger in a car suffers leg and spine fractures when the driver hits a telephone pole. The passenger and the driver's insurance company cannot agree on the amount of compensation for these injuries. Mediation is conducted by a private dispute resolution company.
Typical length of mediation: half day
Typical fees per party: $600

Business contract dispute A computer parts company sues Big Computer, Inc. for $5 million when Big C rejects parts which allegedly conform to a valid contract. Just before the trial is to begin, the parties decide to try mediation. Mediation is provided by a private dispute resolution company.
Typical length of mediation: four days
Typical fees per party: $8,000

Divorce mediation A divorcing couple with a house, two cars, bank accounts, pension plans and three minor children are trying to reach an agreement out of court as to the division of their property and the custody and visitation of their children. Mediation is provided by an independent divorce mediator in private practice.
Typical length of mediation: six two-hour sessions over two months, plus five hours to prepare a written agreement
Typical cost for couple: $2,215 (split 50-50)

How can I be sure mediation will produce a fair result?

Remember that in mediation, you and the opposing parties will work to craft a solution to your own dispute. Unless you freely agree, there will be no final resolution. This approach has several advantages over going to court:

- Legal precedents or the whim of a judge will not dictate the solution.
- If your dispute harbors undiscovered or undisclosed issues, mediation, unlike a structured court battle, offers the opportunity and flexibility to ferret them out.
- Because mediation does not force disputants to undergo the fear and sometimes paranoia of the courtroom, —where a judge or jury can stun either party with a big loss—people who choose mediation tend to be more relaxed and open to compromise.

A piece of paper,
blown by the wind
into a law court may in the end
only be drawn out by two oxen.

—CHINESE PROVERB

How can I find a good mediator?

Much depends on the type of dispute you're involved in. Many cities have community mediation centers which do an excellent job of handling most types of routine disputes (consumer problems, neighbor disputes, landlord-tenant fights). For more complicated disputes (business termination, personal injury, breach of contract) it is often better to turn to a private mediation center. National organizations (JAMS and End Dispute) and a number of regional groups do a good job. Private divorce mediations are usually handled by sole practitioners or small local mediation groups. Get a list from the phone book and check references carefully.

Are there some cases that should not be mediated?

All parties to a dispute must agree to mediate, so if one party refuses or perhaps isn't competent to participate, the case cannot be mediated. Mediation may also not be the best choice if:

- One of the parties wants to set a legal precedent that interprets or defines the law according to its own point of view. Legal precedents cannot be set in mediation because mediation agreements do not establish who is "right" or "wrong," and mediation decisions apply only to the parties involved in that particular mediation.

- A person believes he or she can win a huge verdict against a big company (or even a small company with a big bank account or plenty of insurance). Because of the tendency toward compromise in mediation, hitting a legal "jackpot" is more likely in a jury trial.

- One person feels intimidated or intellectually overwhelmed by the other, in which case it's hard to arrive at a true meeting of the minds. It's often possible, however, to remedy a "power imbalance" by arranging for the more vulnerable person to participate with an advisor—perhaps a lawyer.

If I choose mediation, will I still need a lawyer?

In most mediations, it's not necessary to have a lawyer participate directly. This is because the parties are trying to work together to solve their problem—not trying to convince a judge or arbitrator of their point of view—and because mediation rules are few and straightforward. If your case involves substantial property or legal rights, however, you may want to consult with a lawyer before the mediation to discuss the legal consequences of possible settlement terms. You may also want to condition any agreement you make on a lawyer's approval.

More Information About Mediation

How to Mediate Your Dispute, by Peter Lovenheim (Nolo Press), thoroughly explains the mediation process and shows you how to choose a mediator, prepare a case and conduct yourself during a mediation.

Child Custody: Building Agreements That Work, by Mimi Lyster (Nolo Press), provides a step-by-step method for overcoming obstacles and putting together a practical parenting agreement that everyone—especially the children—can live with.

The Divorce Mediation Handbook, by Paula James (Jossey-Bass), explains how a divorcing couple can use mediation to achieve their practical goals while protecting their legal rights.

When Push Comes to Shove: A Practical Guide to Resolving Disputes, by Karl Slaikeu (Jossey-Bass), is a how-to mediation guide for lawyers, managers and human resource professionals.

Dealing With Your Lawyer

May your life be filled with lawyers.

—MEXICAN CURSE

For any number of reasons, you may be mad at a lawyer you hired to do legal work for you. Perhaps your lawyer has failed to keep you informed about your case, to meet deadlines or to do what you believe is quality work. Maybe your lawyer has sent you a bill for far more than you believe is reasonable. Whatever the specifics of your situation, you're sure that something has gone wrong with your professional relationship. These questions touch on the reasons for most complaints against attorneys and offer suggestions as to what you can do about them.

I've lost confidence in my lawyer. Can I fire him?

You have the right to end a relationship with a lawyer at any time. But unless your lawyer is truly awful, it's not wise to fire him until you have another lawyer lined up or feel that you can handle the case yourself.

I fired my lawyer, but I need my file. How do I get it?

Ask, or sign an authorization allowing any new attorney to get it. Even if you have a fee dispute with your former lawyer or you simply have not paid him, you are entitled to your file. If you have decided to represent yourself, demand that the lawyer turn your file over to you. If the lawyer refuses, contact your state's bar association for help.

I'm pretty sure my lawyer screwed up my case. Can I sue her for malpractice?

Unfortunately, it is very hard to win a malpractice case. Malpractice means that the lawyer failed to use the ordinary skill and care that would be used by other lawyers in handling a similar problem or case under similar circumstances.

To win a malpractice case against an attorney, you must prove four basic things:
- duty—that the attorney owed you a duty to act properly
- breach—that the attorney breached the duty, was negligent, made a mistake or did not do what she agreed to do
- causation—that this conduct caused you damages, and
- damages—that you suffered financial losses as a result.

Causation may be your biggest hurdle. To win a malpractice case, you must prove not only the malpractice action against your attorney, but that you would have won the underlying case that the lawyer mishandled. (This second part is not required in Ohio.) Then, you will have to show that if you had won the underlying case, you would have been able to collect from the defendant. For example, let's say you were hit by a car when you were walking across the street, and you hired a lawyer who didn't file the lawsuit on time. You sue for malpractice and can easily prove the driver's liability. To win the malpractice case against your lawyer, however, you'd also have to show that the driver had money or insurance. If you can't show that the driver had assets which could have been used to pay the judgment, you won't win your malpractice case, even though the lawyer clearly blew it and the driver was clearly at fault.

My Lawyer Won't Call Me Back!

If your lawyer fails to return phone calls, it isn't malpractice, but it's a sure sign of trouble. Try to find out why your lawyer isn't calling you back. (He may be busy, rude, sick or procrastinating.) As you do this, examine the possibility that your lawyer may be avoiding you for a good reason—you may be too demanding. A good way to deal with this situation is to write or fax the lawyer a straightforward letter explaining your difficulty in communicating and asking for a phone call or meeting to re-establish or restore your relationship. If this doesn't work, consider firing the lawyer and/or filing a formal complaint with your state's attorney regulatory agency.

My lawyer seems to have stopped working on my case. Is this malpractice?

The longer your attorney ignores you and your case, the more likely it is to amount to malpractice. You must act quickly to see that your case is properly handled and get another lawyer if necessary. Writing or faxing a letter expressing your concerns and asking for a meeting is a good first step.

My case was thrown out of court because my lawyer did no work. Is this grounds to sue my lawyer?

Maybe. Your lawyer is responsible for whatever money you could have won had the case been properly handled. Your difficulty will be in proving not only that your lawyer mishandled the case, but that if handled correctly, you could have won and collected a judgment.

My lawyer originally said my case was worth six figures and now suggests that I settle for peanuts. Can I sue the lawyer for the difference?

No. Your lawyer may have given you an inflated estimate of the value of your case to encourage you to hire her. Get your file from your lawyer and get a second opinion on your case. If another reputable lawyer believes you are being advised to settle for too little, consider changing lawyers.

Can I sue my lawyer for settling my case without my authorization?

Yes, but you would have to prove that the settlement your lawyer entered into was for less than your case was worth.

Big Bills

If you receive an unexpectedly large bill, your lawyer may have overcharged you. In this situation, you have six options:

- You can pay the entire bill and vow not to go near that attorney again.
- You can pay the part of the bill you think is reasonable with a letter explaining why you are refusing to pay the rest.
- You can refuse to pay any of the bill until the lawyer agrees to accept less as full payment.
- In most states and situations, you can request fee arbitration, usually with a panel made up of local lawyers and perhaps one or two nonlawyers. Arbitration is a process where a neutral decisionmaker resolves your fee dispute. You will want to proceed only if it is "nonbinding," meaning that you are free to reject the arbitrator's decision. If the arbitration is to be conducted by lawyers who may be biased against you, don't agree to a binding result—meaning a result you aren't allowed to reject.
- You can pay the bill and file a complaint with your state attorney disciplinary agency.
- You can pay the bill and sue your attorney for a refund.

I saw my lawyer playing tennis with the opposing lawyer. Is this a breach of attorney ethics?

No. There is nothing ethically wrong with opposing attorneys playing tennis, bridge, golf or enjoying other common social interactions. If they talk about your case (on the tennis court or anywhere else), however, and your lawyer lets slip something that you said in confidence, that would be a clear violation of your attorney's duty to you.

Even though socializing with the opposing counsel isn't a violation of ethical rules, in the real world it can obviously make a big difference how you found out about it. If your lawyer told you he occasionally played tennis with the opposing attorney when you first discussed your case, you clearly had a chance to hire another lawyer if it bothered you. But you'll feel very differently if you head to the tennis court for a match with a good friend after being grilled by the opposing attorney at your deposition, only to run into your lawyer playing tennis with the barracuda who just tried to eat you for lunch. It would have been wise for your attorney to tell you about his social relationship with the other lawyer when you first met. Although in failing to do this your attorney hasn't breached any ethical duty to you, you may wish to change attorneys.

I'm worried that my lawyer may have misused money I paid as a retainer. What should I do?

If you seriously suspect your lawyer has misused any money he holds for you in trust, complain to your state's attorney regulatory agency right away. Although regulation of lawyers is lax in most states, complaints about stealing clients' money are almost always taken seriously, so you should get a prompt response. All states except Maine and New Mexico have funds to reimburse clients when lawyers are caught stealing.

More Information About Dealing With Your Lawyer

Mad at Your Lawyer, by Tanya Starnes (Nolo Press), explains how to handle problems with your lawyer, from poor communication and high bills to stealing your money.

Taming the Lawyers: What to Expect in a Lawsuit and How to Make Sure Your Attorney Gets Results, by Kenneth Menendez (Merritt Publishing), is a guide to choosing and managing a lawyer through various stages of a civil lawsuit.

http://www.nolo.com

Nolo Press offers self-help information about a wide variety of legal topics, including representing yourself in court, small claims court, mediation, legal research and what to do if you have problems with your lawyer.

http://www.legalethics.com/ states.html

The Internet Legal Services provides links to all states' rules of professional conduct and some states' ethics opinions.

Criminal Law and Procedure

IT IS A LESS EVIL THAT SOME CRIMINALS

SHOULD ESCAPE THAN THAT THE GOVERNMENT

SHOULD PLAY AN IGNOBLE PART.

—OLIVER WENDELL HOLMES

The word "criminal" reflects our society's belief that certain acts are unacceptable and that people who commit these acts should be punished. Because we place a high value on freedom, however, our state and federal constitutions make it difficult for the government to take that freedom away from us. As a result—and perhaps as a price—the court system often appears to protect the criminal rather than the victim, and to unduly favor defendants who are blessed with clever attorneys. On the other hand, if the system doesn't place a heavy burden on government prosecutors, we risk sending innocent people to jail and we make it easier for our government to slide into totalitarian practices. One thing is sure: No matter what type of system we have for prosecuting and punishing people who commit crimes, it will always be a matter of great controversy.

Caution!

The material in this chapter is designed to give you a general overview of several important criminal law topics. As you read, keep in mind that the criminal justice system differs in many small but important ways from state to state, county to county and even court to court. This means that some of the material in this chapter may not be applicable in your area.

In addition, the many different players in the criminal justice system—police, prosecutors, defense attorneys and judges—frequently adapt the law to their own uses and contexts. What this gap between theory and practice may mean in a particular case can only be understood by someone who knows the players and who is familiar with how they go about their jobs. Usually, this person would be a local criminal defense attorney.

Because we cannot precisely describe the law in your state and what is likely to happen in your case, consider this chapter a place to get started. To get more specific and reliable information, do some research or consult a knowledgeable criminal defense attorney. For a more in-depth treatment of the topics addressed here as well as other aspects of the criminal justice system—including lineups, arraignments, defenses, plea bargains and sentencing—see *The Criminal Law Handbook: Answers to Everyday Questions About Our Criminal Justice System*, by Paul Bergman and Sara Berman-Barrett (Nolo Press).

Criminal Law and Procedure: An Overview

A crime is any behavior that is punishable by imprisonment or fine (or both). State legislatures have an almost unlimited ability to decide which behaviors are considered crimes, and often their decisions do more than simply define socially unacceptable behaviors—they also reflect the values and judgments of the legislators. For example, most state legislatures define welfare fraud as a crime, and welfare recipients who cheat can end up in jail. On the other hand, no state legislature defines deliberate overcharging by an attorney or other professional as a crime.

While state legislatures have broad powers to decide what constitutes crime, Congress can define behavior as a crime only if the U.S. Constitution authorizes Congress to regulate that type of behavior in the first place. For example, the Constitution gives Congress the power to "regulate commerce . . . among the several States." Congress, therefore, can make many activities—such as racketeering—illegal, if the actions cross state lines or affect commerce that does.

Who decides how the criminal justice system works?

Though legislators have relatively unfettered power to decide whether a certain behavior should be a crime, many rules limit the ways in which the state or federal government can prosecute someone for a crime. These restrictions start with the U.S. Constitution's Bill of Rights, which provides basic protections—such as the right to refuse to testify against oneself, the right to confront one's accusers and the right to a trial by jury—for people charged with crimes. State constitutions may increase (but not take away from) the federal protections. Federal and state legislatures can pass laws governing how criminal procedures work in their jurisdictions, but these laws cannot reduce the protections offered by the federal and state constitutions.

The interplay between constitutional provisions and legislative enactments is regulated by our courts. Courts decide whether or not a particular legislative rule, court practice or police action is permissible under federal and state constitutional law. What may seem like a slight variation from one case to another can be, in the eyes of a court, the determining factor that leads to a vastly different result. For example, a police officer is frisking a suspect on the street and feels a hard object in the suspect's pocket. Suspecting that the object is a possible weapon, the officer reaches into the pocket and finds both a cardboard cigarette box and a packet of heroin. This action by the police officer—reaching into the pocket—would be deemed a permissible search under the rulings of most courts (to protect the officer's safety), and the heroin could be admitted into court as evidence. However, if the object felt by the officer was soft and obviously not a weapon, then reaching into the suspect's pocket might be deemed an illegal search, in which case the heroin couldn't be used as evidence.

What's the difference between a felony and a misdemeanor?

Most states break their crimes into two major groups—felonies and misdemeanors. Whether a crime falls into one category or the other depends on the potential punishment. If a law provides for imprisonment for longer than a year, it is usually considered a felony. If the potential punishment is for a year or less, then the crime is considered a misdemeanor. In some states, certain crimes, called "wobblers," may be considered either a misdemeanor or a felony, because under some conditions the punishment may be imprisonment for less than a year, and in other situations, the criminal may go to prison for a year or more.

Behaviors punishable only by fine are usually not considered crimes at all, but infractions—for example, traffic tickets. But a legislature may on occasion punish behavior only by fine and still provide that it is a misdemeanor—such as possession of less than an ounce of marijuana for personal use in California.

How can I tell from reading a criminal statute whether I'm guilty of the crime it defines?

All criminal statutes define crimes in terms of required acts and a required state of mind, usually described as the actor's "intent." These requirements are known as the "elements" of the offense. A prosecutor must convince a judge or jury that the person charged with the crime (the defendant) did the acts and had the intent described in the statute. For example, commercial burglary is commonly defined as entering a structure (such as a store) belonging to another person, with the intent to commit petty or grand theft (that is, to steal) or any felony. To convict a person of this offense, the prosecutor would have to prove three elements:

1. The defendant entered the structure.
2. The structure belonged to another person.
3. At the time the defendant entered the structure, he intended to commit petty or grand theft or any felony.

You will have to do the same when you read the law. Parse the crime into its required elements to see if each applies in your situation.

What is the presumption of innocence?

All people accused of a crime are legally presumed to be innocent until they are convicted, either in a trial or as a result of pleading guilty. This presumption means not only that the prosecutor must convince the jury of the defendant's guilt, but also that the defendant need not say or do anything in his own defense. If the prosecutor can't convince the jury that the defendant is guilty, the defendant goes free.

The presumption of innocence, coupled with the fact that the prosecutor must prove the defendant's guilt beyond a reasonable doubt (see below), makes it difficult for the government to put people behind bars.

What does it mean to prove guilt "beyond a reasonable doubt"?

The prosecutor must convince the judge or jury hearing the case that the defendant is guilty "beyond a reasonable doubt." This standard is very hard to meet. (By contrast, in noncriminal cases, such as an accident or breach of contract, a plaintiff has to prove her case only by a preponderance of the evidence—just over 50%.) As a practical matter, the high burden of proof in criminal cases means that judges and jurors are supposed to resolve all doubts about the meaning of the evidence in favor of the defendant. With such a high standard imposed on the prosecutor, a defendant's most common defense is often to argue that there is reasonable doubt—that is, that the prosecutor hasn't done a sufficient job of proving that the defendant is guilty.

If I'm accused of a crime, am I guaranteed a trial by a jury?

Yes. The U.S. Constitution gives a person accused of a crime the right to be tried by a jury. This right has long been interpreted to mean a 12-person jury that must arrive at a unanimous decision to convict or acquit. (In most states, a lack of unanimity is called a "hung jury" and the defendant will go free unless the prosecutor decides to retry the case. In Oregon and Louisiana, however, juries may convict or acquit on a vote of ten to two.) The potential jurors must be selected randomly from the community, and the actual jury must be selected by a pro-

cess which allows the judge and lawyers to screen out biased jurors. In addition, a lawyer may eliminate several potential jurors simply because he feels that these people would not be sympathetic to his side—but these decisions may not be based on the juror's personal characteristics, such as race, sex, religion or national origin.

Can a jury acquit me even if I broke the law?

The jury has the ultimate power to decide whether a person is guilty of a crime. As the "conscience of the community," jurors can free a defendant even if they think the defendant actually committed the crime charged. The name for this power is "jury nullification." It has always been a part of our judicial system.

When jurors nullify a law by acquitting a defendant who has obviously broken that law, judges and prosecutors can do nothing about it. A jury's not guilty verdict is final. Jury nullification rarely occurs, but when it does, it most often involves cases that have a political component (such as the refusal to convict draft dodgers during the Vietnam War) or that have harsh punishments the jury does not want to impose on that particular defendant.

If I do not have any witnesses who will testify on my behalf, can I still win at trial?

Yes. Defendants often go to trial without having anyone testify for them. This strategy allows the defendant's lawyer to focus on cross-examining the prosecution witnesses in order to poke holes in the prosecutor's case—thereby creating reasonable doubt. Defense attorneys rely on a variety of arguments to discredit the prosecutor's witnesses. Some common arguments include:

- Prosecution witnesses are biased against the defendant and therefore are lying or grossly exaggerating.
- Prosecution witnesses are mistaken in their observations because the lighting was bad, they were under the influence of drugs or alcohol or they were too far away.
- Evidence from police laboratories is unreliable because the machines were not properly maintained or the technicians were not properly trained.
- Prosecution witnesses are lying to get a good deal on the criminal charges they themselves are facing (witnesses are often criminals who have been offered a deal if they testify against the defendant).

What these arguments have in common is that they do not depend on defense evidence. Rather, they rely on the presumption of innocence and prosecutor's failure to overcome it by proving guilt beyond a reasonable doubt.

I am confused about why a defendant would choose to not testify. If I were innocent, why wouldn't I want to take the stand and tell my story?

A criminal defendant has a right not to testify, and jurors will be told that they cannot assume anything negative if the defendant decides to keep quiet. Of course, some jurors do make assumptions—and they cast their votes accordingly. On the other hand, there are some excellent reasons why a defendant might remain silent in court:

- If the defendant has previously been convicted of a crime, the prosecutor may be able to bring this fact out—but only if the defendant testifies. Evidence of a previous crime may cause some jurors to think that the defendant is guilty of the current crime, too.
- If the defendant testifies, the prosecutor may be able to bring out other information that tarnishes the defendant's reputation and discredits his testimony.
- Some defendants have a poor demeanor when speaking in public. A judge or jury may not believe a defendant who, though telling the truth, is a nervous witness and makes a bad impression.
- The defendant may have a perfectly good story which would nevertheless sound fishy to the average jury in that particular locale.

What is self-defense—and how can a defendant prove it?

Self-defense is a common defense asserted by someone charged with a crime of violence, such as battery (striking someone), assault with a deadly weapon or murder. The defendant admits that she did in fact commit the crime, but claims that it was justified by the other person's threatening actions. The core issues in most self-defense cases are:

- Who was the aggressor?
- Was the defendant's belief that self-defense was necessary a reasonable one?
- If so, was the force used by the defendant also reasonable?

Self-defense is rooted in the belief that people should be allowed to protect themselves from physical harm. This means that a person does not have to wait until she is actually struck to act in self-defense. If a reasonable person would think that she is about to be physically attacked, she has the right to strike first and prevent the attack. But she cannot use more force than is reasonable—if she does, she may be guilty of a crime.

When can a defendant win an acquittal on grounds of insanity?

The insanity defense is based on the principle that punishment is justified only if the defendant is capable of controlling his or her behavior and understanding that what he or she has done is wrong. Because some people suffering from a mental disorder are not capable of knowing or choosing right from wrong, the insanity defense prevents them from being criminally punished.

Despite its ancient origins (England, 1505), the insanity defense remains controversial. Victim-oriented critics point out that a person killed by an insane person is just as dead as a person killed by someone who is sane, and argue that people should be pun-

ished for the harm they cause regardless of their mental state. Critics also question the ability of psychiatrists, judges and jurors to determine whether a person suffers from a mental disorder, and to link mental disorders to the commission of crimes.

The insanity defense is an extremely complex topic; many scholarly works are devoted entirely to explaining its nuances. Here are some major points of interest:

- Despite popular perceptions to the contrary, defendants rarely enter pleas of "not guilty by reason of insanity." On the few occasions that the defendant does raise it, judges and jurors rarely support it.
- Because neither the legal system nor psychiatrists can agree on a single meaning of insanity in the criminal law context, various definitions are employed. The most popular definition is the "McNaghten rule," which defines insanity as "the inability to distinguish right from wrong." Another common test is known as "irresistible impulse": A person who acts out of an irresistible impulse knows that an act is wrong, but because of mental illness, cannot control his actions.
- Defendants found not guilty by reason of insanity are not automatically set free. They are usually confined to a mental institution, and not released until their sanity is established. These defendants can spend more time in a mental institution than they would have spent in prison had they been convicted.
- An insanity defense normally rests on the testimony of a psychiatrist,

who testifies for the defendant after examining him and his past history, and the facts of the case. Courts appoint psychiatrists at government expense to assist poor defendants who cannot afford to hire their own psychiatrists.

Competency to Stand Trial

Aside from insanity as a defense to criminal charges, the question may arise as to whether a defendant is mentally capable of facing a trial. Defendants cannot be prosecuted if they suffer from a mental disorder that prevents them from understanding the proceedings and assisting in the preparation of their defense. Based on a defendant's unusual behavior, a judge, prosecutor or defense attorney may ask that trial be delayed until the defendant has been examined and her ability to understand the proceedings has been determined in a court hearing. If a judge finds that a defendant doesn't understand what's going on, the defendant will probably be placed in a mental institution until her competence is re-established. At that time, the trial will be held.

Can a defendant go free because he was drunk or high on drugs when he committed a crime?

Defendants who commit crimes under the influence of drugs or alcohol sometimes argue that their mental functioning was so impaired that they cannot be held accountable for their actions. Generally, however, voluntary

intoxication does not excuse criminal conduct. People know (or should know) that alcohol and drugs affect mental functioning, and thus they should be held legally responsible if they commit crimes as a result of their voluntary use.

Some states allow an exception to this general rule. If the defendant is accused of committing a crime that requires what's known as "specific intent" (intending the precise consequences, as well as intending to do the physical act that leads up to the consequences), the defendant can argue that he was too drunk or high to have formed that intent. This is only a partial defense, however, because it doesn't entirely excuse the defendant's actions. In this situation, the defendant will usually be convicted of another crime that doesn't require proof of a specific intent—for example, assault with a deadly weapon instead of assault with the intent to commit murder.

If You Are Questioned by the Police

There is plenty of law at the end of a nightstick.

—GROVER A. WHALEN

If a police officer wants to stop and question you, whether or not you must comply depends on the circumstances and the reasons the officer has for questioning you. This section explores some of the common questions people have about their rights and responsibilities when approached by a law enforcement officer.

If an officer wants to stop me while I'm walking on the street and I know I've done nothing wrong, should I comply?

A police officer may interfere with your freedom of movement only if he has observed unusual activity suggesting that criminal activity is afoot and that you are involved. Even if the officer is mistaken, however, you do not have the right to keep walking. As long as the officer has a good faith belief in your connection to criminal activity, he is allowed to detain you. Stopping you is one thing, however. It doesn't mean that you must answer all of his questions. (See below.)

If You Run Away

It is not unusual for people who are approached by the police to run away. Some courts have recognized that people of color, in particular, have a well-founded fear of unfair treatment at the hands of the police, and that many people will avoid contact with the police not because they are guilty of a crime, but because they reasonably believe that they may be mistreated or unjustly accused. Other courts view evasive behavior as evidence of guilt, however, and allow the police to rely on it as grounds for a detention.

If I am legally stopped by a police officer on the street, can he search me?

Yes and no. A police officer is permitted to briefly frisk your outer clothing for weapons if the officer reasonably fears for his safety. If a frisk is later challenged in court as being unreasonable, a judge will usually uphold it.

A frisk is different than a search in that a search may be conducted for evidence of a crime or contraband (an illegal item), and may be much more intrusive than a frisk. An officer who frisks you may not search you unless he has good cause to believe that you committed a crime or that you're hiding an illegal item. (See *Searches and Seizures,* below.)

How a Frisk Becomes a Legal Search—And Possibly an Arrest

When frisking a person for weapons, the police are attuned not only to the feel of possible weapons under clothing, but also to the feel of packaged drugs. Although a frisk may not turn up a weapon, it may turn up a suspicious package which the officer knows is commonly used to carry illegal drugs or some other illegal substance. This suspicion may turn into sufficient cause for a more intensive search of the person's clothing. The lesson here is that a frisk often leads to a search. And if a search produces an illegal substance, it may result in an arrest.

If I am questioned by a police officer after being stopped on the street, do I have to respond to the questions?

The general rule is that you don't have to answer any questions that the police ask you. This rule comes from the Fifth Amendment to the U.S. Constitution, which protects you against self-incrimination. As with all rules, however, there is an exception. Many local and state governments have anti-loitering laws that require people to account for their presence if the police have a reasonable suspicion that they are loitering. Once the police have asked all of their questions about loitering, however, you don't have to answer any others—such as questions about a crime in the neighborhood.

A defense lawyer's most sacred piece of advice is this: Don't talk to the police about a crime unless you clearly weren't involved and you want to help the police solve it.

Searches and Seizures

Most people instinctively understand the concept of privacy. It's the freedom to decide which details of your life are public and which are not. At the same time, most of us acknowledge that society is served when the police, in appropriate circumstances, are allowed to look for and seize contraband, stolen goods and evidence of a crime.

In an attempt to balance our desires for privacy against the legitimate needs of the police, the Fourth Amendment of the U.S. Constitution prohibits "unreasonable" searches and seizures by state or federal law officers. Generally, this means that the police may conduct a search of your home, barn, car, boat, office, personal or business documents, bank account records, trash barrel or any other property if:

- the police can show that it is more likely than not that a crime has occurred and that if they are allowed to search, they will probably find evidence or contraband (this requirement is called "probable cause"), and
- a judge agrees there is probable cause and issues a search warrant, or the police are permitted to search without a warrant because of the particular circumstances involved.

When is a police investigation considered a search?

A police investigation is not a search unless it intrudes on a person's privacy. In other words, if a person did not have a "legitimate expectation of privacy" in the place or thing searched, no "search" has occurred.

Courts ask two questions to determine whether a person had a legitimate expectation of privacy in the place or things searched:

- Did the person expect some degree of privacy?
- Is the person's expectation reasonable—that is, one that society is willing to recognize?

For example, a person who uses a public restroom expects that no one will spy on her, and most people—including judges and juries—would consider that expectation to be reasonable. Therefore, if the police install a hidden video camera in a public restroom, the action is considered a search and must meet the Fourth Amendment's requirement of reasonableness.

On the other hand, if the police glance into a car and see a weapon on the front seat, it is not a search because it is unlikely that a person would think that the front seat of a car is a private place. And even if he did, society is not generally willing to extend the protections of privacy to the front seat of an automobile.

How Private Is Your Property?

Generally, if the police are able to view contraband or evidence on your property without actually entering it, they have not conducted a search. In other words, you cannot have a reasonable expectation of privacy in an area that can legitimately be seen from outside your property. This means that the police can use what they have seen as the basis for getting a

warrant to come in and take a closer look. Or, if the situation calls for prompt action (the need to stop a drug deal, for instance), they may enter without a warrant.

Law enforcement officers are allowed to take aerial photographs or come close enough to overhear your conversations—these actions are not considered searches. On the other hand, without a warrant or an exception to the rule requiring a warrant, officers are probably not allowed to use sophisticated equipment to discover what is on your property or to eavesdrop on your conversations. In general, if the investigation method is highly artificial and high-tech, it's likely to be considered a search. Where the line is drawn, however, is not clear or consistent from state to state.

What is a search warrant?

A search warrant is a kind of permission slip, signed by a judge, that allows the police to enter private property to look for particular items. It is addressed to the owner of the property, and tells the owner that a judge has decided that it is reasonably likely that certain contraband, or evidence of criminal activities, will be found in specified locations on the property.

As a general rule, the police are supposed to apply for a warrant before conducting a search of private property; any search that is conducted without a warrant is presumed to be unreasonable. This means that the police officers will later have to justify the search—and why a warrant wasn't obtained first—if the defendant challenges it in court.

What does it take to get a search warrant?

A judge will issue a search warrant after the police have convinced her that:

- it is more likely than not that a crime has taken place, and
- items connected to the crime are likely be found in a specified location on the property.

To convince the judge of these facts, the police tell the judge what they know about the situation. Usually, the information given to the judge is based either on the officers' own observations or on the secondhand observations of an informant.

The police are limited in their ability to use secondhand information. As a general rule, the information must be reliable given the circumstances. Generally, reliable information is corroborated by police observation. For example, a citizen's tip that someone regularly delivers drugs to a certain location would be corroborated if an officer observes the person's routine. But corroboration is not necessary in every case. Sometimes a judge will issue a warrant if the source of the information is known to the police and has provided trustworthy information in the past.

What are the police allowed to do after they obtain a search warrant?

Once the police have a search warrant, they are entitled to enter the designated property to search for the items listed on the warrant. Legally, the search is supposed to be confined to the specific areas described in the warrant. For example, if the search warrant includes only the living room, the search should not extend into the kitchen, bathroom or bedroom. But there are exceptions to this limitation which are frequently used to justify broader searches. For example, the police may search beyond the terms of the warrant in order to:

- ensure their safety and the safety of others
- prevent the destruction of evidence
- discover more about possible evidence or contraband that is in plain view elsewhere on the property, or
- hunt for evidence or contraband that, as a result of their initial search, they believe exists in another location on the property.

For instance, although a warrant might be issued for the search of a house, the sound of a shotgun being loaded in the backyard would justify expanding the search to the yard in order to protect the officers; similarly, a search limited to the ground floor might legitimately expand to the upstairs if the police, searching for illegal drugs, hear toilets being flushed above. And the police can always seize evidence or illegal items if they are in plain view or are discovered while the officers are searching for the items listed in the warrant.

Do the police always need a warrant to conduct a search?

No. In many situations, police may legally conduct a search without first obtaining a warrant.

- *Consent searches.* If the police ask your permission to search your home, purse, briefcase or other property, and you agree, the search is considered consensual, and they don't need a warrant. The police typically obtain a person's consent by threatening to detain her while they obtain the warrant.

- *Searches that accompany an arrest.* When a person is placed under arrest, the police may search the person and the immediate surroundings for weapons that might be used to harm the officer. If the person is taken to jail, the police may search to make sure that weapons or contraband are not brought into the jail. (This is called an inventory search.) Inventory searches also frequently involve a search of the arrested person's car (if it is being held by the police) and personal effects on the theory that the police need a precise record of the person's property to avoid claims of theft.

- *Searches necessary to protect the safety of the public.* The police don't need a warrant if they have a reasonable fear that their safety, or that of the public, is in imminent danger. For example, an officer who suspected a bomb-making operation while walking his beat might be justified

in entering immediately and seizing the ingredients. And in the famous O.J. Simpson case, the police justified their entry onto O.J. Simpson's property on the grounds that they feared for the safety of other family members.

- *Searches necessary to prevent the imminent destruction of evidence.* A police officer does not need to obtain a warrant if she has observed illegal items (such as weapons or contraband) and believes that the items will disappear unless the officer takes prompt action. This exception arises most frequently when the police spot contraband or weapons in a car. Because cars are moved so frequently, the officer is justified in searching the entire vehicle, including the trunk, without obtaining a warrant. On the other hand, if the police learn about a marijuana-growing operation from a neighbor, they usually would need a warrant, as it is unlikely that the growing plants and other evidence of the operation will disappear quickly enough to justify a warrantless search.

- *"Hot pursuit" searches.* Police may enter private dwellings to search for criminals who are fleeing the scene of a crime.

Can my roommate—or my landlord—give the police permission to search my apartment?

The police may search your apartment if the person in charge of the premises gives permission. If you and your roommate share common areas (such as the kitchen and living room), your roommate can authorize a search of those areas. But your roommate cannot give permission to search your separate bedroom.

Similarly, your landlord cannot give permission to search your apartment. Although the landlord owns the property, your monthly check guarantees your privacy at home. This is true even if you are behind in your rent or your landlord has sued to evict you. Until the landlord has a court order that permits him to enter and retake the premises, he cannot enter without your permission. (But keep in mind that many states allow a landlord to enter for inspections, which usually require advance notice of a day or two.) If the police can point to circumstances that would justify immediate entry, however—such as the sound of a ferocious fight or the smell of burning marijuana—they may enter without permission from anyone.

Arrests and Interrogations

I HAVEN'T COMMITTED A CRIME.

WHAT I DID WAS FAIL TO COMPLY

WITH THE LAW.

–DAVID DINKINS

An arrest occurs when a police officer armed with an arrest warrant utters the magic words "you're under arrest," or when a police officer significantly restrains your freedom of motion. The restraint must be more than a mere detention on the street (discussed above). Although in most situations the police will take you to the police station for booking (photographs and fingerprinting), it is also possible for an officer to arrest and book you at the crime scene, and then release you when you give a written promise to appear in court at a later time.

After the police arrest you, they will often question you in order to find out more about the crime, your role in it and whether there may be other suspects. There are several Constitutional protections that you may invoke during police interrogations.

When do the police need a warrant to make an arrest?

As long as the police have good reason (called "probable cause") to believe that a crime has been committed and that the person they want to arrest committed the crime, they can, with just one exception, make an arrest without asking a judge for a warrant.

The exception? There are few places where the adage "a man's home is his castle" still applies, and an arrest at home is one of them. The police must have a warrant to arrest a person at home if the arrest is for a nonserious offense—such as a simple assault— and there is no fear that the person they want to arrest will destroy evidence or cause harm to the public.

How do the police obtain an arrest warrant?

An officer must present sworn evidence to a judge that a crime has occurred and that the police have probable cause to believe that the crime was committed by the person they want to arrest. If the judge agrees, she will issue a warrant. The police are then entitled to seize the person wherever they can find him.

If the police make an illegal arrest, is the arrested person set free?

No. But if a search of the person or her immediate surroundings is conducted during the arrest and turns up incriminating evidence, the evidence may be kept out of the person's trial on the grounds that it is "fruit of the poisonous tree"—that is, the evidence was found as the result of an improper arrest. Also, if the illegally arrested person makes any statements to the police after being arrested, the statements may not be used as evidence. This is true whether or not the arrested person was "read their rights." (See below.)

Can a person who is charged with a crime be forced to give bodily samples?

Yes. You might think that being forced to give bodily samples—such as blood, hair or fingernail clippings—is a violation of the U.S. Constitution's protection against self-incrimination, found in the Fifth Amendment. But the U.S. Supreme Court thinks otherwise. It has ruled that the Fifth Amendment protects communications only, and that bodily samples are physical evidence and therefore not covered by the Constitution.

If I'm arrested, do the police have to "read me my rights"?

No. However, if they don't read you your rights, they can't use anything you say as evidence against you at trial. What are these rights? Popularly known as the *Miranda* warning (ordered by the U.S. Supreme Court in *Miranda v. Arizona*), your rights consist of the familiar litany invoked by T.V. police immediately upon arresting a suspect:

- You have the right to remain silent.
- If you do say anything, what you say can be used against you in a court of law.
- You have the right to consult with a lawyer and have that lawyer present during any questioning.
- If you cannot afford a lawyer, one will be appointed for you if you so desire.
- If you choose to talk to the police officer, you have the right to stop the interview at any time. (This part of the warning is usually omitted from the screenplay.)

It doesn't matter whether an interrogation occurs in a jail or at the scene of a crime, on a busy downtown street or in the middle of an open field: If you are in custody (deprived of your freedom of action in any significant way), the police must give a *Miranda* warning if they want to question you and use your answers as evidence at trial. If you are not in police custody, however, no *Miranda* warning is required. This exception most often comes up when the police stop someone on the street to question them about a recent crime and the person blurts out a confession before the police have an opportunity to deliver the warning.

Will a judge dismiss my case if I was questioned without a *Miranda* warning?

No. Many people mistakenly believe that a case will be thrown out of court if the police fail to give *Miranda* warnings to the arrested person. What *Miranda* actually says is that a warning is necessary if the police interrogate a suspect and want to use any of her responses as evidence. If the police fail to give you a *Miranda* warning, nothing you say in response to the questioning can be used as evidence to convict you. In addition, under the "fruit of the poisonous tree" rule, if the police find evidence as a result of an interrogation that violates the *Miranda* rule, that evidence is also inadmissible at trial. For example, if you tell the police where a weapon is hidden and it turns out that you gave this information in response to improper questioning, the police will not be able to use the weapon as evidence unless the police can prove that they would have found the weapon without your statements.

What's the best way to assert my right to remain silent if I am being questioned by the police?

If you're taken into custody by the police, you don't have to use any magic words to let police officers know that you want to remain silent. You can simply say nothing in response to police questions. Or, after an officer gives you a *Miranda* warning, you can stop the questioning by saying something like:

- I want to talk to an attorney.
- I won't say anything until I talk to an attorney.
- I don't have anything to say.
- I don't want to talk to you anymore.
- I claim my *Miranda* rights.

If the police continue to question you after you have asserted your right to remain silent, they have violated *Miranda*. As a result, anything you say after that point—and any evidence gleaned from that conversation—will not be admissible at your trial.

How heavy handed can the police get when asking questions?

Information that you voluntarily disclose to a police officer (after you have been properly warned) is generally admissible at trial. The key word is "voluntary." Police officers are not allowed to use physical force or psychological coercion to get you to talk to them. The days of the rubber hose, protracted grilling under bright lights and severe sleep deprivation are pretty much over. If police officers obtain information through any of these illegal means, the information cannot be used by the prosecutor at trial. In addition, under the rule known as "the fruit of the poisonous tree," any evidence that the police obtain as the result of a coerced statement is equally inadmissible.

Reality Check: Cops Usually Win a Swearing Contest

Defendants often claim that police officers coerced them into talking. And it's just as common for police officers to say that the defendants spoke voluntarily. If the police physically coerce a defendant into talking, the defendant can support his coercion claims with photos of marks and bruises. But actual police brutality is unusual, and a defendant cannot usually offer independent evidence to support his claims of psychological coercion. Judges, believing that defendants have a greater motivation to lie than do police officers, usually side with the police and conclude that no coercion took place.

Bail

Those who expect to reap the blessings of freedom must . . . undergo the fatigue of supporting it.

—**THOMAS PAINE**

Many people, especially those arrested for minor misdemeanors, are given citations at the scene of an arrest telling them when to appear in court, and are immediately released. Others, however, are put in jail. Often, a person's first thought upon landing in jail is how to get out—and fast. The usual way to do this is to "post bail." This section answers common questions about the bail system, including its version of Monopoly's "Get Out of Jail Free" card—called release O.R.

What does it mean to "post bail"?

Bail is cash or a cash equivalent that an arrested person gives to a court to ensure that he will appear in court when ordered to do so. If the defendant appears in court at the proper time, the court refunds the bail. But if the defendant doesn't show up, the court keeps the bail and issues a warrant for the defendant's arrest.

Bail can take any of the following forms:
- cash or check for the full amount of the bail
- property worth the full amount of the bail
- a bond—that is, a guaranteed payment of the full bail amount, or
- a waiver of payment on the condition that the defendant appear in court at the required time, com-

monly called "release on one's own recognizance" or simply "O.R."

Who decides how much bail I have to pay?

Judges are responsible for setting bail. Because many people want to get out of jail immediately and, depending on when you are arrested, it can take up to five days to see a judge, most jails have standard bail schedules which specify bail amounts for common crimes. You can get out of jail quickly by paying the amount set forth in the bail schedule.

Are there are restrictions on how high my bail can be?

The Eighth Amendment to the U. S. Constitution requires that bail not be excessive. This means that bail should not be used to raise money for the government or to punish a person for being suspected of committing a crime. The purpose of bail is to give an arrested person her freedom until she is convicted of a crime, and the amount of bail must be no more than is reasonably necessary to keep her from fleeing before a case is over.

So much for theory. In fact, many judges set an impossibly high bail in particular types of cases (such as those involving drug sales or rape) to keep a suspect in jail until the trial is over. Although bail set for this purpose—called preventative detention—is thought by many to violate the Constitution, no court has stopped the practice.

What can I do if I can't afford to pay the bail listed on the bail schedule?

If you can't afford the amount of bail on the bail schedule, you can ask a judge to lower it. Depending on the state, your request must be made either in a special bail-setting hearing or when you appear in court for the first time, usually called your arraignment.

How soon can I appear before a judge?

In federal court, a person taken to jail must be brought "without unnecessary delay before the nearest available . . . magistrate." Most states have similar rules. In no event should more than 48 hours elapse (not counting weekends and holidays) between the time of booking and bringing you to court. Unfortunately, these rules are rarely enforced because the police can simply release the suspect when the time is up and then immediately re-arrest him.

How do I pay for bail?

There are two ways to pay your bail. You may either pay the full amount of the bail or buy a bail bond. A bail bond is like a check held in reserve: It represents your promise that you will appear in court when you are supposed to. You pay a bond seller to post a bond (a certain sum of money) with the court, and the court keeps the bond in case you don't show up. You can usually buy a bail bond for about 10% of the amount of your bail;

this premium is the bond seller's fee for taking the risk that you won't appear in court.

A bail bond may sound like a good deal, but buying a bond may cost you more in the long run. If you pay the full amount of the bail, you'll get that money back (less a small administrative fee) if you make your scheduled court appearances. On the other hand, the 10% premium you pay to a bond seller is nonrefundable. In addition, the bond seller may require "collateral." This means that you (or the person who pays for your bail bond) must give the bond seller a financial interest in some of your valuable property. The bond seller can cash-in this interest if you fail to appear in court.

Nevertheless, if you can't afford your bail and you don't have a friend or relative that can help out, a bond seller may be your only option. You can find one by looking in the Yellow Pages; you're also likely to find bond sellers' offices very close to any jail.

Finally, be ready to pay in cash, a money order or a cashier's check. Jails and bond sellers usually do not take credit cards or personal checks for bail.

Is it true that a defendant who proves his reliability can get out of jail on his word alone?

Sometimes. This is generally known as releasing someone "on his own recognizance," or "O.R." A defendant released O.R. must simply sign a promise to show up in court. He doesn't have to post bail. A defendant commonly requests release on his own recognizance at his first court appearance. If the judge denies the request, he then asks for low bail.

In general, defendants who are released O.R. have strong ties to a community, making them unlikely to flee. Factors that may convince a judge to grant an O.R. release include the following:

- The defendant has other family members (most likely parents, a spouse or children) living in the community.
- The defendant has resided in the community for many years.
- The defendant has a job.
- The defendant has little or no past criminal record, or any previous criminal problems were minor and occurred many years earlier.
- The defendant has been charged with previous crimes and has always appeared as required.

Getting a Lawyer

JUSTICE OFT LEANS TO THE SIDE

WHERE YOUR PURSE HANGS.

—DANISH PROVERB

If you are accused of a crime, you will probably face the possibility of going to jail. This fact alone will most likely drive you to look for a good lawyer.

Unfortunately, private criminal defense lawyers don't come cheap, and you may not be able to afford one. This doesn't mean you'll be completely at the mercy of the government, however. The U.S. Constitution provides that you are entitled to be represented by an attorney if the state is trying to deprive you of your liberty. This means that a court may be required to appoint a lawyer to represent you for free—or for a fee you can afford. This section discusses the role of private and court-appointed attorneys in the criminal process and offers suggestions for finding a private attorney if you can afford one.

How can I get a court to appoint a lawyer for me?

Normally, if you want a court to appoint a lawyer for you at government expense, you must:

• ask the court to appoint a lawyer, and
• provide details about your financial situation.

Typically, your first opportunity to ask the court to appoint a lawyer for you will be at your first court appearance, normally called your arraignment or bail hearing. The judge will probably ask you whether you are represented by a lawyer. If you're not, the judge will then ask whether you want to apply for court-appinted counsel. If you say yes, some courts will appoint a lawyer right on the spot and finish your arraignment. Other courts will delay your case and appoint a lawyer only after reviewing and approving your economic circumstances.

Each state (or even county) makes its own rules as to who qualifies for a free lawyer. Also, the seriousness of the charge may affect a judge's decision as to whether you are eligible for free legal assistance. For example, a judge may recognize that a wage-earner can afford the cost of representation for a minor crime, but not for a crime involving a complicated and lengthy trial.

If you don't qualify for free help but can't afford the full cost of a private lawyer, you may still obtain the services of a court-appointed attorney. Most states provide for "partial indigency," which means that at the conclusion of the case, the judge will require you to reimburse the state or county for a portion of the costs of representation.

Do I need a lawyer at my arraignment?

In most criminal courts the arraignment is where you first appear before a judge and enter a plea of guilty or not guilty to the offense charged. Assuming you enter a plea of not guilty, which almost every defendant does at this early stage, the court will then:

• set a date for the next procedural event in your case
• consider any bail requests that you or the prosecutor make
• appoint your lawyer, and
• ask you to waive time—that is, give up your right to have the trial or other statutory proceedings occur within specified periods of time.

Most people can handle this proceeding without a lawyer. However, if you can get the court to appoint a lawyer for you without postponing the arraignment, or you are able to arrange for private representation before your arraignment, it's always better to have a lawyer.

If I'm poor, will a judge appoint a public defender to represent me?

Because most criminal defendants are unable to afford their own attorneys, many states have Public Defender's Offices. Typically, each local office has a Chief Public Defender and a number of Assistant Public Defenders (P.D.s). P.D.s are fully-licensed lawyers whose sole job is to represent poor defendants in criminal cases. Because they appear daily in the same courts, P.D.s can gain a lot of experience in a short period of time. And because they work daily with the same cast of characters, they learn the personalities (and prejudices) of the judges, prosecutors and local law enforcement officers—important information to know when assessing a case and conducting a trial.

My county doesn't have a public defender's office. How will the court provide an attorney for me?

In areas that don't have a public defender's office, the court maintains a list of attorneys and appoints them on a rotating basis to represent people who can't afford to hire their own lawyers.

Do public defenders provide the same quality of representation as regular lawyers?

Despite the increasingly severe financial constraints on their offices, public defenders often provide representation that is at least as competent as that provided by private defense attorneys. A 1992 study conducted by the National Center for State Courts concluded that P.D.s and private lawyers achieve approximately equal results. For example, in the nine counties surveyed in the study, 76% of P.D. clients were convicted, compared to 74% of clients with private lawyers.

Despite these good points, public defenders are often asked to perform too much work for not enough money, which can cut into their abilities to be effective.

How can I get a second opinion on my public defender's advice?

Like all attorneys, public defenders are ethically obligated to vigorously defend their clients' interests. Undoubtedly, most lawyers live up to their ethical duties. But defendants who think that their court-appointed attorneys are not representing them adequately can buy advice from a private defense attorney. Even a low-income person may be able to pay for a short "second opinion" consultation.

How can I find a private defense lawyer?

Recently arrested people often need to talk to a lawyer as soon as possible. The most urgent priority is often getting a lawyer to help arrange release and provide some information about what's to come in the days ahead.

If you have been represented by a criminal defense lawyer in the past, that is usually the lawyer to call—as long as you were satisfied with his services. If you have no previous experience with criminal defense lawyers, you can look to the following sources for a referral:

- *Lawyers you know.* Most lawyers do civil (noncriminal) work, such as divorces, drafting wills, filing bankruptcies or representing people hurt in accidents. If you know any attorney that you trust, ask him to recommend a criminal defense lawyer. (Some lawyers who do civil work can also represent clients in criminal matters, at least for the limited purpose of arranging for release from jail following an arrest.)
- *Family members or friends.* Someone close to you may know of a criminal defense lawyer or may have time to look for one.
- *Martindale-Hubbell.* Martindale-Hubbell directories identify lawyers according where they work and the type of law they practice. The directories even rate lawyers for competency. All law libraries have Martindale-Hubbell books; many general public libraries have them as well. If you have computer access to the World Wide Web, you can also find Martindale-Hubble online at http://www.martindale.com/.
- *Courthouses.* You can visit a local courthouse and sit through a few criminal hearings. If a particular lawyer impresses you, ask for her

card after the hearing is over, and then call for an appointment.

Should I expect a lawyer to guarantee a good result?

Toasters come with guarantees; attorneys don't. Steer clear of lawyers who guarantee satisfactory outcomes. A lawyer who guarantees a good result may simply be trying a hard-sell tactic to induce you to hire her.

What is a private lawyer likely to cost?

It's impossible to give a definitive answer. Attorneys set their own fees, which vary according to a number of factors:

- *The complexity of a case.* Most attorneys charge more for felonies than for misdemeanors because felonies carry greater penalties and are likely to involve more work for the attorney.
- *The attorney's experience.* Generally, less experienced attorneys set lower fees than their more experienced colleagues.
- *Geography.* Just as gasoline and butter cost more in some parts of the country than others, so do lawyers.

According to a survey of readers reported in the February, 1996 issue of *Consumer Reports*, the median legal fee charged by lawyers in criminal cases was $1,500. Many defendants can expect to pay more than this, however. A defendant charged with a misdemeanor should not be surprised by a legal fee in the neighborhood of

$3,000-$5,000; an attorney may want $15,000-$25,000 in a felony case. And most attorneys want all or a substantial portion of the fee paid up front.

Can I arrange for a contingency fee in a criminal case?

No. A contingency fee is an arrangement where the lawyer gets paid only if he wins the case. These arrangements are not allowed in criminal cases.

Can I change lawyers if I'm unhappy with the one I hired?

Generally, defendants who hire their own attorneys have the right to fire them at any time, without court approval. A defendant doesn't have to show "good cause" or even justify the firing. After firing a lawyer, a defendant can hire another lawyer or perhaps even represent herself. Of course, changing lawyers will probably be costly. In addition to paying the new lawyer, the defendant will have to pay the original lawyer whatever portion of the fee the original lawyer has earned.

Limits on Your Right to Change Lawyers

Your right to change lawyers is limited by the prosecutor's right to keep cases moving on schedule. If you want to change attorneys on the eve of trial, for example, your new attorney is likely to agree to represent you only if the trial is delayed so she can prepare. The prosecutor may oppose delay, possibly because witnesses won't be available to testify later on. In these circumstances, the judge is likely to deny your request to change lawyers.

What if I'm not happy with my court-appointed lawyer? Can I get a new one?

Probably not. Defendants with court-appointed lawyers often ask for new ones. Sometimes the problems are the same as those that would be encountered with any retained lawyer: inability to communicate, personality conflicts or dissatisfaction with the strategy. In addition, clients who are represented by court-appointed lawyers often assume that the representation is substandard.

Requests for a new court-appointed lawyer are rarely granted. A defendant would have to prove that the representation is truly incompetent.

Why do some defendants choose to represent themselves?

Defendants choose to represent themselves for a variety of reasons:
- Some defendants can afford to hire a lawyer, but don't do so because they think the likely punishment is not severe enough to justify the expense.
- Some defendants believe (often mistakenly) that an attorney who represented them previously was ineffective, and figure they can do just as well on their own.
- Some defendants believe that lawyers are part of an overall oppressive system and seek to make a political statement by representing themselves.

- Some defendants want to take responsibility for their own destiny.
- Some defendants who are in jail can
  gain privileges through self-repre-
  sentation, such as access to the jail's
  law library. Also, not bound by
  lawyers' ethical codes, self-repre-
  sented defendants can delay proceedings and sometimes wreak
  havoc on an already overloaded
  system by repeatedly filing motions.

How can I tell whether I should represent myself or not?

The most obvious rule is that the less
severe the charged crime, the more
sensible it is to represent yourself.
Defendants charged with minor traffic
offenses should rarely hire an attorney,
while defendants charged with serious
felonies should rarely be without one.
The most difficult decisions involve
misdemeanors such as drunk driving,
possession of drugs or shoplifting.
Hiring an attorney in these situations
may be wise because jail time and a
fine are possibilities, and convictions
may carry hidden costs, such as more
severe punishment for a second conviction or vastly increased insurance
rates. On the other hand, first time
offenders charged with nonviolent
crimes are not usually sentenced to
jail, and judges and prosecutors often
offer standard deals to all defendants,
whether or not they are represented
by an attorney. Thus, the most critical
piece of information that defendants
should try to learn before deciding
whether to hire an attorney is what
the punishment is likely to be if they
are convicted.

How to Find Out What Your Punishment Is Likely to Be

It can be difficult to learn about judges'
common sentencing practices. Typical
sentences aren't usually listed in statutes
or court rules, unless you're being sentenced in federal court. If you want to
find out what your punishment is likely to
be if you're convicted, you might take the
following steps:

- Pay a private defense attorney for an
  hour of consultation. An experienced
  defense attorney can often make
  accurate predictions as to likely
  punishment.
- Ask a relative or close friend who is or
  who knows an attorney for informal,
  unpaid advice.
- Talk to an attorney from the public
  defender's office.

Can I represent myself and pay a lawyer to advise me as I go?

Yes. If you're thinking about representing yourself, you might want to seek out an attorney willing to serve as a "legal coach." The goal of hiring a legal coach is to combine a lawyer's knowledge with your own time. Because you pay for the lawyer's help only occasionally, the cost of a legal coach can be far less than turning the entire case over to a private attorney.

Not all attorneys are willing to serve as legal coaches. Some are worried about their liability if they give wrong advice based on incomplete information; others do not want to be involved with a case unless they are in control of it. Thus, if you're considering going it alone and you think you'll want a lawyer's help, you should try to line up your legal coach before you make your final decision.

More Information About Crimes and Criminal Procedure

There are many books and publications devoted to the explanation of state and federal criminal law and procedure. Although most of them are written for lawyers, nonlawyers will find them useful, too. Since the practice of criminal law is so intimately tied to state and local laws, we cannot list every resource here. Your best bet is to go to your local law library and ask for practice manuals or digests on the subject.

http://www.findlaw.com
Most states have put their statutes, including their criminal and criminal procedure codes, on the Internet.

Legal Research

YOU ARE BETTER OFF NOT KNOWING HOW

SAUSAGES AND LAWS ARE MADE.

—ANONYMOUS

Legal research is how you inform yourself about the law. It is not a skill reserved exclusively for lawyers; you can find the answers to your own legal questions if you are armed with a little bit of patience and a good road map. The following questions and answers will help you understand what legal research is and how to begin. Once you hit the law library or connect to the Internet, however, you will want a reference guide to help you the rest of the way. Several useful sources are listed at the end of this chapter.

Finding General Information About the Law

Many people want to learn more about a particular legal subject. They are looking for the same level of information commonly found in a general purpose encyclopedia. For example, you might want to know:

- What laws are involved when selling a business?
- What's the difference between a living trust and a will?
- When can you patent a new invention?
- What effect does divorce have on pensions earned during a marriage?

Questions like these can be answered without regard to your specific circumstances. The laws involved when selling a business, for example, are the same for everyone. To find general information about a particular legal topic, you must search for the appropriate background materials.

What exactly are legal background materials and where can I find them?

Legal background materials are books, articles and encyclopedia entries in which experts discuss the basic legal principles involved in a particular

legal subject area, such as bankruptcy, landlord-tenant law or criminal law. Your research may stop with these materials if all you want is a general understanding of a legal subject. Even if you want to go further and find a reliable answer to a specific legal question, these materials give you a foundation so you can understand the more detailed information to come.

You can find these background materials in the law library or, with increasing frequency, on the World Wide Web.

If I go to the law library to look for background information, where should I start?

If you have access to a reasonably well-stocked law library you should begin with a self-help law book such as those published by Nolo Press. These books are written in plain English and are excellent starting points for cracking any legal area that is new to you.

Beyond self-help books, you can often find a good introduction to your topic of interest in a legal encyclopedia. The two legal encyclopedias most commonly found in law libraries—organized from A-Z like regular encyclopedias—are *American Jurisprudence* and *Corpus Juris*. If your state has a state-specific version—for instance, California has a legal encyclopedia called *California Jurisprudence*—then you should use that resource.

Another good source for introductory material is a series of books known as the "nutshell" series, as in *Torts in a Nutshell* and *Intellectual Prop-*

erty in a Nutshell, from West Group (formerly West Publishing). These books should be available in most law libraries.

If you are looking for background information on current or cutting-edge legal issues—for instance, whether DNA tests should be admitted as evidence in court—journals published by law schools, bar associations and legal organizations are an excellent source. The articles in these journals are carefully indexed by subject and keyword in both hardcopy and electronic catalogs.

If you have the time and patience to delve deeply into a subject, you can find comprehensive books—generally referred to as treatises—on virtually every topic of interest. For example, if you wanted to know about some aspect of trademark law, you could use *McCarthy on Trademarks*, a multivolume treatise on all aspects of trademark law.

Finally, it may prove helpful for you to become acquainted with *West's Legal Desk Reference*, by Statsky, Hussey, Diamond and Nakamura. This book lists background materials both by state and by legal topic. For example, if you are in Illinois the *Desk Reference* tells you what background materials have been published specifically for that state. Or, if you're looking for information about drunk driving, you can find many relevant articles, books and encyclopedia entries under "Alcohol." Additionally, *West's Legal Desk Reference* provides key words and phrases that will help you use the indexes to other resources that you encounter during your research.

How to Find a Law Library

Most counties have law libraries in the government buildings or courthouses at the county seat. These libraries are open to the public—you don't have to be a lawyer to use them. County library collections tend to focus on the day-to-day practice of law, so if your question is a practical one (for example, you want to look up a state law), you are likely to find what you need.

Law schools also maintain libraries for their students and staff. Public access to some of these libraries may be restricted, but this doesn't mean you should stay away. Many school libraries are willing to extend help to nonstudents. Law school libraries tend to emphasize the theory, rather than the practice, of law; this will be a big help if your legal question is on the philosophical side—for example, you want to learn about free speech rights under your state's constitution. Also, these libraries are often the best place to look for materials from other states and countries.

How can I find background materials on the World Wide Web?

There are several types of background resources available online. A good starting place is the *Nolo Press Legal Encyclopedia,* which is part of Nolo's Website at www.nolo.com. The *Encyclopedia* explains many common legal issues in plain English, through articles and book chapters written by Nolo authors and editors. The material is reviewed every few months to make sure it's up to date. Often, you'll see links to other helpful Websites right in the articles—a true shortcut for a lucky reader.

How to Get to the World Wide Web

Getting onto the Web requires a computer, a modem, specially designed software and an account with an Internet service provider (ISP). If you want to do research from your home or business, you have to arrange this yourself. You can purchase a modem from any computer store and can sign up with an ISP in your area.

If you are using a law library with a connection to the Web, it will all be taken care of for you. Just look on the screen for the icon or name that tells you that the computer is loaded with a Web browser.

In addition, consider using one of the large number of online catalogs organized by topic. This approach is very much like using a subject matter catalog in a regular library, but you don't have to hunt through the stacks to find what you need. You look for the information you are searching for by placing it within the catalog's topical categories—for example, patent, copyright,

trademark, bankruptcy, family law, estate planning or elder law.

The Best Online Catalogs

Nolo's favorite online catalog is maintained by Findlaw at http://www.findlaw.com. If you click on the "Legal Subjects" link on the Findlaw home page you will pull up a page with a number of legal categories. Once you fit your search issue within one of these categories, you will quickly be able to create a list of potentially helpful background information resources. Other good online catalogs include:

http://www.yahoo.com/
Yahoo

http://www.paralegals.org/ LegalResources/home.html
The National Paralegal Federation Association

http://www.law.indiana.edu/ law/v-lib/lawindex.html
The World Wide Web Virtual Law Library

http://www.law.cornell. edu:80/lii.table.html
The Legal Information Institute

Finding a Specific Law

The 10 Commandments contain 297 words. The Bill of Rights is stated in 463 words. Lincoln's Gettysburg Address contains 266 words. A recent federal directive to regulate the price of cabbage contains 26,911 words.

–THE ATLANTA JOURNAL

When most of us think of the law, we think of specific rules that have been laid down by various governmental bodies. These rules take different forms—such as statutes, cases or regulations—but all are referred to by the legal research community as "primary law sources." To know "what the law is" in a particular instance means that you need to know what these primary law sources say. All discussions by experts, no matter how persuasive they may be with a particular judge, are considered secondary law sources and do not, by themselves, support a judge's decision. It is the law itself that counts, not what somebody says about it.

The primary law sources that most people seek are pronouncements issued by local, state and federal legislative bodies—known as ordinances, statutes and regulations. Another im-portant type of primary law is case law—court decisions that interpret statutes, regulations and ordinances, or make new law.

There are many reasons why you may want to find a particular primary law source. Here are two of the most likely:

- You've learned about a particular new law or court decision through the media or at your job, and you want to read it for yourself.
- You want to know what the law says because you are trying to answer a specific legal question.

If you are searching for the law for the first reason, your research will probably be limited. You will search for the appropriate law source and read the law—and that's all there is to it.

If you are searching primary law sources for the second reason—that is, you want to find a reliable answer to a specific legal question—you usually will have to find and use other legal materials and tools, as well as the law itself. These more advanced research techniques are discussed later in this chapter. (See *Finding Answers to Specific Legal Questions*, below.)

Ordinances, statutes, regulations! What's the difference?

Ordinances, statutes and regulations are written laws or rules issued by government bodies; the differences turn on which council, legislature or agency makes the law. Ordinances, for example, are local laws. They are usually issued by cities and counties and show up in our police codes, city planning codes, building codes, health codes and so forth. Statutes are laws passed by Congress (federal statutes) or state legislatures (state statutes). And regulations are rules issued by administrative agencies (such as the U.S. Department of Transportion) for the purpose of implementing and enforcing federal and state statutes.

I'm looking for a particular ordinance passed by my city council. Where can I find it?

If you are seeking a local ordinance or regulation, you're likely to find what you need at the main branch of your local public library. Once you get there, ask the reference librarian for help.

In addition, many municipalities and local government entities are putting their laws and regulations online. The best place to start is Piper Resources at http://www.piperinfo.com/state/states.html. First, select your state. Then, select your municipality from the list of cities that appears on the page for your state. Click there and search your municipality's Website for local ordinances and regulations.

How can I find a federal or state statute in the law library?

If you have started your research with some background materials, often that information will point the way. Many background resources include the statutes that underlie the law being discussed. For example, *Collier on*

Bankruptcy, the leading bankruptcy treatise, contains a complete set of the federal bankruptcy laws. And even if the statutes are not included, many background resources are likely to provide copious citations (cross-references) to the applicable laws and the books they are found in.

If you aren't using a background resource that includes statutes, most law libraries stock the books you'll need. These books may be called codes, revised statutes, annotated statutes or compiled laws, depending on the jurisdiction. For example, the federal statutes are contained in a series called *United States Code*, and the Vermont statutes are found in a series called *Vermont Statutes Annotated*. (The term "annotated" means that the statutes are accompanied by information about their history and, usually, about court decisions that have interpreted them.) Once you locate the proper set of books, you can use the topical and keyword indexes to look up the law you need. You'll usually find what you need in the hardcover portions of the code books. But it's also important to look at the update pamphlet (called the "pocket part") in the back of the book to see whether your statute has been amended or deleted.

On occasion you may be interested in a brand new statute that has not yet been distributed in a pocket part. (Pocket parts are published only once per year.) Law libraries usually subscribe to services and periodicals that update the law books on a more frequent basis than the pocket parts. Because of the time limitations inherent in printing and mailing hardcopy update materials, however, a law library is typically a week or two behind online resources when it comes to offering the actual text of a new statute. The reference librarian will usually be happy to point you in the right direction as long as you are simply asking about where to find a specific new statute. And, depending on the library, you may be able to use the library's computer to search the Internet. (See below.) But beware: If you ask a law librarian broader questions about your concerns or how a new statute relates to them, they will quickly explain that they can't give legal advice and will suggest you see a lawyer.

Can I find statutes on the Internet?

Absolutely. If you are doing your research on the World Wide Web, you can find the federal statutes and the statutes of more than 40 states by visiting Findlaw at http://www.findlaw.com. For the federal statutes, select the link for "Laws: Cases and Codes." This will take you to another page where you will find the link for "Code of Federal Regulations." That link takes you to a page where you can choose between visiting the House of Representatives Internet Law Library and the Cornell Legal Information Institute. Both of these sites contain the federal statutes. Each has its strengths and weaknesses, so if one isn't working for you, try the other.

For state statutes, go to the Findlaw homepage and choose "State Law Resources." This takes you to a page with a list of all 50 states. Click on the state you want. This will take you to a page that, for most states, offers a "primary materials" link. That link takes you to a page with links for the primary resources for that state, including cases, statutes and regulations. Click the link for statutes (remember, sometimes they're called "codes") and away you go.

If you are looking for a brand new statute, you may need to use the link to "legislation" rather than the link to "statutes" or the code, since there is often a delay between the time a statute is passed and the time it is worked into the overall compilation of laws. See the next question for more guidance.

I recently heard about an interesting bill that my state legislature is considering. Can I find out more about it through the Internet?

Yes. Almost every state maintains its own Website. These sites contain not only the most current version of a bill, but also its history. You can find these sites by using the Findlaw state resources guide described above—but instead of looking for "statutes" or "codes," you'll be looking for "legislation."

What about Congress? Can I use the Internet to locate the most current version of a federal bill?

Yes. Congress maintains a site known as Thomas. This site will help you research all bills pending before Congress as well as bills recently passed and signed into law by the President. You can visit Thomas at http://thomas.loc.gov.

When I asked my lawyer why the judge decided my case in the way she did, the lawyer referred me to a case decided by our state's Supreme Court. How can I find that case?

If you are using a law library, the cases for your state can be found in a series of books called reports or reporters. If you have a citation to the case (the number of the volume and page where the case appears) you can simply locate the correct series, select the appropriate volume and open the book to the indicated page. If you don't have a citation but do know the name of one or both of the parties in the case—for example, in the case named *Jones v. Smith*, Jones and Smith are the names of the parties—you can use a resource available in most states called a case digest. Sometimes these digests are regional (they cover cases decided by the courts in a number of states), and sometimes they are dedicated to a single state. Either way, they come with a "Table of Cases" that provides citations for all cases decided by the courts of the states

covered by the digest. If you don't find an entry for the case name in the appropriate digest, reverse the names and look again. If you still don't find it, look in the Defendant-Plaintiff Table of Cases under both names. If you don't know the name of the case or the citation, then it will be very difficult to find the case in the law library.

If the case is very recent (within the last year or two), you probably will be able to find it on the Internet. There are many ways to do this. We prefer to start our search with Findlaw, at http://www.findlaw.com. Select the link that best describes the category of law you seek—in this case, "State Law Resources." That will take you to a page with a list of all 50 states. Click on the state you are concerned with. Like other Findlaw pages, the next page will give you several options from which to choose. Since cases are a primary source of law, click on the "primary sources" link. Incidentally, the primary resources link has the word "cases" in parentheses following the link.

At the bottom of the next page (you may have to scroll down a little), you will see a "Primary Material" heading. Under this heading there will be a list of the primary resources currently on the Internet for that state. (This page will vary from state to state.) Look for a link that says "cases" or "appellate courts" or "supreme court." This link will take you to a page that will allow you to search for cases decided by your state's appellate courts for the past year or two.

If the case is not recent, you can still find it on the Internet, but you'll have to pay a private company to find it. Versuslaw, at http://www.versuslaw.com, maintains an excellent library of older state court cases that you can research at a cost of $6.95 per month for unlimited use. You'll need a credit card to sign up.

How can I find a U.S. Supreme Court case?

If you are using a law library, U.S. Supreme Court cases are published in three different series of case reporters. The reporters differ according to the type of editorial enhancements they offer. The cases, however, are exactly the same in all three sets. The names of these books are:

- *United States Reports*
- *Supreme Court Reporter*
- *Supreme Court Reports: Lawyer's Edition.*

To find cases in these reporters, follow the same approach discussed in the previous question. There are special digests for U.S. Supreme Court cases if you have a case name but no citation.

If you are using the Internet, you can find and read all U.S. Supreme Court cases decided during the last hundred years by visiting Findlaw at http://www.findlaw.com. Click the link at the top left of the homepage for Supreme Court opinions.

At the top of the next page, you'll see a box in which you can type search terms. Resist the temptation to use this box. Instead, scroll a little further down the page, where you'll see a set of query boxes that helps you direct your search. They provide these options:

- You can browse the database by year. For instance, if you happen to know the year a particular case was decided but can't quite recall the name, you can quickly peruse the names of all cases decided during that year, hoping that one of the case names will jog your memory.
- You can browse the names of all cases reported in a particular print volume of the official *United States Reports*. Sometimes you'll have the volume number but not the page number of a case. This is a way around that difficulty.
- If you have the official citation for a case, you can pull up that case. For instance, if you are reading an article and you are directed to a case at 497 US 497, you can simply enter the numbers in the appropriate boxes and go right to the case by clicking the "get it" button.
- If you know the name of one of the parties to the case, you can pull up all cases where that name is in the case title. For instance, if you wanted to find the famous *Miranda v. Arizona* case, you could simply enter Miranda and Arizona in the query box specified for this search and you would get the Miranda case.
- You can search for a case according to the specific words used in the text of the case—that is, you can search by keyword.

Under each case that you pull up in your search, you'll see a "Highlight Hits" link. This feature gives you a quick look at the places in the case where your search terms appear. From the context, you can determine whether a case is relevant to your search.

How can I find cases decided by other types of federal courts?

The U.S. Supreme Court is the highest federal court. There are also federal appellate courts (they hear appeals from lower or trial courts), U.S. District Courts and specialized courts such as bankruptcy courts and the Tax Court. Decisions from all these courts usually can be found in well-stocked law libraries. Again, if you have a citation to the case, simply ask the reference librarian where the relevant books are located. If you only have a case name, you can use the Table of Cases contained in a series known as the *Federal Practice Digest* to find the citation.

If you are using the Internet, you can use Findlaw to locate recent cases decided by the federal appellate courts (called Federal Circuit Courts of Appeal). To do this, visit the Findlaw homepage and click on "Laws: Cases and Codes." Then, scroll down the next page until you find the "Court of Appeals" link. Below that you'll find links for each Federal Circuit Court of Appeals. If you know which circuit you are looking for, click that specific link. Otherwise, click the "Court of Appeals" link, which takes you to a page with a link for a map that shows which states belong in which circuits.

If you are looking for older federal appellate court cases, you can use Versuslaw, a fee-based service located at http://www.versuslaw.com. Versuslaw charges $6.95 a month, a most reasonable sum.

Cases decided by the U.S. District Courts and specialized courts are not currently available over the Internet on any kind of a systematic basis. However, Versuslaw is working on building a database of these cases as this book goes to print.

Finding Answers to Specific Legal Questions

It's one thing to track down information on a recent case, statute or legal development. It's quite another to confidently answer a question about how the law might apply to your own situation, such as:

• I live in North Carolina, and I've been charged with second offense drunk driving. My passenger was injured as a result of the accident. What penalties do I face?

- My brother is the executor of our parents' estate, and I don't like how he's handling things. What can I do?
- Can I run a home-school in my state (North Dakota) if I've been convicted of a felony?

These are the types of questions that people have traditionally asked lawyers. To confidently answer such questions you must usually turn to a variety of legal resources, including background discussions by experts, statutes, court opinions that interpret the statutes, court opinions that make law of their own (the common law) and techniques to ensure that your information is current. Ultimately, you will be searching for materials that provide the best possible indication of how a judge would rule if presented with the issues and facts of your case.

The Legal Indeterminacy Principle

The principal goal of legal research is to find out how judges have previously decided disputes similar to your own. This information will help you predict the outcome of your dispute, should it end up in court. Predictability arises from a legal doctrine called "stare decisis" (let the decision stand), which basically means that judges are supposed to apply the same reasoning to a current dispute as other judges in higher courts have in previous similar cases. The closer the facts of previous cases are to those of your own, the stronger the element of stare decisis becomes—and the more likely it is that the decision in your case will be similar to the ones in the earlier cases. But keep in mind that the facts never match up 100%, and sometimes the outcome will turn on a single but critical difference.

Put differently, every legal dispute arises from a unique set of facts and may be resolved in a new and unpredictable way. Because of this, legal research can do a pretty good job of answering legal questions, but it can rarely provide a definitive answer. That's why lawyers often hem and haw when asked a legal question.

What materials does a judge use when deciding what the law is and how it should be applied to a particular set of facts?

First, the judge looks to see whether a federal, state or local legislative body or government agency has spoken to the issue in the form of a statute, regulation or ordinance.

If a legislative body or government agency has addressed the issue, the judge's next step is to look for and read written opinions (cases) issued by other judges who previously have interpreted the legislative enactment in ways that are relevant to the current issue. For example, suppose that a state law requires landlords to offer and maintain residential rental property that is "fit and habitable." A tenant has broken his lease and moved out because the heater in his apartment will not raise the temperature above 60 degrees. In order to decide whether this fact renders the apartment "unfit" and constitutes grounds for breaking the lease, a judge would search for a previous case in which a higher court had considered the question of habitability under similar facts.

If there is a statute, regulation or ordinance but no other court has previously interpreted it, the judge does her best to figure out what is intended by its plain language, or if the language isn't clear, she tries to discover what the legislative body or governmental agency had in mind when it established the law.

Often there is no applicable statute, regulation or ordinance—in this case the judge searches for written opinions by other judges who have previously addressed similar disputes.

How does a judge decide a case when there is no legislative enactment or written opinion that speaks directly to the current situation?

In this event the judge will have to break new ground. She will make her decision by reasoning from previous cases that are somehow similar to the current one. This is called "deciding an issue of first impression." (Typically, these issues arise from the use of new technologies, such as the Internet or biogenetics.) When faced with an issue of first impression, judges frequently turn to scholarly articles that have been written by lawyers or law professors who have anticipated the issues and proposed possible resolutions.

So now that I know how a judge sets out to decide an issue, how do I find the right answer to my question?

The best approach is to track the judge's process. After studying relevant background resources (to get the "lay of the land"), you'll want to search for relevant statutory law. Even if you find a statute or code that directly addresses your issues, you're not quite finished. You will want to look a little further to see how the statute has been interpreted by the courts.

If you are using the law library, you may pinpoint cases that discuss your statute (or rule, regulation or ordinance) by using one or more of the following tools:

- case notes that follow the statute in the code book (called "annotations")
- *Shepard's Citations for Statutes* (a book that provides a complete list of each time a particular statute, regulation or constitutional provision has been mentioned in a published decision of a federal or state court), and
- case digests (books that list cases by subject).

Then, see what previous cases have to say about your situation. The closer a case is to yours on the facts, the more likely it is that a judge in your case would follow it.

How can I make sure that the information I find is up to date?

After you read the appropriate secondary sources and find and read the relevant primary law sources, you will want to make sure that all sources you are relying on are completely up to date. Law changes rapidly, and last year's court opinion or statute might make interesting legal history but have very little to do with what a judge will do tomorrow. You'll need to find out whether the principles stated in your cases or statutes are still valid law. To do this, you need to see whether more recent cases have cast doubts on the cases' validity or scope and whether any statutes you are relying on have been amended.

If you are using the law library, you can update your research in the following ways:

- Every book that you use to find background information or statutory authority—such as a legal encyclopedia, a practice manual or a state or federal code—comes with an update pamphlet in the front or back of the book, called the "pocket part." When doing legal research in the law library, always remember to check the pocket part for possible new developments.
- Every case that you find can be updated by using a tool known as *Shepards's Citations for Cases*. This resource contains a list of each time a particular case is mentioned by a later case, and the reasons why it is mentioned. To use *Shepard's*, you find the appropriate volume for the

court that decided your case, locate your case in that volume (according to its citation) and then view the case citations that are listed after the citation for your case. The list of citations will lead you to more recent cases that shed new light on your original case.

If you are using the World Wide Web for your research, it's somewhat harder to update your initial search results. For statutes, you first should find out how up to date the statute site is. If it's a year or two behind the present, you can usually find out whether anything has changed by visiting your state's site for current legislative developments.

For cases, a fee-based service called KeyCite provides the same basic function as *Shepard's Citations for Cases*. This service is located at http:// www.keycite.com. Also, if you are using the Versuslaw fee-based case database (http://www.versuslaw.com), you can simply run the name of your case through that database. If it has been mentioned by more recent cases in the database, you will be informed of this fact and provided an opportunity to review these cases.

Using Lexis and Westlaw to Do Legal Research Online

For many years, it has been possible to do legal research online by using one or both of the major electronic legal databases, known as Westlaw (published by

West Information Publishing Group) and Lexis (published by Reed Elsevier, Inc.). Each of these systems contains the full text of many of the primary and secondary law resources found in major law libraries, including almost all reported cases from state and federal courts, all federal statutes, the statutes of most states, federal regulations, law review articles, commonly used treatises and practice manuals.

As this book goes to print, both Westlaw and Lexis are making their huge databases available over the Internet, primarily on a subscription basis which is still very pricey. However, Westlaw offers some fee-based services to nonsubscribers that are both helpful and reasonably priced. Lexis undoubtedly will follow suit. To find out more about these services— what they offer and what they cost—visit Westlaw at http://www.westlaw.com, and Lexis at http://www.lexis.com.

Finding Legal Forms

If you must take care of a legal matter, chances are good that you'll need to use a form of some sort—that is, a preformatted document that contains standard ("boilerplate") language addressing your specific situation. Leases, wills, trusts, sales agreements and employment contracts are just a few examples of the thousands of forms that are used in the course of our daily personal and business affairs.

Fortunately, there are hundreds of form books available in the law library and thousands of forms available on the Internet. You'll probably be able to find exactly the document that you need.

How do I know which form I need?

Usually someone will tell you. For example, suppose you are handling your own divorce and have used a self-help law book to prepare the initial papers. When you try to file the papers, however, the clerk tells you that you are missing a "disclosure" form. If you are lucky, the court will provide one for you, but you may be told that you'll have to find your own. Another example: You are trying to sell your car and a prospective buyer is unwilling to part with her cash without receiving a bill of sale from you.

If you haven't been pointed toward a particular form, but want to undertake a procedure and suspect it requires forms, you'll have to find a resource that explains the procedure or transaction you're interested in and sets out the necessary forms, with accompanying explanations for how to fill them in and when to use them.

Keep in mind that some forms used by courts or government agencies are "mandatory." This means that they will insist that you use their form, and not a similar form that you or someone else has designed, even though your version might contain the same information. IRS tax forms are mandatory; so are many court forms such as unlawful detainer (eviction) complaints and requests for default judgments. If you need a form for a court or government agency, it's wise to ask a clerk whether an official form must be used.

Where can I find legal forms?

If a court or a business has instructed you to find and complete a particular form, you may be able to obtain it from a stationery store that sells legal forms. Most often, these forms come without detailed instructions—you may need some help filling them in.

Self-help law materials, including those published by Nolo Press, are a good place to find legal forms. Because self-help law materials are published for people without a legal background, the forms used in these materials tend to be in plain English and are usually accompanied by thorough instructions. For example, using self-help law books you can find forms to help you sell your house or car, create a partnership agreement, file for bankruptcy or license your invention. In addition to the bookstore chains and large independent bookstores, you may also find self-help law materials in your local public or law library.

Most law libraries also have a large collection of form books—written primarily for lawyers. These books contain forms for almost every legal transaction imaginable, as well as step-by-step instructions for completing the forms and using them in and out of court. Since lawyers are paid to represent the interests of their clients, they at least are required to understand what's in a form and know

when it's appropriate to make changes in how the form is worded. Forms can hide a lot of important issues in boilerplate language that is difficult if not impossible to understand without the form books stocked by most law libraries. Examples of form books generally available in law libraries are:

- *Bender's Forms for Pleading* (Matthew Bender)
- *California Forms of Pleading* and Practice (Matthew Bender)
- *California Practice With Forms* (Bancroft-Whitney/Lawyers Coop)
- *California Forms—Legal and Business* (Bancroft-Whitney/Lawyers Coop)
- *Commencing Civil Actions in California* (Continuing Education of the Bar)
- *Federal Procedural Forms*, L. Ed. (Bancroft-Whitney/Lawyers Coop)
- *Florida Jur. Forms Business and Practice* (Bancroft-Whitney/Lawyers Coop)
- *Florida Criminal Procedure* (Bancroft-Whitney/Lawyers Coop)
- *Bender's Florida Form—Pleadings* (Matthew Bender)
- *Illinois Forms—Business and Practice* (Bancroft-Whitney/Lawyers Coop)
- *Indiana Forms of Pleading and Practice* (Matthew Bender) Massachusetts Pleading and Practice, Forms and Commentary (Matthew Bender)
- *New Jersey Forms—Legal and Business* (Bancroft-Whitney/Lawyers Coop)
- *New Jersey Criminal Procedure* (Bancroft-Whitney/Lawyers Coop)
- *New Jersey Law With Forms* (Matthew Bender)

- *New York Forms—Legal and Business* (Bancroft-Whitney/Lawyers Coop)
- *Bender's Forms for the Consolidated Laws of New York* (Matthew Bender)
- *Criminal Law of New York* (Bancroft-Whitney/Lawyers Coop)
- *Carmody-Wait New York Encyclopedia of Practice 2d* (Bancroft-Whitney/ Lawyers Coop)
- *Ohio Forms—Legal and Business* (Bancroft-Whitney/Lawyers Coop)
- *Ohio Forms of Pleading and Practice* (Matthew Bender)
- *Pennsylvania Forms* (Matthew Bender)
- *Standard Pennsylvania Practice 2d* (Bancroft-Whitney/Lawyers Coop)
- *Texas Criminal Practice Guide* (Matthew Bender)
- *Texas Forms—Legal and Business* (Bancroft-Whitney/Lawyers Coop)
- *Texas Litigation Guide* (Matthew Bender)
- *Texas Jurisprudence Pleading & Practice Forms 2d* (Bancroft-Whitney/ Lawyers Coop)

Can I use the Internet to Find Forms?

Yes. Many legal forms are also available through the Internet. Go to Findlaw (http://www.findlaw.com) and click on the forms link on the homepage. This takes you to lists of government forms, specific subject matter forms and lists of form collections and indexes. Unlike the form books found in the law library, many of these forms come without detailed instructions. So unless you know what you're doing, you may have to search

for additional information that will explain the function of the form and educate you as to your options.

Researching Current Legal Events

Many people want information related to a current legal event, such as the O.J. Simpson case, the English nanny case (*People v. Woodward*) or perhaps the events surrounding anti-tobacco litigation or the Justice Department's antitrust investigation of Microsoft. The Internet is the best place to find this type of information.

Where can I find legal news online?

There are two types of coverage of current legal events on the Web. Some sites are dedicated to legal information, such as *Court TV* or *Law Journal Extra!* Other sites offer general news coverage, such as *The New York Times* or Yahoo! News. Both are good sources for legal news, though the type of coverage is different.

When searching general news sources, you'll typically find up-to-the-minute coverage of big stories like the Whitewater investigation or Supreme Court opinions. One drawback to general news sources is that they often don't cover the more obscure cases, and instead focus on only major federal cases or those involving politicians or celebrities. Another weakness is that general news media often are skimpy with legal details such as the types of arguments that were made or which statutes or legal precedent governed the case.

Legal information sites, on the other hand, generally do a good job of reporting the nitty gritty legal aspects of news stories. If you want to know specifically what legal arguments Microsoft is making to defend itself from antitrust claims, for example, a legal site such as *Law Journal Extra!* will likely be a better source than *The New York Times*, as it will focus more directly on the legal claims themselves than on other aspects of the story such as the effect of the lawsuit on Microsoft's stock. The downside to legal information sites is that they typically don't cover stories as quickly as general news sites. While *The New York Times* online might issue a story within a half-hour of a court's decision, *Court TV* might take a day or two to cover the same story, though it will generally be more in depth.

That said, legal information sites are starting to focus more on breaking news. A site called Law Street.com, for instance, covers legal news daily with its *Law Street Journal*. And general news sites are good places to go for huge cases like O.J., the JonBenet Ramsey murder case or the Monica Lewinsky drama. When public interest is high, these sites often develop comprehensive archives with tons of stories, analyses, timelines and links to more information.

How do I find news sites?

There are many different ways to find online news sources. We've included a list of our favorite sites at the end of this section. If you want to look for yourself, here are some tips to get you started:

- Check search-oriented sites like Yahoo! and Search.com, which generally have a specific category for news sites. These news categories usually include most major general news sources.

- Use a search engine like Yahoo!, Excite or HotBot to find sites that cover the type of information you need. If you conduct a search using keywords from big news stories, such as "Lewinsky" or "Microsoft antitrust," many of the sites you'll find will be news sites. With some of these search engines, you can restrict your search to news sites only.

- Keep your eyes open in the offline, real world for references to news-related Websites. TV news and print publications often advertise their Web addresses; jot them down when you hear them or look through the print version of newspapers or magazines for a URL.

http://www.ljx.com
Law Journal Extra!

**http://www.lawstreet.com/
journal/index.html**
Law Street Journal

http://www.courttv.com
Court TV

http://www.nytimes.com
New York Times

http://legalnews.findlaw.com
Findlaw Legal News

http://www.wired.com/news/
Wired News

**http://dailynews.yahoo.com/
headlines/**
Yahoo! News

More Information About Legal Research

Legal Research: How to Find and Understand the Law, by Stephen Elias and Susan Levinkind (Nolo Press,) offers a systematic method for doing legal research both in the law library and online, including examples, exercises (with answers!) and sample legal memos. This book is ideal for law and paralegal students and anyone else who wants to learn more about how to find the law.

Another version of *Legal Research* called *Legal Research: Online and in the Law Library* comes with a CD-ROM containing thousands of URLs for law and government Websites.

Legal Research Made Easy (Nolo Press), is an entertaining videotape in which renowned legal research professor Robert Berring explains how to do effective legal research in the law library.

Law on the Net, by James Evans (Nolo Press), is the definitive guide to legal resources on the Internet. It contains listings for thousands of helpful online sites.

Gilbert's Legal Research, by Peter Honigsberg (Harcourt Brace Legal and Professional Publications), is a no-nonsense guide to commonly-used law library resources.

Index

Take 2 minutes & Give us your 2 cents

Your comments make a big difference in the development and revision of Nolo books and software. Please take a few minutes and register your Nolo product—and your comments—with us. Not only will your input make a difference, you'll receive special offers available only to registered owners of Nolo products on our newest books and software. Register now by:

PHONE	**FAX**	**EMAIL**	or **MAIL** us
1-800-992-6656	1-800-645-0895	cs@nolo.com	this registration card

REMEMBER:
Little publishers have big ears. We really listen to you.

fold here

NOLO PRESS — REGISTRATION CARD

NAME		DATE	
ADDRESS			
CITY		STATE	ZIP
PHONE		E-MAIL	

WHERE DID YOU HEAR ABOUT THIS PRODUCT?

WHERE DID YOU PURCHASE THIS PRODUCT?

DID YOU CONSULT A LAWYER? (PLEASE CIRCLE ONE)   YES   NO   NOT APPLICABLE

DID YOU FIND THIS BOOK HELPFUL?   (VERY)   5   4   3   2   1   (NOT AT ALL)

COMMENTS

WAS IT EASY TO USE?   (VERY EASY)   5   4   3   2   1   (VERY DIFFICULT)

DO YOU OWN A COMPUTER? IF SO, WHICH FORMAT? (PLEASE CIRCLE ONE)   WINDOWS   DOS   MAC

☐ If you do not wish to receive mailings from these companies, please check this box.

☐ You can quote me in future Nolo Press promotional materials. Daytime phone number _____

EVL 2.0